CEASEFIRES

CEASEFIRES

Stopping the Violence and Negotiating Peace

GOVINDA CLAYTON, SIMON J. A. MASON,
VALERIE STICHER, ANDREAS WENGER,
EDITORS

GEORGETOWN UNIVERSITY PRESS / WASHINGTON, DC

The publisher is not responsible for third-party websites or their content. URL links were active at time of publication.

Library of Congress Cataloging-in-Publication Data

Names: Clayton, Govinda, editor. | Mason, Simon J. A., editor. | Sticher, Valerie, editor. | Wenger, Andreas, editor.
Title: Ceasefires: stopping the violence and negotiating peace / Govinda Clayton, Simon J. A. Mason, Valerie Sticher, Andreas Wenger, editors.
Description: Washington, DC: Georgetown University Press, 2025. | Includes bibliographical references and index.
Identifiers: LCCN 2024014056 (print) | LCCN 2024014057 (ebook) | ISBN 9781647125387 (hardcover) | ISBN 9781647125394 (paperback) | ISBN 9781647125400 (ebook)
Subjects: LCSH: Armistices. | Peace. | Pacific settlement of international disputes. | International relations.
Classification: LCC KZ6757 .C43 2025 (print) | LCC KZ6757 (ebook) | DDC 341.6/6—dc23/eng/20240409

LC record available at https://lccn.loc.gov/2024014056
LC ebook record available at https://lccn.loc.gov/2024014057

∞ This paper meets the requirements of ANSI/NISO Z39.48-1992 (Permanence of Paper).

26 25   9 8 7 6 5 4 3 2   First printing

Printed in the United States of America

Cover design by Jeremy John Parker
Interior design by Westchester Publishing Services

CONTENTS

List of Illustrations   vii

Acknowledgments   ix

List of Abbreviations   xi

1   Introduction: Exploring the Interaction between the Ceasefire Process
and the Political Negotiation Process   1
Govinda Clayton, Simon J. A. Mason, Valerie Sticher, and Andreas Wenger

2   Ceasefires in the El Salvador Peace Negotiations, 1989–1992:
The Ultimate Bargaining Chip   30
Alvaro de Soto and Owen Frazer

3   Bosnia, 1992–1995: Imposing Ceasefires   59
Christopher R. Hill and Claudia Wiehler

4   Burundi, 1996–2003: Building Peace Step-by-Step from
Arusha to Pretoria   82
Col. Mbaye Faye and Eemeli Isoaho

5   The Government of the Philippines and the MILF in Mindanao,
1996–2014: Paving the Way to Peace?   105
Miriam Coronel-Ferrer, Alma Evangelista, and Malin Åkebo

6   Ceasefires in the Sudan North–South Negotiations, 2002–2005:
From Nuba to the Comprehensive Peace Agreement   133
Jeremy Brickhill, Simon J. A. Mason, and Georg Stein

7   Darfur, 2000–2007: The Perils of Deadline Diplomacy
for Ceasefires   163
Laurie Nathan and Allard Duursma

8 Colombia, 2012–2016: The Benefits and Challenges
of Talking While Fighting 188
Juanita Millán Hernández, Valerie Sticher, and Enzo Nussio

9 Syria, 2012–2018: Addressing Military and Political Issues
Together or Apart? 219
Carsten Wieland and Sara Hellmüller

10 Myanmar, 1989–2020: Conflict Management Ceasefires 244
Anonymous, Cate Buchanan, and Govinda Clayton

11 Conclusion: The Role of Ceasefires in Peace Processes 278
*Govinda Clayton, Simon J. A. Mason, Valerie Sticher,
and Andreas Wenger*

Bibliography 303

Index 321

List of Contributors 327

ILLUSTRATIONS

FIGURES

1.1   Two components of a peace process, shaped by the domestic political context, the international political context, and the military context   2

1.2   Political negotiation process at the core of a peace process   9

1.3   Examples of the interaction between the ceasefire process and the political negotiation process   20

3.1   Bosnia Conflict, 1991–1994   64

3.2   Bosnia Conflict, 1995   68

4.1   Chronology of principal divisions within CNDD-FDD (1994–2001). Adapted from International Crisis Group   86

4.2   Structure of the Burundi negotiation process   94

5.1   The GPH-MILF peace process infrastructure   120

5.2   Government of the Philippines–MILF armed skirmishes, 2008–2015   124

7.1   Two versions of the N'djamena Humanitarian Ceasefire Agreement   168

8.1   Overview of political negotiations (item agreements), conflict violence (battle-related deaths), and ceasefires   192

9.1   Summary of efforts during Lakhdar Brahimi's term   226

9.2   Summary of efforts during Staffan De Mistura's term   230

10.1   Overview of ceasefire agreements in Myanmar by EAO   248

10.2   Overview of fatalities in Myanmar conflict by EAO   248

11.1   Factors shaping use and outcome of ceasefires   279

11.2   A 2 × 2 table of interaction between the political negotiation and ceasefire processes   280

11.3   Key elements of the three context factors conditioning the parties' political and security interests   289

11.4   A 2 × 2 table of interaction between the political negotiation and ceasefire processes across the cases in this book   298

TABLES

1.1   Categories of ceasefires and related arrangements and their defining characteristics   7

2.1   El Salvador timeline   52

4.1   Overview of the three main phases of the Burundi peace process   88

4.2   Main agreements signed between the Government of Burundi and CNDD-FDD (Nkurunziza)   89

5.1   Philippines timeline   110

6.1   Sudan North–South peace process timeline   137

7.1   Darfur timeline   182

8.1   Overview of unilateral ceasefires declared by the FARC   195

ACKNOWLEDGMENTS

This book, a collaborative effort spanning eight years, owes its realization to the generosity of numerous individuals who shared their time and wisdom.

Special thanks go to Julian Th. Hottinger for providing crucial conceptual insights into ceasefire mediation at the project's inception. We express our gratitude to several ceasefire and mediator experts, including Jeremy Brickhill, Georg Stein, Laurie Nathan, Ambassador Ertugrul Apakan, Ajay Sethi, Sean Kane, Owen Frazer, Ian Rigden, Ben Smith, Katia Papagianni, David Lanz, and Anna Hess, who contributed to the design and development of the project. We extend further thanks to researchers, notably Allard Duursma, Enzo Nussio, Corinne Bara, Harvard Strand, Siri Aas Rustad, Håvard Mokleiv Nygård, and Isak Svensson, who provided insights and offered a sounding board throughout the project. Special thanks to Sean Bennett for copy editing, Miriam Dahinden for figure production, Quentin Merle for formatting, and Marc Werner for research assistance. Donald Jacobs, the GUP Senior Acquisitions Editor, deserves recognition for his belief in the project, along with his patience, guidance, and support. Thank you also to the whole Georgetown University Press team for help throughout the production process. Gratitude is also extended to the Centre for Security Studies at ETH Zurich, The Mediation Support Project (CSS ETH Zurich and swisspeace, funded by the Swiss FDFA), and the Centre for Humanitarian Dialogue for making the project possible.

Lastly, we express immense appreciation to all contributors who believed in the project, attended workshops and interviews, and drafted multiple versions of their contributions to ensure coherency and connection between all the chapters.

We hope that this book makes a modest contribution to enhancing peace mediation practice and fostering a more peaceful world.

LIST OF ABBREVIATIONS

AA	Arakan Army
ABSDF	All-Burma Students Democratic Front
ACR	Colombian Agency for Reintegration
AGCH	Agreement for General Cessation of Hostilities
AHJAG	Ad Hoc Joint Action Group
AMIB	African Mission in Burundi
AMIS	African Union Mission in Sudan
AOC	areas of control
ARN	Agency for the Reincorporation and Normalization
ARENA	Alianza Republicana Nacionalista
	Arusha Accords
	Arusha Peace and Reconciliation Agreement
ASEAN	Association of Southeast Asian Nations
AU	African Union
BDA	Bangsamoro Development Agency
BGF	Border Guard Forces
BNDF	Burundi National Defense Force
BIFF	Bangsamoro Islamic Freedom Fighters
CAB	Comprehensive Agreement on the Bangsamoro
CBMs	confidence-building measures
CCCH	Coordinating Committee on Cessation of Hostilities
CDM	Civil Disobedience Movement
CF	ETH/PRIO Civil Conflict CeaseFire data set
CIA	Central Intelligence Agency
	Chair
	Notre Dame University Peace Center
CNDD-FDD	Conseil National pour la Défense de la Démocratie—Forces pour la Défense de la Démocratie
CoH	cessation of hostilities

COPAZ	National Commission for the Consolidation of Peace
CPA	Comprehensive Peace Agreement
CPB	Communist Party of Burma
CPC	Civilian Protection Component
CSS ETH Zurich	Center for Security Studies
CSOs	civil society organizations
	Dayton Accords
	General Framework Agreement for Peace in Bosnia and Herzegovina
DDR	Disarmament, Demobilization, and Reintegration
DOS	U.S. Department of State
DoP	Declaration of Principles
DPA	Darfur Peace Agreement
DRC	Democratic Republic of Congo
EAOs	Ethnic Armed Organizations
ECMM	European Community Monitor Mission
ELN	Ejército de Liberación Nacional
EPL	Ejército Popular de Liberación
ERP	Ejército Revolucionario del Pueblo
EU	European Union
FAB	Framework Agreement on the Bangsamoro
FAES	Armed Forces of El Salvador
FARC	Revolutionary Armed Forces of Colombia
FARC-EP	Fuerzas Armadas Revolucionarias de Colombia—Ejército del Pueblo
FDR	Frente Democrático Revolucionario
FDFA	Swiss Federal Department of Foreign Affairs
FENASTRAS	Federación Nacional Sindical de Trabajadores Salvadoreños
FMLN	Frente Farabundo Martí para la Liberación Nacional
FPNCC	Federal Political Negotiation and Consultative Committee
FRODEBU	Front pour la Démocratie au Burundi
FSA	Free Syrian Army
FTA	Forces Technical Agreement
G20	Group of 20
GDP	gross domestic product
GOES	Government of El Salvador

GoS	Government of Sudan
GRP	Government of the Republic of the Philippines
HNC	High Negotiation Committee
HRDC	Humanitarian, Rehabilitation, and Development Component
ICG	International Contact Group
ICRC	International Committee of the Red Cross
IFFC	Independent Fact-Finding Committee
IFOR	Implementation Force
IGAD	Intergovernmental Authority on Development
IHL	International Humanitarian Law
IMC	Implementation Monitoring Committee
IMT	International Monitoring Team
IS	Islamic state
ISSG	International Syria Support Group
ITM	International Monitoring Team
JCC	Joint Ceasefire Commission
JCPoA	Joint Comprehensive Plan of Action
JEM	Justice and Equality Movement
JI	Jemaah Islamiya
JICA	Japan International Cooperation and Assistance
JMC	Joint Military Commission
JMC	Joint Monitoring Commission
JMC	Joint Ceasefire Monitoring Committee
JNA	Yugoslav People's Army
KIO	Kachin Independence Organization
KNU	Karen National Union
KPC	Karen Peace Council
LAS	League of Arab States
MI	military intelligence
MILF	Moro Islamic Liberation Front
MNLF	Moro National Liberation Front
MOA-AD	Memorandum of Agreement on Ancestral Domain
MoU	Memorandum of Understanding
MPC	Myanmar Peace Center
MTF	Mindanao Trust Fund
MVM	monitoring and verification mechanism
M-19	Movimiento 19 de Abril
NATO	North Atlantic Treaty Organization

NCA	Nationwide Ceasefire Agreement
NCCT	National Ceasefire Coordination Team
NCP	National Congress Party
NDAA	National Democratic Alliance Army
NDFP	National Democratic Front of the Philippines
NGOs	nongovernmental organizations
NLD	National League for Democracy
NMSP	New Mon State Party
NUC	National Unification Commission
OAGs	other armed groups
OAU	Organisation of African Unity
OIC	Organization of Islamic Cooperation
ONUCA	United Nations Observer Group in Central America
ONUSAL	United Nations Observer Mission in El Salvador
PALIPEHUTU-FNL	Parti pour la libération du peuple Hutu—Forces nationales de libération
PKK	Kurdistan Workers' Party
PNP	Philippine National Police
PPT	Puntos de Preagrupamiento Temporal
PSC	Peace and Security Council
PYD	Party of Democratic Unity
QRT	Quick Response Team
RAM	Reform the Armed Forces
RCSS	Restoration Council of Southern Shan
RSF	Rapid Support Forces
SAF	Sudanese Armed Forces
SCCH	subcommittees on cessation of hostilities
SDF	Syrian Defence Forces
SEAC	Socio-Economic Assistance Components
SFOR	Stabilization Force
SNC	Syrian Negotiation Committee
SOC	Syrian National Coalition of Revolutionary and Opposition Forces
SPLM/A	Sudan People's Liberation Movement/Army
TGB	Transitional Governing Body
	The Pretoria Protocol
	Pretoria Protocol on Political, Defense and Security Power Sharing in Burundi
UAE	United Arab Emirates

UCA	Universidad Centroamericana
UCDP	Uppsala Conflict Data Program
UK	United Kingdom
UN	United Nations
UNAMID	African Union–United Nations Hybrid Operation in Darfur
UNDP	United Nations Development Programme
UNFC	United Nationalities Federal Council
UNGA	United Nations General Assembly
UNICEF	United Nations Children's Fund
UNMIS	United Nations Mission in the Sudan
UNPROFOR	United Nations Protection Force
UNSC	United Nations Security Council
UNSG	Secretary-General of the United Nations
UNSMIS	UN Supervision Mission in Syria
UP	Patriotic Union
UPC	Union Peace Conference
UPCC	Union Peacemaking Central Committee
UPRONA	Union pour le Progrès national
UPWC	Union Peacemaking Working Committee
USAID	United States Agency for International Development
US	United States
USSR	Union of Soviet Socialist Republics
UWSA	United Wa State Army
V&M	verification and monitoring
YPG	People's Protection Units
ZAPU	Zimbabwe African People's Union

CHAPTER 1

Introduction

Exploring the Interaction between the Ceasefire Process and the Political Negotiation Process

Govinda Clayton, Simon J. A. Mason,
Valerie Sticher, and Andreas Wenger

Almost all peace processes involve ceasefires. These ceasefire arrangements vary greatly in terms of their timing, content, and connection to the political negotiation process. In Colombia, the government and the Revolutionary Armed Forces of Colombia (FARC) conducted political negotiations in the absence of a bilateral ceasefire, formally agreeing to stop the violence only once they reached an agreement on the main conflict issues. In the Philippines, a ceasefire was put in place very early in the negotiations between the government and the Moro Islamic Liberation Front (MILF), contributing to a drawn-out but successful political negotiation process. Burundi saw initial attempts to install a comprehensive ceasefire between the government and the Conseil National Pour la Défense de la Démocratie—Forces pour la Défense de la Démocratie (CNDD-FDD) fail, yet once an earlier peace agreement began to bear fruit, efforts to stop the violence and resolve the contested issues progressed more smoothly. In Syria, a range of different strategies was tried, but at the time of writing, all ceasefires and political negotiations have failed to stop the war. Why do conflict parties adopt different ceasefire sequencing strategies? What factors condition this choice? And what explains the different uses and effects of ceasefires across these cases?

Ending intrastate conflict peacefully requires that the conflict parties agree to a settlement of the contested issues *and* the terms under which conflict violence will stop. Prior research tended to not make a distinction between these two tasks, instead subsuming both under the broad analysis of "peace processes." As a result, our knowledge remains limited on the relationship between efforts to stop the conflict violence, which we call the "ceasefire process," and efforts to resolve the contested issues (or incompatibility), which we call the "political negotiation process." This book puts the relationship between the conflict parties' attempts at stopping the violence and their efforts focused on negotiating peace front and center, exploring this from a third-party perspective. We seek to understand when and why ceasefire and political negotiation processes foster or impede each other and how various context factors condition this relationship (see figure 1.1).

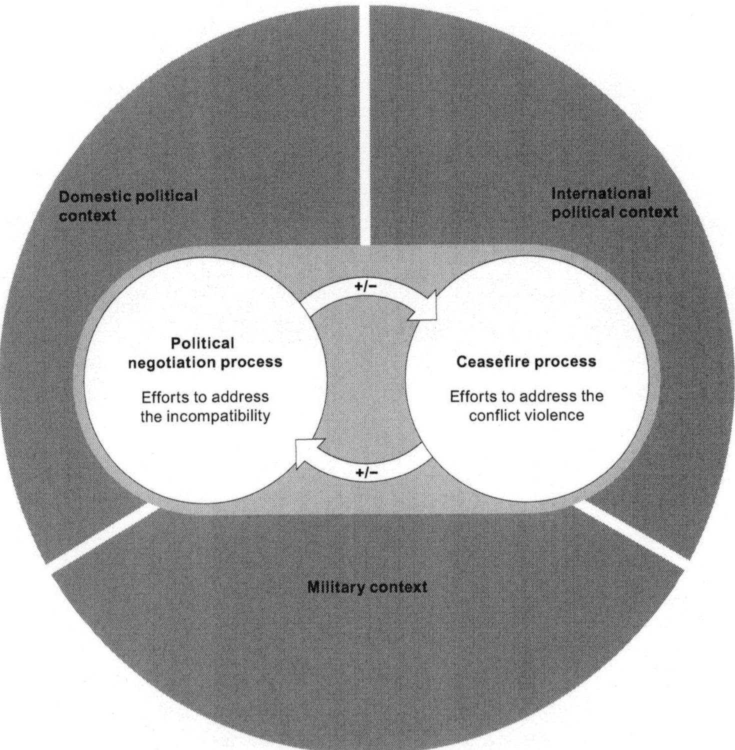

Figure 1.1 Two components of a peace process, shaped by the domestic political context, the international political context, and the military context

We show how the ceasefire process and political negotiations are distinct processes, often involving different actors, strategies, and challenges, yet at the same time being closely intertwined. Rather than considering these two parts of a peace process together, or focusing narrowly only on ceasefires, we explore the dynamic interaction between both processes, focusing on two questions that have previously received little attention:

- When and why do conflict parties adopt a ceasefire at different points of the political negotiation process, and how does this shape political negotiations?
- How do context factors—the domestic political context, the international political context, and the military context—condition the relationship between the ceasefire process and the political negotiation process?

Together, these two questions provide analytical lenses for a structured, focused comparison across cases in the final chapter of the book. Through this approach, this book makes several significant contributions. First, we improve conceptual clarity by advancing understanding of how peace processes function by clearly conceptualizing two constituent parts of the process—the ceasefire process and the political negotiation process. Second, we make a theoretical contribution, developing a framework that captures the key factors that condition the interaction between these two processes. This provides an important foundation for future systematic analysis. Third, we make an empirical contribution, providing a collection of nine case chapters that adopt a common definition of ceasefires and a common analytical approach. As such, we offer detailed knowledge of the role of ceasefires in a wide range of intrastate conflicts. Our cases stretch from the process that ended the conflict in El Salvador in the early 1990s to contemporary cases including Syria and Myanmar.

The book focuses solely on cases of intrastate conflict, aligning with our objective to carry out a structured focused comparison—which necessitates a certain degree of homogeneity among cases. Although we expect that several insights from this book also apply to interstate conflict, there are also significant differences between the two forms of warfare that might influence both the ceasefire and political negotiation processes (e.g., the ability of both sides to withdraw to their territory). Exploring the differences between ceasefires in inter- and intrastate conflict falls outside the scope of our book. We therefore focus on intrastate conflict between armed, organized actors that pursue some political agenda but recognize that such actors are not homogeneous: they are often organized into a military and a political wing and consist of different factions, and there may be important differences in the perspectives of the leadership and rank-and-file soldiers. A key part of our analysis covers how such heterogeneity influences peace negotiations and, ultimately, the interaction between efforts to address contested issues and conflict violence.

This book is written for anyone concerned with promoting peace in violent intrastate conflict. As this book was being completed, calls for a ceasefire in Gaza have been growing stronger. While some argue that the Israel–Palestine conflict does not neatly fit into the category of an intrastate conflict, many of the insights presented in this book are relevant and point to the challenges and (more limited) opportunities for ceasefires as a tool to end the violence and contribute to a political process. In a broader sense, this book is written for anyone concerned with promoting peace in violent intrastate conflicts. That includes academic researchers studying ceasefires, mediation, conflict management, and peace studies, as well as practitioners working to support conflict parties in designing ceasefires and political negotiation processes. One of the coauthors for each chapter was deeply involved in the peace process, providing unique personal insights into the mechanics and inner workings of the negotiations. The book is edited, and each chapter is authored, by a combination of academic researchers and practitioners. It was designed and written in such a way as to speak to both communities, providing a rigorous and systematic analysis that relies on in-depth case knowledge. We seek to adopt ideas and principles used by practitioners and policymakers, thereby helping to move practice to theory.

The remainder of this introductory chapter is structured as follows. First, we discuss the key concepts used throughout this book: the ceasefire process and the political negotiation process. Second, building on existing literature, we set out the various mechanisms through which the ceasefire process shapes the political negotiation process, and vice versa, and articulate the research gap that this book seeks to fill. Third, we set out the analytical framework and the analytical approach used to guide each of the case chapters.

CONCEPTS

Existing research tends to define ceasefires inconsistently, making it hard to undertake cross-case comparisons and identify broader trends. We therefore start by defining three different ideal-type classes of ceasefires, which offer more precision in the subsequent analysis, allowing us to identify the different conditions that shape conflict parties' choice of different types of ceasefires at different points in the overall peace process. We then conceptualize the political negotiation process, differentiating between four ideal-type phases of the political negotiation process that help us explore how the interaction between the ceasefire and political negotiation process changes at different points in a peace process.

What Is a Ceasefire Process?

The ceasefire process is the part of a peace process dedicated to agreeing on the timing, form, and content of arrangements to stop the fighting and to implement such arrangements. While the purpose and scope of ceasefire arrangements are generally set by the conflict parties' political decision-makers, the actual technical aspects of these arrangements are likely to be prepared and negotiated by the conflict parties' military and technical experts who have the necessary knowledge of the situation on the battlefield.

There is no universally accepted definition of a ceasefire, and the use of the term can vary widely. We consider a ceasefire to be **any arrangement in which at least one conflict party commits to a (temporary or permanent) stop in the violence.** Thus, ceasefire is used as an umbrella term throughout this book, covering a variety of related arrangements (e.g., truce, humanitarian pause, window of silence, cessation of hostilities, preliminary ceasefire, definitive ceasefire) that are used to (try and) stop violence.

Our broad definition of ceasefire means that on occasion, the label we use for an arrangement might differ from the name given by the conflict parties. This is because in peace processes, language tends to be contested, meaning that whether an arrangement is referred to as a ceasefire, truce, or some other label can vary for political or cultural reasons beyond the technical characteristics of an agreement.[1] For example, following the onset of the war in Gaza in 2023, the United Nations Security Council debated whether a potential resolution should refer to a ceasefire, truce, or humanitarian pause. These discussions were political rather than technical in nature, looking for a term that would be acceptable to international actors rather than match the characteristics of any proposed arrangement. Peacemakers and conflict parties will always require conceptual and linguistic flexibility when determining the label for ceasefires, meaning names are likely to vary across contexts. At the same time, identifying and comparing similar instruments for analytical purposes necessitates the adoption of a consistent vocabulary across cases. Hence, we adopt a broad but consistent use of language throughout this book and, where applicable, note the different terms used by conflict parties and mediators in a footnote.

Our definition of a ceasefire also differs somewhat from the more stringent approach taken by some ceasefire mediation practitioners, who sometimes reserve the term "ceasefire" for a specific class of formal agreement between two or more conflict parties, in which the actors commit to a monitored or verified, time-bound suspension of hostilities. The advantage of this narrower definition is to more accurately convey that not everything that is labeled as a ceasefire has a realistic chance of stopping fighting; thus, a "ceasefire proper" must fulfill some conditions (e.g., regarding compliance) if it is to be effective over time. However, an important part of our book is comparing and contrasting different forms of arrangement, and as such, we do not wish to restrict our focus to one particular class of agreement. Limiting ceasefires to one specific class of arrangement is also at odds with the bourgeoning body of literature that adopts a broader understanding of ceasefires. We therefore prefer to adopt a broad definition of ceasefire, while maintaining specificity by distinguishing between different forms that ceasefires might take.

Ceasefires can vary in important ways; they can be unilateral (i.e., involving only one party), bilateral (i.e., involving two parties), or multilateral (i.e., involving more than two parties) and may cover an entire country (i.e., nationwide) or only parts of it (e.g., geographical ceasefires limited to parts of the conflict area, or ceasefires between local actors). They may seek to suspend violence temporarily or indefinitely and may range from oral declarations that only stipulate the halt of hostilities to very comprehensive written documents that involve a wide range of military and political provisions. Given the important variation across ceasefires, we further distinguish between three key classes of ceasefire arrangements: cessation of hostilities, preliminary ceasefires, and definitive ceasefires (see table 1.1).[2]

- *Cessation of Hostilities* (CoH) is the least specialized class of ceasefires. They include a temporary commitment from at least one conflict party to stop violence but do not contain provisions to monitor compliance or disarm and demobilize conflict parties. CoH arrangements can range from informal unilateral declarations to more formal bilateral commitments.
- *Preliminary Ceasefires* are a more specialized form of arrangement that—in addition to the commitment to stop violence—also include provisions to support compliance such as monitoring and/or verification.

Preliminary ceasefires are always connected to peace negotiations and are "preliminary" in the sense that they seek to prepare the parties for a final settlement process. To that end, they often include provisions that set out a timetable for future negotiations, define observable benchmarks, and create collaborative ceasefire commissions.

- *Definitive Ceasefires* set out the specific terms through which parties intend to end the violence permanently. In intrastate conflict, such arrangements include compliance mechanisms and provisions to integrate or disarm and demobilize at least one conflict actor. This may be done through disarmament, demobilization, and reintegration of former combatants into civilian life; by integrating them into the state armed forces; or by creating new joint armed forces. Definitive ceasefires are usually a part of or accompany a peace agreement that addresses the underlying conflict issues. For this reason, definitive ceasefires are also referred to as "peace agreement ceasefires," "final status of forces agreement," "final ceasefires," "permanent ceasefires," or the "security clauses" of a peace agreement.[3]

Importantly, we distinguish our three classes of ceasefire from related de-escalation or violence containment mechanisms. These latter arrangements attempt to reduce or contain certain aspects of the conflict violence, but unlike ceasefires, they do not attempt to stop all hostilities between the conflict parties. Examples of such partial efforts to address conflict violence include an announcement by a conflict party to stop kidnapping politicians, or commitments to avoid targeting critical infrastructure. Such mechanisms may be initial tentative steps toward a peace process and a ceasefire proper, or they may not relate in any way to the efforts to move toward peace negotiations. In either case, they are less ambitious and comprehensive than ceasefires according to our definition—even if they are sometimes very close to informal cessations of hostilities.[4]

Table 1.1: Categories of ceasefires and related arrangements and their defining characteristics

	Reduce or contain conflict violence	Stop conflict violence	Stop with compliance mechanisms	Terminate with disarmament and demobilization
De-escalation mechanisms	●			
Cessation of hostilities	●	●		
Preliminary ceasefire	●	●	●	
Definitive ceasefire	●	●	●	●

Table 1.1 provides an overview of our three different classes of ceasefire, and de-escalation mechanisms, and their defining characteristics. This categorization provides conceptually clear, intuitive categories that allow for cross-case comparisons. At the same time, these are ideal-type categories that do not always reflect the messy nature of ceasefires in armed conflicts. As the empirical chapters will demonstrate, actors sometimes seek to negotiate or implement arrangements that fall between the boundaries of these categories, and the class of an arrangement may change over time. When and what type of ceasefire is used at different points in a conflict is likely shaped by various context factors, as we highlight in the conclusion.

What Is a Political Negotiation Process?

The political negotiation process is a series of reciprocal moves between conflict parties aiming to resolve the contested issues underlying their conflict (i.e., incompatibility). Examples of contested issues include the structure and allocation of political power within governing institutions, as well as the composition and governance of the security sector, territorial control, socioeconomic issues, transitional justice, or environmental questions. This process often requires building communication, confidence, trust, and, ultimately, concessions to reach a point of agreement.[5]

We understand the political negotiation process as incorporating the broadest range of "talks" that touch on the incompatibility, including the "talks about the talks" (prenegotiations) and the actual formal talks (negotiation phase). We also consider preparatory steps leading up to these political negotiations (pre-prenegotiations) and efforts to implement a peace agreement (implementation). Given the significant differences in the goals, formats, and likely outcomes at different points of the political negotiation process, we differentiate between four phases throughout this text: pre-prenegotiations, prenegotiations, formal negotiations, and implementation.[6]

- *The Pre-Prenegotiation Phase* is a period in intrastate conflict in which violence is ongoing, and one or more of the conflict parties is unwilling to consider entering political negotiations. At this point, the parties do not even discuss the conditions under which negotiation might occur.[7] Technically, there are no formal negotiations at this moment of the conflict, but we still consider it part of the broader process as it is a key phase leading up to formal negotiations. There are almost always efforts by third parties or factions of conflict parties to foster efforts toward political negotiations.

- *The Prenegotiation Phase* is a period in which the conflict parties have indicated an interest in entering negotiations and engage in discussions to hash out the terms under which formal negotiations can occur, including agreeing on the common objective for any future formal talks. For this reason, this phase is often referred to as a period of "talks about the talks." Since most intrastate armed conflicts have regional or even international actors involved, the identification of a possible negotiation objective needs to consider the interests of these "external" actors as well.
- *The Formal Negotiation Phase* is the period in which the parties negotiate the contested issues. This can occur once the parties have agreed on the objective, structure, and content of the formal process. While the prenegotiation phase often involves shuttle diplomacy, the formal negotiation phase tends to be in person. It is in this phase that a peace agreement would be stipulated.
- *The Implementation Phase* is the period following the signing of a peace agreement in which the clauses are put into place. This might include everything from the disarmament of the nonstate force to the complete reconfiguration of a state's political system.

Figure 1.2 depicts an idealized example of the political negotiation process at the core of the peace process. The arrows depict the transition from one phase to the next. Progress in political negotiations is achieved by moving from left to right on the figure. In this idealized example, the conflict parties move from the pre-prenegotiation through the prenegotiation and negotiation to the implementation phase. Of course, real-life peace processes are far messier. Prenegotiations, negotiations, or the implementation of an agreement may fail for a variety of reasons, which may mean that conflict parties revert to an earlier phase. Different actors may be in different phases in one and the same conflict context, or they may not even know in which phase

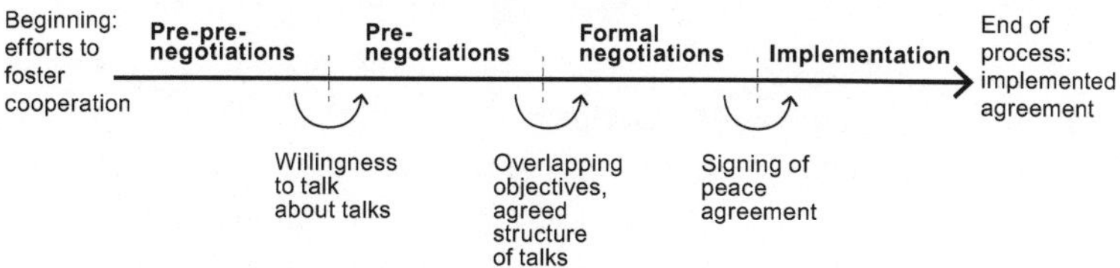

Figure 1.2 Political negotiation process at the core of a peace process

of the conflict they are in. The four phases should therefore not be seen as prescriptive or final but rather serve as a reference for analytical purposes, with deviations from the ideal-typical phases offering important space for exploring variations (see the section on "Analytical Strategy").

The negotiation and implementation of ceasefires and related de-escalation arrangements may happen in any of these phases. The names of the phases therefore refer to progress around efforts to address the contested issues between the conflict parties, and not in reference to how far they have managed to address the conflict violence between them. However, if conflict violence is ongoing in the implementation phase, it is a sign that both the political negotiations and the efforts to address conflict violence are failing.

THE RELATIONSHIP BETWEEN THE CEASEFIRE AND POLITICAL NEGOTIATION PROCESS

Having introduced our key concepts, we now turn to the relationship between the two key components of a peace process: ceasefire and political negotiations processes. First, we discuss several pathways that prior research has detailed through which ceasefires can have a positive or a negative impact on the progress of political negotiations. Second, we highlight how the extent to which conflict parties perceive the political negotiation process as helping them achieve their overall political objectives is likely to be crucial in shaping the onset, duration, and effectiveness of any ceasefire arrangement. Third, we discuss what we consider to be the key innovations of this book against the backdrop of the limitations of the extant literature.

How Does the Ceasefire Process Shape Political Negotiations?

Prior literature has detailed many of the ways in which the presence or absence of a ceasefire impacts the political negotiation process.[8] Parties often use a ceasefire to pursue political objectives beyond the stopping of military violence. The use of ceasefires is then closely related to efforts to address the contested issues between conflict parties. In these cases, ceasefires tend to be an integrated part of a wider negotiation/mediation strategy. In other cases, there may be efforts to deliberately delink ceasefires from efforts to address contested issues. In these cases, a ceasefire might not be a means toward a political goal but serve some limited objective (e.g., humanitarian aid delivery) or be a preferred alternative to both continued war and a negotiated settlement. However, given that in most armed conflicts, parties use conflict violence to achieve (or protect) political goals, all ceasefires are likely to influence the political negotiation process—directly or indirectly, and for better or worse.

How Ceasefires Strengthen Political Negotiations

Prior research reveals several pathways through which ceasefires can have a positive impact on progress in political negotiations, that is, move conflict parties closer to the resolution of the contested issues. The first four pathways directly affect the relationship between the conflict parties; the next two work to do so indirectly through changes that affect the relationship between conflict party leaders and their broader constituencies.

SIGNALING PEACEFUL INTENTIONS

The leaders of conflict parties can use ceasefires to credibly signal their peaceful intent.[9] It is often difficult for a conflict party to credibly communicate their intention to an opponent and to trust any information that their opponent communicates about their intentions. When a conflict party favors a political settlement over continued fighting, a ceasefire can provide an effective signal of their intention to move toward an agreement, while also providing an opportunity to assess the intentions of an opponent. By adhering to the ceasefire and giving up opportunities to take advantage of the opponent in this period, conflict parties can send a strong peaceful signal that can lead to the onset or deepening of peace negotiations.

CREATING A CONDUCIVE ENVIRONMENT FOR NEGOTIATIONS

Ceasefires can also help to create an environment more conducive to peace negotiations.[10] Ongoing violence is often a serious impediment to negotiations.[11] A ceasefire that succeeds in stopping the violence can interrupt the cycle of hatred and anger, removing a key impediment to working toward a joint solution.[12] A break in the violence may save lives, allow the distribution of humanitarian aid, and improve the situation for civilians. This was one of the main arguments put forward for a ceasefire in Gaza during the devastating periods of violence. A ceasefire an also support the negotiation process and make compromise easier. A ceasefire also stabilizes the battlefield, preventing shifts in territorial control that might complicate substantive negotiations.[13]

CONFIDENCE BUILDING

Ceasefires can also be a confidence-building measure, helping to build connections and trust between the leaders of the military forces.[14] By successfully delivering on a ceasefire pledge, conflict parties can demonstrate their commitment and ability to deliver within a process, mitigating problems of credible commitment.[15] This process of collaborating in the context of a ceasefire helps the conflict parties to build confidence and trust in each other[16] and in the peace process. It can also create new structures to enhance communication between the parties.[17]

DEMONSTRATING COMMAND AND CONTROL

Ceasefires can be used to demonstrate command control and internal cohesion of an armed force.[18] For a nonstate force, demonstrating the discipline of their forces is often necessary during a process. A negotiated settlement reflects—at least partially—the military strength and control of conflict parties. Actors thus have an incentive to demonstrate their strengths, including—if in doubt—the cohesion of their forces.[19] Moreover, if an actor suspects that their opponent is unable to deliver on an agreement due to fragmented leadership and forces, they are unlikely to risk participating in a process. Entering into a ceasefire requires an armed force to cease hostilities from a specific point in time and then generally abide by the terms agreed by the leadership.[20] This can provide a useful indication as to whether a group's leadership has control over its forces and is capable of implementing agreements.[21] For example, the short ceasefire called by the Taliban in February 2020 was widely considered a tool through which the Taliban could demonstrate their ability to implement an agreement across their relatively decentralized forces.[22]

PROMOTING INCLUSION

Ceasefires can help to increase inclusion in a peace process. Civilians are those who are most directly affected by conflict, but they are often excluded from political negotiation processes. The ceasefire process, in particular monitoring efforts, can potentially be a space to try to increase roles for the inclusion of overlooked or excluded groups and perspectives, in particular women, young people, religious communities, ethnic or tribal communities, and nongovernmental organizations (NGOs) and civil society organizations (CSOs).[23] However, this is unlikely to be feasible in highly escalated conflicts, as it turns civil society actors into military targets.

INDIRECT EFFECTS

A ceasefire can have several indirect benefits on the substantive negotiations. For example, research has shown that a (successful) ceasefire can increase popular support for a peace process,[24] provide political cover that allows parties to subsequently soften their demands,[25] and produce a cooperative reputation that increases the likelihood of peaceful reciprocation from other actors.[26]

Ceasefires can also help lay the groundwork for more comprehensive arrangements. Preliminary ceasefires often set in place joint structures that pave the way for a definitive ceasefire, while definitive ceasefires set out the terms under which the military aspect of the conflict ends.[27]

How Ceasefires Undermine Peace Negotiations

Yet not all ceasefires move parties closer to an agreement. In many cases, ceasefires have quite the opposite effect. Prior research focuses on four primary mechanisms through which this may occur.

REDUCING RIPENESS

Warring parties are often more willing to settle when conflict is costly and carries significant risks.[28] Fighting also produces important information that might be needed to find a mutually acceptable deal.[29] The intention of a ceasefire is often to restrict the devastating effects of violence without necessarily progressing a peace process.[30] This can then reduce the "ripeness" of the conflict by restricting the flow of information and the costs that create incentives for the parties to move toward peace.[31] This is particularly the case concerning the power holder, who benefits from the status quo, and is thus unlikely to be willing to compromise in the absence of significant pressure.[32] This has led many to question the traditional logic that a ceasefire should be a precondition for peace negotiations.[33]

CONTAINMENT

If a political solution is elusive, a ceasefire can sometimes be used as a way to limit violence. Long-term conflict management ceasefires have occurred in about one-third of all separatist conflicts since 1989.[34] In these cases, ceasefires often contain (rather than stop) the violence, keeping the violence at a level that is tolerable to the elites of the parties, without progress in substantive negotiations. While this can be an important humanitarian imperative, it may risk sustaining a conflict over a longer period.

HIDDEN AGENDA

Ceasefires can also be conceived of as strategic tools to advance political or military objectives inherently at odds with a peaceful political settlement.[35] Ceasefires can be used by a conflict party to rearm, regroup, or consolidate control over a territory.[36] In this way, ceasefires can serve so-called devious intention, where parties engage in peacemaking to further their interests— but not necessarily with the aim of moving toward a peaceful solution.[37] Ceasefires can also serve state-building purposes[38] and facilitate the development of illicit economics.[39]

REDUCING TRUST

While ceasefire compliance may build trust and commitment, a failed ceasefire can undermine trust and worsen relations.[40] When a party commits to an arrangement, but then subsequently fails to honor the deal, or is seen to seek some military advantage through the process, it is likely to undermine and complicate the negotiation process.[41] Ceasefires are usually violated to some degree, yet if it goes beyond a certain level—or if the ceasefire collapses—then it may lead to more distrust than the absence of a ceasefire.

Refusal to engage in a ceasefire may also hinder political negotiations: conflict parties may fight over the sequencing of ceasefires and political negotiations, with one side demanding a ceasefire as a condition to make concessions on the contested issues and the other demanding concessions to agree to a ceasefire. This may result in a deadlock that blocks political negotiations altogether (see also figure 1.3c).[42]

How Do Political Negotiations Shape the Ceasefire Process?

The primary determinant of ceasefire onset, implementation, and outcome is always the political will of the conflict parties. Ceasefires only occur when the conflict parties see a tactical or strategic benefit to ceasing combat, and it will always end if one or more of the conflict parties believe that a better deal can be achieved through renewed violence.[43] Therefore, the extent to which the conflict parties see the political negotiation process helping them achieve their political objectives is likely to be key in shaping whether a ceasefire occurs in the first place and how effective any such arrangement is in stopping the violence.

ONSET/TIMING

Ceasefires are key bargaining chips used by the parties during negotiations. Often one conflict party (usually the power seeker, i.e., in intrastate conflict the nonstate group) will be reluctant to enter a ceasefire in the absence of significant commitment to or progress in the political negotiation process.[44] For entering a ceasefire in effect consents (albeit temporarily) to the status quo in which their opponent maintains their position of ascendency. Violence is the means through which the challenger (in intrastate conflict, the nonstate group) achieves their leverage, and thus in principle, they are likely to be resistant to a ceasefire (in the absence of sufficient concessions) that might alleviate the hard-fought pressure on the state.[45] On some occasions, the onset of political negotiations is sufficient for a preliminary ceasefire; in other cases, more significant progress is required.

EVOLVING TYPES OF CEASEFIRE

Progress (or lack thereof) in political negotiations shapes the salience of different bargaining problems and the likelihood of different forms of ceasefires. Prior to negotiations, or in the earlier phases of political negotiations, ceasefires are more likely to be used to signal intentions or test the waters, and thus cessation of hostility arrangements is more likely. As political negotiations progress and the parties seek to build firmer arrangements with a longer time horizon, a preliminary ceasefire—that is, a ceasefire with a compliance mechanism—is more likely. Finally, once political negotiations draw to a positive close, it is a definitive ceasefire that sets out the disarmament and demobilization or military integration provisions. In this way, the class of ceasefire is always likely to be heavily influenced by the political negotiation process. Yet despite such an incremental logic, different classes of ceasefires do not necessarily build upon each other: conflict parties may agree to negotiate with no cessation in hostilities or a preliminary ceasefire, agreeing only to a (definitive) ceasefire once they solve the contested issues between them.[46]

PROGRESS ON SUBSTANCE

The sustainability and ultimate outcome of a ceasefire are often closely tied to progress in political negotiations. When there is progress on contested issues (and this progress is favored by the relevant conflict parties), ceasefires are more likely to endure. Trust built by progress in the substantive political negotiations may even allow for ceasefires to endure with less heavy monitoring and verification mechanisms. In contrast, when a political negotiation process falters, stalls, or fails to produce the progress a group requires, then a ceasefire is more likely to come under threat. Therefore, ceasefires are more likely to break down if they are imposed[47] or if they occur before the conflict parties recognize the favorability of peace.[48] In the face of strong third-party pressure, it may be easier to sign a political agreement and later discard it, that is, escalating back to open conflict when the third party is no longer watching.[49]

RESEARCH GAP

As just outlined, prior research clearly shows that ceasefires affect political negotiations and that this occurs through various mechanisms that either help or hinder peacemaking. Likewise, political negotiations clearly have an impact on the ceasefire process, and this effect can also be positive or negative. What remains unclear are why different ceasefire sequencing options are adopted, the different effects that different sequencing approaches produce, under which contextual conditions these different interaction effects are likely to arise, and how the technical components of a ceasefire are shaped by politics and vice versa. There are four key reasons why this has been overlooked in prior ceasefire research.

First, much of what we know about ceasefires has arisen through more general analysis of peace processes.[50] This work has been helpful in identifying a number of functions that a ceasefire can perform, but given that the focus is on the peace process—rather than ceasefires specifically—important details regarding the timing, content, and decision-making calculus that surround various types of ceasefires are left undiscussed. Importantly, the broader interaction between political negotiation and ceasefire processes is only considered implicitly.

Second, the most influential research on ceasefires to date comes in the form of guidance notes and briefs tailored specifically to the policy and practice community.[51] The aim of this work is generally to provide accessible summaries of key guidance and process design advice based on the practical experience of the authors. This provides invaluable insight into the inner workings of many ceasefires. Implicitly, much of this work also touches on the relationship between ceasefires and political negotiations, with several studies arguing for ceasefire processes to be better integrated into the mediation process design. But different studies use different understandings and concepts of ceasefires, making it hard to draw comparisons across cases, time, or space.

Third, the nascent field of academic ceasefire research has focused mainly on exploring the outcomes that emanate from ceasefires. This work has been key to identifying the various functions that ceasefires can perform. The availability of new data, most notably the ETH/PRIO Civil Conflict CeaseFire (CF) data set,[52] presents new opportunities to broaden the research agenda on ceasefires, but until now, this research tends to have been limited to analysis of the provisions included within a ceasefire. Quantitative research is well equipped to help us identify which elements of case study results can generalize and are typical of broader trends and can illustrate and help us understand how trends in ceasefires change over time. Yet, this type of research struggles to draw conclusions when there are endogenous relationships or simultaneous causal effects, such as the interaction between the political and ceasefire processes.

Finally, while there is research on how the context (i.e., domestic political context, international political context, military context) may shape political negotiations or the ceasefire process independently of each other,[53] these studies generally ignore an exploration of how context shapes the *interaction* between the ceasefire and political negotiation processes.

With this in mind, this book makes four key innovations. First, we place the analytical focus squarely on the interaction between the ceasefire process and political negotiations over the course of a peace process. Second, we explore the causes and consequences and the advantages and disadvantages of different ceasefire sequencing strategies as well as the role of technical aspects. Third, we explore how contextual conditions—the domestic, international, and military context—affect the role of ceasefires in peace processes (figure 1.1). Finally, we move beyond the commonly discussed contexts (e.g., Sri Lanka, Aceh, and Kashmir) and explore a wide range of cases, covering different conflicts, regions, and time periods. The cases all adopt a common framework and common conceptual definitions, allowing for the most significant comparative case analysis of ceasefires to date.

APPROACH

In this final section, we present our analytical strategy, introduce the framework that guides each of the case studies, and discuss how we selected our cases. We close by highlighting some of the main findings we discuss in the conclusion and offering a series of questions to guide the reader as they work through the cases.

Analytical Strategy

The nine case studies that follow this introductory chapter form the empirical backbone of this book. Each case focuses on a peace process in one particular conflict and is coauthored by a practitioner who was directly involved in the process, as well as a researcher with case expertise. The analyses combine the unique perspective and insights offered by the case expert with careful study of existing research on the cases. The result is a detailed analysis of the relationship between the ceasefire process and the political negotiation process, drawing out the influence of the domestic political, international political, and military contexts, as well as the sequencing and technical approach.

In most cases, the practitioner was involved in the process as a third-party expert, as either a mediator or a technical advisor. Naturally, the analytical perspective taken is then often weighted toward the interpretation of the third party. In three chapters (Colombia, Myanmar, and the Philippines), the authors included members of one (or more) of the parties in the negotiation. In this case, the perspective of the chapters is more in alignment with one of the sides, although every effort was made to ensure a balanced analysis. The authors' perspective should always be considered when analyzing the cases.

Beyond the case-specific insights offered in each chapter, a key empirical contribution of the book is to make comparisons across cases. This allows us to draw generalizable lessons about which context factors shape the use and effects of ceasefires in peace processes—as well as why, how, and when they do so—and how the interaction between the political and ceasefire process relates to the sequencing strategy and technical aspects. To that end, the book is designed as a structured, focused comparison.[54] The approach is "structured" in that case authors were guided by a common analytical framework (see next subsection) and a series of questions to ensure that the analysis clearly maps onto our research objective. It is "focused" in that it deals only with certain specific aspects of the broader process. The actual "comparison" happens in the concluding chapter, where we distill insights on sequencing strategies, context factors, and technical dimensions based on the empirical discussions.

Through a series of workshops and extensive discussions between the editors and the case experts, we ensured that the authors in each case identify commonalities and differences across contexts, apply the terms introduced in the analytical framework consistently, and focus on broadly analogous aspects of the process. Our analytical framework is specific enough to allow for such an approach while leaving sufficient flexibility to the authors to highlight those aspects they view as the most important in shaping peace process dynamics in their specific cases.

Analytical Framework

Figure 1.1 provides a graphical representation of the analytical framework used in this book. At the center of the figure, we depicted the peace process as the combination of the relationship between its two constitutive parts: the ceasefire process and the political negotiation process. Ceasefire processes and political negotiations are distinct but closely intertwined processes, meaning that the processes by which conflict parties commit to stop fighting are likely to shape attempts to address the contested issues, and vice versa. This interaction has critical consequences for the trajectory of the overall peace process: at any point, we observe a positive feedback loop, a negative feedback loop, an impasse, or a disconnection between efforts to negotiate the contested issues and efforts to stop the violence. In our analytical framework, we describe these various feedback loops and discuss the contextual factors that foster or impede momentum in ceasefire and political negotiation processes.

Feedback Loops

Figure 1.3 shows how ceasefire and political negotiation processes can interact in various ways. In some cases, progress in one tract facilitates progress in the other (see figure 1.3a). For example, parties who make progress toward a negotiated resolution of the contested issues might also then become more willing to stop violence (e.g., see chapter 8). Likewise, a successful ceasefire might create the impetus for negotiating concessions in the political negotiations (e.g., see chapter 6). Yet in other cases, progress on one tract can impede the other (see figure 1.3b), as when a ceasefire reduces the pressure on the parties to make the concessions necessary to resolve contested issues (e.g., see chapter 10) or when upcoming agreements in peace negotiations in one part of the country create incentives for spoilers to escalate violence or undermine a ceasefire in another part (e.g., see chapter 7).

In other cases, an impasse over sequencing can emerge, whereby one or several conflict parties prefer to stop violence only once the contested issues

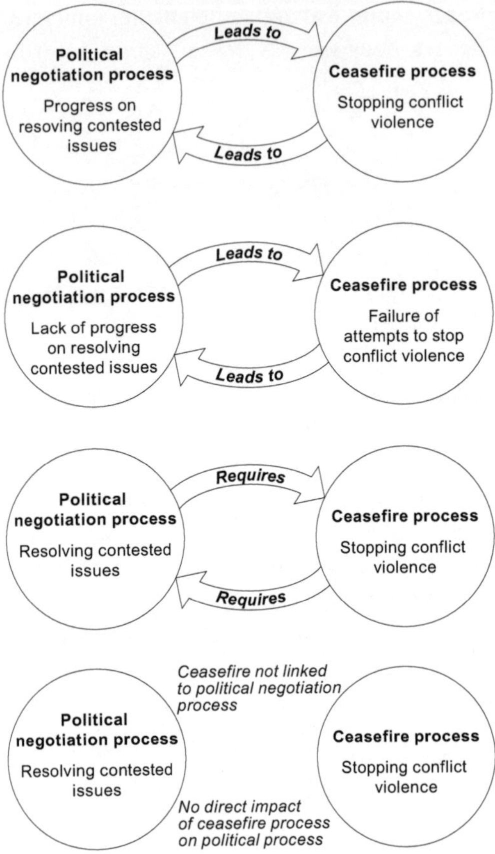

Figure 1.3 Examples of the interaction between the ceasefire process and the political negotiation process

are resolved, while others insist on stopping the violence before addressing the contested issues (see figure 3c) (e.g., early phases of El Salvador). While on yet other occasions, some parts of the ceasefire process might be disconnected from the political negotiation process altogether (see figure 3d) (e.g., early stages of the Colombia process, later stages of the Syrian peace process). Of course, dynamics can change over time, and there may be elements of impasse, as well as positive and negative feedback all within the same process.

These feedback loops provide a simple way to understand the overall relationship between ceasefire and political negotiation processes, allowing us to consider the effects of context factors, sequencing, and technical aspects on the interaction between these two constitutive parts of the peace process.

Sequencing Strategy and Technical Components

In our analysis, we focus specifically on one area that we expect to relate to the nature of the interaction between the ceasefire and political negotiation processes: ceasefire sequencing strategies. Negotiators and peacemakers are likely to have some agency in this area, making it imperative to understand what different sequencing strategies are used, what conditions are most appropriate in what contexts, and how they relate to the feedback loops between ceasefire and political negotiation processes.

Ceasefire sequencing refers to the decisions made by the conflict parties on the point in the political negotiation process at which they chose to adopt different kinds of ceasefires. This may include decisions such as whether a ceasefire is adopted early or late in the political negotiations and how successes or failures are built on. Sequencing can have a big impact on the negotiations, the situation on the battlefield, and often the eventual outcome of a process. It is often a highly contested part of the process. To assess the sequencing strategies that were adopted in each empirical case, the case authors apply the political negotiation phase model introduced earlier in the concept section. More specifically, they discuss how ceasefire processes—the negotiation, content, and implementation of a ceasefire—relate to the political negotiation phases in their case. What types of ceasefires, if any, were adopted in the pre-prenegotiation phase, in the prenegotiation phase, and in the formal negotiation phase? What was the overarching logic behind this sequencing strategy? How was it shaped by and how did it shape political negotiations, and how did it evolve over time? In the concluding chapter, we take stock of the different approaches and develop a framework that details the most common sequencing approaches that we label: conflict containment, talking while fighting, and talking, not fighting.

In addition, as ceasefires are technical agreements, which vary in terms of their "quality," the cases also consider how technical factors shaped the process. Based on practitioner accounts, we would expect that agreements are technically stronger when they are based on a coherent conceptual framework, embedded, and adapted to the specific political, historical, and cultural context, and clearly specify who does what, when, and how. The technical details are likely to be influenced by, and in turn influence, the broader political negotiation process. For example, even if the political process makes significant progress, a process can break down if the technical complexities are not adequately considered. Therefore, it is also a focus for the case studies.

Contextual Conditions

A key aim of this book is to identify the conditions that impact the relationship between the ceasefire and political negotiation processes, in particular the ceasefire sequencing approach. Given the prior lack of research on this topic, it is not clear how to determine the most influential factors. Therefore, we offer a simple framework that provides a common focus across cases, while at the same time being broad enough to allow authors to explore the unique elements of each case. Each of the case chapters focuses on three broad conditions: the domestic political context, the international political context, and the military context. This ensures consistency in the analysis across cases, even though the most influential factors are expected to vary across cases.

International political context covers all elements shaping the peace process that originate outside of the state where the conflict is taking place. This includes the degree of regional and international consensus toward a negotiated process in each case and the nature of external pressure imposed on the parties.[55]

Domestic political context covers all elements shaping the peace process that originate within the state where the conflict is taking place. This includes the political goals of the conflict parties, actor characteristics, political system,[56] public opinion, fragmentation/cohesion of actors,[57] and prior conflict management and peacemaking efforts.

Military context covers all elements related to the ongoing conflict violence.[58] This includes the intensity of the conflict violence, the military balance of power, and geo-spatial-temporal elements such as areas of control and stability of this control over time.

We are primarily interested in how key context factors collectively condition the environment in which the ceasefire process and political negotiations interact (as depicted in figure 1.1). Of note, the ceasefire process and political negotiations may also affect these context factors, for example, if a ceasefire results in increased public support for peace negotiations, or if failure to stop intense fighting triggers international engagement (the "CNN effect"). Each case chapter will reflect on these complexities insofar as they are relevant for that case, but the focus of the analysis clearly lies on how the three broad contexts condition the peace process rather than the other way around.[59]

Case Selection

This book includes nine case chapters, focusing on the processes in

- El Salvador (→ 1992 agreement).
- Bosnia (→ 1995 agreement)
- Burundi (→ 2003 agreement)
- Philippines (→ 1997 and 2017 agreements)
- Sudan (→ 2005 agreement)
- Darfur (→ 2006 agreement)
- Colombia (→ 2016 agreement)
- Syria (2012–2018)
- Myanmar (1989–2020)

The cases selected for this book provide a unique opportunity to study the interaction between the ceasefire and political negotiation processes across several different conflicts. The cases share important commonalities: they are all political, violent intrastate conflicts in which the significant negotiation phases occurred in the post–Cold War era. They all experienced at least one ceasefire arrangement, and in each case, the political negotiation process reached at least the prenegotiation phase. In most cases, the parties stipulated multiple ceasefires and eventually reached a full peace agreement, which allows an analysis of the interaction across different types of ceasefires through different phases of the political negotiation process. However, we also include cases with minimal ceasefires and where a peace agreement remains elusive, to ensure that we do not exclude a specific subset of cases that may, for example, prove particularly hard to settle.

Beyond these shared criteria, the cases exhibit important differences. With regards to the domestic political context, the cases cover conflicts that take place in different political regimes (i.e., democracies, anocracies, and autocracies) and involve conflict parties with quite varied goals (i.e., territorial and governmental incompatibilities), different numbers of armed groups (i.e., one nonstate group and multiparty contexts), and variation in the capacity of the challengers (i.e., strong centralized groups and weak fragmented insurgencies). There is also significant regional variation.

With regards to the international political context: the cases range from the end of the Cold War to the high watermark for liberal peacebuilding in the 1990s, to the post-9/11 war on terror, and ultimately to the present-day return to great power politics. This temporal variation means that the cases exhibit notable variation in the structure of the international system (i.e., unipolar, bipolar, and multipolar periods), forms of international intervention (e.g., mediation, peacekeeping, sanctions, and military interference), and levels of regional and international involvement (i.e., no conflict management, regional or international conflict management). More generally, we have cases where international actors played a supportive or facilitating role, while in other cases, they exerted strong pressure on the conflict parties.

With regards to the military context, the cases cover conflicts that exhibit significant variation in the levels of violence (i.e., high intensity and low intensity), types of violence (i.e., combatant violence and violence against civilians), and geospatial arrangements. There is also variation in the cease-fire sequencing approaches.

Structure

The following case chapters proceed in a chronological sequence—based broadly on when an agreement was reached.[60] Each chapter includes three substantive sections. First, the authors discuss the conflict background, providing relevant details of the domestic, international, and military context. Second, the authors provide an overview of the peace process, discussing if and how the conflict violence and the contested issues were addressed over time, focusing specifically on the sequencing and, when information was available and relevant, on the technical components.[61] Third, they analyze how the interaction between efforts to address conflict violence and contested issues was conditioned by the contextual factors.

The final concluding chapter distills the insights from the structured, focused comparison of the cases. The analysis focuses on what we call the ceasefire opportunity space, a heuristic device that, in any given period, indicates the full spectrum of potentially acceptable ceasefire arrangements and sequencing approaches regarding the political negotiations. We argue that the ceasefire opportunity space is determined by the convergence in the parties' political and security interests, which are shaped by the international, domestic, and military context. We discuss when different opportunity spaces are likely to arise, as well as the advantages and disadvantages of the different sequencing approaches most common in each context. Ultimately, we suggest that whether the opportunity for a ceasefire and any particular sequencing approach is seized depends on various factors. Specifically, we focus on the technical capacity and competence of the negotiating actors and the mediation team. The chapter closes by reflecting on the implications for both researchers and practitioners.

GUIDANCE FOR THE READER

As you, the reader, progress through the cases, it will be helpful to keep the following questions in mind, the themes of which we will return to in the conclusion.

1. How are ceasefires **sequenced** in relation to the political negotiation process—what are the advantages and disadvantages of attempting to stop violence earlier or later in the peace process?
2. How do the ceasefire and political negotiation processes **interact** at various points in the process—positively, negatively, or without direct feedback?
3. What role do **technical components** of the ceasefire(s) play in shaping this interaction, and how are they shaped by the domestic, international, and military context?
4. How do **domestic factors**, such as political goals, actors' characteristics, and prior conflict management, experience shape a peace process and ceasefire sequencing strategy?
5. How do **international factors**, such as international consensus and the nature of external pressure, shape a peace process and the ceasefire sequencing strategy?

   What role does the **military context**, such as the intensity, balance of power, and geo-spatial-temporal dimensions, play in shaping a peace process and the ceasefire sequencing strategy?

NOTES

This book was developed a part of the Ceasefire Project, a collaboration between researchers and practitioners attempting to improve peace mediation practice on ceasefires and security arrangements. For more information, see www.ceasefireproject.org.

1. See, e.g., Aspinall and Crouch, "The Aceh Peace Process: Why It Failed," 15.
2. The categories we propose arose from discussions with Julian Th. Hottinger and Georg Stein from the Swiss Federal Department of Foreign Affairs (FDFA) and are also

found in the practitioner literature on ceasefires such as Brickhill, "Mediating Security Arrangements." See also Clayton et al., "Ceasefires in Intra-State Peace Processes"; Clayton and Sticher, "The Logic of Ceasefires in Civil War."

3. A definitive ceasefire is, however, distinct from an armistice, which in most contexts is understood in relation to the definition set out in the Hague Peace Conference of 1907, which refers to a cessation of active hostilities that may be temporary or permanent. Importantly, under international law, the state of war still exists (e.g., Korea).

4. One might argue that a geographically or temporally limited cessation of hostilities only partially addresses the conflict violence and should thus be considered a de-escalation mechanism rather than a ceasefire. However, in our definition, conflict actors declaring a CoH commit to stopping all conflict violence, including hostilities against the other conflict party—even if only temporally or in a certain geographical area. De-escalation mechanisms, by contrast, deal only with specified parts of the conflict violence.

5. Sisk, "Peacemaking Processes: Preventing Recurring Violence in Ethnic Conflicts"; Zartman, "The Timing of Peace Initiatives: Hurting Stalemates and Ripe Moments," 8–18.

6. Our phase model is consistent with a broad range of literature on the different phases of peace negotiations. One distinct feature of the approach used in this book is that it considers the pre-prenegotiation phase as part of broader peace negotiations. This allows for highlighting the necessity of third-party efforts in the pre-prenegotiation phase and showing how they are different from those in the prenegotiation phase. See Hottinger, "Throw Your Prejudice over Board and Listen," 12–13.

7. At the same time, one can assume that there are always some forms of back-channel contacts—indirect, informal, and deniable—between conflict parties in all phases, be it for intelligence gathering on the armed conflict or exploring if and when to shift into the prenegotiation phase.

8. See Bara, Clayton, and Aas Rustad, "Understanding Ceasefires."

9. Fortna, "Scraps of Paper? Agreements and the Durability of Peace"; Clayton and Sticher, "The Logic of Ceasefires in Civil War."

10. Åkebo, *Ceasefire Agreements and Peace Processes*; Smith, *Stopping Wars: Defining the Obstacles to Cease-Fire*; Sticher, "Healing Stalemates: The Role of Ceasefires in Ripening Conflict."

11. Mahieu, "When Should Mediators Interrupt a Civil War?" 3; Sticher, "Negotiating Peace with Your Enemy: The Problem of Costly Concessions"; Touval, "Ethical Dilemmas in International Mediation," 335.

12. Mahieu, "When Should Mediators Interrupt a Civil War?" 210; Sticher, "The Problem of Costly Concessions"; Touval, "Ethical Dilemmas in International Mediation," 333–337.

13. Mahieu, "When Should Mediators Interrupt a Civil War?"

14. Åkebo, *Ceasefire Agreements and Peace Processes*; Brickhill, "Mediating Security Arrangements in Peace Processes: Critical Perspectives from the Field"; Fortna, "Scraps of Paper?"; Mason and Siegfried, "Confidence Building Measures in Peace Processes."

15. Nathan and Sethi, "Holding the Peace in Intra-State Conflict? The Relevance of Ceasefire Agreement Design."

16. Åkebo, "The Politics of Ceasefires: On Ceasefire Agreements and Peace Processes in Aceh and Sri Lanka," 201–203; Höglund, "Tactics in Negotiations between States and Extremists: The Role of Cease-Fires and Counterterrorist Measures," 238.

17. Brickhill, "Mediating Security Arrangements in Peace Processes: Critical Perspectives from the Field."
18. Höglund, "Tactics in Negotiations between States and Extremists"; Åkebo, "Ceasefire Rationales: A Comparative Study of Ceasefires in the Moro and Communist Conflicts in the Philippines."
19. For example, Fearon, "Rationalist Explanations for War."
20. Clayton et al., "Ceasefires in Intra-State Peace Processes."
21. Sticher and Vuković, "Bargaining in Intrastate Conflicts: The Shifting Role of Ceasefires."
22. Mashal, "Countdown Begins to Possible End of U.S. War in Afghanistan."
23. Pinaud, "Home-Grown Peace: Civil Society Roles in Ceasefire Monitoring," 470–495.
24. Sticher, "The Problem of Costly Concessions."
25. Keels and Wiegand, "Mutually Assured Distrust: Ideology and Commitment Problems in Civil Wars."
26. Bara and Clayton, "Your Reputation Precedes You: Ceasefires, Credibility, and Bargaining During Civil Conflict."
27. Brickhill, "Mediating Security Arrangements: Critical Perspectives from the Field." Strictly speaking, definitive ceasefires are part of the outcome of political negotiations, rather than part of the negotiation process itself, and are thus treated in less detail in this book. We look at definitive ceasefires in as much as their negotiation affected the sequencing and relationship between ceasefires and political negotiation processes but do not cover the implementation of definitive ceasefires in any detail.
28. Zartman, "The Timing of Peace Initiatives."
29. Wagner, "Bargaining and War"; Werner and Yuen, "Making and Keeping Peace"; Luttwak, "Give War a Chance." However, ceasefires can also provide information; see Sticher and Vuković, "The Shifting Role of Ceasefires."
30. Zartman, "The Timing of Peace Initiatives"; Rothchild, "Third Party Incentives."
31. See Sticher, "Healing Stalemates: The Role of Ceasefires in Ripening Conflict" for a comprehensive discussion of the effects of ceasefires on conflict ripeness (which can go either way).
32. Mahieu, "When Should Mediators Interrupt a Civil War?"; Smith, *Stopping Wars*; Zartman, "The Timing of Peace Initiatives."
33. Mahieu, "When Should Mediators Interrupt a Civil War?"; Höglund, "Tactics in Negotiations between States and Extremists: The Role of Cease-Fires and Counterterrorist Measures."
34. Hanson, "Live and Let Live: Explaining Long-Term Truces in Separatist Conflicts," 393–415.
35. Sticher and Vuković, "The Shifting Role of Ceasefires."
36. Toft, "Ending Civil Wars: A Case for Rebel Victory?"; Govinda Clayton et al., "Strategic Suspension: The Correlates of Ceasefires in Civil Conflict."
37. Sosnowski, "Redefining Ceasefires: Wartime Order and Statebuilding in Syria"; for similar examples relating to negotiation and mediation more generally, see Min, "Talking While Fighting: Understanding the Role of Wartime Negotiation", Min, "Painful Words: The Effect of Battlefield Activity on Conflict Negotiation Behavior"; Richmond, "Devious Objectives and the Disputants' View of International Mediation: A Theoretical Framework."
38. Woods, "Ceasefire Capitalism: Military–Private Partnerships, Resource Concessions, and Military–State Building in the Burma–China Borderlands"; Sosnowski, "Ceasefires

as Violent State-Building: Local Truce and Reconciliation Agreements in the Syrian Civil War"; Waterman, "Ceasefires and State Order-Making in Naga Northeast India," 496–525; Kolås, "Naga Militancy and Violent Politics in the Shadow of Ceasefire."

39. Dukalskis, "Why Do Some Insurgent Groups Agree to Cease-Fires While Others Do Not? A Within-Case Analysis of Burma/Myanmar, 1948–2011."

40. Åkebo, "The Politics of Ceasefires"; Åkebo, *Ceasefire Agreements, and Peace Processes*; Åkebo, "'Coexistence Ceasefire' in Mindanao."

41. Crocker, Hampson, and Aall, *Herding Cats: Multiparty Mediation in a Complex World*; Dukalskis, "Why Do Some Insurgent Groups Agree to Cease-Fires While Others Do Not?"

42. Mahieu, "When Should Mediators Interrupt a Civil War?"; Smith, *Stopping Wars*; Höglund, "Tactics in Negotiations between States and Extremists."

43. Smith, *Stopping Wars*.

44. Chounet-Cambas, "Negotiating Ceasefires: Dilemmas & Options for Mediators."

45. Mahieu, "When Should Mediators Interrupt a Civil War?"

46. Clayton and Sticher, "The Logic of Ceasefires in Civil War," 6.

47. Werner and Yuen, "Making and Keeping Peace"; Henderson and Lubell, "The Contemporary Legal Nature of UN Security Council Ceasefire Resolutions."

48. Sticher and Vuković, "The Shifting Role of Ceasefires."

49. Nathan and Sethi, "Holding the Peace in Intra-State Conflict? The Relevance of Ceasefire Agreement Design"; Sticher, "Ceasefire Violations and the Trajectory of Intrastate Peace Processes: A Conceptual Framework."

50. For example, Darby and MacGinty, *Contemporary Peace Making: Conflict, Violence, and Peace Processes*.

51. Haysom and Hottinger, "Do's and Don'ts of Sustainable Ceasefire Arrangements"; Chounet-Cambas, "Negotiating Ceasefires"; Brickhill, "Mediating Security Arrangements in Peace Processes"; Buchanan, Clayton, and Ramsbotham, "Ceasefire Monitoring: Developments and Complexities."

52. Clayton et al., "Introducing the ETH/PRIO Civil Conflict Ceasefire Dataset." See also UN Department of Political and Peacebuilding Affairs (2022) for additional resources.

53. For example, Beardsley, "Agreement without Peace? International Mediation and Time Inconsistency Problems"; Beardsley and Lo, "Third-Party Conflict Management and the Willingness to Make Concessions"; Werner and Yuen, "Making and Keeping Peace."

54. George and Bennett, *Case Studies, and Theory Development in the Social Sciences*.

55. Werner and Yuen, "Making and Keeping Peace." We use the distinction between pressure on process and pressure on conflict issues/outcomes presented by Julian Th. Hottinger MAS ETH MPP 2018.

56. Fearon, "Domestic Political Audiences and the Escalation of International Disputes"; Walter, "Re-Conceptualizing Conflict Resolution as a Three-Stage Process."

57. Stedman, "Spoiler Problems in Peace Processes," 5; Sticher and Vuković, "The Shifting Role of Ceasefires."

58. Reiter, *How Wars End*; Smith, *Stopping Wars: Defining the Obstacles to Cease-Fire*.

59. The context factors may also shape each other: for example, international and domestic support may affect the military situation on the ground. Again, this is not a focus of this book.

60. Cases in which there was no peace agreement at the time of writing are the last to be presented.

61. Interestingly, case studies of conflicts with a weaker international component (such as the Philippines or Colombia) often included a discussion of the technical elements, while the chapters of highly internationalized conflicts (such as Syria or Bosnia) lacked such details. We discuss this in the concluding chapter, showing how technical elements matter, but only if the larger political context provides a conducive environment for negotiations in the first place.

CHAPTER 2

Ceasefires in the El Salvador Peace Negotiations, 1989–1992
The Ultimate Bargaining Chip

Alvaro de Soto and Owen Frazer

The unwinding of the Cold War opened new possibilities for resolving long-running intrastate conflicts. In early 1990 in El Salvador, where a bloody conflict had been raging since the early 1980s, Secretary-General Javier Pérez de Cuéllar embarked the United Nations (UN) on its first mediation of a civil war. Working without a script, the UN mediation team led almost two years of painstaking negotiations. In the process, it learned many lessons about the challenges of mediating intrastate conflicts, not least with regards to the process of agreeing a ceasefire.

Until that point, the standard formula of brokering a ceasefire had consisted of separating armies locked in combat and placing UN blue helmets between them to reduce the chances of friction and flare-up so that negotiators could get on with hammering out a peace deal. However, it quickly became clear that the notion of ceasing fire before tackling political negotiations, which the government of El Salvador (GOES)—whose principal goal was to end the conflict—would have preferred, was not acceptable to its adversary on the battlefield, the Frente Farabundo Martí para la Liberación Nacional (FMLN), which sought far-reaching reforms. The FMLN was convinced that the government had agreed to work for a negotiated solution to the conflict because of FMLN military pressure, and until it had secured the political agreements it was seeking, it was not going to ease the pressure by agreeing to a ceasefire. As such, negotiations mostly took place while fighting continued. Only in November 1991—just two months before the peace accords were formally signed and with a final deal in sight—did the rebels declare a unilateral cessation of hostilities. A definitive ceasefire, conceived as a short, transitional stage that would lead to the formal end of the conflict and the reintegration of the members of the FMLN into society with full legality, was agreed upon six weeks later in a high-pressure final round of negotiations in New York that led to a peace deal being initiated in the opening minutes of 1 January 1992.

The interplay between the political and ceasefire negotiations ran through the peace process, and to illustrate it, this chapter is organized in three main sections. The first section provides an overview of the conflict—including the international political context, domestic political context, and military context in which it was taking place—and relevant developments that preceded the peace negotiations. The second section gives a chronological account of the negotiations that puts the ceasefire discussions in the context of the wider negotiations.[1] In the third section, we reflect on the interaction between the efforts to address the contested issues in the conflict (the political negotiation process) and the efforts to address the conflict violence (the ceasefire process).

THE CONFLICT AND PRECURSORS TO NEGOTIATIONS

Between 1980 and 1992, the FMLN's left-wing insurgency fought the US-backed government of El Salvador in a bitter civil war that cost an estimated 75,000 lives, produced a quarter of a million refugees, internally displaced 25,000 people, and caused over a million people to emigrate.[2] Two issues were at the origin of the conflict: stark socioeconomic inequality and a repressive state apparatus controlled by an alliance of the economic elite and the military, which it viewed as its praetorian guard.

The insurgency began when the dismal failure of an experimental civil-military government led the groups that came together as the FMLN to conclude that there was no chance of achieving political reform and that there was no choice but to take power by force. The early years of the war were the most violent, characterized by both conventional warfare between El Salvador's armed forces (Fuerza Armada de El Salvador [FAES]) and the FMLN, as well as intimidation and assassinations by right-wing death squads with links to the Alianza Republicana Nacionalista (ARENA) party and the military. Starting in 1984, the FMLN switched to guerrilla tactics, and the GOES, with US backing, developed a counterinsurgency strategy aimed at both defeating the FMLN and depriving the FMLN of support.[3] It was only in the late 1980s, when the international environment started to improve, that the parties decided to test the waters to see whether political reform could be achieved through negotiation.

The Parties to the Conflict

The government's original goal was to put down the insurgency. With the ascent to power of the right-wing ARENA party under the presidency of Alfredo Cristiani, it shifted gradually to seeking the disarmament and demobilization of the FMLN through negotiation, not by design or strategy, but in response to the situation on the ground and external pressures.[4] To achieve its goal, Cristiani's government was willing to negotiate with the FMLN on democratic reforms provided that there was no change to their neoliberal economic model, which was later codified through a structural reform program with the International Monetary Fund (IMF).[5] Publicly committed to dialogue with the FMLN, Cristiani's challenge was to bring both the right wing of his party and the armed forces with him during the negotiations.

The FMLN was a left-wing revolutionary movement composed of five distinct armed groups.[6] At its peak in 1983, it comprised 12,000 to 15,000 combatants, including sleeper cells of urban fighters, a network of some 100,000 supporters, and an estimated half a million indirect supporters.[7] Much of the FMLN's support came from grassroots and peasant organizations. However, leaders of the FMLN and that of its political ally, the Frente Democrático Revolucionario (FDR), were largely middle class and college educated, with no experience of rural life. Together with the FDR, the FMLN was very well networked internationally.[8] The FMLN declared that it was fighting for economic and social justice for the people of El Salvador. By the time of the negotiation, this translated into a primary aim of democratizing society through "demilitarization"—extensive reform of the military and security sector.

Pre-Prenegotiations: Dialogue Attempts and a Conducive Environment

A series of developments at the international, regional, and national levels contributed to a conducive environment for negotiations. At the international level, the Cold War was winding down. The United States, which viewed Central America as a frontline in the fight against Communism, had supported the Salvadoran government with both military and economic aid since the early days of the conflict and trained many Salvadoran officers at the notorious School of the Americas in Georgia.[9] In the USSR, Mikhail Gorbachev ascended to power and declared that the Soviet Union was no longer seeking to export revolution and sought cooperation with the West, which opened the door to a fundamental review of the US position regarding the conflicts in El Salvador, Guatemala, and Nicaragua. Although it took a while for the United States to break away from the Cold War mindset, a gradual shift in US thinking meant that the United States began to support a negotiated solution.

At the regional level, peace efforts began in 1983, led by the Contadora Group composed of the foreign ministers of Venezuela, Mexico, Colombia, and Panama, and were followed by a Central American initiative, which became known as Esquipulas II and was led by President Oscar Arias of Costa Rica and President Vinicio Cerezo of Guatemala. Both initiatives were limited by the governments' unwillingness to engage directly with insurgent groups for fear of legitimizing them. However, Esquipulas II produced two important developments that were relevant for the Salvadoran conflict. First, it led to the creation of the United Nations Observer Group in Central America (Grupo de Observadores de Naciones Unidas en América Central [ONUCA]), a regionwide UN field operation designed to monitor Central American countries' compliance with their Esquipulas commitments. Therefore, for the first time in its history, the UN Security Council deployed blue berets in the Americas, breaking a longstanding taboo and making the idea of a deeper UN role in peacemaking in the region less unimaginable than it seemed at first glance. Second, it provided the framework for ending the conflict in neighboring Nicaragua and the elections of February 1990 that brought Violeta Chamorro to power, ending the rule of the leftist Sandinista government. The fact that a peaceful transition of power had occurred, with the Sandinistas maintaining a place in politics, may have provided reassurances to all sides that incorporating the FMLN into politics was a credible and desirable solution to the conflict in El Salvador.[10]

At the national level, there had been several attempts to explore a political solution to the conflict prior to 1989. The FMLN had proposed negotiations as early as 1981 when Daniel Ortega read an FMLN proposal for negotiations to the UN General Assembly. In 1984 and 1987, there were initial talks between the FMLN and the centrist Duarte government under the auspices of the Catholic Church. While these talks could be described as prenegotiations, and they helped to destigmatize the notion of dialogue, the parties never reached an agreement to negotiate, and the process effectively relapsed into the pre-prenegotiation phase until 1989.

"Dialogue without Negotiation"

By the end of the decade, increasing domestic popular pressure to end the war and the conducive international context made it possible to attempt dialogue once again in El Salvador. Alfredo Cristiani won the March 1989 presidential election, and in his inaugural speech on 1 June 1989, he restated his campaign's commitment to opening dialogue with the FMLN. Following a positive response from the FMLN, arrangements for talks between the government and FMLN representatives were quickly made by the Catholic Church. In mid-September, the two sides met at a labor union retreat in Mexico and then met again the following month at a convent in San José de Costa Rica, but no substantive progress was made. The sides agreed to meet again in early November in Caracas. However, in the days after the San José meeting, the government publicly rejected the proposals the FMLN had presented at the meeting. On 31 October, the offices of the trade union Federación Nacional Sindical de Trabajadores Salvadoreños (FENASTRAS) were bombed, killing many participants in a meeting. These developments prompted the FMLN to announce that there was a lack of conditions for serious talks with the government. On 11 November, the FMLN launched a major military offensive, and its forces succeeded in entering the capital for the first time. Until then, the conflict had largely been fought in the rural areas, with the FMLN holding sway in large swathes of the country's territory.

The scale of the FMLN's military successes took both the government and its backers by surprise, especially their incursion into upper-class districts of the capital, where they captured houses of the well-off with little violence, as if defying the armed forces to bomb them from the air as they had done in the poorer districts. Apparently in a panic, the armed forces committed a major blunder by assassinating a group of Jesuit priests, including the rector of the Universidad Centroamericana (UCA), Ignacio Ellacuría, S.J., in cold blood in the early morning of 16 November and tried to pin the blame on the FMLN.[11] It quickly became clear that the perpetrators were members of the armed forces, giving rise to an enormous wave of national and international outrage. Pressure for a thorough investigation into the murders was led by members of the US Congress who sought to condition US aid on progress in investigation of the murders and in the peace negotiations. US military aid was a hugely important source of leverage over the Salvadoran armed forces, and it was to be suspended, reinstated, and reduced at various points in the negotiations that followed.[12]

Despite the FMLN's military successes, it did not take the capital or topple the government. The offensive made clear to both sides that neither side was going to win militarily. The conflict had reached a "mutually hurting stalemate."[13] Sincere efforts began to seek a new format for peace negotiations.

THE UNITED NATIONS-ASSISTED NEGOTIATIONS

A series of diplomatic maneuvers, which had begun while the FMLN offensive was still under way, culminated in separate requests from the government of El Salvador and the FMLN to the UN secretary-general to assist them to restart talks to end the conflict. On 31 January 1990, the secretary-general informed President Cristiani in a personal meeting that the following day his representative, Alvaro de Soto, would travel to Mexico to meet with the FMLN so as to prepare the ground for talks under the auspices of the UN secretary-general (UNSG). De Soto became, in effect, the lead mediator for the next twenty-two months of negotiations.[14]

Prenegotiations: De-escalation Preempts a Precondition

The mediator spent the next eight weeks shuttling between the parties to set the modalities for negotiations. One of the issues to be resolved was the government's insistence that, prior to the start of talks, the FMLN should "renounce any type of violent action that may directly or indirectly affect the civilian population," including sabotage, assassinations, and attacks on economic infrastructure.[15] This ran counter to the FMLN's view that their use of force, and more specifically the November 1989 offensive, was precisely what had brought the government to the negotiating table. They had been transparent with the mediator that military pressure (and the implicit threat of another offensive) would continue and that it would persuade the government to negotiate. It followed that they viewed a ceasefire—or any other limitation of military operations—as a matter for negotiation: why should they unilaterally make such a concession in exchange for nothing? The mediator knew that if he presented the government's demand as a precondition to talks, the FMLN was unlikely to accept it. He also knew that the FMLN valued the fact that the secretary-general had accepted to play the role he had undertaken. Therefore, instead of conveying the government's precondition to the FMLN, he suggested to them that it would strengthen the secretary-general's hand, particularly vis-à-vis the Security Council, if they were to make a gesture of goodwill.

Such gestures were not unprecedented. In earlier phases of the conflict, the FMLN had sporadically declared unilateral cessations of hostilities for limited periods of time, including in advance of the first round of dialogue with Cristiani's government in September 1989.[16] On 13 March, the FMLN announced that it would suspend attacks against economic infrastructure and civilians as a gesture to the UN secretary-general and the archbishop of San Salvador.[17] This goodwill gesture, which was applauded by the government and thus implicitly signaled that their demands had been satisfied, helped to stimulate the process of agreeing negotiation modalities. After a couple more weeks of shuttling, the final details were worked out in a brief unannounced face-to-face meeting in Mexico at the end of March. The framework agreement was then signed on 4 April 1990 in an official ceremony that was presided over by the UN secretary-general in Geneva. It established that the purpose of the negotiation process was "to end the armed conflict through political means as speedily as possible, promote the democratization of the country, guarantee unrestricted respect for human rights and reunify Salvadorian society." It also set out a two-phase process where first there would be political agreements for arranging a halt to the armed confrontation to be monitored by the United Nations, and then they would discuss the "necessary guarantees and conditions for reintegrating the members of FMLN, within a framework of full legality, into the civil, institutional and political life of the country."[18] The substantive negotiation phase was ready to begin.

In the following twenty-two months until January 1992, the UN-mediated negotiations combined shuttle mediation, proximity talks, and face-to-face meetings. Twenty rounds of talks lasting anywhere from a few days to several weeks took place between FMLN representatives and the GOES "dialogue commission."[19] Because President Cristiani refused to negotiate directly with the FMLN, in addition to shuttling between the parties at the various rounds of proximity talks, the mediator also shuttled frequently between San Salvador to meet President Cristiani and Mexico City to meet with the FMLN commanders.[20] Although Cristiani had received political kudos for his call for dialogue in his inaugural speech and sending a "dialogue commission" to meet with the FMLN, he seemed unprepared for a serious negotiation, left his negotiators to their own devices, and handed over the initiative at the negotiating table to the FMLN. The mediation process was supported by four countries whose representatives the mediator consulted with closely but individually from the start and who by July 1991 came to be known as "The Friends of the Secretary General": Mexico, Venezuela, Spain, and Colombia. The mediator regularly briefed other diplomats as well, but the three Latin Americans and Spain were the core.

Sequencing the Ceasefire: A Two-Phase Structure to the Negotiations

The Geneva agreement was followed by a round of talks at Caracas in May 1990 that led to an agreement on the negotiation agenda. The negotiations were to deal with the following issues: armed forces, human rights, the judicial and electoral systems, constitutional reform, economic and social questions, and UN verification. There was also agreement on the overall sequence of a preliminary ceasefire within the negotiations. The FMLN had proposed a two-phase model of negotiations. In the first phase, political agreements would be reached to achieve the conditions necessary for the FMLN to accept a UN-monitored preliminary ceasefire. The second stage would consist of negotiations on the conditions and guarantees for the FMLN to agree to demobilize (without using that word), culminating in the negotiation of a definitive ceasefire under which they would put down their weapons and reintegrate into the social and political life of the country. Surprisingly, the government accepted this proposal, and the two-phase model—already alluded to in the Geneva agreement of 4 April—was detailed in the Caracas agreement that established the agenda for negotiations. The agreement also included a "target date" of 15 September 1990 for the first phase of the negotiations to be completed. This was a suggestion by the mediator with the purpose of spurring negotiations along. The FMLN expressed misgivings, but the mediator reassured them by emphasizing that it was a target rather than a deadline and was therefore nonbinding. In any case, it was contingent on reaching political agreements first.

Over the following months, negotiations stalled on the issue of the armed forces. Although the Caracas agreement explicitly stated that the order in which issues were negotiated could be changed by mutual agreement, as substantive discussions got under way, the FMLN took the position that the armed forces question was so far-reaching and pervasive—they spoke of a "militarization of society"—that, unless it was resolved, there was basically no point in discussing anything else, and they were certainly not going to concede a ceasefire. It later became clear that prevailing on the armed forces question had become an article of faith down the FMLN ranks.

The mediator was able to inject some impetus in the negotiations in July by persuading the parties to switch to the subject of human rights. In just a few days, under the guidance of Pedro Nikken, the legal adviser in the mediation, the parties produced the first substantive agreement of the negotiation, the San José Agreement on Human Rights, which was announced immediately. As noted by astute observers, it contained nothing that was not in force at the time. What was new was the agreement of the parties to the establishment by the UN of a mission on the ground whose purpose would be to monitor compliance by the parties with the agreement they had just signed. However, the mediator, out of an abundance of caution, insisted on including a provision under which this would only be done once there was a ceasefire. This reflected the UN's previous experiences, where missions had been traditionally deployed to monitor ceasefires rather than human rights agreements, and UN monitors only deployed once the fighting had stopped.[21] After the agreement was made public, there was criticism that this provision blunted the agreements' efficacy, and both parties made clear to the UN that they were not opposed to the UN deploying a monitoring mission even before a ceasefire was agreed. The secretary-general was initially cautious, but in December, he proposed to the Security Council to establish the United Nations Observer Mission in El Salvador (ONUSAL). An exploratory mission was conducted in the early months of 1991, and in July 1991, ONUSAL was officially inaugurated.

Pressure for a Preliminary Ceasefire Contributes to Slowing Progress

Meanwhile, in August 1990, the discussions returned to the armed forces question, but for a combination of reasons, no tangible progress occurred. It was a fraught period: the FMLN's room for maneuver at the talks had been reduced and US pressure was building up, and the nontrivial achievement on human rights was not delivering its potential. Some sectors in the FMLN, particularly among field commanders, responded negatively to the human rights agreement. They were dissatisfied that their negotiating team had not been allotted sufficient time for an internal consultation before deciding to switch from their agreed strategy of pressing on with the armed forces question before moving to any other issue on the agenda.

The United States, which interpreted the Caracas agreement's target date of mid-September for a ceasefire as a "deadline," began to apply pressure. With the Cold War ending, the Bush administration was keen to see the Central American conflicts—including El Salvador—ended as quickly as possible so they could focus their attention on developments elsewhere. The United States repeatedly urged the mediator to press the FMLN to declare a ceasefire by the target date and denounce the FMLN if it did not agree. De Soto repeatedly pointed to the Caracas agreement under which the negotiation of a ceasefire would only occur once political agreements had been achieved on all the issues on the agenda. To alter that agreement would require mutual agreement between the parties. As things stood, the FMLN was not in violation of agreements or undertakings, and it would have been unprofessional for de Soto to act as if they were. He declined to denounce them, and 15 September passed without a ceasefire. It was followed by a fair amount of diplomatic activity led mostly by the United States and some public posturing by the government, including the president himself at the UN General Assembly, and responses by the FMLN. None of this was helpful for the negotiations. It soon became clear that the difference of opinion and all the posturing were related not so much to the content or the conduct of the negotiation but to rumblings in the US Congress, where the Bush administration was engaged in a battle to avoid a cut-off or reduction of military aid to El Salvador, imperiled by the progress of the investigation of the murder of the Jesuit priests. The FMLN was enjoying an advantage; US pressure for a ceasefire only hardened the FMLN's negotiating position. To be sure, the FMLN had made it clear to the mediator that they did not entirely rule out the possibility of a ceasefire or some sort of de-escalation—what they would not do is concede a ceasefire for free. FMLN commander Schafik Hándal used the colloquial expression *"amor con amor se paga"* (love must be matched by love). If the government wanted a ceasefire or a reduction in the fighting, they would have to pay for it. The FMLN would have to assess whether what the government offered justified the concession.

Mexico, April 1991: A Breakthrough in the Political Negotiation Process

In the months following the human rights agreement, pessimism grew concerning the prospects of a breakthrough on the armed forces. It became clear that the lack of trust between the parties meant there was not likely to be any progress without an initiative from the mediator. At the end of October 1990—with the consent of the parties—the mediator presented them with a "working paper" on the issue of armed forces. This paper formed the basis for discussions on the armed forces that continued over the following months.

In early 1991, increasingly impatient at the lack of progress toward a ceasefire, the US government once again stepped up the pressure. In representations to the governments of the Group of Friends, the United States— paying no heed to the agreed rules—accused the mediator of bias toward the FMLN and suggested that the GOES was flexible in its negotiating position and that the FMLN had hardened its position. They urged the governments of the Group of Friends to increase pressure on the FMLN for a ceasefire.[22] Accusations of UN mediator bias toward the FMLN were also leaked to the press. This may have been, at least in part, a response to an article the mediator wrote in a major US newspaper explaining the rules agreed by the parties, the comprehensive nature of the negotiation, and the need to avoid a quick fix.[23]

Negotiations reached a make-or-break moment when both sides realized that a very real deadline loomed in the form of the expiration of the Salvadoran legislature on 30 April 1991, due to the constitutional requirement that constitutional amendments be approved in two consecutive legislatures, each lasting three years. If no constitutional amendments were agreed and approved by the legislature and enacted by the president before the end of April, they could not enter into force for another three years. The FMLN refused to accept the GOES contention that the reform could be achieved without a constitutional amendment. Believing that an agreement was possible but accepting the fact that the sole focus on the issue of the armed forces was now hindering the negotiations and that there was need to reassure the government's constituencies that a ceasefire was on the horizon, the FMLN proposed an "initiative to accelerate the negotiations" in March.[24] They proposed a "concentrated agenda" with negotiations on armed forces, constitutional reform, and a ceasefire to take place in parallel. They suggested that if agreement on the political issues could be reached, a ceasefire could be agreed by 30 May.[25] The mediator convened the two sides to a meeting in Mexico City in early April 1991 and used it primarily to tackle, via constitutional reform, issues that had defied solution during the lengthy talks on the armed forces. Following three weeks of intense and dramatic negotiations in April 1991, a package of the required constitutional amendments was finally achieved with the Mexico agreement of 27 April and pushed through the legislature just before the legal deadline. These amendments removed the armed forces' primary responsibility for internal order and subordinated them to the elected civilian authorities. The parties also agreed to the mediator's proposal to create a commission on the truth to investigate the most egregious violations of human rights of the war years. While the Mexico agreement did not guarantee that the negotiations would ultimately be successful, it was abundantly clear that without it, the negotiations would have suffered a severe blow. In Mexico, the parties had come to the edge of the precipice and seen the abyss, stepped back, and reached breakthroughs on the issue of the armed forces, laying the groundwork for the work that needed to be done. It was a turning point.

Rethinking a Preliminary Ceasefire

Following the agreements on constitutional reform, US pressure for a preliminary ceasefire increased further. However, several issues related to armed forces reform remained to be addressed, and the FMLN was unwilling to consider a ceasefire until these had been settled.[26] Nevertheless, the United States kept pushing for a ceasefire by 30 May.[27] As US officials pointed out to the mediator, the negotiations had been going on for over a year with no sign of a ceasefire. The situation was getting increasingly difficult for the government to defend. Cristiani was under a lot of pressure from his party and from the military, who were being pressed to agree to far-reaching reforms while they were under threat of a US military aid cutoff from a Democrat-controlled Congress. They perceived the negotiations as a series of unilateral concessions by the government to the FMLN with nothing in return.[28] There were suggestions that Cristiani was risking a coup—and possibly his life—by persisting with the negotiations. Although the FMLN remained adamant that they would not accept an alteration of the agenda, they were sensitive to the point the mediator made to them that it would not be in their interest to put Cristiani—the best, most pragmatic interlocutor they could expect to have—in jeopardy. Thus, soon after the Mexico agreement, they accepted that "technical" talks should take place at the next meeting, at the Venezuelan beach resort of Caraballeda, Venezuela—if they could bring along key field commanders.

Thus, when the parties met again at Caraballeda in May, a separate ceasefire table was established, chaired by Marrack Goulding, head of UN peacekeeping. Several misperceptions existed on both sides about the nature and role of UN peacekeepers. At the Caraballeda meeting, Goulding therefore briefed the military commanders of both sides about the nature of UN peacekeeping and how a UN monitoring and verification mission could function.[29] However, it was clear to the UN team that these technical talks were something of a pantomime, the audience being ARENA and the FAES hierarchy, serving to maintain the illusion that efforts were being made to secure a ceasefire. Coming to terms would require fulfilling the conditions laid down at Caracas the previous year, before any firm agreement on the ceasefire could be reached.

It soon became apparent that the two-phase structure of the negotiations stipulated in Caracas had become a major obstacle. The GOES saw a ceasefire as a brief period during which both parties would agree to avoid attacking each other militarily and the FMLN would suspend all activities entirely and confine themselves to limited geographical areas in preparation for demobilization. The FMLN agreed that if the ceasefire lasted, there would be no military engagement, but as they saw it, there was no certainty that the political negotiations on the reintegration of FMLN members into civil society during the second phase would succeed, in which case the war would resume. As part of the separation of forces, which was understood by both sides to be necessary for a ceasefire, the FMLN, given the indefinite duration of the ceasefire and the uncertainty whether pending negotiations would end positively, insisted on maintaining control of large swathes of Salvadoran territory and carrying out their activities such as recruitment, training, and exercises to maintain their military readiness in case the ceasefire broke down. This would have required the government to formally acknowledge that there were areas of its own sovereign territory that it did not control, something it could not do. It was one thing to have an informal arrangement of brief duration; it was another to formally sign away sovereign territory for an indefinite period.

In Caraballeda, FMLN commander Schafik Hándal discreetly asked to see the mediator alone. Making it clear that he was not speaking for the FMLN, Hándal wanted to sound him out about his concerns regarding the two-phase structure of the process. He was concerned that it had become an obstacle. What would the mediator think about eliminating the mid-negotiation ceasefire altogether and compressing the two-stage negotiation into one? The goal would be to first finish any political arrangements, including those pertaining to the reintegration of FMLN members into society, and only then would a definitive ceasefire enter into force. The mediator saw that the compression would eliminate the major differences in the parties' notions of what a ceasefire would look like: it would permit the FMLN to come around to the government's conception of the ceasefire as a transitional period of defined duration. Hándal revealed to the mediator that there were differences on this issue within the high command of the FMLN and therefore asked him to treat his approach as a sounding rather than a formal proposal. So, the mediator told Hándal that he would take the matter up with Cristiani—not as an FMLN proposal but as an idea of his own. The mediator went to San Salvador soon after Caraballeda and presented the idea to Cristiani, but he rejected it.

In the summer, the UN mediation team found a way to revive the idea of compressing the negotiations into one phase. At a meeting in Sochi, US Secretary of State James A. Baker persuaded Soviet Foreign Minister Alexander Bessmertnykh to make a joint démarche to the secretary-general. They both appealed to him to take personal charge of the mediation. The secretary-general responded by explaining that he was already personally in charge of the mediation, as made clear by the fact that the mediator was his personal representative. He stood ready to intervene directly should he deem it necessary. He then proceeded to explain that the problem lay elsewhere—in the two-stage structure agreed at Caracas. He informed Baker and Bessmertnykh that, with a view to tackling that problem, he was inviting the leaders on both sides—Cristiani and the FMLN high command—to come to New York in September for consultations on how to break the deadlock by compressing the two-stage negotiations into one. Sure enough, the New York talks undid the "Gordian knot" with the New York Accords of 25 September 1991. The most important agreement was to merge the two phases of negotiations into one and not have a preliminary ceasefire in the middle. They also agreed to a host of other pending matters, including the establishment of the National Commission for the Consolidation of Peace, with equal FMLN participation, that would serve as a transitional forum until the end of the conflict and the reintegration of the members of the FMLN into society, as well as another commission that would make recommendations on purging the armed forces of personnel unfit to continue to serve in the forces as a result of agreed reforms. There was also an agreement on reducing the armed forces and creating a new National Civilian Police, a portion of whose personnel could include up to 20 percent of former FAES or ex-FMLN personnel (since GOES rejected the UN's proposal that both should be barred). The parties now accepted that a ceasefire would not come until the end of the negotiations, but that when it did, it would be within a limited time period.

From Unilateral Cessation of Hostilities to Agreeing a Definitive Ceasefire

Political negotiations continued at a slow pace from October into mid-December. Cristiani was under intense pressure from right-wing forces inside El Salvador. Goulding had to travel to San Salvador to meet with President Cristiani and FAES commanders to help fend off accusations that the New York agreement meant a ceasefire had been pushed aside. He urged the government to try and complete the political negotiations as quickly as possible and demand in return that the FMLN accept a rapid demobilization of its fighters.[30] Nevertheless, since the agreements in New York, it was increasingly clear to everyone that a deal was within reach. Around mid-November, the mediator was approached by one of the FMLN commanders to inform him of their intention to declare a unilateral cessation of hostilities. He explained that they were seeing signs—not unusual as a successful negotiation outcome comes into sight—of fighters still technically locked in combat but not wishing to be the last combatant to be killed in a war. On 14 November, the FMLN declared it was ceasing hostilities, which had the effect of renewing US pressure on the UN mediation team to press for a formal ceasefire. However, there were still matters pending negotiation, and neither side was pressing for a formal ceasefire, so this pressure was unnecessary. General Vargas, the key member of the armed forces on the government's negotiating commission, had articulated the FAES position earlier that a ceasefire would come when the FMLN ceased fire: there was war in El Salvador because the FMLN was waging it against the state. While the Salvadoran armed forces did not immediately reciprocate the FMLN unilateral cessation of hostilities, the mediator intervened with President Cristiani, who soon reciprocated the FMLN's declaration a week later by announcing a de-escalation of the war, with limits on the use of artillery and aerial bombardments.[31]

Come December, however, political issues remained pending, including the whole economic and social item on the agenda and the creation of a National Security Academy to train the future members of the National Civilian Police, which would take over from the public order bodies still under the authority of the FAES. This was behind schedule because the government had failed to take steps necessary to allow this to happen within the near future, which could erode the implementation. Pérez de Cuéllar's term was ending on 31 December, and he had to instill a sense of urgency in the parties to get them to realize that their time was limited if they wished to secure an agreement while a supportive Latin American UNSG was still in office. However, negotiations were at an impasse with the FMLN demanding further progress on pending issues, but the government refused further discussions without an agreement on a definitive ceasefire.[32] The UN mediation team calculated that a final agreement was far more likely to come if President Cristiani agreed to come to New York and that he was more likely to come if ceasefire discussions were already under way.[33]

On Christmas Day, negotiations on a definitive ceasefire began in the conference room on the southwest end of the thirty-eighth floor of the UN headquarters, mediated by Marrack Goulding. Over the next six days, they negotiated from 9:00 A.M. until late into the night.[34] They addressed four main issues: the ceasefire, separation of forces, the drawing down of the FMLN military structure and reintegration of its fighters, and the verification role of ONUSAL.[35] With ceasefire negotiations under way, the secretary-general invited President Cristiani to New York. On 28 December, President Cristiani arrived with a high-level delegation in New York and the final political negotiations continued in parallel to the ceasefire negotiations. An agreement on the outstanding political issues was reached: the creation of the National Civilian Police and the Public Security Academy, as well as provisions for the reintegration of the FMLN—land for arms, as it were—and other social measures.[36] Shortly after midnight on 1 January 1992, as Pérez de Cuéllar's decade in office ended, the New York agreements to end the war were initialed in his presence. The official signing ceremony was set for 16 January in Mexico.

On 5 January, the parties reconvened with Goulding to thrash out the details of the definitive ceasefire and the implementation timetable of interlocking commitments for the implementation of the accords. Although the political agreements had been concluded, working out the details of the ceasefire proved tricky. The parties struggled to finalize the list of sites where forces were to concentrate that would both achieve a separation of forces and respect the parties' established areas of control. It required a strong hand from Goulding. Fortunately, the parties accepted Goulding's directive style, respecting his expertise on technical ceasefire questions and his no-nonsense attitude.[37] He had established his authority when he produced a Gurkha knife he had received as a gift from a Nepali peacekeeping battalion, placed it in the middle of the table, and said, "All right. We are going to come to agreement. I want you to know, if you cannot come to an agreement, I will decide the outcome." Goulding proposed that if the parties could not agree on ceasefire terms by 10 January, then they should accept the arrangements he proposed, which is what ended up happening. Unable to agree, the parties accepted Goulding's decisions on the ceasefire arrangements. Key to the final terms of the ceasefire negotiations was the timetable for implementation drawn up by Goulding. A careful sequencing of steps was stipulated that foresaw demobilization in phases, with progress to the next phase being dependent on GOES implementing particular parts of the political agreements.

Ceasefire Implementation and Demobilization

On 16 January 1992, the parties signed the 122-page Chapultepec Agreement that incorporated all the substantive agreements reached starting with San José.[38] The parties had agreed that an informal ceasefire would come into effect with the formal signing of the peace agreement, putting into writing what was already a reality on the ground. On 1 February 1992, the definitive ceasefire officially began. Monitoring and verification of the ceasefire was overseen by ONUSAL.[39] The initial ceasefire implementation was smooth and took place as set forth in the accords. The separation of forces occurred in two stages over thirty days. In the first five days, the government and FMLN forces concentrated in the key positions they occupied at the end of the war. From the sixth day, the Salvadoran armed forces moved to garrisons and civilian and military sites deemed of national security interest, and the FMLN forces assembled in fifteen designated positions throughout the country.[40]

A hiccup occurred in the demobilization. Because of the failure of the GOES to comply with several commitments according to the agreed timetable, the FMLN suspended demobilization. The GOES had failed to progress on commitments to make plots of government land available for ex-fighters and ex-soldiers, and to comply with the recommendations of the ad hoc commission of the purification of the FAES, which involved the dismissal of many officers. Resolving the impasse required several missions to El Salvador by Goulding and the mediator, which resulted in a delay of two months beyond the nine months that had been agreed upon. Demobilization was eventually completed in time for a ceremony on 15 December marking a definitive end to the war.

The full implementation of the peace agreements took several more years, with several difficult moments along the way. In particular, the purging of the armed forces proved to be a major challenge for Cristiani, and the failure to preliminarily prepare for the creation of the National Security Academy resulted in a delay in setting up the National Civilian Police, during which the army-run security bodies continued to maintain order. The implementation dragged on far beyond the dates set in the implementation package. Nevertheless, sufficient progress was made for elections with FMLN participation to be held in March 1994, and in April 1995, the UN Security Council terminated ONUSAL's mission.

ANALYZING THE INTERACTION BETWEEN THE POLITICAL AND CEASEFIRE NEGOTIATIONS

The challenges that postconflict peacebuilding (a term coined by Secretary-General Boutros Ghali himself) faced in El Salvador have been amply documented elsewhere.[41] However, it is undeniable that the peace negotiations were successful in producing a definitive ceasefire that ended the armed confrontation between the government and the FMLN. Getting to a definitive ceasefire, as we hope our account has made clear, was not a straightforward process. In this section, we reflect on how the El Salvador peace process was characterized by talking while fighting, how domestic political sensitivities shaped the ceasefire sequencing strategy, and how feedback loops between the political negotiation process and the ceasefire process contributed to building the trust that enabled the negotiations to reach a successful conclusion.

Talking While Fighting

Progress toward a ceasefire was inextricably linked to progress in the political negotiations because the FMLN saw military pressure as its main tool for extracting concessions from the government. It was not going to stop fighting, let alone lay down its arms, until an agreement had been reached on its political demands. Had the government fully metabolized this fact sooner, it might have been more forthcoming earlier rather than finding itself pressured into making key concessions on the cliff's edge in April 1991, a truly make-or-break moment. The United States also failed to understand the FMLN's logic and, at points, applied uncalled-for pressure on the mediator to insist on a preliminary ceasefire. However, the UN mediation team and other governments in the Group of Friends understood the FMLN's position and the rules stipulated between the parties and worked to ensure that pressure for a ceasefire did not torpedo the political negotiations.[42]

Knowing that the FMLN's logic was to press for political agreements while their strength was at its peak (i.e., while they were still able to exert military pressure), as soon as they agreed to a ceasefire, their strength would begin to hemorrhage. In UN peacekeeping lore, a preliminary ceasefire was accompanied by a separation of forces to keep them far enough apart that a small incident would not devolve into a wider conflagration, undermining the ceasefire. Although the FMLN held sway over significant parts of the territory, they also employed guerrilla tactics inside government territory and had clandestine urban forces in the cities. They therefore resisted the concentration of these forces in predefined areas. Furthermore, the FMLN was, at least partly, a volunteer fighting force. It could ill afford to have forces concentrated and idle during a ceasefire, owing to likely desertions. As FMLN political ally Rubén Zamora put it when trying to explain to the United States why the FMLN would not accept a ceasefire, the FMLN's troops were unpaid peasants who were likely to be back picking coffee two months after the fighting stopped.[43]

The FMLN was quite open about its strategy of talking while fighting. It used violence at strategic moments to maintain pressure on the government, launching heavy attacks in May, June, and September and a new major offensive in November 1990. In the November 1990 offensive, the FMLN used surface-to-air missiles to bring down planes and helicopters, ending the FAES's dominance of the skies and further altering the military balance in the FMLN's favor.[44] The fighting also served to keep international attention on the conflict and thus pressure on the parties to negotiate. However, it was a delicate balance. Too much violence could undermine the belief that the parties were serious about negotiating, damaging support for the negotiations among both domestic and international audiences.

How Domestic Political Sensitivities Shaped the Ceasefire Sequencing Strategy

It is perhaps not surprising that the interaction between the ceasefire process and the political negotiation process was so central to the course of the entire negotiations. Ending the armed conflict and dismantling the FMLN as a fighting force was, after all, the government's central objective, ostensibly its only one. While technical briefings by Goulding and his team on ceasefire arrangements and UN peacekeeping helped to dispel misunderstandings about what a ceasefire entailed, they could not remove two important political sensitivities to agreeing a ceasefire.

First, ceasefires had a major political significance. For the government, reaching a preliminary ceasefire was already achieving one of their central aims in the negotiations: ending FMLN violence. The FMLN was sensitive to the demand of its political base that it should agree to a ceasefire only once its political demands had been met; it was quick to point out, without fear of contradiction, that it had not been defeated.

Second, progress on the technical side of a ceasefire required agreeing on who controlled what territory. This resulted in a difficult moment in the ceasefire negotiations. The UN mediation had introduced the principle that neither side was going to lose or gain what they had not lost or gained on the battlefield. The problem was that it was exceedingly difficult for the government of a sovereign state to acknowledge that it was not always in full control of parts of its own territory. While the armed forces representatives could accept that they did not control certain areas, politically it was exceedingly difficult to admit this in a formal, written document. Their public position was that the FMLN controlled no territory, but they could hardly deny that they entered parts of Chalatenango, Perquin, and Morazán with trepidation. As described earlier, they said that resolving these issues would depend on progress at the political table. If an agreement would be reached on political reforms, then this might change the connotation of territorial control and it would be possible to move forward on this point.[45] To reach a final agreement on a ceasefire, zones under FMLN control had to be euphemistically be called "conflict zones" (*zonas conflictivas*), which depoliticized the problem. It was also agreed to keep the map showing the final positions of forces secret.[46]

How Positive Feedback Loops Built Trust

In the preliminary stages of the negotiations, there were huge doubts on each side about whether the other side was sincere about its desire to negotiate. So long as suspicion remained that the other side was employing negotiations in a tactical manner rather than seeing them as a strategy for ending the war, the fear that a preliminary ceasefire would be used by the other side to rearm and regroup was high. This may partly explain the government and armed forces' lukewarm response to an initial FMLN ceasefire proposal in February 1989. The FMLN for its part remained highly suspicious of the government's intentions in the early rounds of talks in September and October 1989 as the government position did not seem to have evolved at all since the failed dialogue attempts of 1984 and 1987. While the November offensive helped to make clearer that neither side was going to win militarily, the two sides remained highly suspicious that the other would use any opportunity, including a ceasefire, to gain a military advantage. Positive feedback loops between the political negotiations and the ceasefire negotiations were needed to foster trust.

An early instance of a positive interaction between the ceasefire process and the political negotiations was the mediator's careful orchestration of the FMLN's unilateral declaration of an end to kidnapping and attacks on economic infrastructure as a gesture to the UN (which requested it) and the Church, which preceded the agreement to commence political negotiations (the Geneva agreement of April 1991). However, this did not immediately unlock a virtuous cycle of positive feedback loops.

After the political agreement on human rights in July 1990, the negotiations remained at an impasse over the sequencing of the political and ceasefire negotiations. A lack of progress on a ceasefire made the government unwilling to advance the political negotiations, while the lack of progress on political negotiations meant the FMLN was unwilling to discuss a ceasefire. Only in April 1991 could the impasse be broken with the Mexico agreement on constitutional reforms. The talks in Mexico were preceded by small developments regarding the conflict violence with the FMLN's declaration of a suspension of hostilities during the elections for the legislative assembly in March 1991 and its suggestion that a ceasefire could be reached by 30 May if progress was made in the political negotiations.

The political agreement in Mexico in turn paved the way for the establishment of a ceasefire table at the May 1991 talks in Caraballeda, partly in response to US and government pressure for progress toward a preliminary ceasefire. They argued Cristiani needed to shore up his own constituency by addressing criticisms he was making concessions without achieving anything in return.[47] However, while in other conflicts, preliminary ceasefires have been used to build trust between the parties and help political negotiations to progress, in the El Salvador negotiations this was not the case, owing to the FMLN's resistance to a preliminary ceasefire.

Before the renewed impasse over a preliminary ceasefire could be broken, another important trust-building mechanism was established with the deployment of the UN human rights verification mission in July 1991. The UN, initially cautious about recommending deployment before a ceasefire, decided to take it to the Security Council once an expert mission ascertained that this would be feasible.[48] At that time, the Chinese were said to be averse to issues—particularly human rights issues—beyond a strict literal interpretation of peace and security being raised in the Security Council. To circumvent this, the UN carefully framed this deployment as the first stage in the deployment of what was envisaged as a comprehensive, integrated mission comprising various elements, including ceasefire monitoring and verification. The fact that nobody raised objections or posed questions in the Security Council was a measure of the degree of trust that the Council had in Pérez de Cuéllar. Had they pressed the matter, they would have put the secretary-general and his mediator in some difficulty because he was in no position to assure that that would indeed be the outcome. The mission was to be headed by a special representative overseeing the different components.[49] This framing reassured the parties that the UN would be involved in the monitoring and verification of a ceasefire. ONUSAL officially deployed in July 1991, with a technical preparatory mission preceding it as early as 31 March 1991. Not only did it give the UN mediation team eyes and ears on the ground, but it also got ordinary Salvadorans nationwide and the forces on both sides used to seeing the UN in the country and to working with them. The fact that familiarity and relationships had been established was helpful when it came to the subsequent ceasefire monitoring and verification process that ONUSAL was mandated to carry out in the final peace agreement.

However, the negotiation impasse that had set in since Caraballeda was ultimately only broken when both sides agreed in New York in September 1991 that there would be no preliminary ceasefire. With that agreement, progress could be made toward resolving the remaining contested issues. With a final agreement now in sight, the FMLN sent a positive signal by declaring a unilateral cessation of hostilities, which was eventually reciprocated by the government. The final political agreement in New York followed relatively soon after. From there the path to negotiating the details of a definitive ceasefire was set.

This series of positive feedback loops between the political and ceasefire processes is certainly not the full story of how peace was achieved in El Salvador. However, the interaction between the political and ceasefire negotiations was a crucial dynamic in the peace process. It was supported by careful coordination and a clear division of responsibilities with the UN team. On all the technical aspects of the ceasefire, it was noticeably clear that Goulding was in the lead and was the point of reference. At the same time, even though as an under-secretary-general he was senior to de Soto (who was an assistant secretary-general at the time), Goulding was very clear that he considered de Soto to be the lead mediator with responsibility and authority for all the political aspects and the overall coordination of the mediation effort.

CONCLUSION

The El Salvador peace process proved a watershed moment for UN peace-making in many ways, not least in terms of how it approached ceasefires. Until El Salvador, United Nations ceasefire experience stemmed overwhelmingly from international conflicts, and the traditional UN playbook was to have a preliminary ceasefire in place before commencing political negotiations. The El Salvador experience made it clear that this was not necessarily the only—and undoubtedly not the only practical—approach in the context of civil wars. The intertwined nature of the political and ceasefire negotiations meant that the idea of a preliminary ceasefire had to be abandoned and a definitive ceasefire could only be agreed with the conclusion of a comprehensive political agreement. The need for flexibility in negotiating ceasefires in intrastate conflicts was an important lesson for the UN as it took on an increasing role in mediating civil wars in the post–Cold War world.

Table 2.1: El Salvador timeline

	Efforts to address contested issues	**Efforts to address conflict violence**	**Other key events**
1980	War begins		
1981	Ortega reads FMLN statement at UNGA declaring willingness to talk		
1984	FMLN-GOES conduct dialogue in La Palma and Ayagualo	FMLN temporary unilateral cessation of hostilities	
1987	FMLN-GOES conduct dialogue in La Nunciatura		
1989			
January	FMLN offer to participate in elections if postponed. Proposal rejected		US President Bush takes office
March			President Cristiani elected
June	President Cristiani proposes dialogue with FMLN in inauguration speech		

Table 2.1

	Efforts to address contested issues	**Efforts to address conflict violence**	**Other key events**
August	FMLN accepts Cristiani's offer of dialogue		
September	First round of FMLN-GOES talks during Cristiani presidency, Mexico	FMLN temporary unilateral cessation of hostilities	
October	Second round of FMLN-GOES talks, Costa Rica		
November			FMLN November offensive, murder of Jesuits, fall of Berlin Wall
1990			
January	FMLN and GOES request UN "Good Offices"		
March		FMLN suspends acts of economic sabotage and attacks on civilians	Chamorro defeats Sandinistas in Nicaraguan elections
April	Geneva agreement establishes framework for negotiations		
May	Caracas agreement establishes agenda for negotiations		
July	San José agreement on human rights is first substantive agreement		
September		Target date for a preliminary ceasefire established at Caracas is missed	
October	UN presents working paper on armed forces		US Congress votes to partially suspend military aid to GOES
November			FMLN offensive and use of effective surface-to-air missiles

(continued)

Table 2.1 (*continued*)

	Efforts to address contested issues	**Efforts to address conflict violence**	**Other key events**
1991			
January			FMLN shoot down US helicopter and kill crew. US reinstates military aid.
March			Parliamentary elections in El Salvador
April	Mexico agreement on constitutional reform		End of legislature's term
May	FMLN-GOES talks in Caraballeda	First time a ceasefire negotiation table is established	
July			UN human rights monitoring mission (ONUSAL) deploys
September	New York agreements on the National Commission for the Consolidation of Peace and police reform	Compressed agenda agreed: ceasefire to come at end of political negotiations	
November		FMLN declares unilateral cessation of hostilities. GOES reciprocates.	
December	New York act: political negotiations complete	Definitive ceasefire agreed	
1992			
January		New York II: agreement on ceasefire modalities and implementation timetable	
16 January	Final peace agreement signed, Chapultepec	Informal cessation of hostilities by both sides	
1 February	Implementation begins	Definitive ceasefire comes into force	
December		Disarmament, Demobilization, and Reintegration completed and official end to war declared.	

NOTES

1. For detailed accounts of the negotiations, see Samayoa, *El Salvador*; De Soto, "Ending Violent Conflict in El Salvador"; Martínez Peñate, *El Salvador*; Córdova Macías, *El Salvador: las negociaciones de paz y los retos de la postguerra*.

2. Buchanan and Chávez, "Negotiating Disarmament: Guns and Violence in the El Salvador Peace Negotiations," 14.

3. Byrne, *El Salvador's Civil War*, 145.

4. A US-educated businessman seen as something of a pragmatist, Cristiani was the acceptable face of the ARENA party, as opposed to the charismatic, hard-right founder and leader Roberto D'Aubuisson, whose candidacy had been strongly discouraged by the United States.

5. Following the collapse of the coffee market, the interests of much of the economic elite had changed. They were no longer focused on an agricultural cash-crop export economy dependent on coercion of farm workers. The elites had diversified their business interests toward commerce and were now looking to end the war in order to access domestic consumer markets and encourage the inflow of international capital (Wood, *Forging Democracy from Below: Insurgent Transactions in South Africa and El Salvador*.)

6. See Vickers, "El Salvador: A Negotiated Revolution," 7, for a short overview of the components of the FMLN.

7. Buchanan and Chávez, "Negotiating Disarmament: Guns and Violence in the El Salvador Peace Negotiations," 15, citing Richard A. White, *The Morass: United States Intervention in Central America*, 8. One-third of the FMLN's combatants and 20 percent of its commanders were women (Wade, *Captured Peace: Elites and Peacebuilding in El Salvador*, 28.) Although all five FMLN commanders were men, two women participated regularly in the political negotiations: Ana Guadalupe Martínez and Nidia Díaz. Ana Sonia Medina was the sole female negotiator in the ceasefire talks (Martínez, "Interviewed by Jean Krasno for Yale–UN Oral History Project").

8. The FDR had connections to the Socialist International (indeed Guillermo Manuel Ungo, one of the FDR leaders, was a vice president of the Socialist International). As early as 1981 a Franco-Mexican declaration referred to the combination of the FMLN and the FDR as a "representative political force" (*Joint Franco-Mexican Declaration on El Salvador* annexed to *Letter dated 28 August 1981 from the Permanent Representatives of France and Mexico to the United Nations addressed to the President of the Security Council*, S/14659, https://digitallibrary.un.org/record/23287?ln=en#record-files-collapse -header.)

9. The School of Americas was widely reported to have trained many Latin American military and police officials in practices that were in clear violations of human rights standards. See "School of the Dictators."

10. Aronson, "Interviewed by Jean Krasno for Yale–UN Oral History Project," 18; Samayoa, *El Salvador*, 259.

11. The Jesuits at the UCA were labeled by some elements within the armed forces and, on the political right, as the intellectual leaders of the left-wing insurgency, and their murders may have been an attempt to weaken the FMLN. Ignacio Ellacuría had also recently been involved in discreet efforts to try and restart dialogue between the FMLN and the government, and his murder could have been an attempt to undermine those

efforts. For more information, see Teresa Whitfield's excellent book on the murders that explains why they were such a pivotal event (Whitfield, *Paying the Price*).

12. For a comprehensive account of the internal US political battle around aid to El Salvador, see Arnson, *Crossroads*.

13. Zartman, "The Timing of Peace Initiatives: Hurting Stalemates and Ripe Moments."

14. In this text we have invariably referred to what the UN did in El Salvador as mediation and to the secretary-general's representative as the mediator because that, for all intents and purposes, describes what was done and what he was. However, government sensitivity to the term "mediation" meant that in the negotiations, the terms "good offices," "intermediary," and "facilitator" were preferred.

15. UN internal minutes (1990) *Nota sobre el almuerzo de trabajo del Secretario General con El Presidente de El Salvador*, 31 January, UN archives, document location: S-1024-0160-0012 (15).

16. These were often invoked for humanitarian reasons or in advance of a round of talks. Specific occasions included the papal visit in 1983, the dialogue of La Palma in 1984, a UNICEF child vaccination campaign for three Sundays in 1985, and the holidays of Christmas and New Year in 1985 (Purrer Guardado, *Diplomacia pastoral*, 224–225). In advance of the first round of talks with Cristiani's government, the FMLN also declared a "unilateral truce" of ten days to last from 13–23 September (FMLN "Comunicado del 7 de septiembre de 1989" and FMLN "Comunicado del 10 de septiembre de 1989," available in ECA August–September 1989). See also "Telegrams from American Embassy in San Salvador to SecState in Washington DC," 29 September 1989 and 5 October 1989. However, the truce was not reciprocated, and before the end of September, the FMLN had launched a new series of military attacks (Cronica del Mes p. 740 ECA August–September).

17. *Comunicado Oficial del FMLN*, 13 March 1989.

18. Original text of the Geneva agreement in United Nations Department of Public Information, *The United Nations and El Salvador, 1990–1995*, 4:110, 164.

19. The government objected to the term "negotiations," fearing that this granted too much status to the FMLN and implied that both sides would be making concessions. They preferred to use the term "dialogue."

20. President Cristiani was present at only the two New York rounds of the talks in the later stage of the negotiations, along with the five members of the FMLN high command, although Cristiani was not involved in direct meetings with the FMLN (Samayoa, *El Salvador*, 158). Besides that, the mediator met the full general command on two occasions: during the April 1991 talks in Mexico and on a visit to Havana.

21. At this point, it was by no means certain that the UN Security Council would support the deployment of a UN mission, and so the mediator did not want to undermine the chances of UN Security Council support by leaving open the possibility that a UN mission might deploy before a ceasefire was in place, putting UN staff (including military personnel provided by troop contributing countries) in harm's way.

22. Pérez de Cuéllar, *Pilgrimage for Peace*, 427.

23. De Soto, "UN Negotiations Not among Casualties of War in El Salvador."

24. *Iniciativa del FMLN para acelerar la negociación*, Managua, 16 March 1991.

25. Samayoa, *El Salvador*, 366.

26. Memcon of meeting at the White House between UNSG Pérez de Cuéllar, President Bush, and their teams, 9 May 1991.

27. In a call with the UN secretary-general, President Bush asked him to "insist that negotiations continue towards a ceasefire agreement" (Bush Memcon with Peréz de Cuéllar, 9 May 1991). See also Department of State memo, "Negotiations to End War in El Salvador" (dated as 4 April 1990 but clearly written after end of April 1991 negotiations), in which the United States called for the next round of negotiations to be a "pressure cooker session" in order to reach an agreement on a ceasefire by 30 May.

28. Moreno, "El Proceso de Negociación Salvadoreño Desde La Perspectiva Del FMLN."

29. Goulding, *Peacemonger*, 226.

30. Goulding, *Peacemonger*, 235.

31. De Soto, "Ending Violent Conflict in El Salvador."

32. Sullivan, "How Peace Came to El Salvador," 96.

33. Goulding, *Peacemonger*, 235.

34. Goulding, *Peacemonger*, 236.

35. Buchanan and Chávez, "Negotiating Disarmament: Guns and Violence in the El Salvador Peace Negotiations," 21.

36. On economic and social questions, the FMLN had earlier conceded that they were not aspiring to settle an economic model between the two warring parties: that was legitimately left to a duly elected democratic government; all they sought was the minimum conditions to ensure that FMLN members reinserting into society, many of whom had taken up arms as teenagers, would have proper opportunities to earn a livelihood.

37. Former government negotiator David Escobar Galindo recalled how on the first day of the ceasefire negotiations in December in New York, Goulding asked both sides to present their proposals for ceasefire positions. The next day, both sides presented their proposals. Goulding's reaction was "these are not ceasefire positions but more like battle positions." Galindo had so much respect for Goulding that he even named his dog after him (Interview with David Escobar Galindo, San Salvador, 20 February 2020).

38. Full text of the peace agreement available at https://peacemaker.un.org/elsalvador-chapultepec92.

39. The creation of ONUSAL benefited from synchronization with the winding down of ONUCA, which had been involved in monitoring the peace process in neighboring Nicaragua and overseeing the demobilization of the Contras. Much of the personnel and infrastructure from ONUCA was repurposed and redirected to ONUSAL, facilitating a rapid deployment and scaling up of the mission.

40. *Peace Agreement*, chapter VII: Cessation of the Armed Conflict, paragraphs 11–13.

41. See, for example, De Soto and del Castillo, "Obstacles to Peacebuilding"; Wade, *Captured Peace: Elites and Peacebuilding in El Salvador*.

42. Interview with former FMLN negotiator Ana Guadalupe Martínez, San Salvador, 17 February 2020.

43. Byrne, *El Salvador's Civil War*, 183, citing Cable, "Aronson Zamora meeting on 15 November" from secretary of state to US embassy, 22 November 1990.

44. Samayoa, *El Salvador*, 556.

45. Interview with former FMLN field commander and ERP deputy commander, Jorge Meléndez ("Jonas"), San Salvador, 19 February 2020.

46. Interview with former FMLN Commander Eduardo Sancho, San Salvador, 19 February 2020.

47. In Goulding's view, this decision to involve him and commence technical discussions early on was part of the key to success in the implementation phase. In his view, the

transition from negotiation to implementation had not worked so well in Namibia or Cambodia, precisely because of the failure to make the connection early enough in the negotiations (Goulding, "Interviewed by James S. Sutterlin for Yale–UN Oral History Project").

48. Pérez de Cuéllar, *Pilgrimage for Peace*, 425.
49. To ensure that the human rights monitoring would not be politicized, the mediator insisted that the human rights reporting was sent directly to headquarters with just a copy to the special representative.

CHAPTER 3

Bosnia, 1992–1995
Imposing Ceasefires

Christopher R. Hill and Claudia Wiehler

The Bosnia conflict left more than 100,000 people dead, more than half of whom were civilians. Between 1992 and 1995, multiple peacemaking attempts, including dozens of ceasefires, failed to resolve the contested issues and end the violence. International peacemaking was for long periods extremely ineffective, and only when the conflict began to seriously endanger the Euro-Atlantic relationship did the North Atlantic Treaty Organization (NATO) intervene to push the parties toward the signing of a ceasefire (and, shortly after, the Dayton Peace Accord). This strategy worked out not least because NATO committed itself to enforce the proposed agreements in the long term.

An extensive body of literature details the causes of the peacemaking failures in Bosnia and highlights many of the factors that ultimately allowed the US-led mediation efforts to produce an agreement. This chapter adopts a different focus, centering the analysis on the use of ceasefires throughout the Bosnian conflict, in particular exploring the interaction (or lack thereof) between the ceasefire process and the political negotiations. In line with the framework introduced in chapter 1, it is argued that this interaction can only be understood if the international and military contexts are taken into account. The analysis reveals that the multitude of ceasefires in the Bosnian conflict were almost entirely ineffective because they were largely imposed by outside actors and not in alignment with the military situation on the battlefield and the interests of the conflict parties. A sustainable ceasefire was only possible when the international context shifted, and the (more) united international powers intervened militarily to shift the military balance between the conflict parties, and thereby the incentives of the parties, to move toward peace. When the conflict parties have no genuine interest in a negotiated settlement, imposed agreements without subsequent enforcement were at best ineffective and at worse counterproductive, creating negative feedback loops between the political and ceasefire process.

A second key insight is that ceasefires were ultimately only effective when political issues were agreed, or at least an acceptable resolution was in sight. Once the political terms were (close to) agreed, the incentives to use violence vanished. Thus, progress in the political process facilitated a halt in fighting, which was crucial to reach a stage of "talking, not fighting" during the preparation and signing of the final agreement. This suggests that attempts to impose a stop in fighting are more likely to be rejected, without some framework agreement on how the contested issues might be resolved.

In what follows, we first provide a brief overview of the conflict, discuss the main peace negotiations and attempts to stop the fighting, and then analyze the interaction between the ceasefire process and the political process throughout this case. In so doing, we can provide key lessons for the ceasefire research and practice community.

CONFLICT BACKGROUND

Toward the end of the Cold War, ethnic nationalism was on the increase in Yugoslavia. Under Josip Broz Tito, the former Yugoslavian leader, the dispersion of groups with the same ethnic identity across several republics did not lead to contention, since the groups were connected through an overarching institutional framework, including the party and the military. After Tito's death and the related weakening of the federal government, Serbian attempts to consolidate power triggered fears in other ethnic groups. Serbian nationalist Slobodan Milošević had become president of Serbia in 1989 and gained de facto control over four of the eight republics and autonomous provinces constituting the Yugoslavian federation as well as over the Yugoslavian army.[1]

In response to these developments, and inspired by democratization processes in the wider region, Slovenia and Croatia declared independence. Encouraged by the European Union (EU), the Bosnian Muslims (i.e., Bosniaks) held their own referendum on independence at the end of February 1992. In protest, the Serbian population of Bosnia boycotted the poll, but despite this, Bosniak leader Alija Izetbegović declared independence.[2] In response, a violent conflict erupted between the Bosniak and Serb populations. Bosnian Serbs sought to enlarge their territory to include areas they considered "historically Serbian." Within a few weeks, they had established control over 70 percent of the territory[3] and embarked on a program of ethnic cleansing that drastically shifted the ethnic territorial divisions across the state. Civilian casualties were extensive, with over 80 percent of the victims being Bosniaks.[4]

At the same time, the Bosnian Croats, fearing being sidelined as second-class citizens in a future Bosnia and Herzegovina dominated by the Bosniaks or the Serbs, also took up arms. In 1991, the Bosnian Croats declared the establishment of the Croatian Union of Herzeg-Bosnia.[5] This created resentments among the Bosniaks,[6] and in early 1993, tensions between the two sides escalated, resulting in further fighting and ethnic cleansing.[7] As the conflict progressed, the Bosnian Croats and Serbs joined forces against the Bosniaks, while at other points, they opposed each other violently.[8]

The Bosnian conflict was, from the start, highly internationalized. The Bosnian Serbs profited from their close connection to the Yugoslavian/Serbian government. They received weapons, training, and direct support from the Yugoslav Federal Army. In addition, when the Serbs withdrew from Croatia as agreed in the Vance Plan, their arms were retread into Bosnia. This support was particularly significant because of an international arms embargo imposed on Yugoslavia in 1991, which critically limited the military capacity of the Bosniaks.

Similarly, the Bosnian Croats had a close relationship to the Croatian government of Franjo Tuđman. Croatian elites aimed for a unification of Croatia and the Croatian parts of Bosnia-Herzegovina.[9] To this end, they supported the secession of Bosnia and Herzegovina from Yugoslavia and calculated that the subsequent aggression by the Serbs would lead to a dissolution of the Bosnian territory. This would in turn allow the Croatian republic of Herzeg-Bosnia to declare itself independent.[10] When this did not materialize, Croatia began to support the Bosnian Croats militarily, including through the deployment of Croatian troops to Bosnia and support for irregular Croatian militias.[11]

Other international actors, in particular the Europeans, United States, NATO, and the United Nations (UN), not least via the United Nations Protection Force (UNPROFOR), also played a central role in the conflict. First, third parties sought to pressure the parties into an agreement through high-pressure diplomacy and, as these efforts proved ineffective, stepped up their engagement through NATO military intervention and UN peacekeeping forces. This culminated in NATO's Operation Deliberate Force that included systematic air strikes against the Bosnian Serbs.[12]

The Bosnian conflict and the breakup of Yugoslavia, more generally, were widely understood as the first post–Cold War test to the Euro-Atlantic alliance.[13] The conflict had a particular significance in this regard due to its geographic and cultural position in Europe. After the collapse of the Soviet Union, the Western powers sought to demonstrate the peacefulness and credibility of a new world order based on human rights, while NATO sought to show its value and capabilities in a post–Cold War environment.

THE BOSNIAN PEACE PROCESSES

The Bosnian conflict saw a plethora of third-party initiatives and cease-fire declarations: more than four hundred diplomatic interventions[14] and seventy-nine ceasefire arrangements.[15] For more than three years, these efforts proved extremely ineffective at containing the conflict violence or addressing the contested issues. This failure was largely the result of the disconnect between Western-led peacemaking initiatives and the lack of shared interests of the conflict parties. Until the summer of 1995, the conflict parties had no genuine interest in an agreement, as proposed solutions either failed to match the military realities on the ground—making it unattractive to the Serbs—or undermined the unity of Bosnia and Herzegovina—making the solution unacceptable to the Bosniaks.

Third-party efforts to address the conflict violence involved a variety of different types of ceasefires, mainly involving de-escalation efforts, like no-fly zones, the declaration of Safe Areas, and humanitarian agreements, and cessation of hostility arrangements. As a negotiated settlement remained neither desirable nor feasible, the conflict parties had little incentive to give away their strongest bargaining tool: the unconstrained use of armed violence.

To support the peacemaking efforts, third parties also used economic and military pressure, including the arms embargo on Yugoslavia in 1991, sanctions on the Serbian government in 1992, and limited military interventions by NATO from 1994 onward. Particularly the arms embargo has been criticized for asymmetrically weakening the Bosniaks as the Bosnian Serbs continued to be supported by Serbia.[16] The third-party approach shifted fundamentally with the NATO intervention Operation Deliberate Force, in summer 1995. It was through this initiative that NATO ultimately pressured the Serbs into negotiations and created a situation in which the de facto territorial division resembled the proposed agreements. Under this condition, the conclusion of a comprehensive ceasefire and the Dayton Accords was made possible. An overview of the described efforts in both dimensions of the peace process is provided in figure 3.1 (1991–1994) and figure 3.2 (1995).

The Bosnian case is an example that shows the peace process phases outlined in the framework chapter do not always appear in a linear order. At the beginning, there was no pre-prenegotiation or prenegotiation phase, as the negotiations and security arrangements were imposed on the conflict parties from the outside, even before violence broke out, and thus did not emerge organically from the parties' interactions and interests. However, negotiations were interrupted after numerous failed agreements, and the process relapsed into pre-prenegotiations and later prenegotiations. Similarly, the ceasefire types did not follow the ideal-type sequencing laid out in the framework. In the following, three periods in the peace process are differentiated: first, separate attempts by the EU and the United States to settle the conflict; second, the joint efforts in the Contact Group; and third, the US-led initiative that produced the Dayton Accords in 1995.

Separate Initiatives by the EU and the United States

The first third-party initiatives were led by the EU. The EU considered, and explicitly framed, the Bosnian conflict as a European problem.[17] This fitted well with the US aim to slowly decouple its security relationship with Europe after the end of the Cold War. Anticipating tensions in a weakened Yugoslavia, the EU initially launched a series of initiatives to try and prevent the outbreak of violence, including the establishment of the European Community (EC) Carrington Commission in September 1991 and the Lisbon conference in February 1992, and subsequently the Chapter VI peacekeeping mission UNPROFOR. Originally deployed as part of the Vance Plan in Croatia and only post hoc extended to Bosnia, the mandate of UNPROFOR was to focus on its humanitarian tasks with few strictly military responsibilities.[18] The mission was composed mostly of British and French soldiers.[19]

The Lisbon conference resulted in the Carrington–Cutileiro Plan that foresaw power sharing at all administrative levels. The plan was initially signed by all parties but ultimately failed when Bosniak leader Izetbegović conducted the independence referendum and withdrew from the agreement ten days after the official signature, leading to the onset of war.

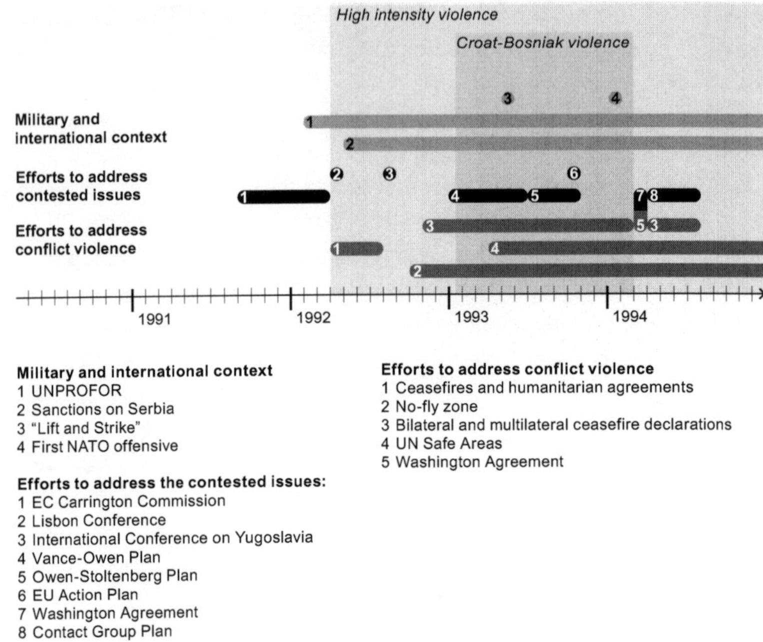

Military and international context
1 UNPROFOR
2 Sanctions on Serbia
3 "Lift and Strike"
4 First NATO offensive

Efforts to address the contested issues:
1 EC Carrington Commission
2 Lisbon Conference
3 International Conference on Yugoslavia
4 Vance-Owen Plan
5 Owen-Stoltenberg Plan
6 EU Action Plan
7 Washington Agreement
8 Contact Group Plan

Efforts to address conflict violence
1 Ceasefires and humanitarian agreements
2 No-fly zone
3 Bilateral and multilateral ceasefire declarations
4 UN Safe Areas
5 Washington Agreement

Figure 3.1 Bosnia conflict, 1991–1994

The onset of war was followed by a series of largely ineffective ceasefires and humanitarian agreements. The ceasefires included monitoring through the European Community Monitor Mission (ECMM), which, similar to UNPROFOR, had been created for the conflicts in Croatia and Slovenia originally.[20] The humanitarian agreements aimed to commit the parties to the principles of international humanitarian law, such as through the Sarajevo Declaration in April 1992, which sought to ensure a humane treatment of displaced persons.[21] The International Committee of the Red Cross (ICRC) initiated agreements on humanitarian principles in this period, but they also proved largely ineffective in shifting conflict behavior,[22] even though several successful agreements on the exchange of prisoners were concluded.[23] In a further attempt to limit conflict violence, a UN Security Council resolution declared the Bosnian airspace as a no-fly zone in October 1992.[24]

Following the failure of the Carrington–Cutileiro Plan, a working group on Bosnia was established at the International Conference on Yugoslavia in London, August 1992. The working group launched three attempts to negotiate a settlement between the Bosnian parties: first, the working group summoned the conflict parties in Geneva, in January 1993, to negotiate the

Vance–Owen Plan, which was based on a similar vision as the previous agreements for power-sharing government. This time, the initiative collapsed due to the rejection of the plan in a referendum of the Bosnian Serbs, who, due to their successes on the battlefield, were unwilling to concede gains in the political process.

The failure of the Vance–Owen Plan led to a further deterioration of the already tense relationship between the Bosniaks and the Bosnian Croats. The plan attributed areas to the Croats that they had lost militarily, enlarging their territorial share significantly. The Bosnian government rejected this proposal, despite pressure from the Croatian government,[25] leading to an escalation in fighting between the Bosniaks and Bosnian Croats.[26]

In response to the stalled peace process, the United Nations attempted further conflict mitigation and de-escalation measures to manage the conflict violence. They established six "Safe Areas" seeking to protect Bosniak civilians in spring 1993.[27] Established through UN Security Council resolutions, the areas covered isolated Muslim-majority cities, including Srebrenica and Goražde, as well as Sarajevo.[28] UNPROFOR was charged with ensuring compliance but ultimately received less troops than asked for.[29] One could argue that the Safe Areas were a signal of the inability of the international actors to contain the violence for generally.

Around the same time, NATO was authorized by the UN Security Council to enforce the no-fly zone that was being violated frequently.[30] The newly deployed NATO forces were tied to UNPROFOR by the dual key agreement that required mutual agreement for military activity. The dual key agreement proved disastrous as it basically eradicated NATO's deterrence effect and its ability to react.[31] Since most of the peacekeeping troops came from European countries, the European governments were reluctant to agree to any military operations that would potentially endanger their troops. This reluctance was exacerbated by the vulnerability of the UNPROFOR forces due to their widespread distribution into small pockets across the country.

The negotiators tried to push the Vance–Owen Plan further throughout the first half of 1993, but Vance finally declared the plan dead in June 1993.[32] Shortly after, the Owen–Stoltenberg Plan was presented but rejected by the Bosniaks, who feared that the plan would undermine the unity of the Bosnian state.[33] This was because the plan foresaw a federation of three ethnic states but also included an exit clause to leave the federation. In a last attempt, the working group suggested the EU Action Plan, also called the Juppé–Kinkel Plan, in October 1993, but equally without success.[34]

The third parties and in particular the UN tried different strategies with regard to ceasefires during this period. The conflict parties were pushed to declare ceasefires before the peace talks, as well as during the negotiations aiming at a "talking, not fighting" scenario. The ceasefires were declared mostly between the Bosniaks and the Bosnian Croats but later also included the Bosnian Serbs. All of them proved ineffective at stopping the violence.

When it became clear that the Bosnian Serbs would not be ready to commit to the solutions proposed by the Europeans, the United States started to pursue its own so-called lift-and-strike policy. The basic idea was to lift the UN arms embargo on the Bosnian government and to strike the Bosnian Serbs until the Bosnian forces were powerful enough to push the Serbs back. This strategy was highly contested within the US administration and equally evoked little support from Europeans. Being afraid of getting drawn into the Bosnian "quagmire," the US government finally dropped the policy in May 1993. It was pursued in parallel with the European-led working group negotiations in 1993 and thereby became a symbol for the complete disconnect between the European and US strategies. As a consequence, the US approach shifted from intervention to conflict containment.[35] Despite the European and US reluctance to get further involved in the conflict after autumn 1993, NATO was drawn into fighting for the first time in early 1994, due to its responsibility for enforcing the no-fly zone. Their intervention was triggered by the bombing of Sarajevo by the Bosnian Serbs.[36]

Given the lack of progress, the United States decided to focus its efforts on the conflict between Bosniaks and Bosnian Croats. US delegates Charles Rodman and Robert Frasure were able to negotiate the Washington Framework Agreement, which established a Muslim–Croat federation in March 1994—a pivotal shift to the domestic conflict context. The signatories included the Bosnian government, the Bosnian Croats, and the Croatian government.[37] The agreement had been supported by a successful preliminary ceasefire between the Bosniaks and the Bosnian Croats concluded the week before and hence allowed the parties, at least for a short period, to talk without fighting.[38] The agreement and preliminary ceasefire was made feasible by the international context, which created a shared interest among the Bosniaks and the Croats in stopping violence and finding a political solution. Specifically, the shared interests resulted from an emerging international consensus and thus mounting international pressure on Croatia through sanctions, coupled with the promise of increased support for Croatia in their related conflict with Serbia.[39] The agreement established a federation in the Croat- and Bosniak-majority areas and included the *possibility* of a confederation with Croatia. The agreement ensured that the Bosnian Croats received equal rights in Bosnia while securing special rights with regard to Croatia. In addition, the agreement addressed the violence between the two sides by including provisions on disengagement and integration of armed forces.[40] The Washington Framework Agreement changed the military situation substantially, as the two groups became much more powerful through the integration of their forces.[41]

The Contact Group

After the failure of the EU action plan in October 1993, no substantial negotiations involving the Bosnian Serbs were attempted for six months. Efforts at conflict containment still proved hard to implement, and violence escalated in spring 1994. On two occasions, a new strategy was tried by declaring temporarily limited ceasefires that were supposed to allow for the negotiation of a ceasefire without temporal restrictions.[42] None of these endeavors bore the desired fruits.

Since the containment strategy had proved ineffective, a Contact Group was established including the permanent members of the UN Security Council (except China), NATO, and the EU member states.[43] The group developed the eponymous Contact Group Plan, which was presented to the conflict parties in summer 1994. Building on the newly established Croat–Bosniak federation, the plan proposed a federation with two states and a 51–49 percent territorial division. However, since the Bosnian Serbs still held around 70 percent of the territory, they had little incentive to accept this proposal.[44] Ultimately, the talks collapsed.

After the failure of the Contact Group Plan in summer 1994, no major peace agreements were brought forward for nearly a year, and the number of proposed ceasefires sharply decreased. US delegate Robert Frasure tried to negotiate directly with Milošević in early 1995, but Milošević blocked these rapprochements as he claimed he would not be able to speak for the Bosnian Serbs.[45] There were no initiatives launched by the conflict parties themselves and no calls for ceasefires, which again demonstrated the lack of interest in managing the conflict violence in this period.

There was one notable exception, however. In January 1995, the conflict parties agreed on the so-called Carter ceasefire that stopped the conflict violence between January and end of March 1995.[46] This was the first sustained break in fighting since the beginning of the conflict. The ceasefire was largely apolitical and driven by the military dynamics in Bosnia and Croatia, as well as the exhaustion of the conflict parties. It collapsed after military offensives by the Bosniak–Croat coalition, and violence escalated again in spring and summer 1995.

The escalation cumulated in the atrocities of Srebrenica, one of the so-called Safe Areas, and began to directly threaten the reputation of the EU, the United States, and the UN as well as the Euro-Atlantic relationship. Coming under pressure from a Bosniak–Croat offensive in the Western Livno valley, the Bosnian Serbs stepped up their attacks against UN-protected areas, including Sarajevo, in May 1995. NATO reacted with the shelling of Bosnian Serb positions, yet the attacks became known as "pinprick strikes" due to their negligible impact.[47] These pinpricks triggered further escalation with the Bosnian Serbs, taking 350 UN peacekeepers hostage. The events culminated in the ethnic cleansing of Srebrenica, during which Bosnian Serbs killed over 7,000 Muslim men. UN peacekeepers were present but outnumbered and did not intervene.

Humiliated by the continuing Bosnian Serb atrocities, the Euro-Atlantic alliance saw its relevance under threat. The alliance could not demonstrate its importance and capabilities in a post–Cold War world without being able to solve something as significant, and as geographically close, as the Bosnian conflict.[48] The international actors were at a crossroads. The UN sought to pull out of Bosnia, pressuring the United States to safeguard this process through the presence of military personnel. Internal plans of the Pentagon foresaw the deployment of 25,000 troops.[49] At the same time, the British, French, and Dutch governments founded the Rapid Reaction Force in

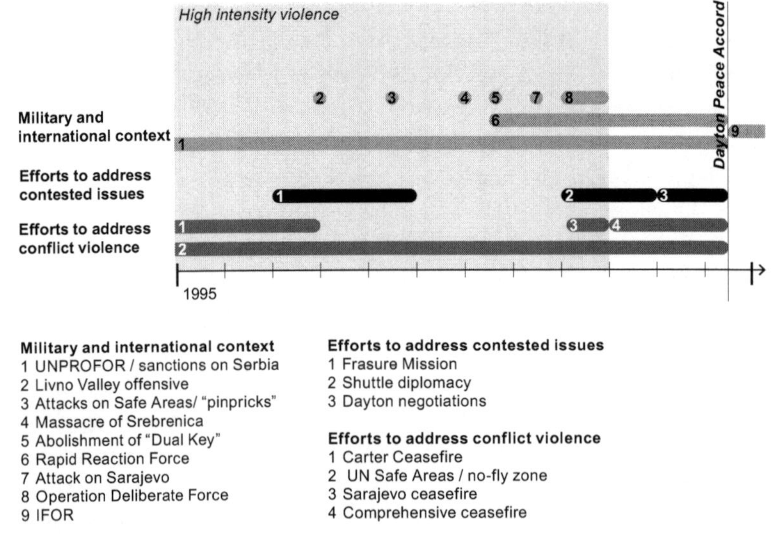

Military and international context
1 UNPROFOR / sanctions on Serbia
2 Livno Valley offensive
3 Attacks on Safe Areas/ "pinpricks"
4 Massacre of Srebrenica
5 Abolishment of "Dual Key"
6 Rapid Reaction Force
7 Attack on Sarajevo
8 Operation Deliberate Force
9 IFOR

Efforts to address contested issues
1 Frasure Mission
2 Shuttle diplomacy
3 Dayton negotiations

Efforts to address conflict violence
1 Carter Ceasefire
2 UN Safe Areas / no-fly zone
3 Sarajevo ceasefire
4 Comprehensive ceasefire

Figure 3.2 Bosnia conflict, 1995

response to the atrocities.[50] This step was complemented with the abolishment of the dual key agreement, strengthening NATO's ability to act.[51]

In combination with rising domestic pressure on President Clinton and a potential US involvement in the case of UN withdrawal, the US and EU joint forces sought to pursue a settlement of the conflict through a combination of diplomatic and military means, overcoming their previous ambivalence in action.[52] The decisive difference to previous initiatives was that the third parties no longer only imposed negotiations or security arrangements but were now also willing to enforce them.

The Road to Dayton: Negotiating the Final Peace Agreement

A twofold initiative was launched by the United States in late August 1995. The initiative came as a reaction to the bombing of a marketplace in Sarajevo that—in combination with the atrocities of Srebrenica—gave the United States the final incentive to intervene.[53] First, military pressure was significantly increased on the Bosnian Serbs through air strikes conducted as part of Operation Deliberate Force. Then second, this military intervention was complemented with the Seven Point Initiative, pursued by a US negotiation team led by Richard Holbrooke. The team initially relied on shuttle diplomacy to establish the basic principles of a potential peace agreement and then summoned the conflict parties in Dayton, Ohio, for the final negotiations.[54] While the United States led this period, the negotiation team ensured close cooperation with their European allies.

The use of shuttle diplomacy was symptomatic of a more fundamental shift in the negotiation strategy. The negotiation team engaged with the parties on the ground, seeking to understand their interests, and hence also the ceasefire opportunity space, in detail. Another major change was the parties involved in the negotiations. While previous agreements had been negotiated between the Bosnian parties, the external powers (i.e., Croatia and Serbia) were now officially involved in the negotiations. The Croatian government was ready to engage because it sought to memorialize the rights of the Croats in Bosnia in the peace agreement and to negotiate the status of eastern Slavonia. Within Yugoslavia, eastern Slavonia had been part of Croatia but had then been occupied by the Serbs during the conflict.

On the Serbian side, in contrast, tensions over the question of representation, between the Bosnians Serbs and the government of Milošević, were complicating the negotiations. The Bosnian Serbs under the leadership of Radovan Karadžić did not accept that Milošević would negotiate on their behalf and feared that he would impose a peace agreement on them. Milošević, in turn, wanted to end the Bosnian conflict. He was paying a high price for his involvement in the Bosnian conflict in the terms of sanctions and international isolation and became increasingly worried that he would be sidelined in the case of direct negotiations between the Bosnian Serbs and the Bosniaks.

Against this background, in a critical breakthrough for the US negotiation team, Milošević brought forward an agreement with the Bosnian Serbs, stating that he would represent them in the peace negotiations. He had leveraged the authority of the patriarch of the Serbian Orthodox church to assert his will over them.[55] This intra-Serbian agreement had a strong signaling effect: Milošević had come up with this agreement based on its own initiative and, in doing so, fundamentally shifted the domestic context by increasing the cohesion of the involved parties. It was also a signal of his willingness to cooperate in finding a negotiated settlement to the Bosnian conflict.

The signaling effect also had a direct impact on the negotiations between the conflict parties. With the Serbian government seemingly willing to compromise, Holbrooke and his team secured the Agreed Basic Principles only a few days later. These principles were based on the Contact Group Plan and adapted the 49–51 percent formula for territorial division.[56] This time, however, the NATO airstrikes and Croat–Bosniak offensives meant that the proposed division more closely corresponded to the military realities on the ground, creating a shared interest in a political solution between the parties.

The effectiveness of the NATO operation was also reflected in efforts to stop the conflict violence, in particular through the agreement by the Bosnian Serbs to a bilateral local ceasefire with NATO, as part of the Geneva signing of the Agreed Basic Principles. In exchange for a withdrawal of the Bosnian Serbian forces from Sarajevo, NATO would suspend its bombardment in the area. This proved largely effective, in sharp contrast to prior efforts to produce a local ceasefire around Sarajevo that had previously failed. Fighting continued in other parts of the country while the second preagreement, known as the Further Agreed Basic Principles, was concluded in New York, outlining a future institutional setup.[57]

It is important to note that violence continued throughout the US shuttle diplomacy efforts: the Bosniak–Croat coalition continued to advance in the West and NATO continued air strikes against the Bosnian Serbs. Only once the two preagreements had been secured did the US negotiation team begin to pursue the conclusion of a comprehensive ceasefire that was ultimately reached on 5 October 1995. Considering the large number of failed ceasefires and the lack of a viable agreement, the US negotiation team consciously decided to *not* aim for a nationwide ceasefire at the beginning of the negotiations but to wait until the political process had progressed sufficiently.[58] While officially limited to sixty days—the negotiation period—it effectively ended the violence in the Bosnian conflict. The conflict parties respected the ceasefire until it was replaced by the Dayton agreement and the corresponding definitive ceasefire.

The final negotiations took place in person in Dayton, a US airbase. Besides the definitive ceasefire, the negotiations focused on the remaining constitutional issues, the Serb withdrawal from eastern Slavonia, and the strengthening of the Muslim–Croat federation.[59] The issue of eastern Slavonia was even taken up before the Bosnian issues, to ensure that Croats represented by President Tuđman would be in full support of the negotiations.

The negotiations ended with the signing of the Dayton Accords on 21 November 1995, after twenty-one days of negotiation.[60] The final agreement resulted in the creation of the Republic Bosnia and Herzegovina consisting of two entities: the Federation of Bosnia and Herzegovina and Republika Srpska. The enforcement of the agreement was guaranteed by the implementation force (IFOR).[61] At its peak, 60,000 troops would be deployed to Bosnia.[62] In addition, pressure on Serbia was upheld by an explicit option to reimpose sanctions should the agreement not be implemented by the conflict parties.[63] The agreement remained relatively vague on the resulting political structures and the question of sovereignty.[64]

The Dayton agreement included a definitive ceasefire and foresaw the establishment of a Joint Military Commission to monitor the compliance with the agreement and specifically with the ceasefire.[65] The commission included members of both sides and was headed by the IFOR commander and could be addressed with allegations of ceasefire violations. The agreement committed the parties to refrain from unilateral actions should a violation occur and explicitly authorized IFOR to enforce the ceasefire in the event of violations.[66] The definitive ceasefires also included Disarmament, Demobilization, and Reintegration (DDR) measures, albeit they were relatively limited.[67]

The primary implementation phase lasted one year and was divided into two parts: first the ceasefire and the disarmament provisions were to be implemented, followed by the creation of "a safe and secure environment."[68] The first implementation phase was a clear success, with the ceasefire holding to this day. The stability of the ceasefire has to be seen against the background of enforcement through the massive deployment of international troops. Still, it was unexpected that not even a single IFOR member was injured and violence terminated as agreed.[69] In contrast, the delay in the implementation of the civilian part, including the prosecution of war crime suspects, and the rise of violence against civilians by loosely organized thugs, endangered the agreement.[70] Nonetheless, IFOR was replaced by the smaller Stabilization Force (SFOR) one year later.

THE INTERACTION BETWEEN THE CEASEFIRE PROCESS, THE POLITICAL NEGOTIATIONS, AND THE INTERNATIONAL AND MILITARY CONTEXTS

An analysis of the Bosnian case reveals that the ceasefire process and the broader political negotiations were blocking each other in a negative feedback loop for several years and that both dimensions are strongly impacted by the international context and military situation on the ground. A sustainable ceasefire is only possible when all parties hold a shared interest in stopping fighting. Whether any party has an interest in stopping fighting is itself dependent on the military context and the likelihood of the actor achieving their goals through the political process. International actors can attempt to change parties' preferences directly (by providing positive or negative inducements, for example) or indirectly (by attempting to shift the military context). The degree to which this is possible is a function of the capabilities and commitment that international actors can credibly signal and the extent of the divergence in the parties' interests. Once the military context pushes the conflict parties to agree on a political solution, a ceasefire can follow because the incentives for violence vanish.

In the Bosnian case, there was a significant divergence in both the interests in political progress and stopping conflict violence. For the initial years of the conflict, Serbian military dominance made the Serbs resistant to any political solution that was not representative of their strong military advantage and the large swaths of territory already under their control. With such an asymmetric power balance, ceasefires were for the Serbians a hindrance to further territorial gains rather than a path to the achievement of their political goals. Similarly, the Bosniaks also saw military contest rather than the political process as the most effective path to achieving their goals. Despite their military inferiority and huge civilian suffering, the leadership remained committed to the unity of the state and hopeful that the support of Western powers would ultimately help shift the military context in their favor. As such, ceasefires of any kind, also for conflict containment, risked consolidating an unfavorable territorial division and tacitly accepting an unacceptable political solution.

Peacemaking in a context with such divergence in political goals, as well as a shared preference of war over ceasefires, was clearly challenging. But this was compounded by the international context as the international actors lacked unity and failed to credibly commit the capabilities needed to shift the military situation on the ground in such a way as to impact the preferences of the parties. Facing a humanitarian disaster and a war in Europe, the divided international community still tried to pressure the parties into negotiations and ceasefire agreements, neglecting the almost complete absence of a ceasefire opportunity space.

Almost all of the more than seventy ceasefires declared in this period failed. Few other de-escalation measures were used beside the numerous ceasefire attempts. This has to be seen in the context of a high level of escalation in which the conflict parties were not willing to constrain the use of weapons at their disposal. For example, the Bosnian Serbs made use of anti-aircraft missiles to attack villages.

A cursory examination of some key failed ceasefires is indicative. First, immediately following the onset of violence, José Cutileiro negotiated a preliminary ceasefire between all three sides on behalf of the EU.[71] The ceasefire was relatively comprehensive, setting the terms for a separation of forces, the dissolution of irregular forces, and monitoring through the ECMM.[72] But the ceasefire was not in the interests of the parties, and the internationals had no capacity to enforce the agreement; thus, while fighting eased shortly around Sarajevo, it continued unabated in other parts of the countries.[73] Heavy fighting was reported the following days, and a week later, the ceasefire was considered to have collapsed.[74]

This pattern continued for several years. For example, a ceasefire between the Bosniaks and Bosnian Croats concluded ad hoc during the Vance–Owen Geneva negotiations in 1993, again sought to impose a stop in fighting to allow talks to occur. This ignored, however, that there was no shared interest between the parties with regard to limiting the use of violence or finding a political solution. As such, the ceasefire (and ultimately the political negotiations) failed.[75] In this context, even short-term arrangements proved challenging to sustain. For example, the Bosniaks and the Bosnian Croats agreed a cessation of hostilities over Christmas 1993 that was limited to twelve days and negotiated between the UNPROFOR commander and the respective heads of the armed forces. It was not explicitly connected to the political process and only sought to create a reduction in violence over the holidays. Yet, even this limited ceasefire was largely ineffective, with 106 fatalities and more than 400 injured across this twelve-day period.[76]

Prior to Dayton, the only effective ceasefire involving the Bosnian Serbs was the Carter ceasefire in winter 1994/1995, which occurred at a time in which all sides were militarily exhausted and so had a brief shared interest in stopping the violence and thus containing the conflict without working on its resolution. The parties' preparations for new military offensives during the ceasefire indicate that the halt in fighting was not driven by a genuine interest in peace, and ultimately this agreement collapsed at the end of March 1995.

Importantly, the imposed political agreements and ceasefires in the first years of the conflict did not only fail in stopping violence but also most likely aggravated it. The imposed negotiations increased fighting because the conflict parties tried to secure gains to improve their bargaining positions, and the high number of failed agreements destroyed trust in the third parties.[77] This points to a negative feedback loop in which the ceasefire and political negotiation process were hampering each other. The only stable ceasefire during winter 1994/1995 was used for preparation of the spring offensives, undermining progress in the political process through the "hidden agenda" of the conflict parties.

Ultimately, a new, more comprehensive strategy was successful in breaking the negative feedback loop and securing the effective ceasefires between the Bosniaks and the Bosnian Croats as well as between the Bosnian Serbs and the Bosniak–Croat coalition, respectively. In both cases, pressure on the international parties (i.e., Croatia and Serbia) was leveraged to advance the political negotiations. Only once a political settlement was basically agreed, the ceasefires were concluded. It was also respectively the first time that Tuđman and Milošević themselves took part in the negotiations. Prior to this, neither had been included, although they were both directly involved in the conflict itself.

In the case of the sustainable ceasefire between the Bosniaks and the Bosnian Croats, positive and negative inducements were used to shift the Croatian incentives (e.g., sanctions, international isolation, and promise of military aid). This, coupled with the Croats' lack of military progress against the Serbs in their bilateral conflict (which was itself, in part, a product of arms embargos), increased the readiness of Tuđman and the Bosnian Croats to pursue a negotiated solution to the Bosniak–Croat conflict. Once a political settlement appeared imminent, the two parties were for the first time willing to commit to a sustainable ceasefire. Thus, one week before the Washington Framework Agreement, a preliminary ceasefire was concluded. This was subsequently superseded by a definitive ceasefire as part of the broader settlement. The ceasefires included the separation of forces, the deployment of UNPROFOR to the frontline, and the commitment to hand over heavy weapons to the UN.[78] The two forces were ultimately integrated, and the ceasefire arrangement (and broader military alliance) proved stable until the end of the conflict.

The sustainable ceasefire as part of the Washington Framework Agreement was made possible by a combination of the international context and a positive feedback loop between the ceasefire and political negotiation process. The international context was critical because it implied that Croatia had an interest in a political solution in Bosnia due to its involvement in another conflict elsewhere—highlighting the importance of the international context. This triggered a positive feedback loop between the processes because the perspective of a political settlement enabled the conclusion of a ceasefire, which in turn safeguarded the signing of the final agreement.

The ceasefire in the Dayton process was similar insofar as it was made possible through a combination of international pressure and the perspective of a political solution. The conclusion of the Dayton ceasefire was at the same time fundamentally different because the third parties intervened militarily to shift the military balance. The military context had already changed because the Bosniak–Croat coalition was able to put serious military pressure on the Serbs within Bosnia, not least through the potential of seizing Banja Luka. In a similar manner, the Croatian government was advancing against the Serbs in Operation Storm and Operation Flash in Croatia and Slovenia.[79] The territorial gains rather emboldened the Bosniaks, however, and the situation was not a hurting stalemate.

Since the conflict parties were still not ready to pursue a political settlement, the Euro-Atlantic parties decided to increase the pressure on the Bosnian Serbs through NATO airstrikes known as Operation Deliberate Force. Importantly, the airstrikes were not only meant to get the Bosnian Serbs and Serbia to the negotiation table in the first place, but they were also constantly upheld during the negotiations.[80] The military intervention was combined with a change in mediation style, now relying on shuttle diplomacy. The military intervention was only possible due to the alignment of interests of the US and the European powers, highlighting the importance of the international context. The case further shows that not only the ceasefire and political negotiation process are dynamic and intertwined but so are the context dimensions, here the international and military context.

The NATO intervention and the territorial advancement of the Bosniak–Croat coalition created a situation on the ground that came much closer to the often proposed 49–51 territorial division and finally allowed for the conclusion of two sets of Agreed Principles in September 1995, codifying the territorial division. Only once this framework for the political settlement and, importantly, the territorial division was agreed were the parties willing to seriously consider stopping the conflict violence. No one wanted to risk their life in combat now that a final agreement was in immediate reach and violence would not change the outcome.

In contrast to earlier efforts, the ceasefire was the last piece of the puzzle and came at the end rather than the start of the negotiations. Bosnia is hence an example how "talking while fighting" can be a successful approach if the agreement between the conflict parties rests mostly on military interests rather than trust and mutual understanding. This, however, also needs to be seen against the background of dozens of failed ceasefires, which meant that any renewed attempt for a ceasefire was encountered with suspicion.

For the first time, all three aspects—the proposed political solution, the military situation on the battlefield, and the preferences of the domestic and international parties—were aligned, creating a ceasefire opportunity space, which allowed for a permanent halt in fighting. The alignment across the political process and the ceasefire process was successfully engineered by the third parties, but it remained challenging for the "mediators" to maintain this delicate balance. This was particularly the case given that the Bosniak–Croat military coalition proved more effective than expected, advancing steadily and regaining so much territory that the envisioned 49–51 territory formula was under threat. By the beginning of October, the coalition advanced on Banja Luka, one of the major cities in Bosnia inhabited by a Serb majority. The capture of Banja Luka threatened to lower the attractiveness of the peace agreement for the Bosniaks and Croats, who would then potentially hold more than their proposed 51 percent allocation. At the same time, there were also tensions among the US officials, in particular between the negotiators and the military. The latter was initially skeptical about the effectiveness of the bombing campaign against the Serbs and later worried that running out of suitable military targets meant they would not be able to sustain the campaign much longer. Yet the precarious balance could be maintained during the negotiations in Dayton.

The negotiations in Dayton were able to secure and refine the terms that had been determined in the Agreed Principles. The definitive ceasefire was central to the Dayton negotiations because it was closely tied to the question of territorial division between the future republics. Indeed, the conflict parties seemed more interested in this territorial aspect than in the constitutional setup. This must be seen in the light of the then prevailing notion of nationalism, which stipulated that each nation should reside on its acclaimed historical territory. Accordingly, great attention was devoted to the technical details of the ceasefire and the inter-entity boundary line separating the future Federation of Bosnia and Herzegovina and Republika Srpska. Drones were deployed to determine the exact demarcation of the line. The lengthy technical discussions had the positive side effect to build confidence between the conflict parties and in the commitment of the third parties.

It was extremely important for the conflict parties to be able to trust the third parties to enforce a potential definitive ceasefire. Since trust in the third parties was critical, the American negotiation team had calculated that an early ceasefire was too large a risk. If the early ceasefire failed, this would have undermined the trust of the conflict parties in the ability of the third parties to enforce a peace agreement. In comparison, trust in the adversaries seemed less relevant. At the beginning, the US negotiation team intended to use confidence-building measures between the conflict parties but then had to realize how well the three leaders knew each other, being on a first name basis. This provides nuance to the risk of negative feedback loops between the ceasefire and political negotiation process: failing ceasefires undermine not only the trust between the conflict parties but also the trust in third parties and, by extension, thus impede the political process.

The third parties gained the trust of the conflict parties by emphasizing their military capabilities and political willingness to enforce the definitive ceasefire. They did so, first, by carefully selecting the negotiation venue. The negotiations took place on the US military base in Dayton, Ohio, and the conflict parties were invited to the weaponry museum for dinner to convince them of the US capabilities. Second, it was decided that NATO should enforce the agreement. This is remarkable, considering the UN mission UNPROFOR had existed since the early days of the conflicts. One could argue that the UN was deployed when NATO would have been needed and NATO was deployed when there ought to have been UN troops. Finally, the detailed and transparent discussions about the demarcation line allowed the third parties to demonstrate that they were serious about implementing the agreement.

The settlement showed that imposed agreements are possible, but only when the military context is fundamentally changed and thereby creates a shared interest between the conflict parties in stopping violence and finding a political agreement. In addition, this engineered change needs to be credibly extended into the implementation phase of the agreement. The long-term use of economic pressure and the short-term use of military force in summer 1995 created the needed readiness of the conflict parties to negotiate and compromise. Yet, it was also their trust in the enforcement capabilities of

NATO, and in particular the United States, that ultimately convinced them to trust in the credibility of the agreement.

CONCLUSION

The Bosnian case demonstrates the futility in imposing ceasefires not in alignment with the interests of the conflict parties. More generally, imposed peacemaking efforts in the earlier phases of the conflict not only failed to improve the situation but likely worsened it by creating negative feedback loops between the ceasefire and political process. The multitude of failed ceasefires likely increased fighting and lowered the trust in the third parties and the process. That international actors nonetheless continued to try and impose ceasefires so many times can be attributed to their drive to stop the humanitarian tragedy that was unfolding in plain sight. But pushing for a stop to the violence out of tune with the progress in the political negotiations and the military context was for a long time counterproductive.

Sustainable ceasefires are only possible when all parties hold a shared interest in stopping fighting. Parties' interests in stopping fighting are dependent on the military context and the likelihood of achieving their goals through the political process. The Bosnian case shows that international actors can shift parties' preferences through positive and negative inducements and by manipulating the military context. But in Bosnia, this ultimately required an unprecedented level of international engagement and unity during and for years after the agreement, underlining the importance of the international context. It is tough to envisage a similar international engagement in the current geopolitical and global economic context. Other cases in this book, in particular the Syrian case study, vividly demonstrate the impact of the changing international context.

This implies that the context dimensions not only impact the peace process directly but also interact with each other. On the one hand, it was the unification of the international actors—and thus a change in the international context—that allowed for an intervention in the battlefield, thereby changing the military context. On the other hand, the conflicts in Bosnia and Croatia were closely linked to each other, showing how the military context goes beyond the individual, country-level case but can also shape the interests of the parties abroad.

Even though the conclusion of the Dayton Accords was ultimately "successful," the agreement produced an imperfect outcome where many substantial issues remained unaddressed. The US team did not see the Dayton Accords as an indefinite agreement but rather as a platform on which the local actors could build a broader period of political change. They expected that the parties would be able come up with a more satisfactory arrangement, maybe on nonethnic grounds later on. Yet to date this has not occurred.

NOTES

We thank Mark Baskin for his thoughtful feedback on the chapter.

1. US Department of State, *The Breakup of Yugoslavia*; Curran, Sebenius, and Watkins, "Two Paths to Peace," 533.
2. O'Ballance, *War in Bosnia*, xviii.
3. Paczulla, "The Long, Difficult Road," 257; Winokur, "Before the Peace," 53.
4. Hartwell, "Conflict Resolution," 445.
5. Dulic, "Perpetuating Fear," 470.
6. Dulic, "Perpetuating Fear," 477.
7. Curran, Sebenius, and Watkins, "Two Paths to Peace," 553.
8. O'Ballance, *War in Bosnia*, 179.
9. Dulic, "Perpetuating Fear," 470.
10. Dulic, "Perpetuating Fear," 471.
11. "Bosnia-Herzegovina: Croat."
12. Winokur, "Before the Peace," 50.
13. Daalder, *Getting to Dayton*, 1.
14. Crocker, Hampson, and Aall, *Taming Intractable Conflicts*, 88.
15. Clayton et al., "Introducing the Ceasefire Dataset."
16. Szasz, "Peacekeeping in Operation," 688.
17. Paczulla, "The Long, Difficult Road," 258.
18. Maloney, "Operation Bolster," 31; Szasz, "Peacekeeping in Operation," 687.
19. Hartwell, "Conflict Resolution," 446.
20. Maloney, "Operation Bolster," 29.
21. Izetbegović, Karadžić, and Brkic, "Sarajevo Declaration."
22. Trnka et al., "Geneva Agreement"; Trnka et al., "Agreement (ICRC Humanitarian Principles)."
23. See Bell and Badanjak, "Introducing PA-X."
24. UN Security Council, *Resolution 781*.
25. Dulic, "Perpetuating Fear," 475.
26. Maloney, "Operation Bolster," 42.
27. Curran, Sebenius, and Watkins, "Two Paths to Peace," 553.
28. UN Security Council, *Resolution 819*; UN Security Council, *Resolution 824*.
29. Curran, Sebenius, and Watkins, "Two Paths to Peace," 553.
30. UN Security Council, *Resolution 816*.
31. Daalder, *Getting to Dayton*, 2.
32. Oberschall, *Peace Building in Divided Societies*.
33. Paczulla, "The Long, Difficult Road," 258.

34. Paczulla, "The Long, Difficult Road"; Debié, "Paper Tiger."

35. Daalder, *Getting to Dayton*, 11–19.

36. Curran, Sebenius, and Watkins, "Two Paths to Peace," 553.

37. "Bosnia-Herzegovina: Croat."

38. Clayton et al., "Introducing the Ceasefire Dataset," CF 346-61.

39. "Bosnia-Herzegovina: Croat."

40. "Framework Agreement."

41. Galbraith, "Washington, Erdut and Dayton."

42. Clayton et al., "Introducing the Ceasefire Dataset," CF 346-64, 346-70.

43. Mahieu, "When Interrupt a Civil War?" 218.

44. Oberschall, *Peace Building in Divided Societies*, 112.

45. Hill, *Outpost*, 70.

46. Karčić, "A Christmas Ceasefire."

47. Oberschall, *Peace Building in Divided Societies*, 113.

48. Hill, *Outpost*, 72.

49. Hill, *Outpost*, 71.

50. Hill, *Outpost*, 70.

51. Curran, Sebenius, and Watkins, "Two Paths to Peace," 533.

52. Paczulla, "The Long, Difficult Road," 259f.

53. Crocker, Aall, and Annan, *The Fabric of Peace in Africa*, 34.

54. Holbrooke, *To End a War*.

55. Hill, *Outpost*, 89.

56. Hill, *Outpost*, 106.

57. Hill, *Outpost*, 109.

58. Hill, *Outpost*, 106.

59. Paczulla, "The Long, Difficult Road," 267.

60. Paczulla, "The Long, Difficult Road," 255–256. The accord was ratified in Paris on 14 December 1995.

61. Holbrooke, *To End a War*, 337.

62. NATO, "Peace Support Operations in Bosnia and Herzegovina."

63. Holbrooke, *To End a War*, 340.

64. Crocker, Hampson, and Aall, *Taming Intractable Conflicts*, 35.

65. Izetbegović, Tuđman, and Milošević, "General Framework Agreement," Annex 1-A, VIII.

66. Izetbegović, Tuđman, and Milošević, "General Framework Agreement," Annex 1-A, II.5, IV.4.

67. Izetbegović, Tuđman, and Milošević, "General Framework Agreement," Annex 1-A, II.3.

68. Izetbegović, Tuđman, and Milošević, "General Framework Agreement," Annex 1-A, II.3; Holbrooke, *To End a War*, 323.

69. Holbrooke, *To End a War*.

70. Holbrooke, *To End a War*.

71. Antonov, "Rival Groups Agree Ceasefire."

72. Boban, Izetbegović, and Karadžić, "Bosnia-Herzegovina Ceasefire Agreement."

73. Antonov, "Rival Groups Agree Ceasefire."

74. Antonov, "New Fighting Dims Hopes"; Antonov, "Bosnian President Asks Army."

75. Clayton et al., "Introducing the Ceasefire Dataset," CF 346-21; Reuters News [Factiva], "Moslems Accept Ceasefire"; Kitchener-Waterloo Record [Factiva], "Pact Fails to Quell Strife."

76. Clayton et al., "Introducing the Ceasefire Dataset," 346-58.

77. Maloney, "Operation Bolster," 42.

78. Maloney, "Operation Bolster," 42.

79. Oberschall, *Peace Building in Divided Societies*, 114.

80. Oberschall, *Peace Building in Divided Societies*, 114; Curran, Sebenius, and Watkins, "Two Paths to Peace," 534.

CHAPTER 4

Burundi, 1996–2003
Building Peace Step-by-Step
from Arusha to Pretoria

Col. Mbaye Faye and Eemeli Isoaho

The Arusha Peace and Reconciliation Agreement for Burundi, which was signed in Tanzania in August 2000, was a crucial step toward solving the bloody civil war in Burundi. While it provided a comprehensive framework for the country's return to constitutional and democratic rule, it did not end the conflict entirely, and in the following years, intense violence continued.[1] The post-Arusha violence mainly involved two nonstate groups: (1) Conseil National Pour la Défense de la Démocratie–Forces pour la Défense de la Démocratie (CNDD-FDD) and (2) Parti pour la libération du peuple Hutu—Forces nationales de liberation (PALIPEHUTU-FNL). In theory, both groups signed the Arusha agreement, but in practice, in both cases, the most significant factions rejected the process and continued violence unabated. In particular, the CNDD-FDD faction led by Nkurunziza had grown in its military power and attracted widespread grassroots support following Arusha, making it the strongest nonstate group in Burundi. In response to the ongoing violence, a series of mediated negotiations were launched between the government and several armed groups. Significantly, these efforts produced an agreement with CNDD-FDD (Nkurunziza) formally ending with the signing of the Global Ceasefire Agreement in Dar es Salaam, Tanzania, in November 2003.

This chapter focuses on the interaction between the political negotiations and the ceasefire process that brought an end to the armed conflict between the government of Burundi and CNDD-FDD (Nkurunziza).[2] We explore how ceasefires were sequenced and which context factors were most influential in shaping the structure and outcome of the process. Through the analysis, we demonstrate the challenges that emerge when the ceasefire process advances more quickly than efforts to address the contested issues and show that premature ceasefire agreements were in this case ineffective due to the absence of agreement on the conflict issues. The case thus illustrates a sequencing feedback loop between the ceasefire process and political negotiations (i.e., progress on the former requires first progress on the latter). We also reflect on the nuances of mediation in fragmented contexts and discuss how this was overcome in Burundi using a gradual step-by-step approach.

The chapter is structured into three sections. First, we provide a basic overview of the civil war in Burundi, highlighting the key actors and prior efforts to address the conflict. Second, we discuss the peace negotiations between CNDD-FDD (Nkurunziza) and the government of Burundi, discussing political negotiation and ceasefire processes during the pre-prenegotiation, prenegotiation, negotiation, and implementation phases. Finally, we draw the discussion together in an analytical section that reflects on the learnings relating to the interaction between efforts to address conflict violence and efforts to address the key contested issues.

CONFLICT BACKGROUND

Burundi's recent past is defined by cycles of violence that entail political assassinations, coup d'états, massacres, and military rule. After independence in 1962, Burundi suffered frequent attacks and, at times, widespread mass killings. This violence was mostly between the country's two principal ethnic groups: the Hutus and Tutsis.[3] The civil war that began in the 1990s is the most violent manifestation of this cleavage. This devastating conflict was the result of regional and ethnic cleavages that stem from the country's colonial period, which were consolidated and deepened by repressive postindependence governments. Burundi, like neighboring Rwanda, was a Belgian colony.[4] Belgium introduced colonial administration reforms, including the systematic elimination of Hutu chiefs and subchiefs, from the colonial administration between 1926 and 1933, as well as the selective schooling of Tutsis to the detriment of Hutu children.

After independence, three successive military presidencies ruled the country from 1966 to 1993, with control over the country's resources concentrated in the hands of a primarily Tutsi political and military elite. The unequal division of power and resources contributed to exacerbating the country's ethnic, identity-based, and regional cleavages, and related cyclical periods of violence. The purging of the Hutu elite from the spheres of power and their consequent political marginalization culminated in 1972 with the killing of at least 150,000 Hutus and their political leaders by the Tutsi-led government. This in turn led to tens of thousands of Hutus fleeing into exile and an even more acute political, economic, and social marginalization of the ethnic majority.

This culminated in the onset of the Burundian civil war in 1993 when the democratically elected Hutu president Melchior Ndadaye was killed, leading to mass killings throughout the country. By 1994, an estimated 300,000 people (the majority being Hutu civilians from the countryside and some from Hutu neighborhoods of Bujumbura) had been killed, while up to 700,000 Burundians, primarily Hutu, fled to neighboring countries of Tanzania, Rwanda, and Zaire (the current-day Democratic Republic of the Congo, DRC). In this context, former president Pierre Buyoya seized power with the support of the mainly Tutsi military in July 1996.

Conflict Actors

The civil war was fought primarily between the pro-Tutsi government and a number of pro-Hutu rebel groups. Although the rebel groups had different regional constituencies within the country and even some Tutsis among their ranks, they shared a common vision of fighting for the country's return to constitutional rule. Most important, they believed in ending the minority Tutsis' disproportionate dominance over the country's politics, economy, and security. In particular, they sought reform of Burundi's armed forces, which had been dominated by the Tutsis since the country's independence.

The pro-Tutsi government, for its part, viewed controlling the country's armed forces and politics as a means to guarantee protection against the existential threat posed by the country's Hutu majority. The armed forces had essentially given the Tutsis a veto power in all decision-making processes: should decisions not be favorable to the Tutsis, they could always retake power through the military. In a regional context of mass violence and increasing ethnic tensions between Hutus and Tutsis, in the broader Great Lakes Region, and in Rwanda in particular,[5] the Tutsi leaders stressed the need for protection and security for the country's minority. Popular, democratic rule, as demanded by the Hutus, was not categorically opposed by the Tutsis, as long as provisions were put in place to protect the rights and security of the minority.

The main pro-Tutsi actor during the civil war was President Buyoya's Union pour le Progrès national (UPRONA), which was established as a political party in 1960 and had ruled the country continuously from independence until Ndadaye's election in 1993. From the 1960s until the end of the civil war, UPRONA dominated Burundian politics and the country's armed forces, effectively creating a one-party state with limited separation of democratic governance and military rule. The line between the political party of UPRONA and the Burundian armed forces was blurred, meaning that even if UPRONA did not have a formal armed wing, it could mobilize the armed forces to advance its goals.

The nonstate actors comprised a series of mobile, agile, and dispersed guerilla movements with bases in Burundi and neighboring countries. The rebellion was marked by their active involvement elsewhere in the region, particularly in the DRC, where groups like CNDD-FDD participated in the First and Second Congo Wars (1996–1997 and 1998–2003). The rebellion was no unified group with a common leadership but rather a relatively fragmented constellation of different pro-Hutu groups of varying sizes. These groups fought not only the government but also each other (i.e., for prominence), with violent attacks being relatively common.

The three most significant Hutu groups during the civil war were Front pour la Démocratie au Burundi (FRODEBU), CNDD-FDD, and PALIPEHUTU-FNL. Historically, FRODEBU was the most significant Hutu political party in Burundi. FRODEBU had its origins in the Burundi Workers' Party and maintained a formally political profile throughout the civil war, even if many of its members were actively involved in the armed struggle. For most of the 1990s, FRODEBU was thus considered the legitimate representative of the Hutu majority. This changed in the aftermath of the killing of President Ndadaye, and while the party maintained its political significance at the national level, well into the early 2000s, its popularity waned in favor of armed rebel groups, particularly CNDD-FDD.

The second major Hutu group was PALIPEHUTU and its armed wing FNL. They were founded in refugee camps in Tanzania in the early 1980s but grew significantly when they mobilized support from displaced peasants in the aftermath of the 1996 coup. PALIPEHUTU-FNL distinguished itself

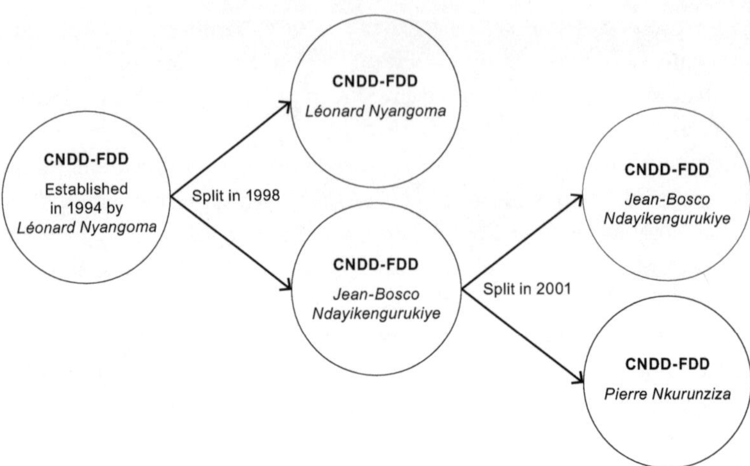

Figure 4.1 Chronology of principal divisions within CNDD-FDD (1994–2001). Adapted from International Crisis Group

from FRODEBU by calling for an armed struggle against the government. Like other groups in the region, it was subject to multiple fractures over the course of the conflict.

The third major Hutu group was CNDD-FDD. It was established in 1994 by a former FRODEBU member and quickly gained popularity.[6] The group also suffered from internal divisions. The political wing of the movement (CNDD) was dominated by Hutus from then-leader Léonard Nyangoma's southern region of Bururi, whereas the armed wing (FDD) attracted members throughout the country. This, coupled with accusations of corruption, led to a split within the movement in 2001, when Jean-Bosco Ndayikengurukiye established a new faction.[7] Divisions within that faction led to another split in 2001, when a group led by Pierre Nkurunziza broke away from Ndayikengurukiye (see figure 4.1[8]). This faction eventually became the biggest and most powerful, with an estimated total of around 20,000 soldiers in 2001.

Previous Efforts

There were several regional and international efforts to end the armed conflict in Burundi between 1996 and 2000.[9] These peacemaking efforts sought a comprehensive solution to end all armed conflict in Burundi, culminating in the signing of the 2000 Arusha Peace and Reconciliation Agreement between the government and eighteen other signatories. The Arusha process started following the outbreak of the civil war, when Julius Nyerere, former president of Tanzania, was appointed by the United Nations (UN) secretary-general, the Organisation of African Unity (OAU), and the broader international community to mediate the growing crisis. Nyerere gave priority to inclusive talks with all parties involved, even if some of the parties were small and relatively insignificant. Following the death of Nyerere in October 1999, the former president of South Africa, Nelson Mandela, was appointed to lead the peace process in December 1999. Mandela's mediation, and the regional sanctions that placed pressure on the actors, led to the signing of the Arusha agreement only nine months later.[10] International and regional pressure in a context of recent mass atrocities in the region, particularly Rwanda, paved the way for a relatively swift yet comprehensive process.

The nineteen signatories to the Arusha agreement included representatives of UPRONA, FRODEBU, PALIPEHUTU, and CNDD. However, the CNDD representative that signed the agreement did not represent the largest CNDD-FDD faction led by Ndayikengurukiye (and later Nkurunziza).[11] The exclusion of principal armed rebel groups meant that, while the Arusha agreement was a landmark political agreement, which had an entire chapter dedicated to a permanent ceasefire and cessation of hostilities, it did not stop the violence on a large scale. Despite its shortcomings, the Arusha agreement paved the way for the country's relatively free elections in 2005, after a transition period, and was vital in building a more unified understanding of the past, as well as a vision for the future.

The agreement also included a number of provisions that inspired and served as a basis for future discussions between the government of Burundi and CNDD-FDD. As a follow-up to Arusha, and in response to the continuing violence, peacemaking efforts switched to a step-by-step approach, whereby individual conflict dyads were managed independently, first involving negotiations between the government and CNDD-FDD from 2002 to 2003 and subsequently between the government and PALIPEHUTU-FNL between 2006 to 2008 (see table 4.1). The following analysis focuses on the 2002 to 2003 peace process between the government of Burundi and the CNDD-FDD faction led by Pierre Nkurunziza.

PEACE NEGOTIATIONS BETWEEN CNDD-FDD AND THE GOVERNMENT

In this section, we offer a detailed analysis of the peace negotiations between the government of Burundi and the CNDD-FDD faction led by Pierre Nkurunziza. The sections are divided chronologically and broadly map the four phases of the political negotiation process: pre-prenegotiations, prenegotiations, negotiations, and implementation. Table 4.2 provides an overview of the agreements signed in each phase of the process.

Table 4.1: Overview of the three main phases of the Burundi peace process

Approximate period Principal Venue(s)		
Key actors	**Chief mediators**	**Agreement(s)**
1996–2000		
Arusha, Tanzania		
Government of Burundi and eighteen other signatories	• Julius Nyerere (1996–1999) • Nelson Mandela (1999–2000) • Working group mediators from the region and the international community	• August 2000: Arusha Peace and Reconciliation Agreement for Burundi
2002–2003		
Arusha, Tanzania and Pretoria, South Africa		
Government of Burundi and CNDD-FDD (Nkurunziza)	• Yoweri Museveni, chairman of the Regional Initiative • Jacob Zuma, facilitator • Working group mediators from the AU and the UN	• December 2002: Ceasefire Agreement • January 2003: Joint Declaration of Agreement • October 2003: Pretoria Protocol on Political, Defence and Security Power Sharing in Burundi • November 2003: Pretoria Protocol on Outstanding Political, Defence and Security Power-Sharing Issues in Burundi • November 2003: Global Ceasefire Agreement

Table 4.1

Approximate period Principal Venue(s)		
Key actors	**Chief mediators**	**Agreement(s)**
2006–2009		
Pretoria, South Africa and Dar es Salaam, Tanzania		
Government of Burundi and PALIPEHUTU-FNL(Rwasa)	• Yoweri Museveni, chairman of the Regional Initiative • Jakaya Kikwete, deputy chairperson of the Regional Initiative • Charles Nqakula, facilitator • Working group mediators from the AU and the UN	• <u>June 2006:</u> Dar es Salaam Agreement of Principles towards Lasting Peace, Security, and Stability in Burundi • <u>September 2006:</u> Comprehensive Ceasefire Agreement • <u>May 2008:</u> Joint Declaration on Cessation of Hostilities • <u>June 2008:</u> Magaliesburg Declaration on the Burundi Peace Process • <u>December 2008:</u> Heads of State and Government Summit Declaration on the Burundi Peace Process Regional Initiative • <u>January 2009:</u> Declaration of the PALIPEHUTU-FNL • <u>April 2009:</u> Declaration of the Political Directorate of the Burundi Peace Process on the Implementation Process for the Joint Decisions Made in Pretoria

Table 4.2: Main agreements signed between the Government of Burundi and CNDD-FDD (Nkurunziza)

Mediation phase	Prenegotiation	Negotiation			Implementation
Ceasefire type	Definitive	Preliminary	Definitive	Definitive	Definitive
Date of agreement	2 December 2002	28 January 2003	8 October 2003	2 November 2003	16 November 2003
Venue	Arusha	Pretoria	Pretoria	Pretoria	Dar es Salaam
Total number of characters	18,094	1,551	7,644	22,632	5,966
Status of implementation	Not implemented. Immediately violated.	Mostly not implemented.	Mostly implemented.	Mostly implemented.	Mostly implemented.

Pre-Prenegotiations

The pre-prenegotiation phase is the period in which violence is ongoing, and one or more of the conflict parties is unwilling to consider entering political negotiations. In this case, the pre-prenegotiation period between the government and CNDD-FDD (Nkurunziza) lasted from the founding of CNDD-FDD in 1994 to around October 2002, during which time the nonstate group remained committed to fighting unabated. While many other nonstate groups joined the Arusha process, CNDD-FDD (Nkurunziza) was unwilling to consider political negotiations or measures to address the conflict violence until approximately two years after the signing of the Arusha agreement.

Primarily, CNDD-FDD (Nkurunziza) was resistant to talks, as they felt that a military victory was possible. Thus, any attempt to limit conflict violence was counterproductive to their goals and fighting continued unabated. The leadership's focus was therefore more on strengthening its ranks and position in the country. Under Nkurunziza's leadership, the social cohesion of the group increased. Meanwhile, its capacity also increased, due to significant support from the country's Hutu peasant population and other Hutu diaspora. Unlike other leaders, Nkurunziza came from the north (versus the southern province of Bururi) and was considered a "man of the people" (as opposed to some distant elite), thereby increasing support for the group. External actors, notably DRC and Sudan, also provided support for the movement, and along with Tanzania, DRC also hosted guerrilla bases. The strength of the movement was evident in its attempts to establish a parallel administration in the country with its own police system and social assistance to peasant populations. By the time the formal peace negotiations were started in Arusha, CNDD-FDD had become the strongest rebel group in Burundi.

In this context, CNDD-FDD (Nkurunziza) primarily concerned itself with intra-Hutu competition, in lieu of a focus on peace talks with the government to save time and energy. From a strategic perspective, the traditionally largest Hutu rebel group, PALIPEHUTU-FNL, posed a more significant threat to CNDD-FDD than the government, as PALIPEHUTU-FNL also competed for popularity among the Hutu majority. Initially, PALIPEHUTU-FNL was stronger and more organized than CNDD-FDD and even provided training for CNDD-FDD officials at the beginning of the civil war. However, as CNDD-FDD grew and overtook the mantle of the biggest Hutu rebel group in the country, friction heightened between the two groups, leading to sporadic clashes between them. In this context (i.e., of intra-Hutu competition), it was important for both CNDD-FDD and PALIPEHUTU-FNL not to be seen as yielding to the Tutsi military, which made both groups hesitant to join the peace talks under Nyerere and Mandela.

More broadly, in this period, CNDD-FDD was also resistant to talks, due to the lack of trust its members had in the mediation process. Nkurunziza and his fellow leaders feared that the mediators might reveal their identities and locations on the ground to the government of Burundi and therefore allowed only relatively low-ranking spokespersons to represent them when the mediation team reached out to try and secure their participation. The CNDD-FDD leadership also felt that the Arusha process did not bring about any meaningful reforms like a transformation of the country's security sector or political life. This perception only began to change in 2003 as the domestic political and military context changed, respectively, with the peaceful transition of power from Buyoya to Ndayizeye and the deployment of a regional peacekeeping mission.

Moreover, CNDD-FDD (Nkurunziza) was actively engaged in the Second Congo War in eastern DRC during this period. The involvement of CNDD-FDD in the Congo Wars worked to strengthen the movement by providing it valuable combat expertise and resources while building regional alliances: President Kabila of DRC provided assistance to CNDD-FDD in exchange for the rebel group's support in fighting Rwandan and Burundian armed forces in eastern DRC. For CNDD-FDD, this meant that the group had an incentive to stay engaged in DRC as it continued to grow in terms of numbers, capacities, and available resources and thus had little interest in talking to the government.

Prenegotiations

The prenegotiation phase—a period in which the parties talk about negotiations—lasted from late 2002 to early 2003. The willingness of Nkurunziza to engage in talks arose from events involving other factions of CNDD-FDD. In October 2002, a cessation of hostilities agreement was signed between the government of Burundi, two smaller factions of CNDD-FDD, and PALIPEHUTU-FNL.[12] The agreement did not change the dynamics on the ground, as these were only minor factions. However, the agreement convinced Nkurunziza to come to the negotiation table, as he and his comrades wanted to be seen as the legitimate representatives of CNDD-FDD. The resulting prenegotiation phase was relatively quick.

First, an agreement was signed in December 2002, under the auspices of the regional initiative with President Museveni as chairman and Deputy President Zuma as facilitator.[13] In practical terms, the agreement was mediated by Deputy President Zuma in his capacity as facilitator, with support from working group mediators from the UN and the African Union (AU). This "prenegotiation" agreement, which identified a list of fifteen agenda items for further negotiations, included a return to constitutional legitimacy, the transition period and its leaders, democracy and good governance, the position of combatants, questions relating to justice, national reconciliation, and civil service reform.

Interestingly, in addition to setting out an agenda for subsequent political negotiations, the agreement also included a definitive ceasefire (as per categorization used in this book): it established compliance mechanisms (e.g., Joint Ceasefire Commission, joint liaison teams, an international monitoring mechanism) and provided for disarmament and demobilization (e.g., the transitional government was tasked with creating new, integrated units for the army, police, and information services, with troops from the army and armed groups). Importantly, the agreement called for the deployment of an African monitoring and verification mission. The specific details on combatants' ranks and hierarchy, which were in reality required for any kind of implementation, were however left for subsequent negotiations. It is surprising that Nkurunziza committed to such a significant definitive ceasefire so early in the process, particularly when the threat of violence remained his main source of leverage. Perhaps it ought to be presumed that there was never a serious intention to implement the ceasefire but, instead, that he would focus on agreeing a substantive agenda for subsequent talks and push for the establishment of an African mission in Burundi. That is, the ceasefire agreement was considered secondary to the list of fifteen agenda items for further negotiations. Or, vice versa, progress on resolving contested issues was considered a requisite for stopping the conflict violence.

Unsurprisingly, then, there was no serious immediate implementation of the 2002 agreement. As such, the peace talks backtracked and were relocated to Pretoria, South Africa, under the auspices of then Deputy President Jacob Zuma. This led to the signing of the second agreement—a joint declaration—a little under two months later at the end of January 2003.[14] As implied by its name, the agreement was merely a declaration, attesting to the fact that the parties met in Pretoria to discuss the implementation of the December 2002 agreement. It did not provide any additional details about the ceasefire and did not refer to any aspects of disarmament or demobilization. The declaration did, however, call for the "urgent establishment of the Joint Ceasefire Commission," suggesting that the parties were concerned with setting up the structures for a more sustainable preliminary ceasefire as part of the subsequent process. The only new detail in the document was the agreement on the locations of two food supply points for CNDD-FDD combatants in the provinces of Bunanza and Ruyigi.[15] All other matters—both addressing conflict violence and solving political issues—were tabled for future negotiations.

Throughout this period, CNDD-FDD continued its armed struggle to keep pressure on the government. Given the proximity of the forthcoming elections in 2005, it was vital for CNDD-FDD to maintain pressure for genuine political reforms, so as to allow it to gain what it considered its role as the country's legitimate ruler.

Negotiations

The negotiation phase lasted from the January 2003 agreement until the end of 2003. The talks were hosted by Deputy President Zuma in Pretoria, South Africa. Relocating the negotiations to South Africa made sense as they were the primary funders of the process. In addition, this offered physical proximity to President Mandela, who had mediated the Arusha agreement and, with his personal credibility and political clout, continued to assert influence over the conflict parties. Mandela was often called into the venue to meet with the parties separately to push them toward agreement. Pretoria also had the advantage of increased isolation (in comparison to Tanzania or Uganda), reducing the media pressures and leaks to the press of unfinished agreements, the likes of which had derailed peace efforts in the past.

Two parallel working groups were formed on security and political issues, respectively. The political and security working groups both had representatives from the government of Burundi and CNDD-FDD. The heads of delegation in the different working groups remained the same throughout the process, but other members of the delegations varied as the technical and political requirements demanded. The security working group was indirectly subordinate to the political group, as the principals, who also served in the political working group, were empowered to vet all decisions taken on security (see figure 4.2).

Two important developments took place at the beginning of the negotiation phase in the domestic political and military context, which helped create a more conducive environment for the nonstate group to engage in the talks. First, as per the power-sharing provisions agreed in the 2000 Arusha Peace and Reconciliation Agreement, President Pierre Buyoya stepped down and handed the presidency to FRODEBU's Ndayizeye in April 2003. In this different political context, Nkurunziza's direct counterpart in the talks in Pretoria was therefore newly appointed President Ndayizeye—a fellow Hutu.

The second important contextual development was in the military context, that is, the deployment of the African Mission in Burundi (AMIB), starting in April 2003. Between April and September, contingents from Ethiopia and Mozambique were deployed to the mission, which also included 1,550 South African troops and more than forty observers from Burkina Faso, Gabon, Mali, Togo, and Tunisia. The presence of foreign troops on the ground was vital in creating a conducive environment for CNDD-FDD to engage in the peace talks, especially since the group continued to view the Tutsi-dominated armed forces of Burundi as an existential threat. In the eyes of CNDD-FDD, the African Mission balanced the security threat posed by the armed forces to some degree.

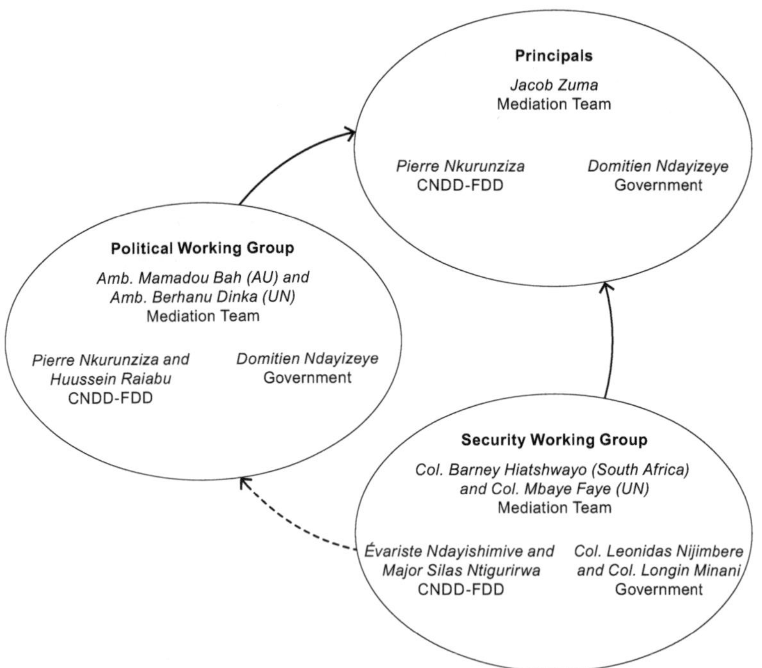

Figure 4.2 Structure of the Burundi negotiation process

Across September, October, and November 2003, two rounds of intense negotiation totaling about fifteen days took place in Pretoria. Between talks, the parties met with their constituencies to share reports on progress and clarify any misunderstandings that had been reported in the media. The mediators also traveled to Uganda and Tanzania to brief the chairman and deputy chairman of the Regional Initiative (President Museveni and President Kikwete, respectively) to ensure their continued support. To keep pressure on the government, CNDD-FDD continued its armed struggle until the signing of the Pretoria protocols, that is, talking while fighting.

The talks produced two agreements. The first agreement, the Pretoria Protocol on Political, Defence and Security Power Sharing in Burundi, was signed in Pretoria on 8 October 2003. On the political front, the agreement set out the terms of a power-sharing arrangement between CNDD-FDD and the transitional government in the Executive, National Assembly, Governors of Burundi's provinces, the Burundian diplomatic corps, local government, and public enterprises. For example, the agreement stipulated that CNDD-FDD would get fifteen members in the National Assembly along with four ministries, notably including a minister of state.[16] Not all issues were resolved, and some important issues were left to be negotiated—such as the status of CNDD-FDD as a political party and CNDD-FDD's participation in the Senate. However, having reached an agreement on power sharing in most decision-making bodies in the country, the Pretoria I agreement paved the way for CNDD-FDD's integration into Burundi's political institutions.

On the security front, the agreement contained within it a definitive ceasefire but this time included more details on the provisions for monitoring and verification, as well as for the disarmament of rebel forces and their integration into the national security forces. The agreement also stipulated a form of cantonment, requiring that CNDD-FDD should move its combatants to areas "designated by the Joint Ceasefire Commission (JCC) under the supervision of the African Mission," after which their size should be verified by the JCC. A lot of the detail in the agreement focused on clarifying how power would be shared within the new Burundi National Defense Force (BNDF). The agreement specified quotas for the security forces, for instance requiring that 60 percent of the general staff and officer corps of the new defense force should be selected from the government's army and 40 percent from CNDD-FDD. For the police and the intelligence services, the quotas stipulated were 65 percent and 35 percent for the government and CNDD-FDD, respectively. For both institutions, the agreement reiterated the principle of a 50/50 ethnic balance.

The second major agreement was Pretoria Protocol II, signed on 2 November 2003.[17] The most detailed and longest of all the agreements signed with CNDD-FDD, this protocol included provisions on the transformation of CNDD-FDD into a political party once the process of cantonment began, offered provisional immunity for all leaders and combatants of CNDD-FDD and the government's security forces, and initiated the reconstitution of the transitional government within three weeks from the signing of the agreement.

Pretoria II also included a detailed Forces Technical Agreement (FTA) as its annex, guided by the principles negotiated in Pretoria I. The FTA defined the name, roles, functions, principles, structure, command, and composition of the new BNDF, as well as the preexisting security forces (e.g., the police and intelligence services). For instance, the FTA distinguished between the roles and functions of the Public Security Police; the Judicial Police; the Police of the Air, Borders, and Foreigners; and the Prison Police and therein also provided for the integration of CNDD-FDD. In addition, the FTA outlined the process through which the defense force should be established under the supervision of the African Mission and the Joint Ceasefire Commission. A general quota of 60/40 between the government and CNDD-FDD was stipulated in the FTA for all defense and security forces. Importantly, the agreement also furthered the implementation of the earlier definitive ceasefire by outlining the Disarmament, Demobilization, and Reintegration (DDR) process pursuant to the provisions included in the December 2002 agreement. During this period, violence in the country continued at a relatively low level of intensity, with CNDD-FDD undertaking only specific targeted attacks to keep up political pressure in order to finalize and implement the agreement.

The final significant agreement between CNDD-FDD (Nkurunziza) and the government of Burundi was concluded in Dar es Salaam in November 2003. The Global Ceasefire Agreement was cosigned by the heads of state of the region (Uganda, Tanzania, South Africa, Mozambique) as well as the African Union and the United Nations. Representatives of Rwanda, Kenya, Ethiopia, Gabon, and the Democratic Republic of the Congo were also present at the signing ceremony. As more of a ceremonial agreement, the Global Ceasefire Agreement reconfirmed the previous agreements signed between the warring parties in Arusha (December 2002) and subsequently in Pretoria (January–November 2003), thereby framing the agreements as "an integral part of the Arusha Peace and Reconciliation Agreement for Burundi."

While the Global Ceasefire Agreement primarily reconfirmed earlier commitments, it did also call on the other major nonstate actor,

PALIPEHUTU-FNL, to suspend its hostilities. The signatories made a strong appeal to the rebel movement to join negotiations with the government and threatened that if the group refused to resume negotiations, "the African Union and the United Nations will deem it to be an organization inimical to the peace and security of Burundi and will treat it as such."

Implementation

Implementation began immediately after the signing of the Pretoria protocols. By mid-November 2003, the first official delegation of CNDD-FDD, including Nkurunziza's deputy, Hussein Rajabu, had joined Zuma on a visit to Bujumbura. In December, Nkurunziza himself paid a personal visit, and many other CNDD-FDD leaders began to travel. As a result, the implementation of the political components of the agreements began swiftly. Violence between the government and CNDD-FDD also waned immediately after the signing of the Pretoria Protocols and the Global Ceasefire Agreement. There was a strong incentive on both sides to implement the agreement, particularly on the part of CNDD-FDD, which wanted to enter Burundian politics in the run-up to the 2005 elections. However, while the violence between CNDD-FDD and the government waned during this period, PALIPEHUTU-FNL (Rwasa) continued its active armed rebellion, partially feeling empowered as the last significant Hutu armed group.

CNDD-FDD members received basic education from the UN and other international actors to build their capacities in the run-up to their inclusion in the country's administration. They were registered as a political party in early 2005 and took part in the parliamentary elections held in the country in July 2005, winning 58.55 percent of the votes, against 21.7 percent of FRODEBU and 7.21 percent of UPRONA. This gave CNDD-FDD an absolute majority of 64 out of the 118 seats in the National Assembly, alongside 32 out of the 49 seats in the Senate. In August, the National Assembly and the Senate voted to elect the next president, and, unopposed, Nkurunziza was elected and sworn in for his first five-year term. In less than two years, Nkurunziza had transformed from the leader of the country's largest armed rebel group to its democratically elected president.

Nkurunziza's relatively rapid transformation took place in the context of the country's broader peace process, in particular the implementation of the 2000 Arusha agreement. An Implementation Monitoring Committee (IMC) had been established in 2000 to monitor and coordinate the provisions of the various protocols of the agreement. Chaired by Ambassador

Dinka of the UN, the IMC was convened regularly and consisted of various members of the signatories to the Arusha agreement and regional and international powers. Importantly, the IMC monitored the redrafting of the country's constitution, which was adopted in a national referendum in February 2005, thereby formalizing the power-sharing principles both in the political sphere (e.g., 60/40 ethnic quotas between Hutus and Tutsis in the National Assembly), as well as in the security sector. The IMC concluded its mandate as the transition period came to an end with the election of the new National Assembly and president in the 2005 elections.

On the security side, a Joint Ceasefire Commission (JCC) was established following the Arusha agreement, with the intention to monitor the implementation of ceasefires and reform of the security sector. Chaired by the UN Operation in Burundi (AMIB was transferred to the UN office in 2004), the JCC worked closely with the Multi-Country Demobilization and Reintegration Program and the newly established National Commission on Demobilization, Reinsertion, and Reintegration to plan and implement DDR programs in the country. After some initial challenges, a Joint Operations Plan was adopted in November 2004 to guide the pre-disarmament, disarmament, combatant verification, and demobilization efforts in the country. At this time, combatants of CNDD-FDD (Nkurunziza) had already been moved to pre-disarmament assembly areas following the signing of the Global Ceasefire Agreement. Thereafter, some 7,000 members of CNDD-FDD (Nkurunziza) joined the transitional government in its efforts to combat PALIPEHUTU-FNL (Rwasa), which served as a confidence-building effect between the government of Burundi and Nkurunziza's forces. The formal DDR process for CNDD-FDD (Nkurunziza) was initiated in the first half of 2005 and continued well into 2008.[18]

INTERACTION BETWEEN POLITICAL NEGOTIATION AND CEASEFIRE PROCESSES

The Burundi case offers several insights into the interaction between political negotiation and ceasefire processes, and how this interaction is shaped by the domestic, international, and military context.

First, the case offers important insights with regard to the sequencing of the ceasefire and political negotiation process. The case shows the importance of marrying the two processes and not trying to progress the security track prior to sufficient progress in the political negotiation process. Armed nonstate groups are unlikely to voluntarily give up their most important leverage—that of the continued armed struggle—prior to agreeing on sufficient political progress. The case thus illustrates the feedback loop 3c ("impasse over sequencing") from chapter 1: progress on stopping conflict violence required progress resolving contested issues between CNDD-FDD and the government of Burundi.

In Burundi, the parties appear to have agreed to the initial definitive ceasefire prematurely. Prior to reaching any substantive agreement on the key contested issues, the initial definitive ceasefire stipulated that CNDD-FDD should move toward integrating their troops into the military and launch a DDR program. Given their military strength and their favorable position on the battlefield, it was unlikely that the group's leadership would give up its military leverage and commit to not fighting prior to agreement on key issues like political power sharing. Instead, these sensitive political matters were listed as agenda items for future negotiations. Thus, as the political negotiations remained in the prenegotiation phase (i.e., the parties were negotiating on what issues would be discussed in the subsequent negotiations), the definitive ceasefire was premature and moreover out of balance with the rest of the process.

The discrepancy between the phases on security and contested issues was in part a result of the different understandings the parties held of the process. CNDD-FDD (Nkurunziza) viewed the December 2002 agreement as the *beginning* of the political negotiations process (i.e., the goal was to identify agenda items to be discussed subsequently). In contrast, the government and the mediation team hoped the agreement would settle all remaining issues and bring the conflict to an end, as the core contested issues had already been addressed in Arusha. This latter perception arose from the belief that the talks were the conclusion of the process initiated in Arusha under President Mandela. The agreement even states that "this Ceasefire Agreement is the final stage of the peace process, itself the culmination of the Arusha Peace and Reconciliation Agreement for Burundi . . . after a process of political negotiations."[19] CNDD-FDD (Nkurunziza) did not consider December 2002 as a "culmination" of a process but as a prenegotiation agreement that marked the beginning of political negotiations.[20] For CNDD-FDD, the list of agenda items provided for in the December 2002 agreement was more important than the relatively detailed ceasefire provisions included therein.

In light of the mismatch in perceptions between the conflict parties, it is not surprising that the initial ceasefire failed to bring about a significant shift in the conflict dynamics and that violence continued. CNDD-FDD (Nkurunziza) did not have an incentive to end its armed struggle in the prenegotiation phase when key political issues remained unaddressed. Nkurunziza had a long-term ambition of ruling the country. This focus led to greater focus being placed on the political rather than the security negotiations. This was reflected in the setup of the subsequent Pretoria talks, where the heads of delegation, including Nkurunziza, sat in the political rather than security working group.[21] The long-term intention was clear: Nkurunziza's ambition was to become a political leader, and the armed struggle was only a means to change the politico-security structure of decision-making in Burundi. CNDD-FDD's unwillingness to progress the security track prior to political progress was perhaps also reflected in the content of the initial definitive ceasefire, which lacked key details necessary for implementation and was therefore unlikely to ever have been considered implementable. Yet after the second Pretoria Protocol, in which the most significant political power-sharing provisions were agreed upon, the parties were ready to operational-ize the earlier ceasefires and flesh out the necessary detail. Having agreed on the key political content, the parties were ready to move beyond fighting, to talk, while thrashing out the final details. Progress on contested issues was therefore a prerequisite for meaningful progress on ceasefire implementa-tion, demonstrating again the sequencing feedback loop between political and security issues in the Burundian case.

Second, Burundi offers a unique example of a step-by-step peacemaking approach in a context with fragmented nonstate groups. Here, the mediators sought to build peace in an accumulative fashion. They did so by shifting the domestic political context and the military situation on the ground (i.e., for the strongest rebel groups) by agreeing and implementing agreements with other actors. Thus, the mediators wisely sought to prevent the self-exclusion of key armed groups from hindering progress in the overall peace process. It is unlikely an agreement would have been possible if the mediators had waited for all rebel groups to silence their guns simultaneously. Instead, agreement was first reached among several small parties that were willing to engage, building confidence in the process and laying the foundations for other armed groups to subsequently join. The earlier agreements shifted the domestic political context, and the broader situation on the battlefield, and created opportunities for engagement with other groups.

In 2003 in particular, the domestic political context shifted with the implementation of the Arusha agreement, which signified significant prog-ress toward political power sharing between Hutus and Tutsis, especially when the presidency was handed over from Buyoya to Ndayizeye. The successful rotation of the executive sent a clear sign to the stronger rebel groups, specifically CNDD-FDD, that the government of Burundi was seri-ous about ending the conflict and moving toward a more democratic rule.

For Nkurunziza, the new political context, in which the president was a fellow Hutu, also made negotiations easier. Similarly, the deployment of the African Mission in Burundi around the same time also had a positive effect on the peace talks. Although not keen on the mission, the government of Burundi allowed it to be established as it sent a clear signal to CNDD-FDD (Nkurunziza) of the government's genuine commitment to the peace talks. It was only after these two developments that detailed discussions on the political content occurred in Pretoria, which in turn created the space for progress in the security track. Thus, important shifts in the domestic context allowed for progress in the political, and subsequently the security, track.

It should also be noted that the step-by-step approach extended beyond the negotiations with CNDD-FDD (Nkurunziza). The November 2003 Global Ceasefire Agreement explicitly called on the remaining armed group, PALIPEHUTU-FNL (Rwasa), to join the peace talks. Following Nkurunziza's appointment as president, negotiations began with PALIPEHUTU-FNL, culminating in ceasefire agreements in 2006 and 2008. The Burundian peace process, therefore, provides an example of a response to situations in which the conflict might not be "ripe" for agreement with all rebel groups, but a gradual approach combining political and security tracks allowed Burundi to reach peace step-by-step, with each phase paving the way for the next. This also shows how in a context with multiple actors, a government might demonstrate commitment to other actors through successfully implementing agreements with other actors. For example, although some of the smaller rebel groups who had signed the 2000 Arusha agreement were already in the implementation phase in December 2002, the CNDD-FDD faction led by Nkurunziza had barely moved from pre-prenegotiations to prenegotiations by that time. But the successful implementation of Arusha shifted the context and helped pave the ground for the subsequent process.

CONCLUSION

In 1996, peace efforts in Burundi were initiated against the backdrop of bloody ethnic violence in the region. There was a sense of urgency to prevent further mass atrocities. The mediators adopted an innovative step-by-step approach, whereby progress in the negotiation and implementation of political arrangements helped pave the way for subsequent progress with other groups. The political agreement reached in 2000 Arusha set the broad political contours of the new Burundian state. While this agreement lacked the participation of the two biggest nonstate groups, key principles, such as minority/majority rights and power sharing in both the political administration and the security sector, were established in that process, and their implementation paved the way to incorporate the excluded armed groups in the process. Attempts to initially rush the security track with CNDD-FDD (Nkurunziza) were ineffective, chiefly because the political negotiation process had not progressed sufficiently for the group to be willing to seriously commit to laying down arms. But once the political details were subsequently agreed upon, the parties were able to quickly commit to the necessary details in the security process. Thus, it must be said, sequencing matters, in particular for rebel groups in civil war contexts, as actors like CNDD-FDD (Nkurunziza) are always likely to be wary of actions that might reduce their military leverage prior to being confident that they have achieved their political goals. The Burundian case also serves as a helpful reminder not to rush the security track and to consider how the sequencing of negotiations and implementation efforts across different armed groups, in a step-by-step manner, might unlock a kind of progress not possible if/when all parties are negotiating simultaneously together.

NOTES

1. The Uppsala Conflict Data Program (date of retrieval: 20 July 2022) UCDP Conflict Encyclopedia: www.ucdp.uu.se. Uppsala University indicates more than 1,000 yearly battle-related deaths from 2000 to 2003.
2. The CNDD-FDD faction led by Nkurunziza is the principal focus of this chapter given its position as the biggest and strongest among various rebel groups at the time, its importance for reducing the levels of violence in Burundi, and the group's political significance. The faction led by Pierre Nkurunziza rose to power and would eventually rule Burundi from 2005 until the present day.
3. Burundi is home to three principal demographic constituencies: Hutu (approximately 85 percent), Tutsi (approximately 14 percent), and Twa (approximately 1 percent). Kirundi and French are the official languages, although Swahili is also widely spoken.
4. Burundi became part of German East Africa in 1894. In 1916, the Belgians invaded Burundi and neighboring Rwanda, establishing Ruanda-Urundi. A few years later, in 1922, Ruanda-Urundi became a class B mandate of the League of Nations. Following the dissolution of the League of Nations and the establishment of the United Nations, Ruanda-Urundi became a "Trust Territory" with continued Belgian rule until its independence in 1962.
5. The 1994 killing of Rwanda's president Habyarimana, a Hutu, heightened preexisting tensions between Rwanda's Hutu and Tutsi, resulting in genocidal killings of Tutsis and those Hutus who were viewed as supporting and/or protecting Tutsis. The approximately 100-day period of intense mass killings between 7 April and 15 July 1994 would later become known as the Rwandan Genocide, in which an estimated

500,000–1,000,000 Rwandans were killed. In addition to Rwanda, the 1990s also witnessed heightened ethnic tensions in eastern parts of the Democratic Republic of the Congo (DRC), which influenced ethnopolitical dynamics in Burundi.

6. International Crisis Group, "The Mandela Effect: Prospects for Peace in Burundi."

7. For a more detailed account of other tensions within CNDD-FDD—ranging from regional differences and personalities to doctrinal disagreements over guerilla war—see Nindorera, *The CNDD-FDD in Burundi: The Path from Armed to Political Struggle.*

8. International Crisis Group, "The Burundi Rebellion and the Ceasefire Negotiations."

9. In addition to the formal peace efforts described herein, there were various civil society peacemaking initiatives as well. Most notably, the Rome-based Catholic organization Community of Sant'Egidio held secret talks between Buyoya and the CNDD-FDD faction led by Nyangoma, leading to the signing of an agreement on 10 May 1997, on the suspension of hostilities and restoration of constitutional order. However, the process failed to bring about sincere change in the conflict dynamics on the ground.

10. See Grauvogel, *Regional Sanctions against Burundi: A Powerful Campaign and Its Unintended Consequences,* and Khadiagala, "Dealing with Conflict in Africa: The United Nations and Regional Organizations."

11. Similarly, the person who signed on behalf of PALIPEHUTU only represented a small faction of the movement.

12. "Cessation of Hostilities Agreement between the Transition Government of Burundi and the Armed Political Parties of Burundi," signed in Dar es Salaam, Tanzania, on 7 October 2002 between the government of Burundi, CNDD-FDD (Ndayikengurukiye), and PALIPEHUTU-FNL (Mugabarabona).

13. "Ceasefire Agreement between the Transitional Government of Burundi and the Conseil National Pour la Défense de la Démocratie–Forces pour la Défense de la Démocratie," signed in Arusha, Tanzania, on 2 December 2002.

14. "Joint Declaration of Agreement Reached between President Buyoya, Representing the Transitional Government of Burundi, and Pierre Nkurunziza, the Legal Representative of the CNDD-FDD in Pretoria on 27 January 2003," signed in Pretoria, South Africa, on 27 January 2003.

15. "Joint Declaration of Agreement Reached between President Buyoya, Representing the Transitional Government of Burundi, and Pierre Nkurunziza, the Legal Representative of the CNDD-FDD in Pretoria on 27 January 2003," Article 7.

16. "Political Power Issues," in "The Pretoria Protocol on Political, Defence and Security Power Sharing in Burundi," 8 October 2003.

17. "The Pretoria Protocol on Outstanding Political Defence and Security Power Sharing Issues in Burundi," signed in Pretoria on 2 November 2003.

18. For more on the DDR process, see Boshoff et al., *The Burundi Peace Process: From Civil War to Conditional Peace.*

19. "Ceasefire Agreement between the Transitional Government of Burundi and the Conseil National Pour La Défense de La Démocratie–Forces Pour La Défense de La Démocratie," 2 December 2002, Article I.3.

20. Interestingly, at the end of the process, Article 1 of the November 2003 Global Ceasefire Agreement between CNDD-FDD (Nkurunziza) and the government of Burundi situates the agreement as "an integral part of the Arusha Peace and Reconciliation Agreement for Burundi." The crucial difference between December 2002 and November 2003

was, however, that CNDD-FDD (Nkurunziza) had taken part in the negotiations itself, moving from prenegotiations to negotiations, rather than having to simply accept the negotiations between other conflict dyads.

21. Interestingly, Pierre Nkurunziza was demobilized eventually with the formal rank of major, which was a relatively low rank for the leader of the largest rebel group in the country. This could be considered a further example of his main intentions having been in the political sphere rather than the armed struggle.

CHAPTER 5

The Government of the Philippines and the MILF in Mindanao, 1996–2014
Paving the Way to Peace?

Miriam Coronel-Ferrer, Alma Evangelista, and Malin Åkebo

The ceasefire between the government of the Philippines and the Moro Islamic Liberation Front (MILF) in Mindanao is arguably one of the longest lasting and most comprehensive ceasefire arrangements in the world today. The bilateral agreement was forged in 1997 in the early days of the peace negotiations, and it remains operational to date, during the implementation phase, and has been a key feature of engagement between the government and the MILF.

The peace negotiation process was drawn out, and it took some seventeen years before a comprehensive peace accord was reached in 2014. Over the years, the parties agreed on several incremental ceasefire guidelines, terms of reference, transitional modalities, and the core substantive matters relating to governance, security, and fiscal arrangements. Conventionally, the cumulative documents reaffirmed and built on older agreements, rather than overturning or revising them. The ceasefire process is still ongoing, alongside the implementation of the 2014 Comprehensive Agreement on the Bangsamoro (CAB). For most of the time, it has prevented or de-escalated hostilities. After the three major ceasefire breakdowns in 2000, 2003, and 2008, the mechanisms were further reinforced.

The relationship between the ceasefire and the negotiations has been multifaceted. Overall, progress in the formal talks has reduced the hostilities on the ground. However, major breakdowns have still occurred due to extraneous triggers outside of the formal talks. Among such triggers were the veto by the Supreme Court of a soon-to-be signed major document and police operations against other armed groups that did not observe ceasefire protocols requiring prior coordination with the ceasefire mechanisms. Shifts in central government policy toward open hostilities also caused major setbacks in both the talks and the ceasefire.

In this chapter, we will examine the linkages between the ceasefire and the negotiation efforts to settle the core conflict issues and end the armed conflict between the government and the MILF in Mindanao. The remainder of the chapter is organized as follows. In the second section, we briefly introduce the background to the armed conflict, including the main actors and issues. The third section gives an overview of the peace negotiations and how the contested issues and conflict violence were addressed over time. In the fourth section, we analyze how the interaction between efforts to address conflict violence and efforts to address the contested issues played out in this case. The fifth section outlines a number of key conclusions and lessons learned with regard to the interaction between conflict violence and contested issues.

This chapter shows how the ceasefire has been an integral part of the peace process from the start. Given the difficult core issues to be settled and prevailing mistrust, a functional ceasefire contributed positively to the talks by building trust in the other party's intentions and allowing the parties to focus on the substantive talks. The ceasefire mechanisms were important for building trust on the ground over the years, both between the parties and with the general public. This chapter also shows how the interaction has changed over time, as reflected in the extension of the ceasefire mechanism and progress in the negotiations.

THE ARMED CONFLICT: ACTORS AND ISSUES

The armed conflict between the government of the Philippines and the MILF is rooted in a struggle for self-determination of the Muslim population in the major island group of Mindanao in the southern Philippines. The differentiation and alienation of the Muslim population can be traced to the cumulative marginalization and discrimination that they endured under 400 years of Spanish colonialism. Islam had arrived in Mindanao, the Sulu islands, and some other parts of the archipelago some three centuries before Spain laid claim of the islands in the sixteenth century. The self-governed

Muslim sultanates in Mindanao were never fully put under the control of the Spaniards. They thus preserved their religious, political, and social institutions and practices. At the turn of the twentieth century, the United States took over the erstwhile Spanish colony and succeeded in putting Mindanao and Sulu under its administrative and military control. After gaining independence in 1946, the Philippine state continued with the colonial policy of aiding the resettlement programs of Christian Filipinos to the island of Mindanao and the development of the plantation economy, providing corporations and settlers with generous land ownership rights, to the detriment of the original populations. As private property relations expanded, eroded traditional communal property rights, and led to dispossession, communal conflicts broke out between Christian and Muslim militias. Moreover, many traditional leaders lost out to migrant upstarts in local electoral contests. The region was caught in the webs of patronage that governed national politics. In the late 1960s, a separatist Muslim rebellion in Mindanao emerged. It was met with massive and violent repression by the Marcos regime, especially in the first four years under martial law.[1]

The Moro National Liberation Front (MNLF) emerged as the largest organized group in this struggle, and over the next two decades, it engaged in war and peacemaking with the government. Already in 1976, the government and the MNLF reached an agreement facilitated by the Organization of Islamic Cooperation (OIC) (formerly the Organization of the Islamic Conference). The MILF emerged as a splinter group of the MNLF in 1977 and was formally organized in 1984 under the leadership of Hashim Salamat. The MILF splintered due to dissatisfaction with the MNLF's approach in the negotiations with the government, as well as differences in ideology and leadership styles between the MNLF's leader Nur Misuari and the MILF's Hashim Salamat. While the MNLF was more secularly inspired, the MILF put greater emphasis on the role of Islam in the self-determination struggle and the governance of Muslim Mindanao.[2]

Since the armed conflict began in the late 1960s, some 120,000 people have been killed, especially during the most intense phase of war in the 1970s. In the later stages, the armed conflict had predominantly been low intensity and characterized by guerrilla warfare, although more large-scale violent eruptions did take place. Skirmishes and tensions on the ground also triggered a large number of temporary displacements over the decades. It is also important to note that the armed conflict between the government and the MILF is embedded in a conflict landscape characterized by multiple armed groups and sources of violence. Although the government signed a new peace deal with the MNLF in 1996, some twenty-three years after negotiations started, and many subsequently joined the military and civilian bureaucracy, ran for elective posts, or joined the private sector, many commanders continued to keep their weapons and followers in their respective localities.

The negotiations between the government and the MILF formally began shortly after the peace deal was forged with the MNLF in 1996. Significantly, a ceasefire agreement was immediately reached. However, the talks took another seventeen years to conclude. While most of the presidents have been in favor of pushing forward a peace agenda, the political will has varied. On the one hand, a change in the presidency provided a fresh start in a slowly moving peace process. At the same time, it also required new trust-building efforts. Notably, it was only in 2011 that for the first time a sitting Philippine president met the chair of the MILF.

The MILF, in their turn, also underwent internal changes. The growth of the MILF was conditioned by the global rise of Islamic revivalism in the 1990s. At that time, the MILF opened up spaces in their areas of control to regional violent extremist groups such as the Jemaah Islamiya (JI). Many MNLF and MILF supporters have ties in the Middle East and were influenced by different schools of thought. Several others had combat experience in the fight against the Soviet Union in Afghanistan. Within this ongoing dynamic, the MILF generally kept to their traditional guerrilla warfare military strategy, although with capacity to mobilize large formations and establish camps. Despite the influential role played by their ulamas, they eschewed violent extremism. The transfer of leadership in 2003 from the religious scholar Hashim Salamat to Murad Ebrahim, who trained as an engineer, further buttressed the moderate track. However, various groups had already been let inside their areas, which contributed to the complex mixture of armed groups operating in the same geographic space.

Finally, the involvement of the international community in the formal talks should be considered. During the first period of peace negotiations, there was no third party involved. This period, from late 1996 until early 2001, is referred to by the MILF as the "domestic stage" of the peace process. In 2001, Malaysia became involved as a facilitator, setting off the "international stage" of the negotiations. In addition, outside of the formal talks, a number of states have invested in the peace process, including Japan, the European Union (EU), the United Kingdom, and Australia. This investment has both been grounded in their normative support of the peace process and as part of the global antiterrorism concern in the aftermath of 9/11.

OVERVIEW OF THE PEACE NEGOTIATIONS

The initial phase of the seventeen-year engagement between the government and the MILF focused on agreeing on the terms of a ceasefire and setting the agenda for the substantive talks (see timeline in table 5.1). The ceasefire agreement was reached first, within five months from the start of negotiations in 1997. It took several more years before the agenda was settled in 2001. In 2012, the agenda was moreover modified. By the time the comprehensive peace agreement was settled in 2014, the negotiations with the MILF had continued across four different administrations.

Despite the relatively short period in hammering out the main ceasefire agreement during the term of President Fidel Ramos, agreeing on the operational terms and implementing these were no easy matter. From late 1997 to 2000, the parties signed around thirty more security-related agreements, approximately half of which were on localized ceasefires. The major documents included the operational procedures and ceasefire mechanisms and safety and security guarantees for MILF negotiators. Specific agreements dealt with the repositioning of troops, managing evacuees displaced by intermittent conflict, and small interim and localized truces in response to localized fighting. It was evident that the main concern at this stage was to manage the violence on the ground, consequently distracting focus on the core issues. Moreover, the whole negotiation process suffered a major setback when then Philippine president Joseph Estrada reverted to a war policy in 2000.

Negotiations subsequently resumed in 2001, and President Gloria Macapagal Arroyo acceded to the MILF's demand to invite a third-party facilitator to the talks. Malaysia became involved as a facilitator, setting off the "international stage" of the negotiations. Foreign third-party participation was further bolstered with the creation of the International Monitoring Team (IMT) for the ceasefire.

In 2004 and 2005, the parties reached several consensus points on central issues of territory and governance in Mindanao. These were eventually consolidated in the Memorandum of Agreement on Ancestral Domain (MOA-AD) of 2008. However, the initialed but unsigned MOA-AD was deemed unconstitutional by the Supreme Court. This setback sparked retaliatory acts from the MILF side, leading to another major ceasefire breakdown.

In an effort to restore the process, the international component of the talks was expanded in 2009 with the creation of the International Contact

Table 5.1: Philippines timeline

	Efforts to address contested issues	Efforts to address conflict violence
1992–1995	Government reaches out to the MILF *(pre-prenegotiation phase)*.	
1996	Exploratory talks *(prenegotiation phase)*.	
1997	Negotiating an agenda for talks. Parallel tracks on agenda setting and ceasefire, but focus is set on a ceasefire.	Agreement for General Cessations of Hostilities (AGCH) *(preliminary ceasefire)*. Coordinating Committees for the Cessation of Hostilities (CCCH), and Independent Fact-Finding Committee (IFFC).
1998		The Quick Response Team (QRT).
1999		Verification and recognition of MILF camps.
2000	Formal negotiations on the substantive agenda January–March. "All-out war," the MILF withdraws from the talks.	Major ceasefire breakdown during the "all-out war."
2001	Malaysia invited as facilitator. Negotiations on core conflict issues *(negotiation phase)*. The Agreement on Peace signed in Tripoli stipulates an agenda for the continuation of peace negotiations.	Local monitoring teams (LMTs). The IFFC and the QRT are removed.
2002		Joint communique on the establishment of the Ad Hoc Joint Action Group (AHJAG).
2003	Peace talks suspended. The Bangsamoro Development Agency (BDA) established.	Major ceasefire breakdown during military operations. Independent civil society–led Bantay Ceasefire is introduced.
2004		The International Monitoring Team (IMT). Violence drops significantly.
2005	Progress in the negotiations of core conflict issues.	The Ad Hoc Joint Action Group (AHJAG).
2006		
2007		

Table 5.1

	Efforts to address contested issues	Efforts to address conflict violence
2008	The Memorandum of Agreement on Ancestral Domain (MOA-AD) is reached but deemed unconstitutional.	Major ceasefire breakdown following the collapse of the MOA-AD.
2009	The International Contact Group is established to assist the Malaysian facilitators.	
2010		Introduction of the Civilian Protection Component of the IMT.
2011	As the first Philippine president, Benigno Aquino meets in person with the MILF chair.	
2012	The Framework Agreement on the Bangsamoro (FAB).	No armed clashes recorded between the parties.
2013		
2014	The Comprehensive Agreement on the Bangsamoro (CAB) is reached (*implementation phase*).	The CAB confirms a *definite ceasefire* between the parties. The ceasefire structure remains during the implementation of the peace agreement.

Group (ICG) and the Civilian Protection Component (CPC) in the IMT. Composed of representatives of four states and four nongovernmental organizations (NGOs), the ICG sat as observers in the talks. The CPC was made up of both international and local NGOs.

In 2012, during the presidency of Simeon Benigno Aquino, the parties reached a major breakthrough when they signed the Framework Agreement on the Bangsamoro (FAB). Following the FAB, the parties negotiated four annexes on transitional modalities, wealth sharing, power sharing, and normalization, as well as the Addendum on the Bangsamoro Waters and Zones of Joint Cooperation. The normalization annex was the last annex signed because apparently the MILF committed to decommissioning their weapons and combatants only after they secured satisfactory terms under the power-sharing and the wealth-sharing annexes.

The aforementioned documents, along with all previously signed documents, constituted the comprehensive accord, the CAB. Based on the terminologies used in this edited volume, the settlement of the CAB marks the transition from a "preliminary ceasefire" to a "definite ceasefire" aiming to permanently end armed hostilities between the parties.

The 1997 cessation of hostilities agreement has lasted for more than twenty years and has remained the reference document for a very long ceasefire and negotiation process. Looking back, the early ceasefire building phase served as a building block for the next even more difficult phases of the negotiations. It fostered trust and confidence on the ground and prevented or de-escalated hostilities between the government and MILF forces for substantial periods of time. It also brought about some changes in the communities themselves through the development projects initiated within the framework of the ceasefire. The ceasefire mechanisms also created a channel for civil society involvement in the peace process through ceasefire accompaniment and monitoring.

The successes in localized conflict management made the negotiating teams confident that they could move forward on the agenda setting. They continued to exchange ideas on agenda items, and the parties began to relax more around each other. This created more room for dialogue and discussion. Thus, in hindsight, many of the ceasefire measures were necessary at the time in order to create the space for the political aspects of the negotiations to prosper.

In the next sections, we delve into the negotiations to cease hostilities, look into the structure of the ceasefire mechanics, and examine the contentious events and issues that confounded the institutionalization and observance of the ceasefire.

Initiating the Peace Negotiation

The inception of the negotiation process can be traced to the first years of the six-year presidency of Fidel Ramos. Soon after winning the presidential election in 1992, Ramos set up a multisectoral National Unification Commission (NUC) with the objective to craft a national peace policy and to find a peaceful resolution to the armed insurgencies in the Philippines. The NUC conducted nationwide consultations over a nine-month period and consolidated the gathered input into a document that they titled "Six Paths to Peace." This outcome document remains the basic government peace framework to date. The NUC also reached out to the leaders of different armed groups, including the main armed groups of the MNLF, the MILF, and the National Democratic Front of the Philippines (NDFP) as well as Reform the Armed Forces (RAM).[3] The armed groups were all initially receptive, and several back-channel processes started. The MILF responded with a wait-and-see stance.

The peace agreement with the MNLF was signed in September 1996, less than two years before the term of President Ramos was to end. However, Ramos wanted it to be his legacy to have started talks also with the MILF. A few months before the peace deal with the MNLF was settled, Ramos gave instructions to his appointed negotiators to explore more seriously the possibility of talks with the MILF. Thus began the first discreet "talks about talks" (the prenegotiation phase) with the MILF. Government emissaries led by the president's Executive Secretary Ruben Torres met with Ghazali Jaafar, who was then the head of the political arm of the MILF. This was followed by discreet meetings between the parties on the structure of the talks. The meetings were held at the level of the technical committees of both sides. They met at different locations in Mindanao (mainly Cotabato, Cagayan de Oro, and Davao), depending on where the MILF was agreeable to meet.

The parties agreed to concurrently pursue two tracks, namely to define an agenda for the negotiations and to hammer out a ceasefire. Under the umbrella of each panel, they created their respective technical subcommittees for each track. The two sets of subcommittees held simultaneous meetings. However, even as the parties were trying to set the agenda for negotiations during the exploratory talks in January 1997, the fighting continued, including very frequently in specific areas. As such, they decided to temporarily set aside the track on agenda setting and concentrated on the ceasefire.

It is notable that there was no external mediator involved in the ceasefire negotiation process. Nonetheless, the crafting of the agreement was aided by insights from civil society organizations in Mindanao and other peace advocates in the country.

Negotiating the Ceasefire Agreement

The agreement can be categorized as a "preliminary ceasefire" because it aimed to stop conflict violence and included compliance mechanisms to facilitate this, such as monitoring and verification.[4] As a bilateral formal agreement to suspend violence, it did not specify a period of duration or any limitation to its effectivity. Moreover, the point of departure was that the commitment was made "with the end in view of finding a just and lasting solution" to the conflict.[5] Thus, the ceasefire was explicitly linked to the broader peace negotiation process. It was negotiated in formal negotiations and preceded the deliberations on the substantive agenda.

President Ramos was keen to rapidly secure a ceasefire pact. He set a two-month target for his negotiators to produce the deal, a time frame that extended to four months. In the back-channel discussions between the MILF and government emissaries, the MILF were told of the pressure from President Ramos. The government negotiators underscored the urgency to seal a deal fast by pointing to the uncertainties in the intentions and policies that a new president might adopt. Pressured by the limited time frame before presidential elections were held, the panels produced an agreement within a short time period. Overall, both sides saw the merit in ceasing hostilities if the peace negotiations were to move forward quickly.

The two parties created their respective subcommittees on cessation of hostilities (SCCH), with six members each. The government team was composed of senior military officers from the armed forces, chaired by the commanding general of the Southern Command (covering all of Mindanao), with active field commanders of conflict-affected areas as members. The Philippine National Police (PNP) was also represented, as was the legal office of the AFP. The MILF SCCH was composed of some members of the MILF Central Committee and legal counsels. The MILF legal counsel initially chaired the SCCH.

The SCCH held several meetings in the second quarter of 1997, resulting in the Agreement for General Cessation of Hostilities (AGCH)[6] in July 1997. Operational details of the AGCH were elaborated in the "Implementing Administrative Guidelines of the GRP-MILF Agreement on the General Cessation of Hostilities" signed between the parties on 12 September 1997 and the "Implementing Operational Guidelines" signed two months later on 14 November 1997.[7]

Contentious Issues

Several contentious issues stalled the ceasefire negotiations. To begin with, support for the ceasefire was not unanimous within the parties. On the government side, especially within the military, the idea of a ceasefire was controversial and considered sensitive because they feared that this would transfer "belligerency status" to the MILF. This outdated thinking that acknowledging and negotiating with an armed group changes its legal standing and vests it with the right to claim "belligerency status" ran through several segments of the military and civilian bureaucracy, creating inconsistent levels of support for the formal talks and for the ceasefire agreement itself. Consequently, the agreement came to be framed as a "cessation of hostilities" instead of as a "ceasefire," as this was more in keeping with the comfort level of the military establishment, even though the MILF initially suggested using the latter term and there may be no major legal difference between the two terms.

For the MILF, a major difficulty concerned laying out details about what acts would and would not be allowed. It contested the provision stating that that the Philippine government would maintain its supervision and enforcement of peace and order in the area. Affirming this was crucial for the armed forces and the police. The MILF, for their part, argued that this responsibility should be under their authority because it concerned their communities. They opposed opening up the communities where they have presence and influence to regular visits and suspected that the presence of government security forces would lead to unwarranted arrests.

Even more contentious was identifying the specific areas of the ceasefire. This implied that the parties had to jointly determine and agree on whether there were indeed MILF "camps" as claimed by the MILF, and where these were to be found, in order to determine the areas in which the ceasefire was to apply. The MILF had provided a list of some forty-seven areas that they claimed to be their "camps," while the Government of the Republic of the Philippines (GRP) asserted that the list needed to be verified.

While the joint CCCH was discussing the verification process, higher-level back-channel talks were taking place toward an agreement between the peace panels to at least commit to beginning formal peace talks. This resulted in the signing of an "Agreement to Reaffirm the Pursuit of Peace" on 10 February 1999 by the chairpersons of the GRP and the MILF peace negotiating panels.[8] On the same day, the "Joint Acknowledgement of 2 MILF Camps" was also signed as "a confidence-building measure in furtherance of the peace process," without a verification process.[9] Unlike previous agreements pertaining to the cessation of hostilities that were signed by CCCH members of both sides, it bore only the signatures of the two chairpersons. The document acknowledged the two main MILF camps, Abubakar and Busrah, as areas to be covered by the cessation of hostilities for the duration of the GRP-MILF talks. The joint CCCH was tasked to determine the limits of these camps, as well as to determine and verify other MILF camps that may be covered by the ceasefire for the duration of the talks. On 17 February 1999, the joint CCCH issued a statement indicating that five "camps" on the MILF list would be jointly verified initially and that others on the list may be verified afterward upon agreement by both parties.

Even prior to the verification process, the government's armed forces had long established that in the view of the MILF, these "camps" covered communities, and even whole municipalities, within which MILF positions or military garrisons in the traditional sense were located. During intense internal discussions within the government, two main views emerged. On the one hand, some saw the acknowledgment of the existence of these camps as ceding territory to a rebel group and therefore as a threat to national sovereignty and territorial integrity. Some key military personnel on the ground expressed the belief that the ceasefire should only extend to MILF "positions" (i.e., locations of military garrisons and their immediate vicinity). To acknowledge "camps" as defined by the MILF would mean that the government would be relinquishing territory to the group. This also became the predominant public view, fueled by media reporting on the matter.

On the other hand, there were those who argued that because these "camps" were in fact communities found within political boundaries established by national law, they would always remain under the legal jurisdiction of the Philippine government—even if they were heavily influenced by the MILF. In fact, legitimately elected officials, government structures, and services, no matter how flawed or lacking, were still to be found in these areas. Based on this premise, it was further argued that the "camps" verification process should include, or should lead to, the identification of key socioeconomic needs that had to be delivered by the government toward addressing the recurrent violent conflict in these areas. Thus, defining the coverage of the ceasefire would also serve to spur government action toward establishing area-specific socioeconomic interventions.

Three months after the joint acknowledgment of camps Abubakar and Busrah as areas for the cessation of hostilities for the duration of the peace talks, on 18 May 1999, the joint CCCH signed the "Rules and Procedures in the Determination and Verification of the Coverage of the Cessation of Hostilities."[10] The document outlined the steps in the verification process, including scheduling, and the designation of an MILF representative to serve as coordinator in identifying areas to be verified and to act as a guide for the verification, among other duties. The document also defined the scope of verification (including demographic data and geographic delineation and other related data pertaining to the areas to be verified), as well as postverification activities. The document used the term "camps/positions" in reference to the areas to be verified, thus reflecting the language of both sides. (Presumably, this language would also imply that while some areas may be verified as "camps" as defined by the MILF, others may be mere "positions" as asserted by the armed forces.) The document also included a section that said that a "participatory process to include the MILF" would "determine and prioritize special areas for development to be discussed by the formal GRP and MILF peace panels."

In October 1999, the GRP-MILF CCCH released a joint statement acknowledging the existence of five more MILF "camps" to be covered by the cessation of hostilities for the duration of the peace talks. This sparked alarm and disagreement within the military and civilian elements of the government, as well as among the media and general public. The claim that doing so was tantamount to granting territory and belligerency to the MILF was raised again and again. In fact, the verification process, while indeed conducted to establish the exact coverage of the cessation of hostilities in support of the peace process, appeared to have served other purposes, with both parties aiming to achieve individual objectives. For the MILF, government acknowledgment of camps, even if only for purposes of a ceasefire for the duration of the talks, was an oblique way of emphasizing their ownership and territoriality around those camps, thus bolstering their ambitions toward a status of belligerency. For the armed forces, the verification process also served to confirm intelligence and to establish new information on MILF troop strength, positions, and movements, as well as firepower capacity, and to establish the scope of influence in the communities around the MILF "camps."

Despite the agreement on the general cessation of hostilities, localized skirmishes had been taking place between the two parties in several areas covered by the ceasefire, with both sides blaming the other for provoking the hostilities. The CCCH intervened in these cases, managing to reduce tensions by signing agreements on repositioning of troops, affirming ceasefire mechanics, and safety guarantees, including protection of returning evacuees. But intermittent skirmishes between government and MILF forces escalated in Maguindanao province in the next two months, and by January 2000, large-scale fighting had broken out in the communities along the highway from Cotabato City to Sultan Kudarat.

Amid escalating hostilities, the peace panels meanwhile managed to forge an agreement on the rules and procedures for the conduct of formal peace talks in December 1999, and they held the first round of formal talks on 15 February 2000, during which the agenda for the peace talks was approved. However, by March 2000, the Philippine government had adopted an "all-out war" policy against the MILF, citing the need to safeguard national sovereignty and territorial integrity as well as national security, given allegations at the time that the MILF was harboring foreign terrorists in their camps. Thus, in a reversal of initial ceasefire efforts early in his term, then-President Estrada ordered a military campaign to capture all MILF camps (not just the seven that had been acknowledged as ceasefire areas). As the president clearly saw "all-out war" as an alternative to a negotiated settlement, peace negotiations were suspended.

Following a military offensive over three and a half months, the armed forces declared victory on 9 July 2000, having captured all the MILF camps, including its headquarters, Camp Abubakar. MILF Chairman Hashim Salamat responded with a call for jihad on 11 July 2000, thus marking the full collapse of the ceasefire as well as the peace negotiations.

Although subsequent efforts were made to restart talks and cease hostilities, by November 2001, Estrada had been impeached by the Lower House on corruption charges. He was subsequently removed from office, resigning on 19 January 2001. His vice president, Gloria Macapagal-Arroyo, took over the presidency and immediately resuscitated the peace process.

In March, the government and the MILF forged the General Framework for the Resumption of the Peace Talks signed in Kuala Lumpur, Malaysia. By June of the same year, the government and the MILF met in Tripoli and, in the presence of representatives of the Gaddafi International Foundation for Charitable Associations and the governments of Malaysia and Indonesia, signed the Agreement on Peace, otherwise known as the Tripoli Agreement. The document outlined three agendas: the security aspect, the rehabilitation aspect, and the ancestral domain aspect. Under the first aspect, they pledged to implement all past agreements.

Structuring the Ceasefire and Its Implementation Mechanisms

After signing the foundational two-page ceasefire agreement in 1997, the government and MILF peace panels organized subcommittees to draw up the longer and more detailed Implementing Administrative Guidelines and the Implementing Operational Guidelines for the formal ceasefire. Prohibited hostile and provocative acts, acts that are exempted from the ceasefire such as law enforcement operations, the coverage of the agreement, and the administrative and organizational setup, including the membership and mandate of different committees, were spelled out in detail in the two implementing guidelines. Several implementing guidelines followed in 2001, notably the Manual of Instructions and the Implementing Guidelines on the Security Aspects of the 2001 Tripoli Agreement.

The Implementing Administrative Guidelines defined the terms of reference and established the CCCH as the main coordinating mechanism for the ceasefire between the two parties. The GRP and the MILF later established their respective CCCHs and CCCH Secretariats, comprising six and three members each, respectively. Both parties provided logistical and administrative personnel to the CCCH, with the government footing the bill for the operational expenses. The Administrative Guidelines also established the civil society organization–led Independent Fact-Finding Committee (IFFC), which was tasked with conducting fact-finding inquiries for alleged violations of the ceasefire guidelines and with submitting its findings to the CCCH.

The IFFC was led by civil society groups and personalities from the Mindanao area. These included the Notre Dame University Peace Center (chair), the Maguindanao Professionals and Employees Association, the Protestant Lawyers' League of the Philippines, and the Cotabato City Media and Multipurpose Cooperative. There were a number of women among them, which otherwise had been limited in the early stages of the process. After a while, the IFFC became inadequate in effectively responding to violent incidents because of its lack of access to the affected areas and concerned actors. Moreover, the armed forces accused it of siding more with the MILF in its reports of alleged violations.

In 1998, the IFFC gave way to the Quick Response Team (QRT). It had the same members as the IFFC but now included representatives of the GRP and the MILF. The QRT had similar functions as its predecessor, and if hostilities broke out, the QRT investigated the incident, produced a report, and submitted it to the CCCH for verification and response. As such, the QRT, rather than being a completely independent mechanism, directly involved the two parties. The rationale for this was that including representatives from both parties facilitated a quick response to halt the hostilities, even before a report on the incident could be brought to the CCCH for deliberation. The IFFC and QRT were instrumental in enabling civil society participation and enhancing civil society's legitimacy as monitors and co-implementers, a practice carried through in the succeeding mechanisms that were introduced.

Although the 2001 Tripoli Agreement invited the OIC to monitor all agreements, this did not materialize. Instead, in 2004, the IMT headed by Malaysia, which was by then also facilitating the talks, was constituted. Its main task was to monitor the implementation of the 2001 Tripoli Agreement and its guidelines, which included both monitoring the observance of the ceasefire and the progress of the rehabilitation, reconstruction, and development of conflict-affected areas. The main assignment of the IMT was to assess and determine the validity of specific reports, protests, and complaints of ceasefire violations picked up by the CCCH and local monitoring teams.

In 2002, the parties issued a joint communique providing for coordination during criminal interdiction through an Ad Hoc Joint Action Group

(AHJAG). The military was concerned with the alleged links between the MILF and regional groups such as the JI, whose operatives were tracked moving around in MILF areas. In the post-9/11 context, from the perspective of the government, it was important that the MILF showed that they were committed to working against terrorism. The MILF also made several efforts in that direction, for instance, by writing directly to President Bush to underline that they reject terrorism.

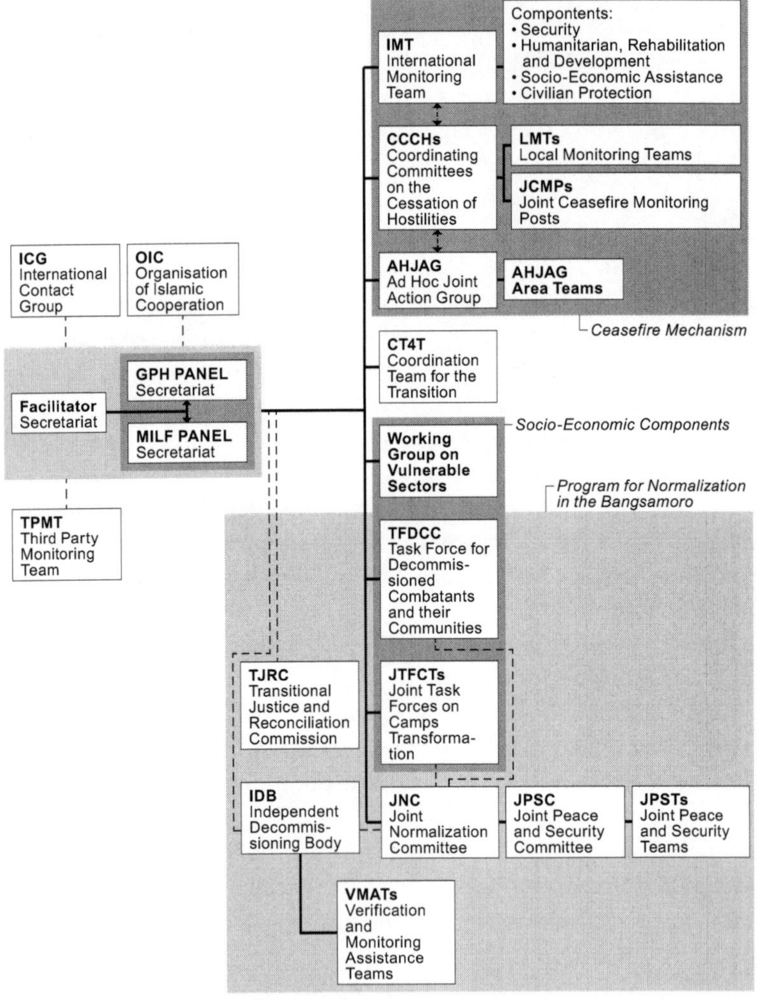

Figure 5.1 The GPH-MILF peace process infrastructure

In 2007, the Humanitarian, Rehabilitation, and Development Component (HRDC) and the Socio-Economic Assistance Components (SEAC) were added to complement the mostly security-focused component of the IMT. The HRDC was tasked with monitoring the observance of the two parties of international humanitarian law and human rights. The SEAC assisted the parties in determining the development needs of conflict-affected communities. After the MOA-AD debacle resulting from the Supreme Court veto in 2008, the Civilian Protection Component (CPC) was established to monitor, verify, and report on the compliance of the two parties with their duty to ensure the protection of civilians and civilian communities. The CPC, unlike the other components, was made up of four selected international and local civil society organizations. The local monitoring teams attached to the security component combined both government and nongovernment individuals from the provincial sites where the IMT's extension offices were based.

By the time the comprehensive accord was signed in 2014, the whole architecture for the ceasefire, the formal negotiations, and the implementation of the agreement had expanded full-blown to ensure the effective implementation of the different aspects of the CAB (see the GPH-MILF peace process infrastructure in figure 5.1).

THE INTEGRAL LINK BETWEEN THE CEASEFIRE AND THE POLITICAL NEGOTIATIONS

The early stage of the negotiation process largely focused on security and ceasefire-related aspects, and formal negotiations on substantive issues lingered. However, from the onset of the negotiation process, the ceasefire and the political agenda for resolving the conflict were clearly linked. The 1997 ceasefire agreement clearly stated in its rationale that the ceasefire was being enforced in view of the goal of "finding a just and lasting solution to the centuries-old problem of the Bangsamoro and native inhabitants of Mindanao."

As such, process-wise, the agenda was not lined up sequentially in terms of addressing conflict violence and addressing contested issues but simultaneously, although one moved farther ahead or was given more attention at a given moment. Indeed, in one of the first meetings, the MILF proposed a succinct agenda item: "to solve the Bangsamoro problem."[11] They submitted a nine-point agenda that revolved around the issues of land or the loss of their ancestral domain, displacement, exploitation of natural resources, and protection of human rights. By February 2000, the technical working groups of both sides were already clustering agenda items and crafting papers to refer to the panel level and their respective principals.[12]

When the talks restarted in 2001, the three aspects of security, rehabilitation, and ancestral domain that comprised the redesigned agenda items were similarly not laid out as sequential steps but rather as simultaneous agenda items to be pursued. The subsequent discussions on the security component generated the major improvements in the ceasefire infrastructure and enabled the formation of a modality for joint coordination in addressing criminality in the region.

The government's negotiating team interpreted the core essence of the nine-point agenda as a desire to establish self-governance that would address the Bangsamoro way of life and having their own systems accepted. From the government's point of view, the biggest challenge was the question of territorial scope for the autonomous region. The claimed Bangsamoro homeland currently encompasses some twenty provinces, and it is far bigger than the current five provinces and adjacent cities where the Moro population still dominate. In the past two referendums to define the scope for regional autonomy—conducted by way of implementing the peace agreement with the MNLF—only the remaining Moro-dominated provinces agreed to inclusion. The other provinces and cities were vehemently against being included in a third referendum. The other challenge was the range of powers that the autonomous region would enjoy, as these were delimited by the constitution. To grant the demands of the MILF would require a constitutional change or risk the whole process being scuttled by another Supreme Court rejection. Lastly, there was the matter of reconciling conflicting interests within the Bangsamoro region such as similar claims to the right to their ancestral domain among the non-Moro indigenous populations in the region and the balancing of allocation of rights between the regional and local governments under the principles of devolution and subsidiarity.

Given the difficult core negotiation issues, opening the parties to fair and viable compromises required a lot of trust building, strong leadership on both sides to generate support and override opposition within their own constituencies and among the greater public, goodwill and creativity in the negotiation process, and appropriate mechanisms to troubleshoot and sustain the talks. The changes in government policy vis-à-vis the MILF across four administrations obviously cast doubts on the government's trustworthiness and intentions. On the other hand, the suspected dalliances with violent extremist groups, the involvement in criminal and other illegal activities of some MILF members, the restlessness among some MILF commanders who were losing faith in the negotiations, and the overall distrust of their agenda made many in and out of government wary of what could be achieved through a peace process. Not surprisingly, the negotiations took almost two decades. The greater the distrust of the other, the less willingness there was to compromise.

In this regard, the ceasefire was an important part of building trust within the two parties' ranks and among the greater public. Being able to implement the ceasefire and exhibit command over one's troops manifested both will and leadership over one's ranks, two things that the parties to the negotiation not only looked for in their counterparts but also were critically assessed by the affected communities and the general public.

The joint efforts to sustain the ceasefire proved beneficial to the high-level talks and vice versa. Aside from building a foundation for a modicum of trust in the other party's intentions, a ceasefire in place relieved the parties from having to defend the process and allowed them to concentrate on the substantive talks.

The CCCHs on both sides were authorized on behalf of the panels to undertake the necessary steps to stop or avert violence. Thus, rather than getting orders from Manila or higher-ranked commanders, the CCCH had the authority to deal directly with their respective local commands in such localized situations. As such, most incidents were effectively managed at the level of the ceasefire committee. Especially in the later period of peace negotiations, from around 2011, the practice was that only major cases were elevated to the panels. This meant that the panel could concentrate on the political process. To buttress respect for and compliance with the government CCCH among the armed forces, notably colonels in charge of infantry brigades, the armed forces appointed generals to the post of CCCH chair.[13]

Consequently, the parties avoided discussing violent incidents at the level of the panel in the plenary sessions. Elevated security issues were predominantly discussed one on one with the facilitator or were confined to a small group at the level of the chairs and the facilitator so as not to disrupt the discussion on the substantive agenda. This approach rested on the understanding that it would not be possible to totally avoid violence.

Progress in the talks in turn assuaged the discontent and doubts on the ground. This was evident in the downward slide in skirmishes between the government and MILF forces in the years when the framework agreement, four annexes, and addendum were negotiated and consolidated into the comprehensive agreement in March 2014 (see figure 5.2).[14]

Moreover, the combination of the ceasefire and progress in the negotiations helped consolidate the ranks of both parties in support of the process.

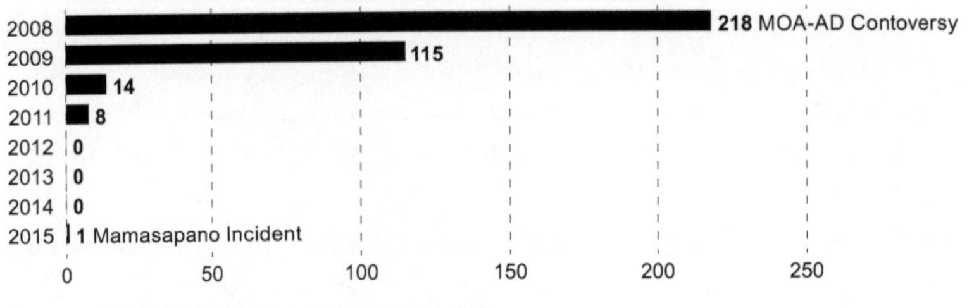

Source: GPH CCCH Data as of 03 November 2015

Figure 5.2 Government of the Philippines–MILF armed skirmishes, 2008–2015

For the government, the combination generated buy-in, especially in the different arms of the security sector and among the politicians, who were probably the most lethal internal "spoilers" to a peace process. Notably, since the last fallout in the ranks of the MILF in 2011 in the form of the splinter group called Bangsamoro Islamic Freedom Fighters (BIFF), the MILF was able to muster the support of its fighters and the communities under its influence. It was only sometime in 2015, when the prospect of legislating the Bangsamoro law that was needed to put in place the new autonomous government under the term of then-President Aquino dimmed, that some rapture within the ranks happened, this time more decisively aligned to the global extremist groups. This setback was due to the disastrous Mamasapano misencounter, which we will discuss later.

On the other hand, it was evident that violent acts by either party that were deemed to be a violation of the ceasefire disrupted the substantive negotiations to different degrees. As a consequence, and as already described in the previous section, new mechanisms were added to further buttress the management and prevention of hostilities.

In this section, we will further illustrate how ceasefire breakdowns negatively affected the political process. Then, on the more positive side, we will illustrate how the ceasefire mechanisms expanded to include other forms of security cooperation, especially in relation to addressing the threat posed by other armed groups and, given the long process, how development goals were integrated in the infrastructure and context of the ceasefire.

Consequences of Violent Ceasefire Breakdowns on the Talks

The first two of three major ceasefire breakdowns in the course of the peace negotiations were the result of military operations against MILF camps.

The Armed Forces of the Philippines (AFP) references these attacks as a response to alleged armed actions by the MILF. The breakdown in 2000 directly led the peace negotiations to collapse. The parties stopped discussions on the agenda as fighting went full blast. On the government side of the negotiations, the armed forces chief of staff became the controlling voice in the process. Camp Abubakar, the MILF's largest camp, fell in the offensives, and several other MILF encampments were scuttled. Although the MILF lost these battles, they were able to withdraw to other areas, and the leadership relocated to their other smaller base camps. The CCCH was not operational during the big offensive, and contacts between their respective chairs and secretariats became difficult.

Subsequently, government agencies had to address the massive displacement of about 900,000 people. Civil society groups called for a ceasefire in order to be able to address the humanitarian impact of the months-long fighting, and back channels were used to pave the way for the reinstatement of the ceasefire. People from the negotiating teams held secret meetings at the Marco Polo hotel in Davao, and this had to be done quietly because a large section of the armed forces was opposed to it.

The second major ceasefire breakdown was in 2003. The policy shift happened in the context of the post-9/11 war against terror, President Arroyo's efforts to align herself with the Bush administration, and the distrust in the peace process of her defense secretary (who was the previous president's AFP chief of staff). This involved another military offensive, this time against the MILF leader Hashim Salamat's headquarters in the Buliok complex, where suspected JI and Abu Sayyaf elements were allegedly harbored.

The operation was launched on the very same day as a draft peace proposal was scheduled to be presented by the government's peace negotiators. By that time, the parties had reached some substantial progress on security and rehabilitation, while the issues of ancestral domain, which addressed the very core of conflicting issues, remained largely unresolved. After the military offensive, the MILF also intensified its violent attacks. Although in July of the same year, the parties agreed to restore the ceasefire,[15] very slow progress was made in terms of negotiating contentious issues over the next seven years.

The third major ceasefire breakdown was, in contrast, precipitated by the act of a separate branch of government, notably the Supreme Court. In response to a petition filed by several local government officials, the Supreme Court declared the MOA-AD unconstitutional. This resulted in the longest break ever in the ceasefire mechanism. It even led the Malaysian government to withdraw its contingent in the IMT for about a year. In protest of the court decision and the aborted signing of the MOA-AD, three influential MILF commanders launched separate attacks on several villages near their areas of operation. Umbra Kato, one of these three commanders, decided to eventually break ranks from the MILF in 2011. No longer believing in the peace talks, he organized the BIFF from among his followers. The two other commanders, Commander Bravo and Commander Pangalian, stayed within the MILF.[16] Still, a year later in 2009, the ceasefire was reestablished. The fact that the political process was sustained made it easier to restore the ceasefire. After all, it was not the executive branch negotiating with the MILF that blocked the peace agreement but the Supreme Court that had decided against it.

The setback in the negotiations in 2008 not only caused another round of displacements but also set back the negotiation process. As discussed in previous sections, new elements in the ceasefire mechanisms were added to reinforce its capacity after each of these major breakdowns. These different components further bolstered the ceasefire structure so as to more ably respond to challenges on the ground.

It was not until the term of President Simeon Benigno Aquino from 2010 to 2016 that large-scale fighting was averted and the main substantive documents that now make up the comprehensive agreement were finally forged. However, throughout this period, violence sparked by other armed threats that in turn led to hostilities between the government and MILF forces also occurred. While these events destabilized the talks and created public uproar, both parties stayed the course and defended the value and continuity of the process, thus preventing another major breakdown in the negotiations.

An illustrative example is the unintended encounter in 2011 involving government troops and MILF commanders on Basilan Island. The military was going after the Abu Sayyaf but entered MILF areas, which led the MILF to join the Abu Sayyaf in fighting the military. As a consequence, the ceasefire was broken locally on the island and several soldiers were killed. In response, the ceasefire mechanisms were activated and a joint investigation was initiated together with the independent civil society monitoring group called the Bantay Ceasefire (Ceasefire Guards). This resulted in a joint report that found violations on both sides. The colonel who led the operations disregarded prior coordination with his military command as well as with the government ceasefire committee as was required in the ceasefire protocols. The president court-martialed the colonel, and the MILF sanctioned the local MILF commander. After this, the negotiations continued despite the public outcry against the negotiations and the MILF. But as seen in this instance, the government and the MILF were able to put a closure to the incident through the ceasefire mechanism, although it did not necessarily get the public's approval.

The Mamasapano incident in 2015, nine months after the CAB was signed, faced a similar outcome. The breakdown resulted from a raid against a wanted high-value JI operative named Marwan who had a multimillion-dollar price on his head. Marwan was located in the marshlands where various armed groups, including the BIFF and MILF, reside. The police-led raid was not coordinated with the CCCH and AHJAG. While it succeeded in killing Marwan, backup police forces in another village were met with gunfire. Only afterward were the ceasefire committees and the IMT called in to stop the fighting. By the time they were able to enter the area, the firefight had killed forty-four of the Philippine National Police's Special Action Force, seventeen MILF fighters, at least five civilians, and an unknown number of other armed men.[17] This was the only violent outbreak between the parties since negotiations moved forward in April 2012 and was the most serious in terms of deaths since the 2008 ceasefire breakdown.

The Mamasapano misencounter had significant consequences. Like the 2011 Basilan incident, the public backlash against the peace process was harsh, affecting the actuations of the legislators who at that time were deliberating on the draft of Bangsamoro Basic Law that would implement the governance aspects of the agreement. Because of the public outcry, the process lost the support of politicians who did not want to risk losing votes in the upcoming election of 2016. This put the process of passing a draft law on the Bangsamoro in Congress on hold. The incident was also utilized by the opposition at that time against the incumbent president.

To conclude, in the latter phases of the peace process, violent incidents on the ground seemingly had more of an indirect effect on the parties but consistently negatively affected public perceptions and politicians' actuations. These incidents, especially if they involved both parties, destabilized the talks and broke the momentum but did not break the process given the strong interest of the parties to maximize their gains through political negotiations. In these instances, the ceasefire mechanisms lived up to their tasks of responding by de-escalating or stopping the violence in order to restore both the ceasefire and the confidence of the parties in the whole process.

"Ceasefire and Development" in the Context of Slow Progress in the Peace Talks

The lack of progress on the core issues of a political settlement saw the tighter interlinking of the ceasefire with development and rehabilitation concerns from 2001 onward.

As stipulated in the 2001 Tripoli Agreement, the parties agreed to establish the Mindanao Trust Fund (MTF), and the MILF created its development arm called the Bangsamoro Development Agency (BDA) to co-implement development projects under the MTF. The BDA became operational in 2003.[18] The BDA reported to the MILF, and all development interventions were accordingly implemented with the latter's consent. This was important for the MILF not to perceive the development initiatives as counterinsurgency measures but rather attuned to their wider aspiration for self-governance. A key condition that enabled the implementation of the development programs was that the ceasefire was more or less holding.

Interestingly, the reconstituted Implementing Guidelines issued in August 2001 also included the agreement "to implement all necessary measures to normalise the situation in the conflict-affected areas, to pave the way for and ensure successful rehabilitation and development of said areas." As such, the ceasefire was seen not only as a measure to support the political negotiation but also as a condition to enable the rehabilitation and socioeconomic development aims of the peace process.

The MTF was set up to manage the foreign development assistance given for the socioeconomic recovery of conflict-affected areas of Mindanao. Its programs included building community infrastructures, supporting local enterprises and other job-generating endeavors, grassroots empowerment, and training programs. Another introduced framework for development interventions was the Sajahatra Bangsamoro, shortly after the Framework Agreement was signed in 2012. This consisted of short-term projects identified by the MILF and jointly implemented with the government, as well as partly supported by the MTF.

The MTF also financed the drafting of the Bangsamoro Development Plan that was launched in a big ceremony in 2014, eight months after the CAB was signed. The World Bank, under the rubric of the MTF, also provided technical and logistical support for the projects identified in the camps' transformation component of the normalization annex of the agreement.

There were some serious incidents in the course of the twelve-year life of the MTF-BDA collaboration, but most were managed within the framework of the ceasefire arrangement. Moreover, it should be recalled that built into the IMT structure since 2007 is the socioeconomic assistance component occupied solely by a representative of Japan. In this regard, Japan International Cooperation and Assistance (JICA) projects were facilitated, supported, and monitored through this component.

It should be noted that the positive perception of the MILF regarding these development initiatives ebbed and flowed with progress on the political front. During the long impasse on the substantive negotiations from 2003 to 2011, rancor was evident against the very long ceasefire without any substantial output. Those who were increasingly critical among their ranks raised the specter of counterinsurgency over the development initiatives.

Expanding the Scope of Security Cooperation through a Functional Ceasefire Infrastructure

The joint CCCH mechanism established good working relations and eventually dealt with security concerns beyond its intended function. This is best understood within the broader conflict landscape of the region. In addition to the vertical conflict between the government and the MILF, the government has been involved in conflict with other organized armed groups, including splinter groups of the MNLF and the MILF. In addition, communities were plagued by horizontal violent conflicts, including family or clan feuds (*rido*) and private armies of politicians and criminal groups.

A good number of localized sparks of violence were dealt with through the government CCCH, which in turn called on its MILF counterpart to collaborate if necessary. Thus, the CCCHs became useful beyond the vertical government–MILF conflict. This enhanced the confidence around the security partnership and the common objective of reducing community violence. The CCCH did not necessarily solve whatever the conflict or friction was about, but it was able to respond by, among other means, convening local government officials or community leaders to assist and investigate an incident, ease tensions, and contribute to the de-escalation of the violence. The track record established by the CCCH built its reputation as a local dispute-resolution mechanism. Increasingly, it received calls for assistance from local governments, police commands, tribal elders, and civil society organizations. It aided rather than determined the settlement of horizontal conflicts in a process that was built on collaboration. Acting together, dialoguing with other actors, and even providing cover or support for pursuit operations against criminal elements altogether generated more confidence and trust in the benefit of the ceasefire and the promise of the peace process.

Another mechanism for security cooperation is the AHJAG. Agreed on in 2002 and activated in 2005, the AHJAG served as a coordinative body between the two parties during government operations against lawless elements in areas where the MILF is also present. It was primarily designed to avoid misencounters between the government and the MILF forces that would seriously harm the ceasefire while ensuring unhampered law enforcement operations. According to its guidelines, the army and police units concerned should inform the government AHJAG of an impending police operation. At a prudent time, the government AHJAG shall inform the MILF AHJAG, who will then inform the MILF CCCH. Through advance warning, MILF forces are assured that they are not the object of the manhunt. They must therefore refrain from attacking the government forces.

In many instances, proper observance of the AHJAG protocols resulted in effective law enforcement, in some cases with backup support from the MILF as, for example, a blocking force. On the other hand, on occasions when the protocols were not observed, serious harm befell the law enforcers, such as in the case of the unfortunate Mamasapano incident.

It should be noted that the AHJAG mechanism was drawn up during a time of serious crime incidents in the region involving kidnappings, drugs, piracy, and JI penetration into the region (although terrorism was not mentioned in the AHJAG agreement). For the government, this was an instrument to gauge MILF commitment to disavow criminality in their own backyard. Equally important, it provided a practical approach to meet the twin objectives of law enforcement and the ceasefire implementation. This was against the backdrop of a police force who felt that the ceasefire agreement tied their hands in doing their job. Altogether, the AHJAG created opportunities for greater cooperation, albeit not devoid of complications given the complex setting of multiple armed threats.

The ceasefire infrastructure also conveniently served as a joint security force for large gatherings that brought together the MILF and the government. For example, during the launching of the Sajahatra Bangsamoro that witnessed the president, his cabinet, and the diplomatic community entering an MILF camp for the first time, the joint CCCH, together with the Presidential Security Guard and the local police and military command, jointly designed the security plan. The same went for the travel and attendance of MILF commanders and central committee members during the signing of the Framework and the Comprehensive Agreement at the Malacanang Palace in Manila 2012 and 2014. The security of visits, meetings, and projects of the IMT, other third parties, foreign diplomats, and the government panel and other officials in MILF areas was guaranteed through this joint security provided by the ceasefire mechanisms.

CONCLUSION

The bilateral ceasefire was initiated at an early stage of the peace negotiations and has been a cornerstone in the engagement between the conflicting parties. The level of trust and its efficient operational modalities are the product of an elaborate ceasefire infrastructure that has evolved over decades. The formality and early institutionalization of the ceasefire arrangement promoted cooperation, established regularity in protocols, and enhanced trust among the people within its mechanisms. A key aspect is that the ceasefire arrangement revolved around doing everything jointly. These developments on the ground also influenced the elite-level negotiations, and progress or lack of outcomes in the latter affected the former.

A functioning ceasefire was important for the high-level talks because it created trust in the other party's intentions and allowed the negotiators to focus on substantial issues. An observed ceasefire was also important to build trust in the negotiations among the general public, which meant that the parties did not have to spend time defending the talks. Moreover, the ceasefire mechanisms provided a channel for peace advocacy and developmental initiatives in ways that contributed positively to progress in the political negotiations. The civil society involvement in the ceasefire process linked to the broader peace movement in Mindanao helped keep the parties on track.

Progress in the talks, in turn, eased tensions on the ground. Illustratively, from the leadup to the signing of the FAB and in the succeeding fifteen months, there were zero hostilities between the government and the MILF. In these later phases when the negotiations were significantly moving forward, ceasefire violations had lesser effects on the peace talks compared to earlier phases. The ceasefire mechanisms were continuously expanded to manage ceasefire violations that would otherwise disrupt the talks.

The ceasefire was sensitive to the political dynamics of the talks and the core concerns underlying the conflict as it responded to contentious conflict issues in the context of a self-determination struggle embedded in a complex and violent landscape. In this respect, it should be stressed that already from the onset, both parties saw advantages of engaging in a ceasefire process, although both parties' political leaderships and military and police officers' appreciation of what could be achieved through the security arrangement and the talks varied over time and as such caused breakdowns and difficulties.

NOTES

1. For a background of the violent conflict, see, for example, Abinales, "War and Peace in Muslim Mindanao: Critiquing the Orthodoxy," 39–61.
2. For an analysis of the emergence of the MILF, see, for example, Coronel Ferrer, *Region, Nation and Homeland: Valorization and Adaptation in the Moro and Cordillera Resistance Discourse*; Santos, "War and Peace on the Moro Front: Three Standard Bearers, Three Forms of Struggle, Three Tracks (Overview)," 58–90.
3. This was a group of military officers who had launched a series of coup d'états against the Corazon Aquino administration.
4. Clayton et al., chapter 1.
5. Retrieved from the PA-X Peace Agreements Database, https://www.peaceagreements.org/viewmasterdocument/244.
6. Retrieved from the PA-X Peace Agreements Database, https://www.peaceagreements.org/viewmasterdocument/244.
7. Retrieved from the PA-X Peace Agreements Database, https://www.peaceagreements.org/viewmasterdocument/400, https://www.peaceagreements.org/viewmasterdocument/403.
8. Retrieved from peacemaker.un.org.
9. Retrieved from peacemaker.un.org.
10. Retrieved from the PA-X Peace Agreements Database, www.peaceagreements.org.
11. Retrieved from the PA-X Peace Agreements Database, https://www.peaceagreements.org/viewmasterdocument/944.
12. The government side was willing to continue with the whole agenda set out by the MILF (but wanted to recluster the items) and also to add the disposition of MILF forces and weapons to the agenda. The MILF were initially not receptive to the idea, citing that this was outside the scope of the core issues of the Bangsamoro problem. However, they agreed that when the broader socioeconomic, political, and historical aspects of the Bangsamoro problem had been discussed, they would also address the matter of disposition of forces and weapons.
13. The government's CCCH put a lot of effort in developing good relationships with the colonels and generals. While the military officials at the infantry brigade and division levels were temporarily positioned, the ceasefire secretariat had been there for the longest time and developed longstanding relations with key MILF army officers and commanders as well as the military officials who rose through the ranks.
14. Note that while there were no skirmishes, there were other filed ceasefire violations that were relatively minor. Usual charges against the MILF were carrying firearms outside of their homes, resulting in arrests and confiscation of these weapons by government troops, and the conduct of unauthorized law enforcement activities. Typical complaints against the government included uncoordinated movement of troops and alleged illegal arrests. The ceasefire guidelines provided for a system of filing and responding to such complaints. Not all complaints were addressed or settled, but this did not cause fatal damage to the ceasefire or to the talks proper.
15. Rood, "Forging Sustainable Peace in Mindanao: The Role of Civil Society," 8.
16. Both commanders are now members of the Bangsamoro transition authority.
17. De Jesus and Quintos de Jesus, "The Mamasapano Detour," 159.
18. Abubakar and Askandar, "Defining the Bangsamoro Right to Self Determination in the MILF Peace Process."

CHAPTER 6

Ceasefires in the Sudan North–South Negotiations, 2002–2005

From Nuba to the Comprehensive Peace Agreement

Jeremy Brickhill, Simon J. A. Mason, and Georg Stein

This chapter focuses on the North–South peace process in Sudan between 2002 and 2005. It explores the multiple interlinkages between the political negotiations of the conflict cleavages that were tearing the country apart and the ceasefire processes that aimed to stop the violence. These closely interlinked processes did not happen in a void and were shaped by the broader international, domestic, and military contexts.

Sudan's colonial legacy of a strong center in the North, and its marginalization of the South, East, and West, has shaped political, socioeconomic, and military developments in Sudan[1] and two wars between the North and South from 1955–1972 and 1983–2005. Sudan has experienced not one but multiple armed conflicts, which are partially interlinked. While we focus on the peace process that ended the Sudan North–South war in this chapter, we need to keep in mind the connections between the North–South process and the armed conflicts and peace negotiations in the West, in Darfur (see chapter 7, this volume), and the efforts to deal with conflict in the East of Sudan.

The chapter is structured as follows: First, we provide a basic background to the conflicts in Sudan. Second, we describe the efforts that aimed to address the North–South conflict between 2002 and 2005. We begin by exploring the process that led to the Nuba Mountain Ceasefire in January 2002 and the subsequent Machakos Protocol in July 2002. We then

133

explore the main negotiation process between July 2002 and the final signing of the Comprehensive Peace Agreement (CPA) in January 2005. We highlight the efforts of the mediation team and its security advisors to equip the parties with the necessary knowledge and trust to negotiate and prepare for the definitive ceasefire. These efforts occurred in parallel to the ongoing political negotiations that dealt with the contested conflict issues that were agreed upon in the protocols of the final CPA. Thus, the CPA included the Machakos Protocol and power-sharing agreement, the agreement on wealth sharing, the resolution of the Abyei conflict, the resolution of conflict in southern Kordofan and Blue Nile states, and the security arrangements.[2] Third, in our final discussion, we highlight the incremental nature of the processes aimed at addressing the violence and how this was affected by interactions between (1) political negotiations on conflict issues and cleavages, as well as (2) ceasefire processes and related security arrangements, and (3) how this was influenced by, but also influenced, the military (e.g., nature of fighting), domestic (e.g., political goals of parties), and international (e.g., US policy) context. We end with some key insights that we argue are likely to also be of relevance to other comparable cases.

BACKGROUND

The first Sudanese North–South war lasted from 1955 to 1972, with southerners demanding more representation and regional autonomy. The war ended with a peace agreement that was never implemented and only partially addressed some of the basic grievances that had led to the war in the first place.[3] The second Sudanese North–South war lasted from 1983 to 2005. An estimated two million people lost their lives and four million people were displaced.[4] Besides direct battle deaths, many people died due to the indirect consequences of war, including displacement, poverty, famine, and disease. The war ended with the signing of the Comprehensive Peace Agreement (CPA) between the Sudan People's Liberation Movement/ Army (SPLM/A) and the government of Sudan (GoS) in 2005. In addition, in the West, the Darfur War started in 2003 and is still not resolved today. In the East, armed conflict involving the Fierce Lions and the Beja Congress was less escalated, especially after they lost support from the SPLM/A with the signing of the CPA in 2005. Nevertheless, the Eastern Front still constituted another battleground. Finally, war broke out again within South Sudan in 2013, after South Sudan had reached peace with the North in 2005 and gained independence in 2011. The war in South Sudan has cost the lives of between 50,000 and 380,000 people (depending on estimates) and has led to millions of displaced, while many issues remain unresolved to this day.[5] In the North, conflict later took the form of street protests, which started in 2019 and have led to the ousting of longstanding President Omar Al Bashir, the founder of the National Congress Party (NCP), to a political transition period and a coup in 2021, as well as armed conflict between the Rapid Support Forces and Sudanese Armed Forces that started in April 2023.

Militarily, it is hard to get a clear estimate of the size of the respective forces, as these changed over time and vary depending on the definition of "armed force." In the South, estimates in the early 2000s were that the SPLA consisted of a standing army of about 60,000, complemented by additional seasonal combatants with estimates of the total forces being as high as a quarter of a million. Culturally, it is normal in many regions of Sudan and South Sudan to carry a weapon, making the distinction between formal forces and informal combatants difficult. The divergent definitions of what constituted an "SPLA combatant"[6] became a negotiation challenge when the question of disarmament, demobilization, and reintegration (DDR) arose in the peace process. Beyond light weapons, the SPLA also had a range of heavy weapons,[7] as the SPLA received military assistance from neighboring states. Up until 1998, the United States had followed a regime-change agenda toward Khartoum, supporting neighboring states as part of what was termed the frontline strategy, with military supplies indirectly ending up in the hands of the SPLA.[8] John Garang de Mabior, leader of the SPLM/A, who died in a helicopter crash on 30 July 2005, shortly after the signing of the CPA, had himself received military training in the United States. In the North, the standing army constituted about 100,000 soldiers, numerous conscripts, and a fully-fledged range of armament, including an air force.[9] The military complexity of the Sudan's conflicts also relates to its interconnectedness with the region, as armed conflicts in the Sudan, Chad, Democratic Republic of the Congo (DRC), Eritrea, and Uganda periodically spill over national borders. Uganda and the Sudan, for example, have accused each other of harboring armed nonstate actors fighting insurgencies within their countries, crossing borders to avoid state military retaliation.

A change in the international context helped to unblock the Intergovernmental Authority on Development's (IGAD's) peace process that had started in 1994. After almost thirty years of civil war, the Iron Curtain of the Cold War had lifted, and the world had started getting used to a more functional United Nations (UN). With this came the belief in the capacity of the international system to be able to help settle armed conflicts peacefully. At the same time, fear of violent Islamic fundamentalism grew in the West, related to a number of attacks on US assets abroad. The United States seems to have been motivated to push for peace in Sudan by at least three factors: First, after 9/11, pressure increased on the Sudan, as then US president George Bush called for an immediate end to any type of support for Al Qaida (Osama bin Laden had previously lived in Sudan). Already in May 2001, Sudanese and US officials had agreed that Khartoum would provide the United States with intelligence on terrorist networks that had been based in Sudan in the 1990s. They would do so in exchange for normalized relations and support for the peace process.[10] The degree to which Khartoum provided such information is likely to have decreased US pressure on Khartoum. Second, the United States wanted to diversify its oil sources, and thus a peaceful Sudan would allow it to access another source of oil.[11] Third, the focus on Sudan was prompted by an effective Christian lobby in Washington, DC, providing information about the plight of Christians in Sudan and raising concerns about slavery. All this led to a substantive increase of pressure on the warring parties in Sudan. In addition, there was growing donor fatigue in relation to the ongoing delivery of humanitarian aid in the Operation Lifeline Sudan.

In summary, the change in the international context provided opportunities to deal with the conflict through negotiations. These opportunities were actively used by the mediators when designing and running the process.

THE PROCESS

We zoom in now on the peace process between the North and South of Sudan. The timeline in table 6.1 is provided as orientation. Agreements related to ceasefires and security arrangements are marked in bold.

Nuba Mountains Ceasefire

In the context of the end of the Cold War and the post-9/11 situation, US Senator John Claggett Danforth, an ordained Episcopal priest, was appointed special envoy to Sudan in the Department of State. Danforth pronounced four "tests" in 2001 to see if the GoS and the SPLM/A were willing to try serious peace negotiations or if the United States would have to increase pressure. The four tests included (1) the prevention of aerial attacks on civilians, (2) periods of tranquility for immunization and humanitarian relief, (3) an examination of slavery, and (4) a ceasefire in the Nuba Mountains.[12]

Table 6.1: Sudan North–South peace process timeline

1956	Independence of Sudan
1955–1972	First Sudanese war between North and South, ends with a peace agreement, yet only partially addressing issues that led to the war
1983–2005	Second Sudanese war between North and South, ended with the Comprehensive Peace Agreement
1983	Addis Ababa agreement collapses
1989	Operation Lifeline Sudan
1994	IGAD-led talks
1997	Signing of the Declaration of Principles under IGAD
2002	
January	**Signing of the Nuba Mountains ceasefire agreement (Burgenstock negotiations)**
May–July	Machakos negotiations, signing of the Machakos Framework on 20 July
September	Battle of Torit
October 15	**Signing of a MoU on a cessation of hostilities for the duration of the talks**
2003	
September 25	**Signature of the security arrangements framework agreement**
2004	
January 7	Signature of wealth-sharing protocol
May 26	Signature of the protocols on power sharing and the three conflict areas
December 31	**Signature of the annexes on detailed security issues, ceasefire and DDR, and the implementation schedule**
2005	
9 January	Signing of the CPA

Note: Bold = security-related provisions.

It was in these circumstances that President Omar al Bashir was prompted to do something about the situation in the country at the domestic level and to signal to the United States, in particular, that it was willing to change or at least explore what negotiations could offer.

It was then that Ambassador Joseph Bucher from Switzerland was able to offer his tightly knit network of contacts in Sudan and the region to join with the United States in bringing together representatives of the GoS and the SPLM/A to discuss possibilities of a ceasefire in the Nuba Mountains. Due to the prevailing situation and the need to signal to the United States that there was a certain readiness for change in Khartoum, the parties came together in January 2002, in the cold of the Swiss winter. Here, over the course of seven days, from the 13 to 19 January, they discussed the ins and outs of a ceasefire in the Nuba Mountains. This occurred under the auspices of a Swiss/US team, headed by Swiss ambassador Josef Bucher and involving the Swiss mediator and ceasefire specialist Julian Thomas Hottinger, as well as the head of the US delegation, Col. Dennis Giddens, among other US experts. The team worked together with the parties on a detailed plan for a temporary, geographically limited, preliminary ceasefire in the Nuba Mountains. Once under way, the implementation of the ceasefire was supported by the Joint Military Commission (JMC) and a mixed international team led by the Norwegian general Jan Erik Wilhelmsen. The ceasefire functioned well in practice, and it continued to be implemented until the end of the status of war brought about by the security-related clauses in the CPA in 2005.

The Nuba Mountains ceasefire signaled that there was a willingness to talk about ending the conflict in Sudan—responding to one of Danforth's tests. At the technical level, the ceasefire was also a clear signal of feasibility that a ceasefire could be implemented in Sudan. It meant that, even if limited in scope, a ceasefire agreement could function amid the Sudanese civil war. Several factors seemed to have contributed to the effective implementation of the Nuba Mountains ceasefire agreement. It was crafted in such a manner as to separate the forces effectively, redeploying them to their respective zones of control, government troops in and around settlements, chiefly in the valleys and along roads, and the SPLM/A troops in the hills in so-called goose eggs. This differs from traditional cantonment arrangements, in which troops are concentrated in one specific location, making them an easy target for attack if/when a ceasefire is broken. The novel approach allowed the SPLM/A to control territory, at the same time making them responsible for security in their zones. For this to function, the permitted and prohibited acts under the ceasefire were clearly defined, as, for instance, a prohibition to overfly the area covered by the ceasefire.

A risk that is specific to geographic ceasefires, such as that in the Nuba Mountains, is that troops are pulled out of the area and used elsewhere in the country. To avoid this dilemma—a ceasefire in one location leading to the escalation of violence in another—the Nuba Mountains ceasefire included regulations on the movement and rotation of troops. It clarified that they had to stay in the area covered by the ceasefire and, were they to be rotated, had to be replaced by other troops. This regulation was key to making sure troops could not be taken out of the area covered by the ceasefire and deployed in other areas of conflict in Sudan.

What distinguishes a cessation of hostilities from a preliminary ceasefire is the question of monitoring or verification. The Nuba Mountains ceasefire entailed a monitoring mechanism that required the parties to work together, aided by an international component. This mechanism, known as the "three-in-a-jeep" kind, also allows the parties to begin learning how to work together and thereby build trust. Incidents would be reported by the monitors. They would in turn be investigated and discussed by the JMC and qualified as a violation of the ceasefire or not. When an incident was qualified as a violation of the ceasefire—and since such violations are more or less inevitable—the goal was not to mete out punishment but to discuss what had happened and to make sure that this type of violation would not recur. The emphasis was therefore on trust building, and the understanding was that if any sanctions were needed, they would be carried out by each party using their own internal procedures. The implementation of the ceasefire allowed the sides to get used to working together. It also showed the local population that the situation was changing and their lives might in some ways get back to normal.

In the manner explained above, the effective implementation of the Nuba Mountains ceasefire helped to build trust on the local level, demonstrating to the rest of the country that it was possible to effectively stop the violence. What it did not do—and what it was never designed to do—was address the cleavages that were tearing society apart. For this to happen, political negotiations were needed. As a preliminary ceasefire, the Nuba Mountains ceasefire contributed to restarting political negotiations as it brought about an understanding between the warring sides that cooperation even among enemies is possible. Building initial trust between two belligerent parties is the first in a number of steps toward reaching a negotiated solution to a conflict. It ultimately reflects the realities on the ground and the readiness of parties to take the next step. A realistic effort to contain or stop violence, properly implemented, is much more effective in the longer-term trajectory from war to peace than that of an overly ambitious ceasefire agreement that collapses. The Nuba Mountains ceasefire helped to instill a sense of trust between the sides that it was possible to cooperate, at least in a limited area. This said, such preliminary ceasefire agreements are not stand-alone and need to be accompanied by at least the prospect of political negotiations in the future, else they risk rapid collapse.

Machakos Protocol

The Nuba Mountains ceasefire agreement paved the way for what was to come, namely, a renewal of the IGAD's[13] efforts to mediate peace between

North and South Sudan, a process that started in 1994. Leadership for the Sudan peace process came from Kenya, whose president chaired the IGAD Subcommittee on the Sudan and appointed Kenyan Lt. General Lazaro Sumbeiywo as chief mediator of the peace process. The peace process was further supported by the "Troika," which consisted of the United States, United Kingdom, and Norway. One of the main funders of the process was the European Union (EU).[14] At the start of the process, UK Foreign Office officials estimated the chances of success of peace between the SPLM/A and the GoS were poor, at about 10 percent.[15]

It often helps a peace process to be guided by a "vision of society." This is usually developed during the prenegotiation phase and provides orientation, in the form of clarifying the process objectives and the political, judicial, socioeconomic, and security content to be negotiated. In the case of Sudan in 2002, however, there was more than one vision for the future. While John Garang de Mabior represented those actors who shared a vision of a "Unified Sudan," his deputy, Salva Kiir Mayardit (later to become president of South Sudan), represented those who had a vision of an independent South Sudan. Khartoum had the vision of keeping the largest country of Africa intact and getting off the list of potential troublemakers as perceived by the West. It also aimed to end a costly conflict and stabilize the situation to develop oil resources. The way to negotiate an agreement, despite competing visions of the future, was found in the framework agreement signed in Machakos in July 2002, seven months after the signing of the Nuba ceasefire agreement.

The Machakos Protocol contained the key aspirations and political goals of the conflict parties from both the South and the North. It set out the basic principles of the political agreement to come. A key clause was the following: "At the end of the six (6) year interim period there shall be an internationally monitored referendum, organized jointly by the GOS and the SPLM/A, for the people of South Sudan to: confirm the unity of the Sudan by voting to adopt the system of government established under the Peace Agreement; or to vote for secession."[16] Thus, the unity of the Sudan was to be given priority, but the option of secession of the South was foreseen by the agreement. Crucially, this secession could only happen after the transition period, so that unity could be made feasible and attractive. Another key clause was the following: "Nationally enacted legislation having effect only in respect of the states outside Southern Sudan shall have as its source of legislation Sharia and the consensus of the people." This allowed the religious aspirations of the North to be respected, without imposing them on the people in the South.[17]

Regarding security, the Machakos Protocol simply stated that for the pre-transition phase, during the period when the details of the Machakos framework were to be negotiated: "If not already in force, there shall be a cessation of hostilities with appropriate monitoring mechanisms established." Further, it stated, "Preparations shall be made for the implementation of a comprehensive ceasefire as soon as possible." Thus, the principles and parameters of the political agreement between the North and South were agreed early on in the 2002–2005 peace process in the Machakos Protocol. Nevertheless, it took another 2.5 years to negotiate the details behind the principles.

Building Mediation Strategy and Teamwork

It was during the Machakos negotiations that the IGAD special envoy, Lt. General Lazaro Sumbeiywo, established the basic parameters of his mediation strategy. These continued throughout the following thirty months of negotiations and were to have a major impact on the process.

As a professional soldier who had risen to the most senior command posts in the Kenyan Army, Lt. General Lazaro Sumbeiywo was a highly experienced, competent commander, fully capable of exercising his authority when required. His military knowledge was an important additional factor. Such experience is certainly an important quality for a special envoy in a mediation process. A necessary addition to this, however, is the capacity to develop an appropriate mediation strategy, to be implemented by a team operating in an effective, complementary, and disciplined manner. It was these particular areas of strategic planning and team building in which Lt. General Lazaro Sumbeiywo excelled. Thus, he made his own particular contribution to the CPA.

A core element in Lt. General Lazaro Sumbeiywo's strategy was to build national ownership, ensuring that the parties to the conflict owned the agenda and agreements arising in the process and were assisted in making meaningful decisions, which they understood and were capable of implementing. In pursuit of this goal, Lt. General Lazaro Sumbeiywo protected the negotiating parties and the negotiation process from external pressures, preventing external actors and donors from constantly interfering in the process. The venue at which the Sudanese delegates were located was sealed off by Kenyan security, and external access was allowed only within a stipulated schedule each week. He and his team provided donor briefings on a regular basis, but he insisted that "observers should only observe the process" and not interfere in the mediation. When donors attempted to unilaterally impose their own national experts to support the negotiations, he rejected this assistance and insisted that the IGAD mediation team should determine when and how advisory support was provided to the parties. This helped maintain mediation cohesion and limited confusing, contradictory influence and other input to the negotiating parties. Instead, Lt. General Lazaro Sumbeiywo provided his own carefully selected expert advisors and resource persons to support the process under his guidance and within his strategic framework.

Fortunately, the major international actors involved pursued a broadly complementary and positive approach to the IGAD mediation process, but inevitably there were political differences, and even fairly sharp disputes, from which the negotiating parties and process needed to be protected. These included elements of competitiveness between various external actors and donors and even internal tensions between headquarters and field perspectives in the same camp. One example of external pressure occurred toward the end of 2003, as US officials pushed SPLM/A and the GoS to sign an agreement in a Rose Garden ceremony in Washington, DC before the president's State of the Union Address in January 2004.[18] This can be seen in relation to the optics of the domestic political situation in the United States, with President George W. Bush heading for elections in 2004. Rather than give in to this external pressure, however, Lt. General Lazaro Sumbeiywo was able to protect the process, telling the US officials, "You may be a superpower, but you do not understand this very well. It is the Sudanese to decide on how to progress and how they want the peace deal clinched, not the Americans."[19] Instead, the mediation welcomed a high-level visit by Colin Powell, giving visibility to the United States, but not short-cutting the needed time to negotiate the implementation modalities.

Commencing at Machakos and continuing throughout the CPA negotiation process, Lt. General Lazaro Sumbeiywo insisted that extensive and thorough preparations were undertaken to support both the negotiating parties and the content and process of negotiations. Regarding the two negotiating parties, Lt. General Lazaro Sumbeiywo arranged extensive expert input through training workshops prior to each negotiation session and topic. This ensured that the parties had adequate knowledge and background on the topic at hand, understood the available options, and felt confident to take decisions. Thus, before every round of ceasefire negotiations, for example, Lt. General Lazaro Sumbeiywo arranged workshops at which expert resource persons, including experienced peace support personnel, provided input and advice, including comparative experience in previous peace processes. This undoubtedly improved the capacity and confidence of the parties to reach effective agreements. In the later stages of the negotiations at Naivasha, Lt. General Lazaro Sumbeiywo consolidated this support to the parties by providing advisors and extending the capacity building to include training for officers of both armies in the field, as will be discussed in more detail below.

As far as team building was concerned, the chief mediator encouraged internal and critical discussion in the development of mediation strategy and plans. At the same time, he demanded unhesitating and effective implementation and compliance once a plan had been adopted, insisting on a remarkably high level of discipline. Information was carefully protected, and Lt. General Lazaro Sumbeiywo managed all personnel with a close eye on security. Under his direction, a need-to-know rule applied to any confidential encounter, ensuring adherence to a strict code of confidentiality within the mediation team. If Lt. General Lazaro Sumbeiywo wanted a team member to pass a message informally to a donor, or to one or both of the negotiating parties, he issued a clear instruction. Otherwise, he insisted on radio silence, tolerating absolutely no gossip or idle banter.

Lt. General Lazaro Sumbeiywo exercised great care with regard to team functions and roles, including relations with the parties and external actors. Each member of the mediation team was required to focus on their own task and not interfere in the responsibilities that fell to other team members. He understood the importance of differentiating roles in the team and therefore the need to protect the independence and impartiality of advisors. This, in turn, enabled them to build effective relationships with the parties.

He used his advisors effectively and discreetly, in order to monitor the situation and the perceptions of the negotiating parties. On occasion, he did so to subtly pass messages or prepare the ground for negotiations, but he never compromised their independence in providing impartial support and expertise to both parties. He never once used his advisors to apply pressure. Thanks to this, he enhanced the integrity of the advisors in the eyes of the parties and ensured that the parties had confidence in the advice they were receiving. At the same time, he skillfully deployed his mediators to help parties move toward agreement or, on occasion, used external actors to apply pressure when necessary. Meanwhile, he reserved the possibility of his own personal involvement when absolutely necessary. In his own words, "The role of the Special Envoy is to oversee the whole process. The role of mediators is to mediate and find a compromise. The role of advisers is to provide the best impartial advice to the negotiating party. These are very different functions."

The basic structure of the negotiations was to negotiate topics in sequence, sealing an agreement thereafter. The disadvantage of this approach is that it is harder to make linkages between topical agreements once an agreement has been signed and sealed. The advantage of this approach is that if the process collapses, at least there may be a partial agreement the parties can hold onto. It also allows parties to begin implementing early, which in turn gives the populations affected a sense that something is changing on the ground and the prospect of a relative return to normalcy in their lives.

In summary, one can say that the effective leadership and teamwork of the Sudan CPA mediation team, the deployment of technical support within a comprehensive strategic vision, and the basis of a competent evaluation of the domestic, international, and military context were all major positive factors in the successful conclusion of the CPA process. In contrast, the African Union (AU) mediation process on Darfur (which began in Abuja shortly after the conclusion of the CPA) has been criticized for shortcomings in precisely these areas, namely, poor leadership and the absence of teamwork, an incoherent mediation strategy, and failure to provide technical support to the negotiating parties.[20]

From Machakos to Torit

During the early days of the negotiations, the parties continued to fight. This began to increasingly affect the process. At a certain point, the parties understood that negotiating while fighting at the same time could only bring them so far. In general, there is a point at which violence on the battlefield needs to be addressed if negotiations are to continue meaningfully. In the Sudan, this point was reached with the events around the city of Torit, a town about 150 km from Juba and strategically located on the road to Lokichoggio on the Kenyan border. The SPLM/A attacked the town of Torit in South Sudan in September 2002 (just two months after Machakos). Upon hearing this, the GoS negotiation delegation walked out of the negotiation room. It proved impossible to continue negotiations when one side was cheering its success on the battlefield, while the other side found itself deeply depressed and angry in defeat. The town was retaken shortly after by government troops, and the dynamics reversed. There was no way to continue discussing issues of substance, so long as these dynamics persisted.

Following the Machakos process, and specifically in response to the consequences of the battle of Torit in September 2002 (which led to the suspension of negotiations), discussions within and between IGAD, the Troika, and the mediation team focused on the urgent need to discuss with the parties how to effectively halt hostilities and resume negotiations. After some discussions, the parties agreed to a memorandum of understanding (MoU), which requested the mediators "to establish a channel of communication . . . to facilitate the implementation of a cessation of hostilities."[21] This was signed in October 2002. While this agreement did not explicitly establish a formal cessation of hostilities (CoH) or contain specific content to enable the parties to implement a CoH—indeed, while the content referring to a CoH amounted to no more than a single page—it did in fact have the desired effect, halting the hostilities and enabling negotiations to resume. Having agreed in Machakos on the basic political compromise, there was sufficient understanding of an objective to be achieved by both sides that negotiations could actually lead to a viable agreement. The military situation on the ground, at least between the SPLM/A and the GoS forces, did not spoil the negotiations from that time onward.

This illustrates just how significant political will and commitment can be and that the framing and outcome of a security agreement between parties can differ. In this case, a lightly framed agreement with limited detail on the obligations of the parties yielded a substantive result, because the parties had understood that they couldn't continue to negotiate unless they were committed to stopping the fighting.

Advising Parties and Preparing for an Effective Ceasefire

As part of these discussions, noting that Lt. General Lazaro Sumbeiywo had made successful use of external resource persons to provide background briefings to the negotiating parties at Machakos, the question arose as to whether to deploy an advisor to operationalize the requested "channel of communication" on security arrangements. A Zimbabwean former liberation fighter who had delivered the Machakos briefings on the ceasefire process and DDR was recruited into the IGAD mediation team as an advisor. His terms of reference required him to provide expert advice to the IGAD mediation team, to the negotiating parties, and to any other appropriate party as directed by Lt. General Lazaro Sumbeiywo.

The October 2002 MoU enabled Lt. General Lazaro Sumbeiywo to introduce the newly appointed advisor to the parties on this basis. The advisor then began a consultation process with both parties, which led to two initial training workshops (one in Khartoum for GoS and one in Rumbek for SPLM/A) focusing on the two major issues that were of immediate concern to both parties, namely, the ceasefire frameworks and DDR. These initial workshops were attended by senior military, intelligence, and political functionaries of the parties, and this high-level attendance clearly signified the importance that both parties attached to the ceasefire frameworks and DDR.

The subsequent negotiations on ceasefire issues (in September 2003) enabled the parties to frame the necessary and important detail of a cessation of hostilities. A formal ceasefire agreement was signed in October/November 2004, the designs of which were already largely being implemented. The agreement also included provision for a verification and monitoring mission, which was largely modeled on the highly effective three-in-a-jeep model that had been developed and deployed in the Nuba Mountains.[22]

The ceasefire model and framework themselves were essentially based on freezing military forces and halting all offensive actions as a first step, followed by effective disengagement and withdrawal to main bases and barracks. Both SPLA and GoS military forces were thereafter contained in their own generally agreed areas of control (AOCs). As had been the case in the Nuba Mountains, meaningful commitment by the parties to cease hostilities, supported by an effective and joint verification and monitoring system, was quite sufficient to ensure the fighting stopped. While there were occasional violations of the cessation of hostilities, these were usually minor local ones, and no further significant military engagements occurred after Torit.

Among various other innovative measures taken by Lt. General Lazaro Sumbeiywo was his decision to deploy an additional security advisor embedded directly into the SPLM/A structures to assist the SPLM/A in preparations for security arrangements negotiations. This advisor was recruited specifically on the basis that he had been a guerilla fighter himself (in Zimbabwe), understood the context, and could relate to the SPLM/A leaders and commanders. He developed a strong relationship with both the political and military leadership and played an important role in assisting the SPLM/A to understand the process and negotiate with confidence.

Lt. General Lazaro Sumbeiywo used both his security sector advisors to maintain his assessment of developments in the field. They had access to commanders, as well as rank-and-file fighters, and made regular trips into both North and South Sudan. They had developed close relationships and bonds of trust with their Sudanese colleagues in both GoS and SPLM/A. Their assessments of the mood, morale, realities in the field, and responses to the negotiation process assisted Lt. General Lazaro Sumbeiywo in his continuous assessment of progress both within the confines of the talks and in wider Sudan.

In this regard, it was noted that commanders in the field, most obviously in the SPLA, were suspicious about what exactly was being conceded by their leaders in Naivasha, where the negotiations were taking place, and, indeed, about what the ceasefire process (which they were expected to implement) would look like. With this in mind, the advisors proposed that the training workshops on ceasefires and DDR could also be delivered to senior officers and commanders in the field.

This idea was quickly endorsed by Lt. General Lazaro Sumbeiywo, who understood that this initiative would assist the parties to manage their own constituencies and would build capacity for the effective implementation of agreements in the future. As has been noted, "Maintaining understanding, support and command loyalty from the field towards the leadership is a major challenge in a negotiating process. The lower levels of leadership and command will be understandably worried and nervous about what concessions are being made by their leaders. In Sudan, both parties—but most obviously the SPLM/A—struggled with this problem throughout the negotiations. A significant element in this problem is about managing information flow. This of course was routinely done by the leadership of both parties themselves, but the request to conduct security arrangements training workshops in the field was an innovative idea. . . . It strengthened understanding and confidence and helped the field feel more connected to the process."[23]

Lt. General Lazaro Sumbeiywo also clearly operated in a manner that enabled him to look ahead and prepare for future needs and challenges. In this regard, the early reconnaissance he encouraged, alongside the relationships developed by his security advisors, was useful, chiefly in subsequent stages of the ceasefire and peace process when verification and monitoring teams were being established inside Sudan and when the UN mission was eventually deployed after the signing of the CPA.

Lt. General Lazaro Sumbeiywo specifically encouraged his advisors to establish a relationship with the Nuba Mountains verification and monitoring (V&M) mission, headed by the Norwegian general Jan Erik Wilhelmsen, and to undertake an assessment there that could be applied to the ceasefire in southern Sudan. The highly successful and cost-effective Nuba Mountains V&M strategy was based on a light footprint three-in-a-jeep model in which the primary responsibilities rested on the conflict parties themselves. The lessons learned from the Nuba Mountains V&M mission were intensively studied and usefully applied to the deployment of the North–South V&M mission (see section above). These linkages between negotiation and implementation assets and processes from the various conflict theaters in Sudan were assiduously assessed and applied by the IGAD mediation team. When the AU established its own Darfur mediation process, these useful lessons were neither considered nor applied, despite the efforts of both Lt. General Lazaro Sumbeiywo and his security advisor, who was seconded to the AU for this purpose.

Preparing Parties for DDR Negotiations

Both parties had significant and purposeful interests in DDR, more specifically in the demobilization of forces. For the GoS, the possibility of downsizing the conventional one hundred thousand standing army (including conscripts) was a potentially significant political and financial objective, albeit with the caveat that it could be done safely. The SPLA, comprising sixty thousand guerilla fighters, relied heavily on a very large, irregular seasonal military capacity (varying in size over the years but notionally a quarter of a million strong). The prospect of demobilizing, or more realistically containing, these disparate forces by providing some form of financial reward or incentive was an important internal political and security objective. Both parties were aware of the potentially substantial donor investment in DDR and were anxious to ensure they received an appropriate share of any financial incentive for ending hostilities. Finally, both parties had obvious intelligence interests and security concerns regarding any DDR process.

Aside from basic introductions to concepts, tools, and methods, the first DDR training workshops were largely focused on stripping away the illusions and simplistic assumptions with which the parties approached the issues. In this manner, the initial workshops provided participants with some idea of the harsh realities and the challenges they would face. The workshops included presenters who were former commanders and managers of DDR programs from other African countries, who were therefore credible in their communication of such difficult ideas.

Among the key messages delivered at these workshops, as well as in the bilateral consultations with senior officials and commanders that accompanied them, were the following: (a) Do not let external actors control or manage these processes or the programs they might finance. You must ensure effective national ownership. (b) You need to develop meaningful national capacity to understand and manage these processes, which will require significant attention to training. (c) All aspects of the security arrangements must be negotiated and agreed to by the parties in detail, including and specifically any DDR process (which is frequently left out of the negotiation process with very negative consequences). (d) You need inclusive national ownership, engagement, and participation, especially in DDR programming, so do not let the military/security apparatus dominate and prevent broad-based civilian participation.

These were not easy messages to convey, and some aspects, such as building inclusive civil participation in security-related processes and programs (such as DDR), were directly threatening to historically authoritarian beliefs and systems. Nevertheless, some key participants heard the message and understood its implications and importance, and following further consultations, both parties participated in further workshops on DDR, which incorporated community and religious leaders, academics and researchers, and even women's organizations. The DDR commissions eventually constituted by both the North and the South were diverse, including various elements of civil society as had been recommended.

The challenges of designing and implementing an effective DDR strategy and program in Sudan were complex, most obviously in South Sudan. Considerable time and effort were devoted to analyzing and discussing the issues. Direct disarmament was clearly not an achievable objective, especially in South Sudan, where decades of conflict, and indeed longstanding culture and tradition, ensured that most male adults carried weapons. These armed men provided military capabilities for both defensive and offensive purposes based on localized geographical and community interests, in the first instance. Larger military formations comprising combinations of these smaller community units could be mobilized when required and essentially represented ethnic identities. The largest part of the military capacity of the SPLA comprised the temporary mobilization of a range of local and community-based military formations, as required for specific military purposes. US complex political and economic relationships and interests underpinned the collaboration required to mobilize the informal SPLA military seasonal forces, and these were replicated, to some degree, even within the formal military formations.

The SPLM/A had no intention of significantly downsizing its standing army, at least not immediately, following a peace agreement. However, some specific issues concerning a DDR process could be applied to the existing guerilla army. These included the retirement of overage and injured fighters and the future development of more professional and conventional military forces appropriate for peacetime defense purposes. There were also prominent issues regarding the regional and ethnic concerns and tensions within the SPLM/A, which needed to be considered and could potentially be addressed through the establishment of some form of part-time territorial force (a halfway house DDR process).

The major, and most immediate, challenge, however, involved the so-called harvest guerillas. This large number of SPLA fighters essentially comprised part-time reservists whose primary occupation usually involved agricultural production or cattle rearing. Other, primarily rural, livelihoods included mining and various trades and services. These men could be regarded therefore as fundamentally integrated into society and did not require formal demobilization or reintegration. However, both the SPLM/A leadership and the part-time combatants themselves anticipated that some sort of compensation or incentive might be provided to the part-time fighters as part of the agreement to end the conflict. Any DDR program in South Sudan had to address the enormous problems that would be created by raising expectations among, and in effect remobilizing, these already settled fighters. A key challenge for DDR in South Sudan was therefore to avoid attracting already settled part-time fighters and increasing the scale of the problem, while focusing on the real DDR tasks.

Issues of community defense and potential localized threats, often involving various longstanding resource conflicts, added another dimension to this already complex situation. Further challenges were posed by political and economic interests, which had been developed around resource opportunities in a war economy, and these extended into the wider regional context. Child soldiers were another complication in a context in which underage recruitment had become a cultural norm, despite previous efforts by UNICEF and others to demobilize children from the SPLA. This is one reason the topic of child soldiers was addressed early in the process as there were concerns about the fate of the children. This process thus took place long before the main negotiations.

Variations of this range of complex challenges, and others, existed in parts of northern and eastern Sudan and obviously in the emerging sharp conflict in Darfur. In this regard, a major issue in the context of ceasefire and DDR planning and implementation concerned the advantages that could be obtained by either side through a de-escalation of conflict in one area, which could thereby enable the redeployment of forces and escalation of conflict in another area. This issue had been specifically considered and addressed in the earlier negotiations establishing the Nuba Mountains ceasefire and was an important issue in the North–South context, too.

These challenges, which were sensitive issues for both negotiating parties, required thorough and frank assessment and discussion. This could only take place if specific institutional capacity was developed by both parties and authority was thereby given to those responsible to discuss and negotiate the issues. On this basis, the IGAD security advisor recommended that both the

GoS and the SPLM/A should be assisted to establish their own specialized DDR commissions as soon as possible and therefore before a final agreement was reached.

In this regard, noting the basic principles already agreed at Machakos and considering the directions in which the ongoing political negotiations were taking the parties, Lt. General Lazaro Sumbeiywo agreed to allow a separate, parallel mediation process to be initiated by the security advisor. This involved direct consultations and negotiations between the two putative demobilization commissions. The aim was to enable a joint or at least collaborative DDR framework to be developed.

At this stage, approaches were made through the UN system to recommend that the United Nations Development Programme (UNDP) should establish a small support unit to assist both the GoS and SPLM/A to establish formal demobilization commissions, which would enable substantive planning to take place and attract donor funding. While each separate DDR commission would obviously need to develop its own particular focus and strategy, a joint DDR coordination framework, including agreement on funding allocations and processes, was also necessary.

The joint DDR coordination framework would be a conditionality for UNDP institutional support and subsequent donor funding. It also provided the leverage to persuade the parties to attempt to develop a joint approach to DDR. Lt. General Lazaro Sumbeiywo, however, insisted on maintaining control of this parallel mediation process to ensure that the UNDP DDR initiative operated within the broad CPA mediation strategy and did not take steps that might threaten or undermine it. In these circumstances, the head of the newly established Sudan DDR support unit would be required to mediate the negotiations between the parties to establish a joint DDR coordination framework acceptable to the UNDP. This said, his efforts would be supported and effectively supervised by Lt. General Lazaro Sumbeiywo's security advisor. On this basis, his advisor was appointed in an advisory role to the UNDP unit, supervising recruitment and program implementation on Lt. General Lazaro Sumbeiywo's behalf and discreetly overseeing the mediation process while remaining available to the parties as an advisor.

Following a series of joint consultation meetings and further trainings over a period of several months, both GoS and SPLM/A made progress toward establishing their own demobilization commissions and reaching agreement on a joint DDR framework, which was then submitted to the senior negotiating teams at the Naivasha talks. Here it was endorsed by the political leadership, resulting in the establishment of a joint Sudan DDR commission, comprising both northern and southern components. The joint DDR commission was able to present a funding proposal to the UNDP, which received donor support provided through the UNDP Sudan DDR support unit.

This type of creative approach to mediation, alongside the innovative deployment of his technical team, was a hallmark of Lt. General Lazaro Sumbeiywo's ability to maintain the core mediation process and strategy. It was also emblematic of his desire to seek out opportunities to strengthen and deepen the broad mediation process. In this particular case, establishing the joint Sudan DDR commission while negotiations were still ongoing had a major positive impact on the overall mediation process. As Lt. General Lazaro Sumbeiywo's security advisor himself has noted, "This development represents the best-case scenario of what mediators hope to achieve. It opened space to begin planning and preparing for the implementation of anticipated peace-building processes. Furthermore, it created opportunities for the parties to work together on practical implementation issues in parallel with the negotiation process. Finally, it built relationships and confidence between the belligerent parties."[24]

In the final stages of the negotiations, Lt. General Lazaro Sumbeiywo also used the joint Sudan DDR commission to host the first major conference with multilateral and international donors and implementation agencies. It focused on both DDR and postconflict recovery and development planning, encouraging post agreement implementation processes to commence.[25]

The joint DDR commission made substantial progress in the following months, undertaking preparations and training and submitting content to the negotiation process in Naivasha. The definitive ceasefire agreement signed by the parties in July 2004 contained specific details on DDR developed by the joint DDR commission over the previous months. It essentially followed the format of the final status of forces agreement establishing two separate DDR commissions overseen by a joint coordination mechanism.

The security arrangements framework agreement, signed in September 2003, contained the principal ideas of the definitive ceasefire agreement that was signed in July 2004. A definitive ceasefire silences the arms for good; it ends the status of war and it ultimately marks the transition from war to peace. The core idea of the final status of forces agreement was to keep two standing armies for the duration of the transition, as well as having joint units comprising SPLA and GoS forces for specific hot spots and the border areas. The definitive ceasefire agreement also included content on DDR, as well as to initial security sector reform.

In order to highlight one of the risks that come with large DDR programs or the prospect thereof, there is an anecdote to be told, which is that when it became publicly known that the Naivasha negotiations were dealing with questions of future disarmament, the market price of unserviceable weapons in neighboring countries increased, in anticipation of disarmament programs where weapons (serviceable or not) might be handed over in exchange for DDR packages. This highlights the importance of careful negotiation of DDR programs, including their implementation schedules and adapting them to the realities and needs on the ground, as well as establishing programs that realistically can be financed and that donors actually are willing to finance.

Moving to Implementation

Issues related to the implementation process of the CPA were problematic, as donors were anxious to rapidly move toward a final agreement and dismissed the need for a detailed implementation schedule to be negotiated and incorporated into the final agreement. Lt. General Lazaro Sumbeiywo and his team were adamant, however, and managed to obtain donor agreement and finances to complete the negotiation of an implementation schedule. This was, however, at the cost of various other important issues, which were neglected in the final stages of the negotiations and had negative consequences.

The most significant of the issues that were not satisfactorily completed because of this donor impatience was the threat posed by other armed groups (OAGs), as they were called, and whose issues and interests had not yet been addressed in the ceasefire process or planning for DDR. More broadly, the serious problems of military balance and potential internal conflict, reflecting the multiethnic and regional complexities of the various armed formations in South Sudan, both within the SPLA and outside it, were not adequately addressed. Various proposals addressing these challenges, including specific plans to establish part-time regional reservist formations that could assuage security concerns, were never pursued.

In tandem with this aspect of neglect at the last moment was the inadequate time allocated for an effective handover between the long-established and experienced mediation team and the newly arriving UN mission with its multiple program components and international nongovernmental organization partners. These included the newly recruited UNDP and UNICEF DDR consultants who inherited the national Sudan DDR organizations and plans, but it did not include advisors, who knew the terrain and had gained the confidence of the Sudanese colleagues involved in DDR. The relationships of trust that had enabled frank discussions between the advisors and their Sudanese colleagues were replaced with more formal donor/recipient relationships, and inevitably, the incumbent UN DDR consultants were inclined to take traditional approaches to DDR, which were not entirely appropriate to the unique circumstances in Sudan.

Most obviously, this transfer of, and necessary interconnection between, conflict theaters and processes in Sudan were not sufficiently applied to the Darfur mediation efforts. Although the security arrangements advisor to IGAD was seconded to the Darfur mediation process for a period before his resignation, no other attempt was made to transfer knowledge and experience from Naivasha to Abuja.[26] Furthermore, independent of third-party efforts, the main approach taken by the GoS and the SPLM/A seems to have been to try and isolate the CPA process from the Darfur conflict by keeping the existing North–South bilateral setup, rather than enlarging the negotiation delegations to include representatives of Darfur. It is likely that the GoS felt it had more control by trying to negotiate bilateral agreements with the different areas, rather than one peace agreement with all three regions.

One of the lessons from the collapse of the Addis Ababa agreement of 1972 was that implementation modalities must be crystal clear if an agreement is to be implemented. For this reason, the mediation team pushed heavily for negotiating the details of the implementation modalities of the CPA agreement before the final signature on the entire agreement. While there was pressure from the United States to end earlier (as discussed above), sufficient time was set aside to negotiate the implementation modalities. This also allowed the mediation team to bring on board UN actors early enough to clarify how the implementation of the agreement could be supported by the UN. Implementation of agreements in conflicts like the Sudan takes a lot of external third-party support. The United Mission in Sudan (UNMIS) had an authorized strength of up to 10,000 military personnel, with a mandate to support the implementation of the CPA. Acting under Chapter VII of the UN Charter, UNMIS was also able to take the necessary action to protect UN personnel and civilians.[27]

The CPA—an agreement of 241 pages—was finally signed on 5 January 2005,[28] outlining an initial pre-interim period of six months. Then, after an interim period of six years, there was to be an internationally monitored referendum for the people of South Sudan, organized jointly by the government of Sudan and the SPLM/A. Unexpected obstacles to the implementation arose with John Garang's death in a helicopter crash on 30 July 2005 at the end of the pre-interim period. This changed the situation fundamentally, as the principal South Sudanese leader in favor of the vision of "one Sudan" was no longer there to explain the reasoning behind this to the population or to work toward implementing the agreement that had six years to make unity attractive. It was then that the cohesion of the SPLM/A became more fragile, and those voices in favor of an independent South Sudan became stronger, leading up to the referendum in 2011 whose outcome was independence. While the CPA did end the war between the North and the South, in December 2013, civil war broke out in the Republic of South Sudan, and in April 2023, war began between the Sudan Armed Forces and the Rapid Support Forces in the North.

CONCLUSION

The Sudan CPA process demonstrates how the international and military context influenced the parties' political decisions at the domestic level and influenced efforts to address the conflict violence. At the same time, efforts to address conflict violence (e.g., Nuba) helped to create the space and trust for political decisions to be taken (e.g., Machakos), which allowed the political negotiation process to advance. The two processes, therefore, were intertwined and incremental in nature, thereby creating a positive feedback loop between the ceasefire process and the political negotiation process. Examples of the interaction between these processes and how they were shaped by the evolving context are discussed here for illustrative purposes.

Long before the CPA negotiations began in 2002, efforts occurred to address or at least contain the violence, such as Operation Lifeline Sudan in 1989. Such early humanitarian efforts helped to get the actors used to the idea of negotiation and establish trust that could later be built on. Another such example was UNICEF's Child Soldiers Rehabilitation Programme (largely in southern Sudan), which was implemented in the period immediately before and during the CPA negotiations. Like Operation Lifeline Sudan, this provided training and experience, which was invaluable during the CPA ceasefire implementation. The Sudanese (SPLA) head of the UNICEF child soldiers program became the South Sudan DDR commission director. Thus, early steps to address conflict violence helped create capacity and build up to more substantive steps later. At the same time, if violence is contained or reduced but no political process occurs to deal with the contested conflict issues and incompatibilities fueling the violence, such measures are either likely to collapse or may even be seen as prolonging the war. The broader ceasefire process cannot be seen as a stand-alone undertaking but needs linking to a political negotiation process.

The Nuba Mountains ceasefire was geographically limited. It helped create trust to move ahead with the political negotiations that led to the Machakos Protocol. After the Machakos Protocol was signed, the political negotiations on the details to fill the framework continued, until they were blocked by the military situation on the ground, namely, by the battle of Torit. At the level of the ceasefire process, a CoH/declaration of principles was then negotiated to stop the violence contaminating the political negotiation process. The CoH specifically stated the aim for the parties "to resume negotiations." Political negotiations restarted, on security, power sharing, wealth sharing, and social issues. These political negotiations took time, but with the CoH in place and some progress having been made on the political level, they advanced. Without progress in the political negotiations, it is likely the CoH would have collapsed or would have had to have more robust monitoring and verification mechanisms.

At the same time, the reduction of violence also allowed the security advisors of the Naivasha mediation team to start working with the parties to prepare them for the negotiation of more contentious security issues, such as those related to DDR and the final status of forces. As part of the political negotiation process, the definitive ceasefire was first agreed upon in principle, and then the details were hashed out until the definitive ceasefire could be included in the final CPA package. Since the definitive ceasefire entailed so many highly contested issues (such as those related to DDR), elaborate training workshops were required to prepare not just the politician leaders but also the military officers. Thus, the horizontal component of the negotiations was complemented by the efforts of the mediation team, vertically.

In 2003, a domestic and military context factor—albeit indirectly also shaped by the CPA negotiation process—appeared with the escalation of the Darfur conflict. With hindsight, one of the main problems seems to have been that it was impossible to address the different violent conflicts ongoing in the country at that time in a single negotiation process. While the IGAD-led negotiations on the North–South conflict proceeded well, the AU-mediated negotiations on Darfur proved thorny, leading to a piecemeal set of agreements with a number of opposition groups, which ultimately did not last. The conflict in the Beja region in the east of the Sudan remained unaddressed. Would the approach of bundling all conflicts into one negotiation process have helped to solve all of them, or would the complexity of three conflicts have led to the collapse not just of the Darfur process but also of the North–South process? It is impossible to say, but it is understandable that the GoS wanted to maintain maximum control over the negotiations, negotiating separately with the South and the West. At the level of third parties, however, more could have been done to learn lessons from one process to be used in another.

At different points during the process, pressure from donors and key international states was exerted. Yet the international community learned at least partially to respect the needs of the process. The last phase of the negotiation process—thanks also to the protective hand of the chief mediator Lt. General Lazaro Sumbeiywo—could therefore be sufficiently isolated from international pressure for the agreement to come to a reasonable end, including the negotiations of the implementation modalities. More time, however, could possibly have led to a more solid agreement, for example, by also addressing some key questions related to the OAGs. At the start, pressure from the United States helped push the parties to negotiate, while at other moments, it nearly derailed the process.[29] Soon after signing the CPA, the death of John Garang de Mabior threatened the implementation of the peace agreement. While the agreement and its implementation were robust enough to survive the loss of one of its main protagonists, the driving force from the South for unity and the vision of a "New Sudan" was lost, and in 2011, the people of South Sudan chose to secede from the North.

It is impossible to explore the many other interactions between political negotiation process, ceasefire process, and international, domestic, and military contexts, yet the few examples highlighted above show how they do affect each other, and often in unexpected ways. Seeing examples of such interactions in a specific case can help one to be aware of their importance in other contexts.

The ways to address violence and create space for political negotiations are specific to each context. No template approach should be applied. This is also why such case studies looking into past negotiation processes to establish in hindsight what conditioned the negotiations, how they played out, and what results could be achieved are dangerous. We do not know today what the specific realities on the ground were at the time, what mindset the negotiators and decision-makers had, and how this affected how the negotiations were conducted and evolved. Avoiding copy-and-paste from one case to another, however, does not mean reinventing the wheel in each new case. The challenge is more to try and see the essence of basic patterns that occur in multiple cases and then adapt and contextualize them in new cases. In the following, we conclude with some insights from the Sudan case that we argue are also likely to be relevant in other more or less comparable contexts.

First, the political negotiation and ceasefire processes are ideally designed to be sequenced and intertwined, so that developments can occur incrementally and in a mutually reinforcing manner: The Sudan case shows how the parties' political decision to attempt to negotiate a way out of the violent conflict was the key factor shaping both the political negotiation process and the ceasefire process. There is no magic wand that will simply make parties stop their fighting. It is their political decision, based on their own assessment of whether they would like to resolve their conflict through negotiations, that may make it possible to address the violence. The ceasefire process thus served the political goals of the parties. Yet this political decision was not enough; it had to be supported by technical steps to address the conflict violence in practical terms to establish the initial trust required to proceed with the political negotiations. Without this, the military situation on the ground would likely have contaminated and impeded the progress of the political negotiation process. For political negotiations to proceed, violence had to be addressed at multiple points in time and in multiple different ways. In this case, one key moment was after the battle of Torit. This case indicates that the situation on the ground has to sometimes evolve in a certain way until the parties are ready to take the necessary steps to address the violence through a cessation of hostilities or preliminary ceasefire. At the same time, the Sudan case also shows that multiple measures short of a ceasefire can be useful to reduce violence, as well as build trust and expertise early on, such as a battlefield truce, aiming to halt fire for the exchange of the dead and wounded or to allow civilians to leave the zone of combat, or confidence-building measures (CBMs)[30] to contain or restrict certain forms of violence.

As the Sudan case shows, agreements that address the violence do not resolve the conflict. They are there to establish the trust and the space necessary, between the warring parties, to engage in, or proceed with, a political negotiation process, which aims to resolve the cleavages that are tearing society apart. This is why ceasefires are not stand-alone documents and why their respect and implementation also depend on the prospect of progress in the negotiations on those other issues at hand.

Second, the need for a coherent mediation strategy, a mediation team with clear roles, and ongoing analysis: The Sudan CPA process showed how the chief mediator was able to develop a strategy and team that was clearly structured and that respected the roles that were attributed to them in a coherent manner. Thus, much depends on how a mediator and their team—if negotiations are meditated—design and implement their mediation strategy. It also depends on how they seek to foster parties' technical expertise and trust in the process in a dynamically evolving context. The choice of when and how a security arrangement is introduced is shaped by the readiness of the parties in the ceasefire process to address security, but also by the political context, progress in the political negotiations, and the military situation on the ground. Thus, the process calls for ongoing, in-depth analysis by the mediation team. Analysis by the mediation team is key to developing a mediation strategy, which is oriented to the process goals agreed to by the parties. Such a strategy allows the team to be prepared to respond to the needs of the negotiations early on, adapt to different scenarios as they arise, determine required participation, and organize upcoming meetings. A strategy fosters awareness of the interlinkages of the different themes (e.g., security, political power sharing, economy) and how they condition each other. A mediation strategy is key to organizing tasks and roles in the team, and to respond to pressures and events from the international, domestic, and military contexts in a proactive and coordinated manner.

Third, discussing and preparing before negotiating: One option used in the Sudan process was to start discussing how to address violence before actually negotiating the topic. By introducing questions about different ways of addressing violence early on, parties get used to the idea, as well as to the need for thorough preparation. If the topic of "ceasefires" is too threatening, it may, in the first instance, be more realistic to start discussing initial steps that would help regulate and reduce the fighting. When introducing the many different possible ways of addressing violence, it is often helpful to clarify with the parties the different meanings and nuances of CBMs, CoH, preliminary ceasefires, and definitive ceasefires. It is also helpful to introduce them to the basic logic of an incremental move from informal to more formal and binding steps, highlighting how the initial, informal, and nonbinding steps allow parties to withdraw from the process and go back to fighting if they lose trust in the other side. Such discussions on different approaches to addressing violence in a peace process focus on increasing the parties' options of what can be done, in a manner that is appropriate to the context and phase they find themselves in. If parties see such steps as potentially helping them negotiate their political goals, they may consider them.

Fourth, technical knowledge must be built for parties to understand and develop options and build trust: Related to the point above, the Sudan North–South process showed that it is essential to prepare and engage parties on a technical level for purposes of knowledge and confidence building. One simply cannot expect actors who have been waging war to know how to craft technically sound ceasefire agreements, as the knowledge of how to begin or fight wars is different from the knowledge of how to end wars. This is a technical process, based on a political decision to engage in ceasefire negotiations, and it aims at building an understanding of the options available to address certain forms of violence and then to work toward a preliminary and then a definitive ceasefire. Technical knowledge can be construed in parallel formats to the political negotiations, where the knowledge is built ahead of the time when it is negotiated. In some circumstances, this building of capacity also enables a "normalization" of discussions around topics as sensitive as security—leaving the actual decisions to a later stage or for the parties' political leadership. Both the leadership, who make the final decisions, and rank and file, so they follow along, need to be involved in such discussions and capacity building.

Fifth, ceasefires and political negotiations require a delicate role division between domestic and international actors: The case shows how domestic, national ownership of ceasefires and peace agreements is key to legitimacy and sustainability, and thus all decisions on content must remain in the hands of national conflict parties, as they are the ones to live with the agreement. International actors, nevertheless, can also play a key role, as they can support conflict parties to make better-informed agreements by providing technical expertise, bringing in comparative insights from other cases, mediating the process, and supporting the process financially. International actors can also highlight to national actors the minimal requirements an agreement needs to fulfill for it to be technically viable and to respect international legal frameworks. This is key for the agreement to be implemented and internationally accepted and financially supported.

In conclusion, the shifts in international, domestic, and military contexts may provide opportunities to start working toward stopping and ultimately ending the violence, as well as resolving the conflict, but these opportunities can only be effectively used if engagement with the parties happens discreetly, early on, and continues in a manner that is adapted to the needs of the parties. Such engagement requires thorough and ongoing analysis of the conflict at hand. This includes trying to understand the actors, the content, the context, and the military situation on the ground, as well as the experiences from previously failed attempts at stopping violence or resolving the conflict. If the parties agree that mediation is what they want, the mediation must involve a carefully crafted strategy, regularly updated and implemented by a team with clear roles and tasks. Both the political negotiation process and the ceasefire process in and of themselves need to be integrated into the overall mediation strategy to make best use of any linkages between the two processes.

NOTES

The views expressed are those of the authors and not those of any of the institutions mentioned.

1. Sudan, which then became Sudan and South Sudan on 9 July 2011.

2. The Comprehensive Peace Agreement between the Government of the Republic of the Sudan and the Sudan People's Liberation Movement/Sudan People's Liberation Army.

3. International Crisis Group (ICG), "God, Oil and Country Changing the Logic of War in Sudan."

4. UN Sudan, *United Nations Mission in Sudan (UNMIS) Background.*

5. Center for Preventive Action, "Civil War in South Sudan."

6. Some argued that if a combatant had fought once for the SPLA, they were considered a combatant for life and should therefore be treated like all other combatants. Others argued that someone had to have been trained, fought, and served a certain number of years and still be integrated into the SPLA forces to define as an "SPLA combatant."

7. Global Security.org, Sudan People's Liberation Army (SPLA), Sudan People's Liberation Movement (SPLM), https://www.globalsecurity.org/military/world/para/spla.htm.

8. Duursma, "He Who Pays the Piper, Calls the Tune? Non-African Involvement in Sudan's African-Led Mediation Processes, Perceived by the West."

9. "The Sudanese army numbered 105,000 soldiers in 2004, including 20,000 conscripts, organized into 10 divisions, including 1 armored, 1 mechanized, and 6 infantry divisions. By then, the army had 270 tanks, 218 reconnaissance vehicles, 316 armored vehicles, 470 artillery pieces, 635 multiple rocket launchers, 40 recoilless launchers, 40 attack guns, 1,000 air defense guns, and 54 surface-to-air missiles." Global Security.org, Sudan Army, https://www.globalsecurity.org/military/world/sudan/army.htm Global Security.org, Sudan Air Force, https://www.globalsecurity.org/military/world/sudan/air-force.htm.

10. Duursma, "He Who Pays the Piper, Calls the Tune? Non-African Involvement in Sudan's African-Led Mediation Processes, Perceived by the West."

11. Duursma, "He Who Pays the Piper, Calls the Tune? Non-African Involvement in Sudan's African-Led Mediation Processes, Perceived by the West."

12. Advisor to the United States Institute for Peace (USIP), interviewed by Haven North, "Interview # 26," 4 October 2006.

13. IGAD is a regional organization, comprising, in 2002, the states of Djibouti, Eritrea, Ethiopia, Kenya, Somalia, Sudan, and Uganda.

14. Van der Zwan, "Evaluating the EU's Role and Challenges in Sudan and South Sudan. Sudan and South Sudan Case Study."

15. Duursma, "He Who Pays the Piper, Calls the Tune? Non-African Involvement in Sudan's African-Led Mediation Processes, Perceived by the West."

16. Machakos Protocol between the Government of Sudan and the Sudan People's Liberation Movement/Army, 20 July 2002.

17. Machakos Protocol between the Government of Sudan and the Sudan People's Liberation Movement/Army, 20 July 2002.

18. Duursma, "He Who Pays the Piper, Calls the Tune? Non-African Involvement in Sudan's African-Led Mediation Processes, Perceived by the West."

19. Waihenya, W. "The Mediator." Nairobi: Kenway Publications, 2006. Quoted in: Duursma, "He Who Pays the Piper, Calls the Tune? Non-African Involvement in Sudan's African-Led Mediation Processes, Perceived by the West," 6.

20. Brickhill, "Protecting Civilians through Peace Agreements: Challenges and Lessons of the Darfur Peace Agreement."

21. Memorandum of Understanding on Cessation of Hostilities between the Government of the Sudan and the Sudan People's Liberation Movement/Army.

22. "Three-in-a-jeep" refers to a V&M structure in which both conflict parties participate in the V&M organization alongside an impartial third party at every level from the field to headquarters, ensuring that the conflict parties are present, involved, and responsible for investigating and resolving any violations of their ceasefire agreement.

23. Brickhill, *Mediating Security Arrangements in Peace Processes*, 35.

24. Brickhill, *Mediating Security Arrangements in Peace Processes*, 56.

25. Brickhill, *Mediating Security Arrangements in Peace Processes*, 64.

26. See Brickhill, "Protecting Civilians through Peace Agreements: Challenges and Lessons of the Darfur Peace Agreement."

27. UN Sudan, *United Nations Mission in the Sudan Mandate*.

28. The Comprehensive Peace Agreement between the Government of the Republic of the Sudan and the Sudan People's Liberation Movement/Sudan People's Liberation Army.

29. Duursma, "He Who Pays the Piper, Calls the Tune? Non-African Involvement in Sudan's African-Led Mediation Processes, Perceived by the West."

30. See "Ten Guidelines for Mediating CBMs," based on interview with Julian Th. Hottinger, in: Mason, Simon J. A. and Matthias Siegfried, "Confidence Building Measures (CBMs) in Peace Processes," in *Managing Peace Processes: Process Related Questions. A Handbook for AU Practitioners*, 57–77, 76.

CHAPTER 7

Darfur, 2000–2007
The Perils of Deadline Diplomacy
for Ceasefires

Laurie Nathan and Allard Duursma

This chapter examines the various ceasefires concluded for Darfur in response to the civil war that began in western Sudan in 2002. It focuses on the mediated negotiations between the Sudanese government and the Darfurian armed opposition movements between 2003 and the conclusion of the Darfur Peace Agreement (DPA) in May 2006. It first examines the ceasefires concluded during the initial mediation efforts by Chad and then covers the subsequent mediation process led by the African Union (AU). None of the ceasefires in this period achieved peace. There were several reasons for this: the conflict was not ripe for a political settlement, and the conflict parties therefore saw no benefit in a provisional ceasefire; the international community pursued a strategy of deadline diplomacy, applying pressure on the mediators to produce "quick agreements" contrary to the will of the parties; and the mediators, under pressure from the AU and donors, were preoccupied with producing peace texts rather than attempting to mediate genuine agreements among the parties. The main lesson from this experience is that conflict parties will not faithfully adhere to peace agreements they have been compelled to sign under duress. Their genuine ownership of their agreement is a necessary condition for the implementation and sustainability of the agreement.

CONTEXT

Darfur has a long history of marginalization that dates back to colonialism and was exacerbated by the authoritarian rule of the National Congress Party (NCP). The NCP came to power via a coup in 1989 and governed with an Islamist and Arab nationalist orientation. In response to a high level of marginalization, several opposition movements were formed in the 1990s.[1] To draw more attention to the marginalization of the peripheries of Sudan, a group of regime insiders—who called themselves the Seekers of Truth and Justice—produced the *Black Book* in 2000 (see table 7.1 at the end of this chapter for a timeline). The *Black Book* supported the claim that Sudan was ruled by only a small part of the population and that political power was concentrated in the North. More specifically, it argued that most government positions in Khartoum were held by members of three tribes, representing only 5.4 percent of the population.[2]

The *Black Book*'s fundamental message was strongly reflected in the stated goals of the two rebel movements that took up arms in Darfur in late 2002. Both the Justice and Equality Movement (JEM), which had an Islamist ideology, and the Sudan Liberation Movement/Army (SLM/A), which reflected strong ethnic identities, highlighted the marginalization of Sudan's peripheries.[3] In fact, many of the authors of the *Black Book* would later join JEM.[4] Abdul Wahid, the leader of SLM/A, declared on 14 March 2003 that his movement demanded a "united democratic Sudan based on equality, the separation of religion and the state, complete restructuring and devolution of power, even-handed development, and cultural and political pluralism."[5]

The structural causes of the rebellion also included communal conflicts. The Fur, Zaghawa, and Masalit accused the government of supporting pastoral nomadic groups that took over their homelands. In the late 1980s, the Fur, Zaghawa, and Masalit communities formed self-defense forces to protect their villages against the attacks of Arab militias.[6] These communal conflicts escalated in the early 2000s, and many of the self-defense forces would later fight under the banner of the SLM/A or JEM (hereafter "the movements").[7]

One of the proximate causes of the rebellion was the 2002–2005 peace process to end the decades-long North–South civil war in Sudan. In that process, the NCP government and the Sudan People's Liberation Movement/Army (SPLM/A) were negotiating a new distribution of political power and economic wealth at the national level. The negotiations excluded the Darfur communities, deepening their marginalization. Although the Darfur movements were weak militarily, they hoped their rebellion would compel the government to enter into negotiations for a greater share of power and resources for Darfur.[8]

The North–South peace process helped to keep the initial phase of the Darfur rebellion off the radar of the international community. The US Department of State actively tried to keep the Darfur conflict from being discussed during the North–South negotiations, fearing that it might undermine the fragile process. One US official allegedly told members of the Sudanese government that Washington would "accept a military solution to Darfur, if it was a quick, surgical approach."[9]

One of the first organized attacks on the government took place in June 2002, when the movements targeted a police station in Golo.[10] In early 2003, the armed conflict escalated when several coordinated attacks led by SLM/A leader Abdul Wahid were launched on government army units.

When the movements took up arms, the government initially kept the communication channels open. In March 2003, when attacks on government targets became more frequent, the governor of North Darfur, Ibrahim Suleiman, formed an ad hoc Darfur Security Committee to negotiate an end to the violence.[11] However, the dialogue between the movements and the government was terminated as soon as government officials had successfully negotiated the release of the commander of the Sudanese Air Force, who had been captured during an attack on El Fasher airbase.[12]

To crush the rebellion, the government pursued a ferocious counterinsurgency campaign that relied on local Arab militia known as the Janjaweed. Their scorched-earth measures laid waste to entire villages, with mass killings and displacements gradually drawing the attention of the international community. The destruction of people and villages was so intense and systematic that, on 19 March 2004, Mukesh Kapila, the United Nations' (UN's) humanitarian coordinator in Sudan, publicly stated that ethnic cleansing was taking place in Darfur.[13] On 9 September 2004, US Secretary of State Colin Powell testified in front of the Foreign Relations Committee of the US Senate that "genocide has occurred and may still be occurring in Darfur."[14] By 2006, an estimated 350,000 people had been killed and almost two million people had been displaced.[15]

INITIAL CEASEFIRE NEGOTIATIONS

The movements were initially more successful on the battlefield than the Sudanese government had anticipated. Data from the UN and the United States suggest that the movements won thirty-four out of the thirty-eight encounters with government forces in the middle months of 2003.[16] Hence, it became increasingly evident to the government that a quick military victory was not within reach. As it became clear that fighting was likely to be protracted, Chad offered to mediate the conflict. Chad was concerned about increased insecurity in its own country due to the many Darfurian refugees fleeing across the border. In addition, affiliated ethnic groups lived in the border region of Chad and Sudan, which made fighting spilling over from Darfur to Chad seem likely.[17]

The first round of peace talks mediated by Chad took place in Abéché in late August and early September 2003. It focused almost exclusively on concluding a ceasefire. JEM boycotted the talks, accusing Chad of being biased in favor of the Sudanese government, but the SLM/A participated in the process. On 3 September 2003, after five days of negotiations, the conflict parties signed the Abéché Ceasefire Agreement.[18] Only a few days later, the SLM/A accused the government of breaking the ceasefire, which the latter denied. Heavy fighting followed the talks, with both sides trying to gain the upper hand on the battlefield.[19]

While the Abéché negotiations focused on a ceasefire rather than the political dimensions of the conflict, the agreement called for comprehensive peace talks.[20] Consequently, official negotiations—which came to be known as the Abéché ceasefire renewal talks—resumed on 29 October 2003, one day prior to the scheduled expiry of the September ceasefire.[21] The SLM/A presented a set of political and economic demands. The most important political demands were autonomy for the Darfur region and rotation of the national presidency among the different regions of Sudan. On top of the list of economic demands was an equitable distribution of development projects across Sudan. However, the movement negotiators insisted that before any substantive negotiations could take place, the government had to create a conducive security environment for talks by ending attacks, demobilizing the government-sponsored militias, and allowing the deployment of international observers. Hence, the failure of the Abéché ceasefire prevented substantive negotiations from taking place.

Both the Sudanese government and the Chadian mediators were eager to rush the movements to sign an immediate peace agreement, whereby they would lay down their arms and accept cantonment of their forces in designated areas under the supervision of a joint ceasefire commission. The movements rejected this proposal since cantonment would make them static targets for the Sudanese army. The parties signed a ceasefire renewal, which was not respected by either side, because all of them wanted to avoid being perceived internationally as spoilers.

As the fighting in Darfur intensified, international actors started paying closer attention to the peace process. They were concerned that the fighting was jeopardizing the negotiations between the Sudanese government and the SPLM/A aimed at ending the war in southern Sudan. As a result, the UN, the AU, and the United States wanted Khartoum to solve the crisis in Darfur as soon as possible.[22] Moreover, the worsening humanitarian situation in Darfur was reaching catastrophic proportions. In March 2004, Mukesh Kapila, the UN's humanitarian coordinator in Sudan, stated that ethnic cleansing was taking place in Darfur.[23]

Against this backdrop of greater international involvement and pressure, the Chadian minister of foreign affairs opened the next round of negotiations in N'djamena on 31 March 2004.[24] Talks were chaired by President Déby and the director of the AU Department of Peace and Security, Sam Ibok. The negotiations continued to focus on security matters, such as the conclusion of a ceasefire and the deployment of a small African peace support mission. On 8 April 2004, the parties signed the N'djamena Humanitarian Ceasefire Agreement, which included a forty-five-day cessation of hostilities.[25] The agreement also called for the deployment of a monitoring team to observe compliance with the ceasefire, as well as the formation of a Ceasefire Commission consisting of representatives of the Sudanese government, the SLM/A, and JEM. The Ceasefire Commission would be chaired by the AU, while the EU acted as deputy chair and the UN and the United States were granted observer status.[26]

The agreement had significant flaws. First, it had no maps. The government had promised that it would accept the deployment of around 120 observers to oversee the implementation of the ceasefire, accompanied by around 300 peacekeeping soldiers. However, since the ceasefire had no maps, it was impossible for the African Union Mission in Sudan (AMIS) observers to monitor the locations of the conflict parties. Proceeding without maps was the result of a rushed mediation process aimed at a quick fix. The Chadian government wanted to end the hostilities as quickly as possible because the conflict in Darfur was creating instability in Chad. Other international actors, and the United States in particular, also pushed for a quick ceasefire because they wanted to safeguard the peace process in southern Sudan.[27] The Sudanese government, in turn, was willing to sign a ceasefire as a result of a shifting balance of power in its favor. Concluding a ceasefire would confine the movements to mountain areas and the desert. The movements, on the other hand, only signed the ceasefire to buy time to relocate the fighting to the eastern and southern parts of Darfur, where there had previously been relatively little fighting.[28] In short, the conflict parties did not sign the ceasefire with the aim of establishing a conducive security environment for substantive negotiations.

A second major flaw of the N'djamena Agreement was that it was not a genuine agreement. In fact, two versions of the agreement existed. When the mediators presented the draft agreement to the government delegation, it refused to sign the document, insisting that it had agreed to demobilize the militias on condition that the movements would be cantoned. The mediators supported the government and asked AU mediator Sam Ibok to add this extra clause by hand.[29] Without the consent of the movement negotiators, Ibok added the clause and put a mediation stamp on it, after which the government delegation signed the agreement. Ibok claims he expected the changed text to be passed back to the movements for approval, yet it was not.[30] As shown in figure 7.1, the original sentence in this paragraph, to which both parties agreed, was "The Sudanese government shall commit itself to neutralize the armed militia." The added sentence stated, "The forces of the armed opposition should be assembled in clearly identified sites."[31] It is highly unlikely that the movements would have agreed to the added provision, since it would make them static targets for the Sudanese troops. However, after the agreement, Khartoum linked the two sentences and argued that based on the agreement, they only had to neutralize the militias if the movements assembled in clearly identified sites.[32]

This debacle increased the movements' distrust of the Chadian mediation team. Indeed, the SLM/A and JEM refused to participate in any future rounds of mediation in Chad.

While the intensity of the conflict dropped significantly in the period surrounding the signing of the N'djamena Agreement, fighting did continue. The period from June 2004 to January 2005 saw violations of the ceasefire by both the movements and government forces.[33]

With mediation by Chad no longer viable, the AU took over the role of lead mediating organization. The AU Commission chairman, Alpha Konaré, appointed Sam Ibok as the AU chief mediator.[34] The first round of talks,

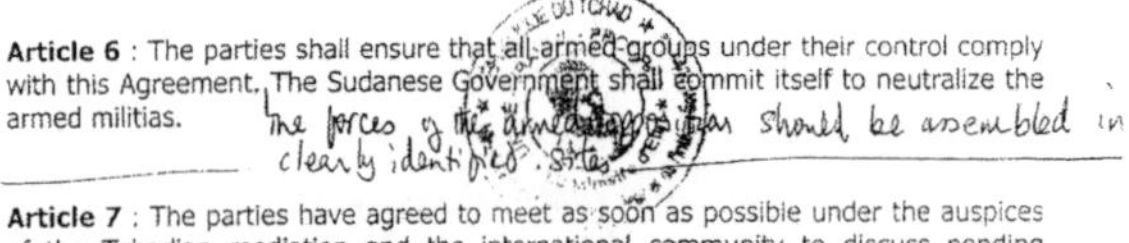

Figure 7.1 Two versions of the N'djamena Humanitarian Ceasefire Agreement

which later became known as the Abuja peace process, started in Addis Ababa between 15 and 17 July 2004. The negotiations mainly focused on the implementation of the N'djamena Humanitarian Ceasefire Agreement, as fighting continued in Darfur.

The second round started in Abuja on 23 August 2004, under the auspices of President Olusegun Obasanjo of Nigeria, the chairperson of the AU Assembly at that time. The mediation team began by trying to formulate an agenda for substantive negotiations. Little progress was made over the ensuing six months. However, the conflict parties signed the Protocol on the Improvement of the Humanitarian Situation in Darfur, which aimed to improve the humanitarian situation and strengthen AMIS to ensure effective monitoring. The talks were concluded on 17 September.[35]

The third round started on 21 October 2004. Following two days of seminars, the mediation team organized a plenary session on 25 October, at which the conflict parties outlined their vision for a Declaration of Principles (DoP). Separate consultations between the mediators and the parties continued until 31 October, when the parties submitted their views on a DoP. On the basis of these views, the mediation team drafted a preliminary DoP, which was presented on 2 November 2004.[36] The DoP stated that the Sudanese government should refrain from hostile military flights in and over Darfur. While the government negotiators objected to this provision, the movement negotiators demanded a total no-fly zone in Darfur as a confidence-building measure. The disagreement about security provisions, specifically regarding military flights, prevented the conclusion of DoP as the basis for resolving the political dimensions of the conflict. The mediators could not bridge the disagreement about military flights in the subsequent days. As a result, it was decided to continue to discuss the DoP at the next round of talks.[37]

The fourth round began on 11 December 2004. Three days prior to this, the Sudanese government launched a military offensive in Darfur. This made it impossible to finalize the draft DoP. Consequently, the fourth round of talks was suspended on 21 December.[38] Negotiations were scheduled to resume in early 2005, but tensions within the SLM/A delayed this. The SLM/A leadership repeatedly requested more time to organize a congress that would appoint the leader of the SLM/A and designate a new negotiating team. The efforts to reorganize the SLM/A leadership failed, and tensions between two factions, led respectively by Abdul Wahid and Minni Minnawi, grew more intense.

While no formal rounds of negotiations were held because of tensions within the SLM/A, informal discussions on security arrangements continued. The most challenging issue was the question of what to do about the Sudanese government-sponsored militias, generally referred to as the Janjawiid. The movements demanded a complete demobilization of these militia. Vice President Ali Osman Taha discussed the issue in a private meeting with Abdul Wahid in Abuja on 7 April 2005, but the meeting failed to produce a compromise. Abdul Wahid asserts that Taha "offered nothing on the Janjawiid" and that this undermined the entire Abuja peace process: "Security is everything. Then we can come to power-sharing and wealth-sharing."[39] The failure to get agreement on security arrangements thus constrained the mediators from focusing on the substantive issues.

Nevertheless, fighting decreased significantly during the middle months of 2005. This helped to move the peace process forward during the fifth round of negotiations, which started on 10 June 2005.[40] These negotiations were mediated by Salim Ahmed Salim, the former secretary-general of the Organisation of African Unity (OAU), who had been appointed as the AU special envoy for the Darfur talks and chief mediator in May 2005. On 5 July 2005, after more than three weeks of negotiating and high-level involvement of African leaders, the DoP was signed. It marked the start of the negotiation phase as the negotiations from then onward began to focus on the contested issues.

COMPREHENSIVE NEGOTIATION PHASE

The sixth round of AU-mediated peace talks began on 15 September 2005. In order to build on the DoP, the mediation team set up three commissions that focused on wealth sharing, power sharing, and security arrangements, respectively.[41] The chief mediator was Salim, while Sam Ibok served as the chief of staff and a team of diplomats, mediators, and resource people supported them by facilitating negotiations, providing expert input, and developing strategy and tactics. The support team included UN officials and military officers from AMIS. Based in a dingy hotel in downtown Abuja, the mediation was funded mainly by the government of the United Kingdom. The formal negotiating sessions were usually conducted through simultaneous translation as several of the mediators did not speak Arabic, the lingua franca of the conflict parties. Wracked by divisions, the rebels devoted considerable time and effort to inter- and intramovement negotiations.

The dominant dynamic that drove the process was not the parties' negotiations but rather a steady stream of unrealistic deadlines emanating from the international community. The UN Security Council initially set a deadline of 31 December 2005 for the conclusion of a comprehensive agreement; in January 2006, Jan Pronk, the UN secretary-general's special representative for Sudan, proposed a new cutoff date of February; in early February, the AU commissioner for peace and security, Said Djinnit, told the mediators to wrap up by the end of the month; in March, the AU Peace and Security Council (PSC) called for the conclusion of a comprehensive agreement by the end of April, and the UN Security Council (UNSC) thereafter endorsed this date as the final deadline.[42]

These monthly deadlines to conclude a comprehensive agreement were utterly unrealistic. According to one informed commentator, "The best of the AU's experts in Abuja believed [that the deadline of] April was off by a couple of months at least."[43] There were at least two motivations for the "deadline diplomacy." First, the international community was distressed at the high level of violence and suffering in Darfur. This concern was dramatically reinforced by the US administration's accusation that genocide was being perpetrated in Darfur.[44] The mass atrocities led to the formation of the Save Darfur Movement, a formidable pressure group in the United States.[45] Consequently, the US government was under a lot of domestic pressure to act in Darfur. As soon as the AU-led Abuja peace process began, the United States deployed diplomats and CIA personnel to Abuja.[46] Second, international actors were frustrated at the lack of progress in the Abuja talks. The United Kingdom, which was funding the talks, was annoyed at the apparent waste of taxpayers' money.[47] Andrew Natsios, the administrator of USAID from 2001 to 2006, estimates that funding for the humanitarian relief effort, the African peacekeeping mission, and the peace negotiations was costing Western governments around US$1 billion annually at the peak of the crisis.[48] In return for this financial aid, Western government officials wanted a greater say in the peace process. Hillary Benn, the British secretary of state for international development at the time of the Abuja talks, remarked in this regard that "there was an acute situation in Darfur. People were dying and there was a huge humanitarian effort ongoing. So the question was, what are we going to do about it? . . . We were the good guys. The US and the UK provided most support and effort to the humanitarian operation to save the people in Darfur. We were the ones pressing to bring the conflict to an end."[49]

The international actors believed that the pressure of deadlines, accompanied by threats of sanctions, would yield positive results. The parties, though, dismissed the threats as bluff. One government official reflected on the pressure exerted by the United States that "the only carrot the US could provide was not using more sticks, and the only stick would be not using more carrots."[50] Similarly, in July 2006, for example, a senior Sudanese government official observed that "the United Nations Security Council has threatened us so many times, we no longer take it seriously."[51]

Another reason why the United States and the United Kingdom were unable to push the Sudanese government toward compromise is that many officials in Khartoum held a grudge against the United States for not keeping its promise of normalizing relations when the Comprehensive Peace Agreement (CPA) was signed between the Sudanese government and the SPLM/A. US officials acknowledge that relations were indeed not normalized, pointing out that the situation in Darfur did not merit normalized relations. Nevertheless, the Sudanese leaders had anticipated that because of the concessions they had made in the CPA, the United States would lift the economic sanctions and Sudan would be taken off the list of countries supporting terrorism. Ghazi Salah al-Din al-Atabani states that "every single US statesman that participated in Sudan's peace process promised to normalize relations if the government would sign the CPA. These US statesman used Darfur as an excuse to break their promise."[52] Believing that Western countries would never normalize relations with Sudan, no matter what the Sudanese government did, the government attached little value to Western promises of normalizing relations during the Darfur peace talks.

The lack of concerted and sustained external leverage was a major reason why the parties ignored the donor deadlines and generally refused to engage in serious negotiations. According to a firsthand account from a member of the mediation team,

> The parties made no attempt to accommodate each other's concerns and showed no interest in trying to find common ground. None of them was willing to make concessions to its opponents. There was no bargaining, let alone collaborative problem-solving. Instead, the parties merely reiterated their demands ad nauseum, rejected the claims of their adversaries, traded accusations, recriminations and insults, indulged in grandstanding for the benefit of the international observers, and endeavored to win support for their positions from the mediators.[53]

No Serious Negotiations

There were four main reasons for the parties' unwillingness to pursue a negotiated settlement. The first was the parties' intense hatred and suspicion of each other.[54] The movements regarded the government as an evil regime that had come to power through a coup and that had never honored a single peace agreement it had signed.[55] The government, on the other hand, viewed the movements with undisguised contempt. It was frustrated that the Abuja process did not reflect the balance of power and was under way only to appease the international community. It was also concerned that making political and economic concessions to the movements would intensify similar demands from marginalized communities elsewhere in Sudan.[56] The mediation team was unable to foster the reconciliation necessary for a sustainable settlement.

Second, the divisions among the movements made it difficult for them to develop unified negotiating positions. There was disagreement and mistrust between the SLM and JEM; the two SLM factions were fighting each other in Darfur while the talks were under way in Abuja, and these factions were themselves loose and tenuous alliances of local leaders rather than cohesive groupings.[57] Salim identified the splits and fragmentation of the movements as major constraint on the talks.[58]

Third, the negotiations proved difficult because the conclusion of the Comprehensive Peace Agreement between the Sudanese government and the SPLM/A in 2005 left little room for power sharing with Darfurian leaders and communities. In January 2006, the SPLM/A made it clear that the CPA, which governed the entire country and not only North–South relations, could not be revised.[59] Hence, the Darfurian movements and the newly created Government of Unity had to share power within the framework of the CPA. The ruling National Congress Party was not willing to give up any of its seats within the executive and legislative bodies. This meant that the Darfurian movements could only obtain seats within the executive and legislative bodies at the expense of the SPLM/A. This constrained the Darfurian rebels in terms of what they could achieve in Abuja.[60] Another rebel demand that was impossible to meet as a result of the CPA was the desire of the SLM/A to separate religion and politics in northern Sudan; the CPA, however, preserved Sharia laws in this region.[61]

Fourth, most of the parties in Abuja were not interested in a negotiated settlement because they believed they could still make gains through fighting. They viewed the battlefield as the strategic arena of conflict and the negotiations as merely a tactical arena.[62] Given the international outcry over the humanitarian crisis in Darfur, the parties had to be seen to be engaged in peace talks, but this was not their primary means of defending and advancing their interests.

The movements suffered from the delusion that time was on their side as international pressure on Khartoum mounted. Minnawi was sure he could win a war of maneuver against the militarily weaker grouping of Abdul Wahid. The government, on the other hand, was convinced it would win a war of attrition against the movements; it was not in fact overly troubled by the international pressure and it was not under any great military threat from the movements. For its part, JEM had a national political agenda that would not be met by a peace agreement for Darfur. Although it lacked a sizable fighting force, its military activities in western (and eastern) Sudan helped to maintain its profile as a liberation movement. JEM was also bolstered by military support from Chad.[63]

The only leader who keenly wanted a settlement was Abdul Wahid, whose community and soldiers were being hammered by the Janjawiid, the government, and Minnawi. But in his interactions with the AU mediators and the government negotiators, he was erratic and indecisive, constantly projecting confusion and backtracking on promises he had made.[64] In early 2006, he entered into secret talks with the government and then pulled out just as an agreement looked imminent.[65] He ended up being seen by the AU and its partners as the main spoiler in Abuja.

Undue Pressure on the Mediators

Whereas the deadline diplomacy was ignored by the parties, it put undue pressure on the mediators, who were obliged to conform to the instructions of their principals and donors. The mediators' strategy therefore shifted from attempting to facilitate negotiations among the parties to drafting the text of the DPA by the stipulated date.[66]

One of the negative consequences of this approach was that the mediators inadvertently became negotiating parties. In order to meet the deadlines, they produced papers that aimed to bridge the parties' divergent positions. As a result, the parties treated the mediators as arbitrators rather than as facilitators of negotiations. They applauded what they liked in the mediators' papers, rejected the rest, and devoted much time and energy to lobbying the mediators. To the great frustration of the mediation team, the parties' most strenuous negotiating efforts were directed at the mediators and not at each other.[67]

Another negative consequence of the deadline diplomacy was that it severely constrained the mediators' flexibility, options, and ability to make strategic decisions on the basis of their best judgment. In late February and early March 2006, confronted by the deadlock in Abuja and the fierce fighting in Darfur, the mediation team debated at length whether it was more likely to make progress by putting forward a comprehensive peace agreement aimed at addressing the root causes of the conflict or by tabling an enhanced humanitarian ceasefire agreement aimed at reducing the level of violence and improving the climate for negotiations. This debate was rendered moot by the AU's decree that the comprehensive agreement had to be concluded by the end of April.

More specifically, the mediators did not have time to develop viable ceasefires. The movements' negotiators were unfamiliar with the relevant concepts and options, and they requested training on these issues. Salim rejected the request on the grounds of insufficient time. In addition, the parties disagreed vehemently on the demarcation of their respective areas of control, they resisted the efforts of AMIS to map the location of their forces, and there was no realistic strategy for demobilizing the Janjawiid. These problems posed potentially fatal impediments to the anticipated disengagement and redeployment of forces under a ceasefire. Moreover, as noted above, the movements were completely mistrustful of the government's willingness to honor its ceasefire commitments. The mediation team could offer no meaningful assurances in this regard. It was clear to all that AMIS did not have the capacity to deter and manage ceasefire violations and breakdowns.

Given the tight deadlines, there was no opportunity for the mediators to inform Darfurian communities about the nature of the talks and invite these communities to offer their own perspectives. Nor were the movement negotiators able to brief and consult their constituencies adequately. As Pronk later observed, the perception of many Darfurians was that the DPA had been imposed on them.[68] The geographical and political distance between Abuja and Darfur was so great that when violent protests against the DPA broke out after the signing ceremony in May 2006, the mediators were convinced that much of the opposition was based on an incomplete and inaccurate reading of the document.[69]

The most severe consequence of the rushed mediation process and lack of serious negotiations was that the parties had no sense of ownership of the DPA, which was therefore bound to be unsustainable. At the end of the failed Abuja process in 2006, this perspective was articulated explicitly by Abdul Wahid's faction: "The legitimate question is on what basis the Movement have to sign an agreement, which it did not participate in its discussion?"[70] According to a JEM official, "We have rejected the proposed peace accord because we do not think that the document is a product of a negotiated settlement. In fact, we think that this document is a product of intimidation, bullying and diplomatic terrorism."[71]

Final Flurry

Five days before the 30 April deadline set by the AU and the UN Security Council, the mediators presented the draft DPA to the parties on a take-it-or-leave-it basis, giving them less than a week to read, comprehend, debate within their ranks, and then endorse an eighty-six-page English-language document that encompassed a set of complicated security, political, economic, and administrative arrangements. Compounding the difficulty this posed for the parties, the Arabic version of the DPA was only completed on 28 April and contained significant mistranslations and ambiguities.[72]

The five-day time frame for the approval of the DPA would have been unreasonable and impractical in almost all negotiations to end a civil war. It was especially so in the context of the Abuja process: the parties disagreed profoundly on many of the DPA provisions, they were confronted in the document by mechanisms and arrangements they had not considered previously, they loathed each other and doubted that their opponents would implement their undertakings in good faith, and, as noted, the movement negotiators had no confidence in the envisaged ceasefires.

The movement negotiators asked the mediators for a three-week extension in order to study the draft DPA.[73] When they were turned down, they rejected the document.[74] They complained that the draft agreement diluted proposals made earlier by the mediation team, favored Khartoum, and did not address adequately the rights and demands of Darfurians. They also objected to the imposition of a fanciful deadline. The government, on the other hand, stated that it was prepared to endorse the agreement despite its reservations. This was a shrewd move because it painted the government in a positive light and made it difficult for the movements to negotiate changes to the document. The head of the government delegation, Majzoub El Khalifa, arranged for a meeting with the press so that he could be photographed holding the document in front of his chest.[75]

At the request of the international partners and President Obasanjo, Salim extended the deadline by forty-eight hours and then a further forty-eight hours.[76] In this brief period, the lethargic pace of the talks changed dramatically. There was a frenzy of behind-the-scenes deals, counterdeals, offers, and threats, as various international leaders and officials—including Obasanjo; Robert Zoellick, the US deputy secretary of state; and Hilary Benn, the British secretary for international development—took over the mediation.[77] Hilary Benn recounts that "things had clearly reached a critical point. The cork came out. We dropped everything and off we went. The negotiations had dragged on and we tried to achieve critical mass."[78] The AU mediators were rendered mere spectators.[79] The international players offered the movements guarantees regarding the implementation of the DPA, tabled a list of nonnegotiable amendments aimed at meeting the movements' concerns, and threatened them with sanctions.[80]

In the last days of the Abuja process, Minnawi still had reservations. At the final meeting, which was held at Obasanjo's presidential villa and started in evening of 4 May 2006 and would last until early in the morning of the next day, Zoellick allegedly told Minnawi, "Have no doubt where I stand. I am a good friend and I am a fearsome enemy."[81] Minnawi buckled under the pressure and joined the government in signing the agreement the next morning, on 5 May 2006. Abdul Wahid and JEM refused to sign, objecting to both the content of the agreement and the imposition of an inappropriate deadline. According to a JEM negotiator, the agreement "does not address the root causes of the conflict and was not the result of a negotiation between the parties."[82] One of Abdul Wahid's negotiators argued similarly: "Above all the [rebel] Movements have been given an ultimatum of five days to sign the document or leave it and this is clearly against the prevail[ing] understanding of negotiation norms world-wide which allow the parties to negotiate every issue and reach a compromise position, where everybody is a winner."[83]

Hoping that Abdul Wahid and Khalil Ibrahim, the leader of JEM, would change their minds, Obasanjo announced that the nonsignatories would have until 16 May to sign the DPA. To this end, several members of the AU mediation team remained in Abuja to bridge the differences between the nonsignatories and the Sudanese government.[84] A few days after the signing of the DPA, Abdul Wahid proposed a "supplementary agreement" to the DPA, demanding greater representation at the legislature and executive bodies of Darfur.[85] However, government chief negotiator Majzoub El Khalifa rejected this option, insisting that Abdul Wahid had to sign the DPA first, after which some of the remaining issues could be negotiated.[86] Abdul Wahid rejected this option. Hence, negotiations between the Sudanese government and Abdul Wahid ground to a halt.[87]

IMPLEMENTATION PHASE

The DPA did not achieve peace, and in the following respects, it exacerbated the conflict. After the signing ceremony, there were violent protests against the agreement in Darfur. More seriously, the government and Mninawi formed a military alliance and attacked communities that supported

Abdul Wahid, while the Janjaweed's rampages continued unabated.[88] There was widespread opposition to the deal within the Minnawi group, with some commanders announcing a suspension of the DPA and joining JEM or Abdul Wahid.[89] According to the International Crisis Group, the DPA "accelerated the break-up of the insurgency into smaller blocs along loose ethnic lines."[90]

With the political process surrounding the DPA becoming increasingly strained, calls to deploy a robust UN peacekeeping mission grew stronger. Many Western diplomats had attached great value to the conclusion of the DPA because they assumed this would pave the way for a UN mission.[91] However, at no time during the Abuja negotiations had the issue of AMIS's transition to a UN mission been discussed formally.[92] Instead, US deputy secretary of state Zoellick held a secret meeting with Sudanese Vice President Taha in Paris on 8 March 2006, at which Taha promised Zoellick that a UN mission could be deployed following the conclusion of the DPA. Yet, when it became clear that the United States would not normalize relations with Sudan after the conclusion of the DPA, Khartoum backtracked on its promise.[93]

With the formal peace talks ending in May 2006, the only forum for discussion on peacemaking was the Ceasefire Commission established under the 2004 Humanitarian Ceasefire Agreement. Although JEM and the SLM/A led by Abdul Wahid (SLM/A-AW) had not signed the DPA, they initially remained involved in Ceasefire Commission meetings convened by the AU. However, at the request of the United States, the nonsignatories of the DPA were excluded from the commission in August 2006.[94] Jan Pronk recalls how in the wake of the conclusion of the DPA, the nonsignatories were marginalized: "Initially the Sudanese delegation labelled the nonsignatories as spoilers, but soon this changed to outlaws, and finally they were labelled as terrorists."[95] In short, the decision to exclude the DPA nonsignatories from the Ceasefire Commission led to the loss of a forum for interaction among all the conflict parties.

Notwithstanding these negative consequences of the Abuja process, the unsuccessful ceasefires had a number of positive effects. The N'djamena Agreement was used by the UNSC and the AU PSC as a basis for holding the parties accountable for continuing hostilities and human rights abuses.[96] It also paved the way for the deployment of AMIS and AU ceasefire monitors. The ceasefire design contained in the DPA survived the collapse of the agreement and laid the foundation for operational planning for the UN-AU Hybrid Operation in Darfur (UNAMID), which eventually replaced AMIS in 2007.[97] Although UNAMID did not bring peace to Darfur, it restrained local perpetrators of violence and thereby reduced the number of one-sided civilian killings by the government and the movements.[98]

CONCLUSION

In the period under review, the peace process for Darfur failed to achieve a negotiated settlement and peace. Although the mediators and international partners contributed to this negative outcome by imposing unrealistic deadlines, the responsibility for the failure lies principally with the conflict parties. It is a matter of debate which of them bears the greatest responsibility in this regard. The AU and its partners laid the blame on Abdul Wahid's indecisiveness and the movements' internal divisions.[99] Still, the Sudanese government's policies were the main cause of the rebellion in the first place, and the government unquestionably had the power and resources to end the conflict by offering the movements a reasonable political and economic deal. In the context of acute power asymmetry, the government had abundant means, but insufficient incentive, to accommodate the movements' demands and address the marginalization of Darfur. It was also concerned that a reasonable deal might encourage other marginalized groups in Sudan to take up arms in order to improve their situation.

William Zartman's theory of conflict ripeness provides an appropriate framework for explaining the mediation failure.[100] Zartman maintains that conflicts are ripe for resolution through negotiations only when there is a mutually hurting stalemate. Where the conflict parties find themselves locked in a conflict from which they cannot escape and cannot win, and this deadlock is painful to all of them, they may become receptive to negotiating a settlement. If, on the other hand, a party is convinced it can achieve military victory, or at least make military gains, it will eschew negotiations and remain engaged in hostilities.

Most of the Darfur parties did not perceive a mutually hurting stalemate and believed they would benefit from continued fighting. As discussed, JEM had a national political agenda rather than a regional agenda and enjoyed military support from Chad, Minnawi was intent on reducing Abdul Wahid's political influence and support by weakening him militarily, and the government had no doubt it would eventually defeat the movements. Only Abdul Wahid, who was suffering losses on the battlefield to both Minnawi and the government, wanted a negotiated settlement. Yet he lacked the political and negotiating skills to achieve a satisfactory deal, even when this appeared to be within reach.

However, as emphasized in the introduction of this book, the military context is not the only component shaping peace processes. The domestic and international political contexts matter too. Indeed, Zartman suggests that external actors can induce ripeness, where it does not exist, by applying leverage that heightens the costs of the conflict for one or more of the parties.[101] In the wider mediation literature, there is no consensus on what kind of leverage is most appropriate under different circumstances.[102] In the Darfur case, international pressure was not applied in a concerted and systematic manner.[103] This was partly because the international community did not have a unified position on Darfur. Russia and China repeatedly diluted and blocked proposals from the United States and the United Kingdom for tough action to be taken by the UN Security Council.[104] Moreover, the position of the United States was itself ambivalent. While the United States was keen to see a halt to the Darfur violence, it did not want to lean too heavily on Khartoum lest this undermine the fragile peace process of 2002–2005 to end the North–South war in Sudan.[105] Bereft of an effective leverage strategy, the United States focused its efforts on persuading the AU, the UN, and the Sudanese government to accept the replacement of AMIS with a UN peacekeeping mission that would constrain the belligerent forces in Darfur.[106] An unintended consequence of this focus was that it gave Khartoum some international leverage since a UN mission was politically feasible only if the government consented to it.

In the absence of systematic leverage that targeted the parties' vulnerabilities, the external actors' approach of deadline diplomacy was a counterproductive strategy. It put intense pressure on the mediators without putting any real pressure on the parties. The net result was that external leverage, such as it was, did not substantially increase the costs of the conflict for any of the parties.

Since most of the parties were intent on improving their positions militarily and were not ready for a comprehensive settlement, they had no need for a meaningful provisional ceasefire. They signed a number of provisional ceasefires only in order to avoid being accused by the international community of being spoilers. The government naturally wanted some kind of CSA in order to contain, if not end, the rebellion, and the movements naturally wanted some kind of CSA in order to end the merciless government attacks on their communities. But none of the parties wanted a provisional ceasefire for the common purpose of establishing security conditions conducive to substantive negotiations.

In contrast to some of the cases in this edited volume that show that ceasefires can have a positive impact on political negotiations, the ceasefire agreements in the Darfur peace process illustrate that these agreements can also have a negative effect if they are concluded insincerely. This is in line with a point made in the introduction that ceasefires can undermine trust. The parties to the Darfur conflict had no intention of honoring the ceasefire agreements they signed, and the constant violations of the agreements reinforced the parties' conviction that their enemy was untrustworthy and disinterested in peace. The violations also reduced their confidence in the mediation process. Whereas provisional ceasefires are often intended to build the parties' confidence in substantive negotiations,[107] the Darfur provisional ceasefires had the opposite effect. The Darfur peace process between 2003 and 2006 is thus in line with what Clayton et al. in the introduction of this edited volume refer to as a "negative feedback loop." The failed ceasefires led to a lack of progress in resolving contested issues, which, in turn, at least partly explains the subsequent failures to stop conflict violence.

This does not mean that the agreements had no positive effects at all. The positive effects of the agreements included the formation of AMIS, the deployment of AU ceasefire monitors, and the creation of a conceptual and political foundation for the establishment and design of UNAMID. The impact of the ceasefires on the political process was, however, mainly negative.

Indeed, the outstanding lesson from the peace process is that it is unproductive, even counterproductive, to compel conflict parties to sign ceasefire accords and comprehensive peace agreements to which they are not committed. The deadline diplomacy failed to recognize the basic distinction between the parties' signatures on an agreement and their actual resolve to end hostilities, either temporarily or permanently. Neither ceasefires nor enduring peace agreements can be forced on conflict parties. They have to be shaped and owned by the parties for the pragmatic reason that they cannot be implemented and sustained without the parties' consent and cooperation. The Abuja experience demonstrates that the *process* by which agreements are drafted, negotiated, and concluded determine their acceptability and legitimacy and is therefore no less critical than the content of the agreements. This aligns with a point made in the introduction of this book that the primary determinant of successful ceasefires is the political will of the conflict parties. Ceasefires are likely to fail if one or more of the parties believe that they can continue to make military or political gains through the use of violence.

It should be stressed that the perspective offered here is not a matter of wisdom with hindsight. In January 2006, Salim told the UNSC that the negotiations had thus far been wracked by frustratingly slow progress, deep distrust, and an unacceptable level of inflexibility by the parties.[108] In March, Sam Ibok complained that while the mediators had been attempting to facilitate a peace agreement, the parties had continued to fight it out in Darfur and had violated the 2004 ceasefire agreement repeatedly and with impunity.[109]

Table 7.1: Darfur timeline

2000	The *Black Book* is released. It supports the claim that Sudan is ruled by only a small part of the population and that all the power is concentrated in the North.
2002	
June	The SLM/A and JEM take up arms against the Sudanese government, targeting a police station in Golo.
2003	
Early	The armed conflict escalates when several coordinated attacks led by SLM/A leader Abdel Wahid were launched on government army units.
3 September	The conflict parties sign the Abeche Ceasefire Agreement.
2004	
January	The Sudanese army moves to quell uprising in western region of Darfur; hundreds of thousands of refugees flee to neighboring Chad.
March	UN says progovernment Janjawid militias are carrying out systematic killings of African villagers in Darfur.
8 April	The conflict parties sign the N'Djamena Humanitarian Ceasefire Agreement on the conflict in Darfur.
28 May	The conflict parties sign the Agreement with the Sudanese Parties on the Modalities for the Establishment of the Ceasefire Commission and the Deployment of Observers in the Darfur.
September	Colin Powell, US secretary of state, describes Darfur killings as genocide.
9 November	The conflict parties sign the Protocol between the Government of the Sudan (Sudanese government), the Sudan Liberation Movement/Army (SLM/A), and the Justice and Equality Movement (JEM) on the Enhancement of the Security Situation in Darfur in Accordance with the N'Djamena Agreement.
2005	
January	The Sudanese government and the SPLM/A sign the Comprehensive Peace Agreement (CPA).
2006	
5 May	The Sudanese government and the SLM/A led by Minni Minnawi sign the Darfur Peace Agreement. The SLM/A led by Abdul Wahid and the JEM refuse to sign the agreement.
August	Sudan rejects UN Resolution 1706 calling for a UN peacekeeping force in Darfur, saying it would compromise Sudanese sovereignty.
2007	
July	UN Security Council approves a resolution authorizing a 26,000-strong force for Darfur. Sudan says it will cooperate with the United Nations–African Union Mission in Darfur (UNAMID).

Ibok concluded that "our experience over the past sixteen months has led us to conclude that there is neither good faith nor commitment on the part of any of the Parties."[110] On 24 April, the day before the draft DPA was tabled, Ibok again expressed doubts about the parties' interest in peace.[111] Nor was he optimistic when interviewed the day before the DPA was signed by the government and Minnawi.[112]

In short, the mediators rushed the process toward an outcome they doubted would succeed. The case underscores the fact that mediators are not free agents, at liberty to design negotiating processes as they see fit. Instead, they are agents of the organizations that appointed them, and they are obliged to adhere to the mandates they receive from those organizations, their donors, and the UNSC.[113]

On 7 May 2006, Ibok and other members of the mediation team issued a 3,000-word "Open Letter to Those Members of the Movements Who Are Still Reluctant to Sign." They sought to ease the movements' objections and fears by explaining aspects of the DPA and they suggested that "many of the suspicions about this Agreement are based on misunderstanding and the fact that many of you have not had time to study the text in detail, and understand what it provides."[114] This statement, made *after* the DPA had been signed by the government and Minnawi, is an indictment of the deadline diplomacy strategy.

There is no way of telling whether an extension of the Abuja mediation process—by several weeks or even months—would have borne fruit. According to ripeness theory, progress or the lack thereof in peace negotiations depends on battlefield dynamics, external leverage, and major developments affecting the balance of power between the conflict parties. Despite the uncertainty regarding future scenarios in the Darfur case, it seems clear that the AU was mistaken to have ended the formal talks and closed the DPA to negotiation and amendment before the parties had had a proper opportunity to comprehend and embrace the document.

NOTES

1.   El-Tom, *Darfur, JEM and the Khalil Ibrahim Story*, 168; Arabie, *Darfur: Road to Genocide*, 89.

2.   Flint and de Waal, *Darfur: A New History of a Long War*, 16–17.

3.   On the history and causes of the Darfur conflict and rebellion, see De Waal, "Sudan: The Turbulent State"; Burr and Collins, *Sudan in Turmoil: Hasan Al-Turabi and the Islamist State 1889–2003*; Flint and de Waal, *Darfur: A New History of a Long War*.

4. Flint, "Darfur's Armed Movements," 150; Flint and de Waal, *Darfur: A New History of a Long War*, 16–17.

5. Lounsbery, Pearson, and Pearson, *Civil Wars: Internal Struggles, Global Consequences*, 106.

6. Abdul-Jalil, Azzain, and Yousuf, "Native Administration and Local Governance in Darfur: Past and Future"; J. Tubiana, "Darfur: A Conflict for Land?"

7. Abdul-Jalil, Azzain, and Yousuf, "Native Administration and Local Governance in Darfur: Past and Future"; J. Tubiana, "Darfur: A Conflict for Land?"

8. Brosché and Duursma, "Hurdles to Peace: A Level-of-Analysis Approach to Resolving Sudan's Civil Wars."

9. Cockett, *Sudan: Darfur and the Failure of an African State*, 180.

10. Flint and de Waal, *Darfur: A New History of a Long War*, 81; Prunier, *Darfur: The Ambiguous Genocide*, 92.

11. Collins, *A History of Modern Sudan*, 288.

12. Flint and de Waal, *Darfur: A New History of a Long War*, 120–122.

13. Prunier, *Darfur: The Ambiguous Genocide*, 127.

14. Powell, "The Crisis in Darfur—Secretary Colin L. Powell's Testimony before the Senate Foreign Relations Committee Washington, DC. 9 September 2004."

15. UN High Commissioner for Refugees, *The State of the World's Refugees 2006*, April 2006, www.unhcr.org.

16. Flint and de Waal, *Darfur: A New History of a Long War*, 120–121.

17. De Waal, "Sudan: Darfur," 286; Flint and de Waal, *Darfur: A New History of a Long War*, 173.

18. Toga, "The African Union Mediation and the Abuja Peace Talks," 215.

19. Flint and de Waal, *Darfur: A New History of a Long War*, 97–99.

20. Toga, "The African Union Mediation and the Abuja Peace Talks," 215.

21. Prunier, *Darfur: The Ambiguous Genocide*, 107.

22. Flint and de Waal, *Darfur: A New History of a Long War*, 143.

23. Prunier, *Darfur: The Ambiguous Genocide*, 127.

24. De Waal, "Sudan: Darfur," 87.

25. Toga, "The African Union Mediation and the Abuja Peace Talks," 216–217.

26. Toga, "The African Union Mediation and the Abuja Peace Talks," 218.

27. Allard Duursma, "When to Get out of the Trench: Using Smart Pressure to Resolve Civil War."

28. De Waal, "Sudan: Darfur."

29. De Waal, "Sudan: Darfur," 288; Toga, "The African Union Mediation and the Abuja Peace Talks," 217.

30. Flint and de Waal, *Darfur: A New History of a Long War*, 175.

31. A scan of the document with the added passage is available in the Sudan peace Archive of the World Peace Foundation; see http://dl.tufts.edu/bookreader/tufts:MS201.001.001.004.00001.00005#page/3/mode/2up.

32. Flint and de Waal, *Darfur: A New History of a Long War*, 175.

33. Flint and de Waal, *Darfur: A New History of a Long War*.

34. Flint and de Waal, *Darfur: A New History of a Long War*, 215–216.

35. Flint and de Waal, *Darfur: A New History of a Long War*, 221–223.

36. Flint and de Waal, *Darfur: A New History of a Long War*, 225–226.

37. Flint and de Waal, *Darfur: A New History of a Long War*, 226–229.

38. Brooks, "Enforcing a Turning Point and Imposing a Deal: An Analysis of the Darfur Abuja Negotiations of 2006," 417.

39. Flint and de Waal, *Darfur: A New History of a Long War*, 216.

40. Toga, "The African Union Mediation and the Abuja Peace Talks," 231.

41. Interview with Alex de Waal in Boston, 3 September 2014; interview with Mulugeta Gebrehiwot Berhe in Addis Ababa, 13 February 2015. See also Toga, "The African Union Mediation and the Abuja Peace Talks," 232.

42. Nathan, "No Ownership, No Peace: The Darfur Peace Agreement," 3–5.

43. Flint, "Without Foreign Chancelleries and Hollywood's Finest, Can Darfur Peace Deal Succeed?"

44. See Kristof, "Genocide in Slow Motion."

45. Hamilton and Hazlett, "Not on Our Watch: The Emergence of the American Movement for Darfur."

46. Interview with Alex de Waal in Boston, 3 September 2014; interview with Luca Zampetti in Addis Ababa, 4 February 2015. See also Duursma, "He Who Pays the Piper, Calls the Tune? Non-African Involvement in Sudan's African-Led Mediation Processes," 436.

47. Nathan, "No Ownership, No Peace."

48. Natsios, *Sudan, South Sudan, and Darfur*, 2–3.

49. Interview with Hilary Benn in London, 21 November 2014. See also Duursma, "He Who Pays the Piper, Calls the Tune?" 436.

50. Interview with Ghazi Salah al-Din al-Atabani in Khartoum, 7 December 2014.

51. Quoted in John Prendergast, "A Dying Deal in Darfur," *Boston Globe*, 13 July 2006.

52. Interview with Ghazi Salah al-Din al-Atabani in Khartoum, 7 December 2014.

53. Nathan, "No Ownership, No Peace," 8.

54. "AU Mediators Address Open Letter to Reluctant Darfur Rebels," *Sudan Tribune*, 9 May 2006, https://sudantribune.com/spip.php?article15568.

55. Nathan, "No Ownership, No Commitment," 10.

56. Nathan, "No Ownership, No Commitment."

57. International Crisis Group, "Unifying Darfur's Rebels: A Prerequisite for Peace."

58. African Union, "Briefing by Dr. Salim Ahmed Salim, AU Special Envoy and Chief Mediator for the Darfur Conflict, to the U.N. Security Council on 13 January 2006," press release, https://sudaneseonline.com/epressrelease2006/jan19-70147.shtml.

59. Hottinger, "The Darfur Peace Agreement: Expectations Unfulfilled," 48.

60. Brooks, "Enforcing a Turning Point and Imposing a Deal: An Analysis of the Darfur Abuja Negotiations of 2006," 423–424.

61. De Waal, "The DPA and Its National Context," 51.

62. Nathan, "No Ownership, No Commitment," 11.

63. Marchal, "The Unseen Regional Implications of the Crisis in Darfur," 191.

64. "AU's Salim Reveals Abuja Handicaps, Last-Minute Compromise," *Sudan Tribune*, 22 May 2006, https://sudantribune.com/spip.php?article15793.

65. International Crisis Group, "Darfur's Fragile Peace Agreement," 2.

66. Nathan, "No Ownership, No Commitment."

67. Nathan, "No Ownership, No Commitment."

68. Jan Pronk, "Darfur Agreement Is Severely Paralysed," *Sudan Tribune*, 1 July 2006.

69. "AU Mediators Address Open Letter to Reluctant Darfur Rebels," *Sudan Tribune*, 9 May 2006.

70. Abaker Mohamed Abuelbashar, "On the Failure of Darfur Peace Talks in Abuja," *Sudan Tribune*, 25 August 2006, 5.

71. Interview with Abdullahi Eltom in "Darfur: Inside the Crisis," 15 May 2006, www.democracynow.org.

72. Nathan, "No Ownership, No Commitment," 5.

73. Abuelbashar, "On the Failure of Darfur Peace Talks," 5.

74. "Darfur Rebel SLM Rejects Integration of Its Forces in the Army," *Sudan Tribune*, 30 April 2006, https://sudantribune.com/spip.php?article15358; "Darfur SLA/JEM Joint Press Statement on Proposed Peace Deal," *Sudan Tribune*, 1 May 2006, https://sudantribune.com/Darfur-SLA-JEM-joint-press,15395.

75. Flint and de Waal, *Darfur: A New History of a Long War*, 218; Toga, "The African Union Mediation and the Abuja Peace Talks," 241; De Waal, "Darfur's Deadline: The Final Days of the Abuja Peace Process."

76. "AU's Salim Reveals Abuja Handicaps."

77. De Waal, "Darfur's Deadline: The Final Days of the Abuja Peace Process."

78. Interview with Hilary Benn in London, 21 November 2014.

79. De Waal, "Darfur's Deadline: The Final Days of the Abuja Peace Process," 270.

80. Glenn Kessler, "Darfur Peace Accord a Battle of Its Own," *Washington Post*, 9 May 2006; Brooks, "Enforcing a Turning Point and Imposing a Deal: An Analysis of the Darfur Abuja Negotiations of 2006."

81. De Waal, "Darfur's Deadline: The Final Days of the Abuja Peace Process," 273. Confirmed in an interview with Hilary Benn in London, 21 November 2014.

82. "A Rebel Walks Out for Peace: The Satya Interview with Tadjadine Bechir Niame," Satya, June/July 2006, www.satyamag.com/jun06/niame.html.

83. Abuelbashar, "On the Failure of Darfur Peace Talks."

84. Toga, "The African Union Mediation and the Abuja Peace Talks," 242; De Waal, "Darfur's Deadline: The Final Days of the Abuja Peace Process," 280.

85. Toga, "The African Union Mediation and the Abuja Peace Talks."

86. Flint and de Waal, *Darfur: A New History of a Long War*, 227.

87. De Waal, "Darfur's Deadline: The Final Days of the Abuja Peace Process," 281–282.

88. International Crisis Group, "Darfur's Fragile Peace Agreement," 5.

89. "After 5 May Deal, SLM Minnawi Faces Divisions and Defections," *Sudan Tribune*, 19 June 2006; "Tension Mounts within the Darfur SLM-Minnawi Streams," *Sudan Tribune*, 1 July 2006.

90. International Crisis Group, "Darfur's Fragile Peace Agreement," 1.

91. De Waal, "Darfur and the Failure of the Responsibility to Protect," 1046.

92. Interview with Nurudin Azeez, military liaison officer of AMIS to the Abuja peace talks, in Addis Ababa, 17 February 2015; interview with Abdul Mohamed, AU mediator during the Abuja talks, in Addis Ababa, 17 February 2015.

93. Interview with Vladimir Zhagora, UN Senior Political Affairs Officer, in Hawassa on 16 January 2016.

94. Interview with Vladimir Zhagora, UN Senior Political Affairs Officer, in Hawassa on 16 January 2016.

95. Interview with Jan Pronk in The Hague, 1 June 2015.

96. Interview with Kenny Gluck, former chief of staff of the AU-UN mediation team for Darfur.

97. De Waal, "Darfur and the Failure of the Responsibility to Protect," 1053.

98. Phayal, "UN Troop Deployment and Preventing Violence against Civilians in Darfur."

99. "AU's Salim Reveals Abuja Handicaps."

100. Zartman, "The Timing of Peace Initiatives."

101. Zartman, "The Timing of Peace Initiatives."

102. Wallensteen and Svensson, "Talking Peace: International Mediation in Armed Conflicts."

103. De Waal, "Darfur and the Failure of the Responsibility to Protect."

104. Holslag, "China's Diplomatic Manoeuvring on the Question of Darfur," 81–82.

105. Flint, *Rhetoric and Reality: The Failure to Resolve the Darfur Conflict*, 28–29.

106. De Waal, "Darfur and the Failure of the Responsibility to Protect."

107. Clayton, Nathan, and Wiehler, "Ceasefire Success: A Conceptual Framework," 1–25.

108. African Union, "Briefing by Dr. Salim Ahmed Salim."

109. African Union, "African Union Presents Ceasefire Proposal to Sudan Government and Darfur Movements: AU Tells the Sudanese Parties in Abuja—Time Is Up," press statement, Abuja, 12 March 2006.

110. African Union, "African Union Presents Ceasefire Proposal."

111. "AU to End Darfur Peace Talks If No Agreement by End of April," *Sudan Tribune*, 24 April 2006.

112. "International Envoys Push Rebels to Back Darfur Peace Deal," AFP news report, 4 May 2006, www.sudan.net.

113. Nathan, "The Mandate Effect: A Typology and Conceptualization of Mediation Mandates."

114. "AU Mediators Address Open Letter to Reluctant Darfur Rebels," *Sudan Tribune*.

CHAPTER 8

Colombia, 2012–2016
The Benefits and Challenges of Talking While Fighting

Juanita Millán Hernández, Valerie Sticher, and Enzo Nussio

In 2016, the government of Colombia and the Revolutionary Armed Forces of Colombia (FARC)[1] reached a final peace agreement to settle the armed conflict with the FARC that had lasted more than half a century. Past efforts to negotiate a settlement with the largest insurgent group in the country had been futile, with dynamics related to conflict violence and ceasefires contributing to their failures. In the Havana peace negotiations between 2012 and 2016, there was no bilateral ceasefire until the very end of negotiations, showing that this is a viable alternative to the more common model of silencing the guns before or during negotiations. But even though the parties agreed to "talk while fighting," conflict violence at times threatened to disrupt the peace negotiations, highlighting the tight interaction between political negotiations and conflict violence.

This chapter provides an overview of these dynamics. It is divided into three main sections. The first section describes the conflict background, the broader context, and prior efforts to negotiate a settlement. The second section focuses on the Havana peace process, describing the sequencing strategy and how events on the battlefield and in political negotiations affected each other. The third section offers a unique reading of the case from the perspective of both conflict parties, highlighting the distinct challenges and choices that each side faced. Therefore, while the second section lays out facts, concepts, and sequence, the third section discusses why each side took or refused specific measures and how they were each affected by these dynamics. The concluding section summarizes the main insights and discusses how measures short of a preliminary ceasefire replaced some of its functions and enabled talking while fighting.

CONFLICT AND PRIOR NEGOTIATIONS

The armed conflict between the FARC and government forces can be traced back to the 1950s civil war known as La Violencia, which pitted Liberals against Conservatives but also involved a series of communist guerrilla groups. The FARC emerged as a rebel group in the 1960s out of the remnants of these groups.[2] The proximate causes of conflict are related to political exclusion of the political left after the National Front elite pact to stop La Violencia, limited land access for impoverished peasants, and the example of the successful Cuban revolution in 1959.[3] From the FARC's perspective, the government attack on Marquetalia in 1964 marks their birth as an armed insurgency. Afterward came a low-intensity conflict, which, during its course, involved a series of other rebel groups (including the Ejército de Liberación Nacional [ELN], Ejército Popular de Liberación [EPL], Movimiento 19 de Abril [M-19], and other smaller groups).[4] However, it was not until the 1980s with the emergence of drug trade and the appearance of paramilitary groups—some of them aligned with government forces, political elites, and countryside businessmen[5]—that this low-intensity conflict became increasingly complex and violent. From then onward, the government and the FARC faced each other alternately on the military battlefield or the negotiating table without finding a solution until 2016.

Previous Negotiation Attempts

The first political negotiations with the FARC were launched in the early 1980s, but the process eventually faltered.[6] Thousands of members of the Patriotic Union (UP)—a political party founded by the FARC as part of the negotiations—were assassinated by paramilitaries, drug traffickers, members of the security forces, and due to quarrels between FARC members, leading to widespread skepticism within FARC about the possibility of a political solution to the conflict.[7]

At the beginning of the 1990s, the FARC and two other guerrilla groups (ELN and EPL) worked on a joint negotiating position[8] and again engaged in exploratory talks and later political negotiations, but ongoing violence and two high-level assassinations eventually led to the suspension of talks.[9]

After these failed attempts, the conflict became more intense and the room for peace negotiations was more limited. By that time, the FARC had accumulated so much power that they could dominate large areas of Colombia. It was always the FARC's stated aim to take government power, and the second half of the 1990s was the time when it was closest to achieving it, which put the government under enormous pressure of finding a solution.

Against this backdrop, around the turn of the century, the Pastrana administration engaged in a renewed effort to settle the conflict with the FARC politically. Peace talks were held in a demilitarized zone in the Caguán region, southern Colombia, an area corresponding roughly to the size of Switzerland. The war continued in other parts of the country, and the talks were marked by a lack in progress, while the FARC was widely suspected of using the demilitarized zone to rearm and regroup. Amid escalating tensions, decreasing public support, and strong opposition from senior military figures, the FARC hijacking of a civilian airplane in February 2002 triggered the breakdown of the talks[10] and set the stage for a new phase of confrontation.

Plan Colombia and a Change in the Military Balance

One important factor that changed during this new confrontation was the international context. Due to its geographical proximity to the conflict, the United States had sought to influence politics in Colombia for decades, first as part of its efforts to curb the spread of communism and later focusing on the war on drugs. In the late 1990s, US–Colombia relations deteriorated, and economic aid was withheld.[11] However, in 2000, US Congress approved aid to Plan Colombia, a Colombian blueprint that had been rewritten to suit the US priority on the war on drugs.[12] In the aftermath of 9/11, a shift in US policy under the banner of counterterrorism enabled further financial and military assistance to Plan Colombia, and freshly elected President Uribe pursued an aggressive war against the guerillas.[13]

This time, the government forces were expected to have the upper hand on the battlefield thanks to an internal operational transformation of the military forces and the US-sponsored Plan Colombia. The FARC suffered major military setbacks after 2002, which decreased their membership from an estimated 21,000 armed members in 2002 to fewer than 10,000 in 2008.[14] In 2008 alone, their historical leader (Manuel Marulanda) died of natural causes and their number 2 (Raúl Reyes) was killed in a military operation. In the same year, some of the most high-profile kidnapped hostages, including Íngrid Betancourt, were liberated in the stunning Operation Jaque. Generals of the armed forces talked about the "end of the end" of conflict and a military triumph seemed close. However, the FARC also began a major strategic reorientation in 2008,[15] which stabilized their organization on a smaller scale for the ensuing years and stalled the military confrontation.

While US support played an important role in shifting the military balance and thus ripening the conflict for political negotiations, the United States played a largely hands-off but supportive role once the Havana peace process was launched.

NEGOTIATION AND BATTLEFIELD DYNAMICS

The public phase of the Havana peace negotiations was officially launched on 18 October 2012 in Oslo, Norway, and culminated in a final peace agreement in August 2016. After its rejection in a plebiscite in October and renegotiations by the parties to the conflict, Congress ratified a revised peace agreement at the end of November 2016.

The parties to the conflict engaged in direct negotiations, with a limited role for third parties. Throughout negotiations, no bilateral ceasefire was put in place, although there were multiple arrangements that addressed conflict violence while the parties negotiated the agenda items. Figure 8.1 provides an overview of how ceasefire and de-escalation mechanisms corresponded with actual violence on the battlefield and with progress in the political negotiations.[16] Compared to other successful peace processes, Colombia saw a relatively late end to the violence, with fighting ongoing in the first three years of the peace process. Nonetheless, conflict violence all but subsided in mid-2015, more than a year before a bilateral ceasefire was put in place. What led to this shift in battlefield dynamics?

This section details the sequence and relation of events at the negotiation table and in the battlefield, laying out how these dynamics changed as parties moved from a situation with no willingness to explore a negotiated settlement (pre-prenegotiation phase) to talks about how peace negotiations may be held (prenegotiation phase) to a structured discussion of six agenda items (negotiation phase).

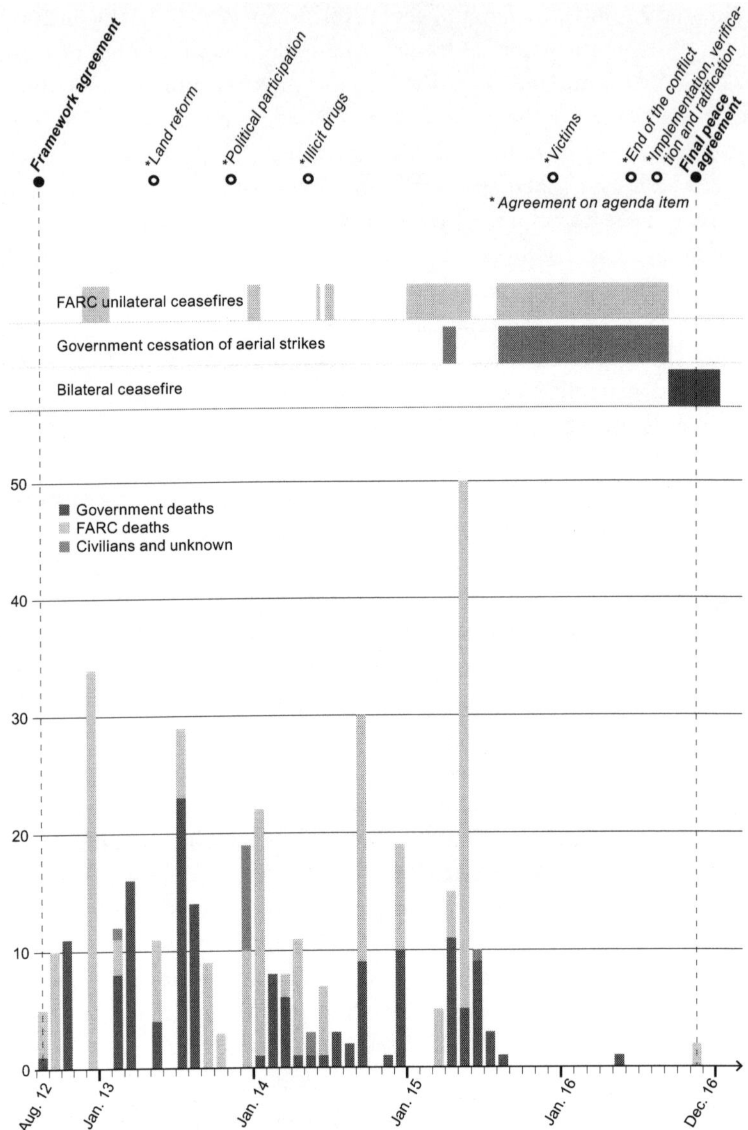

Figure 8.1 Overview of political negotiations (item agreements), conflict violence (battle-related deaths), and ceasefires. See endnote 16.

Pre-Prenegotiation Phase

After the collapse of the Caguán talks in February 2002, the armed conflict between the Colombian government and the FARC relapsed into the pre-prenegotiation phase, that is, a phase of violent conflict in which neither side appeared ready to consider negotiating the contested issues between them, and open warfare resumed. There were informal contacts between the two sides,[17] even during the Uribe administration. However, the conditions posed by President Uribe—which effectively equated FARC surrender—meant that there was no serious opening to explore peace negotiations.

Prenegotiation Phase

As soon as Juan Manuel Santos began his term as president in 2010, he said that the "key to peace was not lost on the ground of the sea." Shortly after his inauguration, he was contacted by a Colombian economist who had been exchanging letters with a member of the FARC secretariat—the same person who led the informal contacts during the Uribe administration. Santos responded by inviting FARC representatives to meet with government representatives for confidential discussions. As a result of this first secret meeting, a series of communication exchanges began between President Santos and FARC chief Alfonso Cano.[18]

In preliminary meetings between September 2010 and February 2011, the parties decided on the security, logistics, and delegations for exploratory talks in Cuba.[19] Throughout the period of preliminary contacts, attacks and military operations on both sides continued, with some important victories on the government side. Most important, on 4 November 2011, only months before the scheduled start of the exploratory talks, the security forces killed FARC commander Alfonso Cano, who had been personally involved in the informal exchange of letters. On 15 November 2011, the FARC secretariat announced that Timoleón Jiménez had been designated as its new commander.

Subsequently, a series of preparatory meetings were held in which details were defined for the start of the exploratory phase. The phase of preliminary contacts ended in January 2012.

Despite the leadership change in the FARC, the exploratory (secret) talks went ahead as planned. They formally began on 24 February 2012 and comprised ten rounds of talks. No ceasefire was put in place, but—as a unilateral de-escalation measure—the FARC announced that it would give up its longstanding practice of kidnapping for ransom shortly after the start of the talks. It also promised to release ten members of the security services, some of which it had held captive for over a decade.[20] In March 2012, the FARC launched a deadly attack on government forces and two large-scale military operations killed dozens of FARC members, including five high-level members.[21] Yet the talks continued uninterrupted, and in early April, the FARC delivered on its promise to release the ten security service members.[22] In other words, throughout the exploratory phase, the conflict parties managed to disentangle ceasefire and political negotiation processes.

The only real temporary breakdown of the exploratory talks was related to the content of the negotiation agenda and not due to battlefield dynamics: the government insisted on including disarmament in the negotiation agenda, while the FARC refused to do so. With the help of third-party diplomacy, the parties to the conflict managed to overcome this crisis (see below).

At the end of the exploratory talks, which lasted six months, the parties had reached agreement on the guiding objective, venue, operational rules, and the negotiation agenda in the form of a framework agreement. The negotiation agenda consisted of six agenda items, five of which were of substantive nature and one mainly procedural.[23] One of the substantive items—called the end of conflict—included the discussion of a definitive bilateral ceasefire, as part of which the parties would also discuss the conditions and modalities for the FARC to lay down its weapons.

Negotiation Phase

The negotiation of the contested issues started in November 2012 in Havana, Cuba, with the land reform item. There was an explicit understanding on both sides that conflict violence would continue during negotiations—the political negotiation process was to take place without any accompanying ceasefire. Opposition to the talks emerged quickly under former president Uribe, who formed an organization and later a political party to mobilize against the peace negotiations. Uribe and his followers criticized, among other things, that the government had agreed to negotiate amid continued FARC hostilities, claiming that the government was being too lenient toward the FARC.

The negotiations proceeded relatively smoothly in the first year and a half, with the parties reaching agreements on three agenda items. In this period, conflict violence continued largely unabated. As an exception, the

Table 8.1: Overview of unilateral ceasefires declared by the FARC

Declared	Effective	Declared time period	Type	Comment
19 November 12	20 November 12	Two months	CoH	
8 December 13	15 December 13	One month	CoH	
16 May 14	20 May 14	Until 28 May 14	CoH	Electoral ceasefire, announced jointly with ELN
7 June 14	9 June 14	Until 30 June 14	CoH	Electoral ceasefire
17 December 14	20 December 14	Indefinite	CoH	Suspended on 22 May 15
8 July 15	20 July 15	One month, later extended indefinitely	CoH	Superseded the bilateral ceasefire on 29 August 16
23 June 16	29 August 16	Indefinite	Definitive ceasefire	

Note: Table adapted from Sticher, "Ceasefires as Bargaining Instruments in Intrastate Conflicts: Ceasefire Objectives and Their Effects on Peace Negotiations," 69.

FARC announced a few temporally limited unilateral ceasefires that lacked official monitoring mechanisms (see overview of all ceasefires during the public phase of the talks in table 8.1). In line with the terminology used throughout this book, we refer to them as cessations of hostilities, although the term has a different connotation in Spanish-speaking countries.[24]

The first cessation of hostilities coincided with the start of the talks in Havana and lasted for two months. On the day the ceasefire expired, the FARC resumed hostilities.[25] The second cessation of hostilities was limited to a month and began a year into the negotiation process. While compliance was solid,[26] a deadly FARC attack the day after the ceasefire expired drew widespread criticism and condemnation. During the two rounds of presidential elections in 2014, the FARC declared short cessations of hostilities, the first together with the second largest guerrilla organization, the ELN, and the second one alone. The election became the first real test for public support of the peace process, as the peace negotiations were a key campaign issue. President Santos received less votes than his contender, who opposed the negotiations in the first round but secured his reelection in the second round.

None of the temporary unilateral cessations of hostilities were reciprocated by the government. In fact, some of the largest military offensives during the peace negotiations, such as two operations killing thirty-four FARC members in December 2012, took place in these time frames.[27] Again, at this stage in the peace process, the conflict parties managed to disentangle battlefield dynamics from the political negotiation process relatively successfully.

A Shift in Negotiations and in Battlefield Dynamics

The pace of the negotiations shifted with the negotiation of the Victims item, which started in June 2014. The parties made little progress toward agreement. The issue was not only complex but also highly sensitive, as it required consensus on how to address justice for crimes committed during half a century of armed conflict.[28] While discussions of the Victims item took place and to speed up the political negotiations, the parties decided that it was necessary to create new mechanisms. They established a technical subcommittee tasked with studying possible ceasefire models and preparing options for an eventual definite ceasefire as part of the final agreement.[29] The creation of the subcommittee to end the conflict and the gender subcommission was a big change in how the agenda topics were addressed. One of the main new approaches for Colombian negotiations was the inclusion of active military members to lead the ceasefire discussion in the subcommittee to end the conflict.

In November 2014, the FARC captured a serving Colombian general who had entered an area with known guerrilla presence in civilian clothes. Despite the explicit understanding that battlefield dynamics would not affect the peace negotiations, President Santos ordered the suspension of the talks. Yet, despite the strong reaction at the negotiation table, the two sides quickly agreed on the conditions for release, and talks resumed in December 2014. A week later, the FARC announced an indefinite unilateral ceasefire. The guerrilla group asked several organizations to monitor compliance with the ceasefire, but in the absence of an official and formal monitoring mechanism, we view this ceasefire as a cessation of hostilities.

In its statement, the FARC indicated that the ceasefire would end "only if it is found that our guerrilla structures have been attacked by the public force."[30] Some interpreted this to suggest that the cessation of hostilities would end if it was not replicated by the government. However, the group continued to maintain the cessation of hostilities as military offensives continued. In March 2015, President Santos ordered the military to suspend its air strikes for a one-month period with the option of an extension. Other types of operations on the ground continued and, in some accounts, even intensified.

Shortly after an extension of the suspension in air strikes, in mid-April 2015, the FARC killed eleven soldiers in a major violation of their unilateral cessation of hostilities during the peace negotiations. President Santos immediately announced the resumption of air strikes. The FARC initially continued with the unilateral cessation of hostilities, but after government forces killed twenty-six FARC members in a large-scale military operation on 22 May, they suspended the arrangement and resumed fighting.

There were some delays in the negotiations after the mid-April FARC attack, but despite the return of hostilities in the battlefield, the talks were never suspended. In May 2015, the representatives of the government and the FARC announced the start of a joint pilot plan for demining one of the rural areas of Antioquia. And after a year of impasses, important progress was made in Cuba on the negotiation agenda, as the parties reached agreement on a symbolically important issue on the Victims agenda point.

Meanwhile in Colombia, where conflict violence had resumed, public backing of the peace talks dropped to an all-time low.[31] Observers noted this tension between events at the negotiation table and on the battlefield, warning that any major incident could spark a breakdown of the peace negotiations.[32] It was in this context that the FARC, in early July 2015, announced another one-month cessation of hostilities. Shortly after, on 12 July 2015, the government and the FARC jointly and formally committed to de-escalation for the first time.

The parties signed an agreement in which they laid out steps to de-escalate the conflict violence in Colombia and speed up the political negotiation process in Havana. These measures were taken to strengthen "the confidence of Colombian men and women in the peace process and trust between delegations"[33] and effectively introduced a positive feedback loop between ceasefire and political negotiation processes. The government announced a renewed suspension of air strikes, and the FARC declared that it would maintain its unilateral cessation of hostilities beyond the one month it had initially announced. In November 2015, the Ministry of Defense announced that the individual demobilization campaigns were going to stop as a confidence-building measure.[34]

Following the 12 July 2015 agreement, conflict violence came to a de facto halt, with only a handful of battle-related deaths on both sides in the remainder of the peace negotiations (see figure 8.1).

Negotiating the Definitive Ceasefire

The negotiation of the definitive ceasefire took almost two years and happened in parallel with the negotiation of the two other remaining agenda items. The first meeting of the subcommittee to end the conflict was on 22 August 2014. After this first encounter, and due to the aforementioned situation on the ground, the subcommittee was only able to work continuously from early March 2015. This was the first time ever that negotiations between the government and the FARC had proceeded so far, so the subcommittee considered the process very seriously, and it took seven months to agree on the structure and basic outlines of the definitive bilateral ceasefire. After this, they created six smaller teams—each composed of three members from each side—to work on the individual ceasefire chapters. The members of these subgroups collaborated closely to work out the details of the chapters, leading to a sense of teamwork and establishing trust between members of the two opposing sides of the conflict.[35]

In June 2016, the parties signed the agreement on the end of the conflict,[36] which laid out the rules, steps, and practical details "to end in a definitive manner the offensive actions between security forces and FARC-EP."[37] The ceasefire and laying down of FARC weapons would be the first steps following the signing of the peace agreement, creating the conditions to implement the provisions addressing the contested issues between the conflict parties.

One of the chapters of the ceasefire agreement was on the monitoring and verification mechanism (MVM). A few months earlier, delegates from the United Nations (UN) had traveled to Havana to explore the possibility of a UN involvement as one of the three parties to the MVM. After the conclusion of the agreement on the end of conflict, the parties and the UN started working on setting up this mechanism.[38] Two months later, on 24 August 2016, the parties formally announced that they had reached a full peace agreement. Another five days later—in line with the timeline provided in the agreement—the bilateral and definitive ceasefire formally came into effect. Once this happened, several important security and logistical procedures started taking place, including the initial training for the members of the MVM, reconnaissance visits of the lands for the Transitional Zones for Normalization,[39] and the analysis of the necessary logistics for its construction.

The Aftermath of the Plebiscite

On 23 September 2016, the FARC National Guerrilla Conference unanimously ratified the peace agreement. Three days later, the two parties held a public signing ceremony. However, on 2 October 2016, following a highly polarized campaign, voters narrowly—and unexpectedly—rejected the peace agreement in a plebiscite. This posed a major challenge to the ceasefire. The parties had no agreement on how to proceed in the case of a rejection at the ballot. Leaders on both sides quickly announced that they would maintain the ceasefire. On 20 October 2016, the president issued a decree that provided the legal ground for the military to maintain the ceasefire and for the monitoring mechanism to continue its preparation and deployment. The decree also created the legal basis to start building the Temporal Pre-grouping Points (Puntos de Preagrupamiento Temporal, or short PPT), as a place to locate FARC members before they could move to the Transitional Zones of Normalization once a new agreement would be reached.

In the period that followed, the government first negotiated with the political opposition and subsequently renegotiated with the FARC, resulting in over fifty amendments to the original peace agreement.[40] However, key issues—including the text on the ceasefire, the laying down of weapons, and their verification—remained unchanged.[41] The revised agreement signed on 24 November 2016 was ratified in Congress but faced continued opposition under Uribe's leadership.

The relocation of FARC combatants in early 2017 was a monumental undertaking. In three weeks, around 7,000 FARC members in the first phase—followed by 2,256 militia members in a second phase—arrived safely to the Transitional Zones of Normalization through thirty-six routes. It involved around 14,000 people from the MVM, security forces, and other institutions.[42] The active phase of the definitive ceasefire had to be extended, as the original time frame had been too optimistic. Yet overall, the "process of decommissioning and removing weapons in Colombia was exemplary,"[43] demonstrating the high level of preparedness and commitment on both sides.[44]

CONFLICT PARTY PERSPECTIVES

Why was the government so adamant about not having a bilateral ceasefire in place? How did events in the battlefield shape political negotiations and vice versa? And what did the absence of a bilateral ceasefire mean for the FARC? This section offers a unique discussion of these questions from the perspective of each conflict party, showing their reasons for engaging in the chosen sequencing strategy and how it affected the government and the FARC in very distinctive ways.

Government Perspective

Past administrations had shifted between a military and a political approach to the conflict like a pendulum, with each failed peace process followed by intensive warfare. As defense minister under President Uribe, Santos had overseen some major offensives against the FARC. He understood that while the balance of power favored the government, defeating the guerrillas would take decades and claim many more lives.[45] In-depth analyses conducted by the government and the security forces came to similar conclusions: that the FARC was highly resilient and would be hard to defeat. But although both the political and the military leaderships understood that the armed conflict could only be ended through negotiations, the initiative to engage in prenegotiations was purely driven by the political leadership. The military followed the political instructions to continue to pursue a military strategy called point of inflection, aimed at pushing the guerrillas to an edge through "surgical operations" that specifically targeted high- and mid-level guerrilla commanders. It was highly successful in these operations, killing at least thirty high-ranking members of the FARC between 2007 and 2012. This included the FARC commander Alfonso Cano in November 2011. When in the aftermath of the killing, the FARC confirmed that everything stood as agreed upon, the government read this as a strong sign of their commitment to the talks.[46]

While the government continued military operations until years into the peace negotiations, President Santos changed the *discourse* on the conflict from the day he took office. In the aftermath of 9/11, and particularly after the breakdown of the Caguán process in early 2002, the political leadership of Colombia had consistently referred to the FARC as terrorists and delegitimized them as a political actor.[47] This essentially limited the space for a negotiated settlement to terms and conditions of surrender. President Santos understood that a change in perception would be necessary to create public support for an eventual settlement.[48] He acknowledged the existence of an internal armed conflict and largely refrained from referring to the FARC as *terrorists* or *narcoterrorists*, instead using terms such as guerrillas, insurgents, or violent groups.[49] Haspeslagh calls this narrative shift a "linguistic cease-fire" that set the stage for envisioning a political solution with the FARC.[50]

Ceasefire Considerations during the Prenegotiation Phase

From the government's perspective, a ceasefire or other changes in the bat-tlefield were never even considered during the exploratory talks, as this phase of the negotiation had to remain in complete secrecy.[51] Only a few people in the military leadership knew about the talks. Shortly before the second round of exploratory talks, the FARC killed seventeen soldiers in an attack in Arauca. The FARC Eastern Bloc, under the command of the FARC delegation head to the exploratory talks, was active in this area. Yet the government did not lose a word about the incident. Similarly, when the government killed thirty-six FARC members in a bombardment of an Eastern Bloc camp shortly before the third round of the talks, the FARC delegation did not raise the incident in the talks. To the government, this confirmed that the rules were clear: both sides understood that the negotiations would not be affected by events on the battlefield.[52]

A key point for the government delegation was to include disarmament into the negotiation agenda: its goal—to end the armed conflict—could only be reached if the FARC was prepared to give up its arms. When the FARC refused to include this point in the negotiation agenda, the government walked out of the exploratory talks and prepared to leave Cuba. Through shuttle diplomacy, agreement was reached to include the point (albeit under a different name).[53] This was another encouraging sign for the government: in none of the previous peace efforts had the FARC agreed to discuss its disarmament, and the government understood that this was a hard sell inter-nally for the FARC.[54] From the government's perspective, it was also key to establish a principle of "simultaneity," in which the disarmament process would be initiated with the signing of the final peace agreement, against the FARC preference of "armed verification" of a peace agreement.[55]

Ceasefire Considerations during the Negotiation Phase

The Santos administration was keen on avoiding past mistakes. A key lesson from the Caguán process related to the use of ceasefires during political nego-tiations. The demilitarized zone constituted a de facto ceasefire, albeit one that was geographically limited to the Caguán region. In the government's reading, the FARC had strongly profited from this arrangement, using it to organize, purchase arms, grow and traffic drugs, and kidnap people. It feared that the FARC would again use any ceasefire—whether geographically limited or nationwide—to its military advantage and thus refused to engage in one.

The government was also wary that a ceasefire would remove pressure from the FARC to negotiate. They may feel comfortable negotiating in Havana without feeling the need to make any concessions. In an interview in 2014, President Santos argued,

> If we agreed to a ceasefire there would be a reason for [the] FARC to prolong negotiations eternally. And if by any chance those talks fail, I don't want to be seen by history as another president who was naive and stupid and gave the guerrillas all the opportunity to gain strength and keep fighting.[56]

From the government's perspective, conflict violence should only be addressed at the very end of negotiations and definitively. A ceasefire would be a key outcome of the peace process, rather than a way to enable political negotiations.

The political leadership also understood that the military leadership was strongly opposed to a bilateral preliminary ceasefire, given the past negotiation experiences and the recent successes of the military approach. At this point, there was no sign that the FARC had honest intentions about the peace talks, and mistrust was all over the place. In this regard, the military leadership had cautioned the president to refrain from a ceasefire, arguing that the FARC would take advantage of such a concession. In contrast to some of his predecessors, President Santos was acutely aware of the need to gain the support of the military leadership. Not only were the military the ones who had been fighting the FARC for fifty years, but they were the ones who really knew them deeply, and President Santos was aware of this.

In previous processes, the military and political approaches had been clearly separated, which had led to tensions. In some cases, the military was even seen as a spoiler to negotiation efforts.[57] To avoid this, President Santos sought to engage the leadership and rank and file early in the process. He personally assured the military leadership that there would be no demilitarized zone.[58] He also included a retired army general and a retired national police general in his negotiation delegations, sending an important message to the security forces.[59] A couple of teams were formed within the Ministry of Defense and the Office of the High Commissioner for Peace, where members of the security forces started analyzing alternative options, previous peace processes, and cases that could be of help. Simultaneously, some of these military members started traveling abroad to receive training on several topics related to negotiation, such as ceasefires and disarmament, demobilization, and reintegration (DDR). There was also permanent communication between the president, the military and police leadership, and the negotiators. Later, when the technical subcommittee on the end of conflict was formed, the government team included the deputy commander of the armed forces, four generals, one admiral, nine officers and noncommission officers from all forces, and a couple of civilians, ensuring that those who would have to implement the ceasefire agreement were also in charge of designing it.

The clear strategy of the government to have a ceasefire as the outcome, rather than part of the peace process, also indirectly limited the choice of the negotiation venue to a place abroad. In the absence of a ceasefire or a demilitarized zone, it would not have been feasible to hold political negotiations inside Colombia, as the government needed to ensure the safety of the FARC negotiating delegation to enable them to participate. In the government's calculation, Cuba was an ideal host because it had an interest in ending the armed conflict: "Cuba gave the FARC the necessary security guarantees, offered us a place to conduct negotiations far from the media, and provided us with all the resources to make the process a success."[60]

In the first three years of negotiations, the political and military leadership converged in their assessment that there should not be a bilateral ceasefire. They viewed the unilateral ceasefires by the FARC as an effort to make them feel comfortable and were adamant to not let down their guard or reciprocate. Knowing the FARC and its organizational structure well, the government understood that—in contrast to the smaller guerrilla organization ELN— the FARC was a hierarchically structured organization with solid command and control. The unilateral ceasefire announcement provided the opportunity for the government to test the FARC's will and capacity in this regard. The compliance with the ceasefires confirmed their assessment. It also gave the government some confidence regarding negotiations in a more general sense—the hierarchical structure and tested command and control suggested that any eventual agreement would be implemented by the rank and files. FARC efforts to include commanders of all major geographical areas of the organization in the talks were further encouraging signs in this regard.

A Shift in Dynamics

While conflict violence did not affect the events at the negotiation table during the confidential phase of the talks, the connection between the two became more visible during the public phase of the talks. For parts of the population, it was difficult to understand why the government negotiated with a group that kept on launching attacks. The Uribe camp, which mobilized against the negotiations, further fueled such perceptions.[61]

These dynamics contributed to the first and only formal suspension of the negotiations, following the FARC kidnapping of a serving general. Never had a general been abducted by the guerrilla organization. The public outcry that followed would have made it virtually impossible for President Santos to simply continue the talks. Despite all previous assurances that battlefield dynamics would not affect the peace negotiations, Santos suspended the talks. But he also publicly asked his own minister of defense to explain the breach of security protocols by the general,[62] suggesting that he did not necessarily blame the FARC leadership for the incident. Importantly, military leaders did not pressure Santos to suspend the talks. They understood the rules of the negotiations—that battlefield dynamics should not affect negotiations—and blamed the general for (almost literally) walking into the guerrillas' hands.

The FARC announcement to indefinitely cease fire was perceived as a smart move: the FARC had thrown the ball into government's court. While previously, the government was united in its opposition to a bilateral ceasefire, Santos—who was under a lot of pressure domestically and internationally—started to consider a bilateral ceasefire as talks were ongoing. In January 2015, he ordered the negotiation delegation to prioritize the discussion of a bilateral ceasefire. Meanwhile, the military leadership opposed such an idea, cautioning that a bilateral ceasefire would only prolong negotiations.

In March 2015, as an initial, formal de-escalation measure, Santos ordered the suspension of air strikes against the FARC camps. While the military followed all orders, they were highly skeptical of the move, as air strikes had been the most effective tool in the fight against the guerrillas. They perceived the suspension of this tool as a huge concession to the FARC. Following the president's order, the military announced that they would continue to fight the FARC with "all available means"[63] (i.e., with everything except aerial bombings).

The mid-April 2015 FARC attack was terrible news to the government. President Santos condemned the attack and immediately ordered the military to resume air strikes. At the same time, he argued that the attack was "precisely the reason why the war needs to end."[64] Government delegation members were saddened and upset about the killings, but it was even harder for the military ones, particularly upon hearing that the soldiers had been killed in their sleep. They understood that battlefield dynamics should not affect the negotiations but found it challenging to adhere to. There was also a public outcry, with many Colombians not understanding why the government would continue to negotiate in these circumstances. After some initial delay to let tensions cool off, the negotiation delegations soon continued to work on the details of the agreement, but the first meetings after the killings were incredibly difficult and tense; it was possible to sense the feelings of anger and frustration in the room of the subcommittee on the end of conflict. Furthermore, the public and political pressure made the negotiation process more complicated. Many had lost trust in the possibility of a ceasefire—and some in the negotiation process itself—demonstrating the perils of a "unripe" ceasefire.[65]

The military offensive that killed dozens of FARC on 22 May 2015 was seen as justice for those killed in the April FARC attack. But in a conciliatory tone, President Santos cautioned not to celebrate the deaths of the war.[66] The attack was personally difficult for many negotiation delegation members, as among the killed were two FARC members who had previously participated in the negotiations.[67]

The political leadership decided to engage in a formal de-escalation process in July 2015 against the backdrop of a strong decrease in public support for the talks. Although on the government side, the order was only to suspend air strikes, the fighting came almost to a halt. Amid a feeling that the end of the armed conflict was near, mid- and low-level commanders sought to avoid confrontations with the FARC, as no one wanted to be the last victim of the armed conflict.

Following the 12 July 2015 agreement, the concern of the government—and particularly the military leadership—that a lack of military pressure would slow the negotiations did not materialize. The parties had already agreed on the main parameters of agreement and put all their eggs in one (and the same) basket. If anything, the calm in the battlefield facilitated the process of negotiating the end of conflict item, with parties now able to fully focus on the technical details of the deal—an almost textbook example of a positive reinforcement feedback between ceasefire and political negotiation processes, even if no bilateral ceasefire was in place.

From the beginning of the negotiations, the government had insisted that some form of popular endorsement was needed to legitimize the agreement.

Once the peace agreement was finalized, the government was fully convinced that it would gain popular support. However, the opposition ran a campaign full of trickery to convince people to vote against the agreement. At the same time, President Santos refused to have a contingency plan in case of rejection, believing that this would send a signal of noncommitment. This posed a significant challenge in the aftermath of the defeated plebiscite.

The result of the plebiscite vote was a very hard blow to all those who believed in the process, but it was especially difficult for the members of the Monitoring and Verification Mechanism of the security forces who were already collaborating with members of the FARC. The day after the plebiscite, you could see sadness and concern in the faces of many members of both the government and the FARC, mainly because of the latent possibility of having to fight against each other once again.

Both sides quickly sought options to save the agreement. The president announced that he would call all political forces to adjust the agreement—a process that lasted a month until a new final agreement was reached. For some people, the revised agreement had introduced some specific improvements. For others, however, the government's decision to go ahead with the (slightly altered) peace agreement by ratifying it in Congress felt like a "betrayal of the will of the people."[68]

The rest of the implementation of the bilateral and definitive ceasefire agreement started when Congress ratified the revised peace agreement. From the government's perspective, the relocation of FARC members and decommissioning was a major success. Particularly to members of the Subcommittee on the End of Conflict, it confirmed that the drawn-out process of going over each detail of the definitive ceasefire had been worth the effort, as there were little ambiguities during the process.

FARC PERSPECTIVE

Readers should note that the FARC perspective presented in this section is partly based on an in-depth interview with Julián Gallo Cubillos (also known as Carlos Antonio Lozada), a former member of the FARC secretariat, negotiator in the peace process, and, since 2018, senator for the FARC party (today called "Partido Comunes").[69]

The FARC had participated in a series of peace negotiations since the 1980s. In their view, war was not an objective but a means to achieve changes in Colombian society. Hence, they claim to have always heeded the calls of the government to enter negotiations, precisely to push for deep-seated reforms.

Compared to the previous Caguán process between 1998 and 2002, the Havana process was marked by a very different context. In the FARC's reading, even though the two parties to the conflict met to negotiate in the Caguán process, there was an expectation on both sides to tip the military balance in one's favor. According to the FARC, the government of Andrés Pastrana had already decided to pursue a military victory, whereas the FARC itself was at the peak level of its military development. This setup ultimately led to the failure of the process.

After 2002, the government side gained momentum supported by US military help under Plan Colombia. However, the new government strategy lost steam toward the end of the Uribe government,[70] as the FARC learned how to adapt to the technological and military advantage of the government side and strategically reoriented its struggle to irregular activities in 2008. Even so, the FARC had to expend an enormous amount of energy in their resistance to the superiority of government forces. By 2010, both sides were thus fatigued by years of intense confrontation, setting the stage for a new negotiation process under the government of Juan Manuel Santos.

One could say that, while both parties joined the Caguán negotiations convinced that they would eventually reach a military triumph, both participated in the Havana negotiations convinced that they would be *incapable* of achieving victory on the battlefield. According to the FARC, they could have continued the struggle and may have eventually turned the military momentum to their side, but seeking a political solution was the preferred alternative in this context. They also noted that public opinion did not favor continuing the conflict at that time.

The FARC not only were well aware of their own preference for negotiations but also had a clear understanding of the opposing side in the run-up to the Havana negotiations. "When they said that they were close to defeating us, *we knew that they knew* that this wasn't true." They had also noted a reduced impetus of government forces on the battlefield because of fatigue. Military operations were undertaken more frequently with the aim to establish a presence rather than to enter in direct confrontation. Hence, from a FARC perspective, the conditions for negotiations were present on both sides.

Bilateral Ceasefire and Unilateral Cessation of Hostilities

In all negotiations, the FARC wanted to establish a bilateral ceasefire at the outset. A bilateral ceasefire would show the "benefits of peace" to the wider public, which was very important for the FARC as Marxist insurgency, given that they intended to gain the support of the broader population. In their view, a bilateral ceasefire would have opened a space for civil society, reduced the impact of conflict violence, and generally created a different environment for the talks. Hence, the government's condition of "talking while fighting" was clearly against the preference of the FARC leadership. While this condition was hard to swallow, the FARC saw no alternative to accepting it in the case of the Havana negotiations. Behind the government's veto to a bilateral ceasefire, they saw the opponents of the peace process, "extreme right-wing political sectors and the high military command," who think that the FARC only wants to use bilateral ceasefires as "perverse incentive"[71] to gain military advantage. With the benefit of hindsight and a successful peace agreement, they still believe that an early bilateral ceasefire would have been the right course of action.

In the absence of a bilateral ceasefire, the FARC ordered their troops a temporally limited unilateral cessation of hostilities on several occasions, including during Christmas holidays and national elections. When announcing the first such arrangement, they stated that "this political decision of the FARC represents a resolute contribution to strengthening the climate of understanding necessary to the parties who initiate the dialogue, so that they can achieve the desired outcome for all Colombians."[72] The FARC recognized that, beyond the agenda points and the military balance on the battlefield, public opinion was a decisive factor to tip the balance in one's favor. Hence, they wanted to demonstrate their commitment to a peaceful resolution and show the benefits of peace to a broader public even in the absence of a bilateral ceasefire.

The decisions to cease hostilities were preceded by internal discussions to reach a consensus, which was very important to avoid tensions within the FARC. The hierarchical and disciplined organization of the FARC helped to comply with the announced cessations of hostilities. As part of their implementation strategy, FARC units moved into their heartlands, where they held territorial control, and adopted a defensive position. This approach, combined with not conducting offensive operations, helped them to actively evade confrontation with military forces. From a FARC view, this strategy implied enormous risks as it put the FARC in a less favorable position in terms of military confrontation. Hence, the FARC always perceived unilateral cessations of hostilities as a costly strategy.

The FARC therefore tried to reap the benefits of their achievements as much as they could. Once the first cessation of hostilities was over, they publicly announced, "Nobody with a head in the right place cannot recognize that during the last two months, the FARC has not realized one sole attack on bases and installations of the military forces, nor on police posts."[73] After stressing the continued violence by the armed forces, they further mentioned in the same statement that "the Colombian population and the international community are aware how the Colombian oligarchy responds to manifestations of peace by the people in this country."

Hence, the objective of the unilateral cessation of hostilities was to put pressure on the government side and to push public opinion to their side. Aware of the importance of the public debate, they believed that this would ultimately strengthen their position at the negotiating table. Moreover, showing commitment to their own cessations of hostilities provided them with an argument based on actual military behavior to continuously call the government for a bilateral ceasefire.[74]

Disarmament as Initial Stumbling Block

The negotiations between the FARC and the government experienced a series of crises. Some of these were directly related to battlefield activities in Colombia. However, from a FARC perspective, the moment that was most critical for the continuity of the talks actually came during the secret negotiation phase. While it was not related to anything happening on the battlefield, it was about the wider security arrangements that both sides envisioned, namely, the disarmament of FARC members. From the FARC's perspective, the initial government proposal consisted basically of "surrender and disarmament." This was completely unacceptable for the FARC, as they entered the negotiations to reach structural changes for the Colombian society and repeatedly stated that they were not defeated by the government forces.

The FARC had been reluctant to talk about disarmament in previous negotiation processes. In addition to concerns about perceptions of a defeat, the early disagreement about including disarmament in the negotiation agenda needs to be understood in the light of the government's longstanding policy to incentivize individual demobilization from among the ranks of the FARC. According to government sources, more than 19,000 members of the FARC deserted after 2002.[75] The FARC have long seen this policy and the implementing Colombian Agency for Reintegration (ACR in its Spanish acronym) as a "criminal" counterinsurgency strategy.[76] In fact, they are cited as telling the government to "not give us the model for deserters and traitors."[77]

According to the FARC, the peace negotiations only continued thanks to the facilitation of Cuba and Norway. The agreement on agenda points that resulted from the secret negotiations presented a language that departed from the terminology hitherto used by the government. Instead of "reintegration," it used the term "reincorporation," and instead of "disarmament," it used the term "laying down of arms" (*dejación de armas*). While these seem to be minor semantic points, they refer to deeper disagreements. The broader question was whether the FARC was going to surrender to the government or seek an agreement as an equal negotiation partner.

Eventually, the laying down of arms took place at the very end of the process, after the ratification of the peace agreement. The agency in charge of ex-combatants was renamed as the Agency for the Reincorporation and Normalization (ARN). Moreover, to avoid any impression of surrender to the government, the FARC prohibited any pictures of combatants surrendering their weapons, which were delivered to UN representatives.[78] Hence, the two sides overcame initial difficulties by finding a common language and postponing the details of "disarmament" to the end of the negotiations.

Battlefield Dynamics and De-escalation

Despite the agreement that the two sides would not discuss battlefield dynamics at the negotiation table, a series of military events interfered with the negotiations. From the FARC's perspective, the most notable of these were the killing of FARC leader Alfonso Cano in 2011, when the two sides were assessing the ground for negotiations, the confusing retention (the media used the term kidnapping) of a military general by the FARC in Chocó in 2014, and a series of military strikes on both sides. Perhaps the most consequential sequence of military events occurred in Cauca in April 2015. It had a direct and eventually positive impact on the course of the negotiations.

At the time of the attack, a FARC ceasefire had been in place for several months. While previous unilateral ceasefires by the FARC had been temporally limited, in December 2014, following the public outcry after the retention of the military general, the FARC had declared a cessation of hostilities for an indefinite period. It repeatedly called on the government to cease its military offensive, arguing that "if the government really wants to get to the signing of a Final Agreement, its deeds should be consistent with the discourse of peace."[79] FARC leaders also repeatedly warned that the truce was "under siege,"[80] highlighting the difficulties of implementing a unilateral cessation of hostilities while government offensives were ongoing.

The cessation of air strikes in early March 2015 brought some much-needed respite to the FARC, but the group questioned the credibility of this move, as other offensive measures continued.[81] So while it may have been an important gesture, the government's cessation of air strikes appeared to be "too little, too late" to maintain the calm in the battlefield.[82]

The FARC attack that triggered the collapse of the ceasefire took place on 14 April 2015 in the municipality of Buenos Aires, resulting in the death of eleven members of the armed forces. The FARC quickly declared that it was not in violation of their own protocols as it was a defensive act.[83] However, the Santos government reinstated the use of aerial bombings on 15 April, which later led to a major air strike on 22 May when twenty-six guerrilla combatants were killed, which is when the FARC reciprocated and ended its unilateral cessation of hostilities. Hence, these battlefield events quickly escalated and threatened the negotiations.

However, the effect on political negotiations was limited. According to the FARC, this was largely thanks to the presence of high representatives of the armed forces in the Subcommittee on the End of Conflict. After the first attack against the armed forces, the FARC did not receive one complaint from the side of the officials at the table. In fact, it was the initiative of the FARC to express their pain for the loss of soldiers. They felt that there was understanding on both sides, and the same happened after the bomb strike against FARC combatants. The FARC felt that everybody was aware that these situations could happen and followed the implicit rule of not complaining about war acts. In their view, this understanding in the face of tragic battlefield events was rooted in the common language of warriors, who looked at it from a *logic of war* rather than a *logic of politics*. This explains why the FARC deemed it crucial for high-ranking members of the armed forces to be present in Havana.

In an unexpected turn of events, this episode created a sense of urgency to advance political negotiations. The government and the FARC agreed on a plan to "expedite in Havana and de-escalate in Colombia" on 12 July 2015. Also, they started with humanitarian demining, as one activity that could be put in place by both sides together and demonstrate the benefits of cooperation. While this episode thus marks one of the lowest points of the negotiations and could have led to its failure, the negotiations actually received a new impetus. However, in the FARC's view, without the presence of government negotiators with real battlefield experience, the negotiations could have ended there. Instead, from July 2015 onward, with a new cessation of hostilities by the FARC and the promise to de-escalate by the government, a de facto bilateral ceasefire was suddenly in place.

After this episode, there was a sense that an agreement was just a question of time. However, timing was a controversial issue during the negotiations. President Santos initially asked for an agreement "within months and not years."[84] While the government was mainly interested in demobilizing the FARC, the times of the FARC were much more extended as they wanted to achieve deep reforms to change Colombian society and were therefore against what they called an "express peace."[85] This inconsistency in timing was less pronounced toward the end of the negotiations, when the FARC was also interested to reach an agreement, including a bilateral ceasefire.

After the peace agreement was signed, the upcoming congressional and presidential elections provided an incentive for the FARC to lay down weapons quickly, as they were only allowed to campaign in these elections once they had completed this process.[86] At the same time, there were some trust issues that the FARC had to overcome. While many within the FARC leadership had established some trust in their military counterparts on the government side during the negotiation process, particularly during the lengthy negotiation of the definitive ceasefire, the same was not true for mid-level commanders and rank-and-file soldiers. In the absence of a preliminary bilateral ceasefire, which often provides an opportunity to build trust between opposing forces,[87] most ordinary FARC members could not experience or test the commitment of the government forces during the negotiation process.[88] The UN involvement in the tripartite monitoring verification mechanism and the smooth implementation of the process of laying down arms helped overcome some of these barriers.

However, even after FARC combatants collectively transitioned from an armed group to civilian life, doubts about the future of the agreement remain among the FARC leadership. Although they trusted their military counterparts during negotiations, they still do not trust politicians. They view changes to the final agreement and noncompliance with some provisions as proof of the inherent bad faith of the political class. However, their hope is that the agreement will help to mobilize the Colombian society and ultimately transform Colombian politics. In this sense, the FARC have not given up on their objectives but changed their method for achieving it.[89]

CONCLUSION

Colombia did not follow the classical sequence of many peace negotiations, as the conflict parties negotiated in the absence of a bilateral preliminary ceasefire. It also defied another common pattern: while it is often the nonstate actor that refuses to enter into a bilateral ceasefire and the state actor that pushes for one, it was precisely the opposite in the case of Colombia. The government was clear from the beginning that it would not stop military operations during negotiations, viewing a bilateral ceasefire as an outcome rather than a precondition of the negotiation process. The FARC accepted the "talking while fighting" principle reluctantly but continued to raise the issue of a bilateral ceasefire throughout the talks.

Two main factors shaped this sequencing strategy: the experiences of past peace processes, in which the FARC was perceived to have benefited from a cessation in fighting, and the military balance between the two actors, as the ongoing fighting was favoring the government rather than the FARC.

The negotiated sequencing strategy was eventually successful: after more than four years of peace negotiations, the two parties to the conflict agreed on a comprehensive peace agreement. From the government's perspective, maintaining the military pressure on the FARC—by delinking the ceasefire from the political negotiation process—was key to this success. From the FARC's perspective, it would have been preferable to agree earlier to a bilateral ceasefire to avoid unnecessary loss of life, facilitate the negotiation process, and build trust before the phase of laying down arms.

Yet, while Colombia is often portrayed as a case without a ceasefire, the analysis in this chapter shows there were indeed multiple ceasefires—just not in the sequence and format that we might expect from other cases. The FARC engaged in several cessations of hostilities that evolved from time-limited arrangements to indefinite ones in the second half of the process. The government—despite advice from the military and outrage by the opposition camp—suspended its air strikes twice. Especially toward the end of the negotiations, when there was a general feeling that a peace agreement was near, these measures were sufficient to end the violence. This ceasefire process positively reinforced the political negotiation process: the calm on the battlefield facilitated the conclusion of the agreement and helped keep the process on track, even when the agreement was rejected in a public plebiscite vote.

Additional measures were taken to replace the functions normally offered by a preliminary ceasefire. The military's involvement in the negotiations, particularly in the technical subcommittee tasked with negotiating the definitive ceasefire, allowed the leaderships of both the armed forces and FARC represented in the subcommittee to establish working relations and a shared sense of trust in each other's commitment to end the conflict. One might argue that at the level of rank-and-file soldiers, the functions of a preliminary ceasefire were only fulfilled *after* the peace agreement was reached—that is, with the relatively smooth implementation of the definitive ceasefire. This raises some questions as to what degree the "Colombian model" is replicable in cases where the nonstate actor does not have the same strong hierarchical structure as the FARC.

Despite the overall success, the late end to the violence came with some important challenges: on the government's side, there was a disconnect between what happened in Cuba and in Colombia, which at times undermined public support for the negotiations. Continued hostilities and the images of dead soldiers provided fuel for the opposition camp to mobilize against the government strategy in the negotiations. And while unilateral arrangements by the FARC brought some calm and helped change the discourse, it proved difficult for the FARC leadership to maintain these arrangements as long as government offensives continued.

The way in which the government and the FARC managed to overcome these challenges—including efforts on both sides to unilaterally address conflict violence despite internal skepticism—is a testament to their commitment to find a negotiated settlement. The Colombian case provides a specific example of how conflict parties may shift their conflict behavior to create space for a negotiated settlement, even when a preliminary ceasefire is not an option. Yet, it also reveals that, ultimately, conflict parties must transition to negotiations without fighting to achieve a durable peace agreement, even if they initially chose to separate battlefield events from political negotiations.

NOTES

The government perspective on this chapter solely and exclusively expresses the arguments and personal opinions of the authors and in no way represents the official position of the Armed Forces, the National Defence Ministry, or the Government of the Republic of Colombia.

1. Fuerzas Armadas Revolucionarias de Colombia—Ejército del Pueblo (FARC-EP). We use the short version of their acronym.
2. CNMH, *¡Basta Ya! Colombia: Memoria de Guerra y Dignidad*; Medina, *FARC-EP. Temas y Problemas Nacionales 1958–2008*.
3. Pizarro, *Una Democracia Asediada: Balance y Perspectivas Del Conflicto Armado En Colombia*.
4. ELN: Ejército de Liberación Nacional—National Liberation Army (exists until today); EPL: Ejército Popular de Liberación—Popular Army of Liberation (demobilized in 1991, dissident group exists until today); M-19: Movimiento 19 de Abril—19th of April Movement (demobilized in 1990).
5. Gutiérrez Sanín, *Clientelistic Warfare: Paramilitaries and the State in Colombia*.

6. See Chernick, "Negotiated Settlement to Armed Conflict"; Posso, "Negotiations with the FARC: 1982–2002."

7. ICG, "The Day after Tomorrow," 6; Posso, "Negotiations with the FARC: 1982–2002," 48.

8. Posso, "Negotiations with the FARC: 1982–2002," 48.

9. See Rabasa and Chalk, *Colombian Labyrinth. The Synergy of Drugs and Insurgency and Its Implications for Regional Stability*; Posso, "Negotiations with the FARC: 1982–2002."

10. Tate, *Drugs, Thugs, and Diplomats*.

11. Council on Foreign Relations, "1903–2022. U.S. Colombia Relations."

12. Tate, *Drugs, Thugs, and Diplomats*; Schirmer, "To End the War in Colombia," 203.

13. Council on Foreign Relations, "1903–2022. U.S. Colombia Relations."

14. Nussio and Ugarriza, "Why Rebels Stop Fighting. Organizational Decline and Exit from Colombia's Insurgency."

15. Cortés and Millán Hernández, "The Role of the Armed Forces in the Colombian Peace Process," 3.

16. Battle-related deaths are from the UCDP Georeferenced Events Dataset. Figure adapted from Sticher, "Ceasefires as Bargaining Instruments in Intrastate Conflicts: Ceasefire Objectives and Their Effects on Peace Negotiations," 64.

17. See Segura and Mechoulan, "Made in Havana: How Colombia and the FARC Decided to End the War," 10.

18. OACP, *Biblioteca Del Proceso de Paz Con Las FARC*, 1:65.

19. See Segura and Mechoulan, "Made in Havana: How Colombia and the FARC Decided to End the War," 10–12.

20. Forero, "Colombia's FARC Rebels Say They'll Stop Kidnapping."

21. Daugherty, "'FARC Has Suffered 2 Historic Blows': Santos"; Jaramillo, interview about the use of battlefield violence in the context of the Colombian peace negotiations. Conducted by Valerie Sticher in Zurich (Switzerland) on 24 June 2019.

22. Neuman and Gonzales, "Colombian Rebels Free 10, Raising Hopes of Peace Talks With Government."

23. The substantive agenda items were land reform, political participation, the end of the conflict, illicit drugs, and victims. The procedural agenda item included implementation, verification, and ratification.

24. In Spanish, the term *cese de hostilidades* is sometimes used to specifically refer to a suspension of hostilities against civilians.

25. ICG, "CrisisWatch. Colombia, January 2013."

26. ICG, "CrisisWatch. Colombia, January 2014."

27. Högbladh, "UCDP GED Codebook Version 19.1"; Sundberg and Melander, "Introducing the UCDP Georeferenced Event Dataset."

28. See IFIT, "The Colombian Peace Talks: Practical Lessons for Negotiators Worldwide," 7, 17–19; Jaramillo, "The Possibility of Peace."

29. "Joint Communique # 42."

30. FARC-EP, "Unilateral Cease-Fire for an Indefinite Period: FARC-EP."

31. GALLUP, "Gallup Poll #115 Colombia," 103.

32. ICG, "On Thinner Ice."

33. FARC-EP and Government of Colombia, "Expedite in Havana and De-Escalate in Colombia."

34. The central purpose of the individual voluntary demobilization policy was to dismantle the guerrillas. Through these programs, between 2002 and 2015, 25,193 guerrilla members had laid down their weapons individually. Of those, 82 percent belonged to the FARC-EP. Hence, this was a strategic tool of the Colombian state to combat the FARC. See Nussio and Ugarriza, "Why Rebels Stop Fighting. Organizational Decline and Exit from Colombia's Insurgency."

35. Millán Hernández, "Connecting Practice and Research: What Can We Learn from the Colombian Ceasefire between the Government and the FARC (2016 to 2017)?" 28.

36. Note that while the end of conflict agreement was signed in June, the protocols were only ready on 5 August 2016.

37. "Terminar de manera definitiva las acciones ofensivas entre la Fuerza Pública y las FARC-EP," "Acuerdo Sobre Cese al Fuego y de Hostilidades, Bilateral y Definitivo y Dejación de Las Armas Entre El Gobierno Nacional y Las Farc-EP," 2.

38. Tripartite monitoring operations started formally on 7 November 2016. Mecanismo de Monitoreo y Verificación, "Informe de Cierre de Actividades Del Mecanismo de Monitoreo y Verificación," 2.

39. The official name for those zones is Zonas Veredales Transitorias de Normalización, or Transitional Veredal Zones of Normalisation. Veredas correspond to rural areas within larger municipalities, similar to hamlets.

40. ICG, "In the Shadow of 'No.'"

41. IFIT, "The Colombian Peace Talks: Practical Lessons for Negotiators Worldwide," 25; Millán Hernández, "Connecting Practice and Research: What Can We Learn from the Colombian Ceasefire between the Government and the FARC (2016 to 2017)?" 35.

42. Mecanismo de Monitoreo y Verificación, "Informe de Cierre de Actividades Del Mecanismo de Monitoreo y Verificación," 4–5.

43. Barometer Initiative, Peace Accords Matrix, "State of Implementation of the Colombia Peace Agreement," 36.

44. Barometer Initiative, Peace Accords Matrix, "State of Implementation of the Colombia Peace Agreement"; Mecanismo de Monitoreo y Verificación, "Informe de Cierre de Actividades Del Mecanismo de Monitoreo y Verificación"; Millán Hernández, "Connecting Practice and Research: What Can We Learn from the Colombian Ceasefire between the Government and the FARC (2016 to 2017)?"

45. Von Mittelstaedt and Zuber, "'Waging War Is More Popular Than Negotiating'. SPIEGEL Interview with Colombian President Juan Manuel Santos."

46. Segura and Mechoulan, "Made in Havana: How Colombia and the FARC Decided to End the War," 13.

47. Haspeslagh, "The Effect of Proscription on Pre-Negotiation: A Comparative Analysis of Making Peace with Colombia's FARC before and after 9/11," 130–32; Haspeslagh, "The 'Linguistic Ceasefire.'"

48. Haspeslagh, "The Effect of Proscription on Pre-Negotiation: A Comparative Analysis of Making Peace with Colombia's FARC before and after 9/11," 137–139.

49. Haspeslagh, "The Effect of Proscription on Pre-Negotiation: A Comparative Analysis of Making Peace with Colombia's FARC before and after 9/11"; Nussio, "Violencia, terrorismo y guerra de discursos. Dos décadas de amenazas a la seguridad vistas por los presidentes colombianos"; Canal and Aponte, "A Collaborative Peace," 12.

50. Haspeslagh, "The 'Linguistic Ceasefire.'"

51. Jaramillo, interview about the use of battlefield violence in the context of the Colombian peace negotiations. Conducted by Valerie Sticher in Zurich (Switzerland) on 24 June 2019.

52. Jaramillo, interview about the use of battlefield violence in the context of the Colombian peace negotiations. Conducted by Valerie Sticher in Zurich (Switzerland) on 24 June 2019.

53. Cooper, "Dag Nylander on Salmon Diplomacy."

54. Jaramillo, "The Possibility of Peace"; Jaramillo, interview about the use of battlefield violence in the context of the Colombian peace negotiations. Conducted by Valerie Sticher in Zurich (Switzerland) on 24 June 2019.

55. Jaramillo, interview about the use of battlefield violence in the context of the Colombian peace negotiations. Conducted by Valerie Sticher in Zurich (Switzerland) on 24 June 2019.

56. Von Mittelstaedt and Zuber, "'Waging War Is More Popular Than Negotiating'. SPIEGEL Interview with Colombian President Juan Manuel Santos," 1.

57. Tate, *Drugs, Thugs, and Diplomats*; Schirmer, "To End the War in Colombia."

58. Schirmer, "To End the War in Colombia," 230.

59. See Cortés and Millán Hernández, "The Role of the Armed Forces in the Colombian Peace Process," 5; IFIT, "The Colombian Peace Talks: Practical Lessons for Negotiators Worldwide," 6.

60. Jaramillo, "The Possibility of Peace," 4.

61. See Sticher, "War of Narratives: Elite Framing and Peace Negotiations."

62. Santos, "Tweet by @JuanManSantos: Mindefensa y Cdte Gral: Quiero Que Me Expliquen Por Qué BG Alzate Rompió Todos Los Protocolos de Seguridad y Estaba de Civil En Zona Roja."

63. Colombia Reports, "Timeline," sec. 2015.

64. Santos, "Tweet by @JuanManSantos: Lamento Muerte de Soldados En Cauca. Esta Es Precisamente La Guerra Que Queremos Terminar."

65. Jaramillo, interview about the use of battlefield violence in the context of the Colombian peace negotiations. Conducted by Valerie Sticher in Zurich (Switzerland) on 24 June 2019.

66. Santos, "Tweet by @JuanManSantos: Dejemos de Felicitarnos Por Las Muertes de La Guerra. Todos Somos Colombianos. Recordemos a Ghandi: 'Ojo Por Ojo y El Mundo Quedará Ciego.'"

67. Cooper, "Dag Nylander on Salmon Diplomacy."

68. Nussio, "The Colombian Trap: Another Partial Peace," 2.

69. The interview was conducted via videoconference by Enzo Nussio on 28 September 2021.

70. This interpretation is consistent with independent analysis by Granada, Restrepo, and Vargas, "El Agotamiento de La Política de Seguridad."

71. FARC public announcement, 4 September 2012.

72. FARC public announcement, 18 November 2012.

73. FARC public announcement, 20 January 2013.

74. See, for example, FARC public announcements from 9 June 2013 and 19 May 2014 before electoral ceasefires.

75. Nussio and Ugarriza, "Why Rebels Stop Fighting. Organizational Decline and Exit from Colombia's Insurgency."

76. FARC public announcement written by Timoleón Jiménez, 13 December 2013.

77. Bermúdez, *Los Debates de La Habana: Una Mirada Desde Adentro*, 143.

78. Bermúdez, *Los Debates de La Habana: Una Mirada Desde Adentro*, 148.

79. FARC public announcement, 11 January 2015.

80. FARC public announcement, 30 December 2014.

81. FARC public announcement, 14 March 2015.

82. ICG, "On Thinner Ice," 5.

83. "Colombia: FARC Aseguran Que Ataque a Batallón Fue Una Acción Defensiva."

84. Verdad Abierta, "La Hoja de Ruta Para Lograr La Paz."

85. FARC public announcement, 1 October 2012.

86. Jaramillo, "The Possibility of Peace," 7.

87. See Brickhill, "Mediating Security Arrangements."

88. An exception worth mentioning are the joint demining activities, in which both sides cooperated as part of a confidence-building mechanism.

89. While the bulk of the FARC members transitioned into civilian life, dissident organizations have emerged shortly after the implementation of the peace accord started.

CHAPTER 9

Syria, 2012–2018
Addressing Military and Political Issues
Together or Apart?

Carsten Wieland and Sara Hellmüller

It has been said that being a United Nations (UN) mediator on Syria is "the toughest job in the world."[1] Indeed, UN mediators have faced great challenges in addressing the armed conflict in Syria. Ongoing for more than a decade, it has become one of the worst humanitarian crises of the twenty-first century, with a staggering death toll. Ending this overwhelming human suffering has thus been on top of the UN's agenda. At the same time, the UN has also tried to mediate a political solution to the conflict. This chapter explores how the efforts to end the conflict violence and the efforts to address the incompatibility between the conflict parties interacted.

The chapter focuses on the time from 2012 to 2018 when the UN secretary-general subsequently appointed Lakhdar Brahimi and Staffan De Mistura as special envoys for Syria. In this period, the Syrian peace process oscillated between pre-prenegotiations and prenegotiations, but the parties arguably never arrived at the stage of formal negotiations, defined in the introduction to this book as a situation in which they "have agreed on the objective, structure, and content of the formal process."[2] In De Mistura's words, "there have been no substantive negotiations between the two parties."[3] Similarly, while de-escalation mechanisms, cessation of hostilities, and preliminary ceasefires were negotiated, there was no definitive ceasefire as all agreements to end violence were limited either in time or in geographical scope.[4]

The chapter provides two main insights. First, it shows that the sequence of ending violence and addressing the political issues is not linear. It is sometimes assumed and even expected by the parties that an end to violence needs to be negotiated before political talks can start. However, the case of Syria shows a more circular relationship defined as feedback loops in the introduction to this book. While the UN mediators used violence reduction measures as confidence-building measures (CBMs) to create a more propitious environment for talks on the political issues, they also used the political talks as a forum to discuss, among other things, a reduction of violence.

Second, the chapter shows the benefits and risks of addressing military and political issues in a process managed by one convener as compared to different conveners in parallel processes. In the case of Syria, while both issues were addressed in the same forum in the beginning (namely, in the UN-led mediation process), they were increasingly separated over time, with Russia, Turkey, and Iran opening an alternative track to address the conflict violence. The chapter outlines this development and shows its advantages and challenges. Separating the military from the political issues can allow for focused negotiations on ending the violence, and—if successful—provide much-needed relief to the thousands of people suffering. However, it can also prevent a coherent overall strategy and de-politicize ceasefire negotiations. In other words, it can lead to a situation where the reduction of violence is seen as an end in itself, without addressing the underlying political issues in terms of the incompatibility, thereby favoring a "victor's peace."

The chapter is based on several conversations with Carsten Wieland, who was senior advisor in both Lakhdar Brahimi's and Staffan De Mistura's teams and is a long-term expert on Syria. It also draws on an in-depth interview with Staffan De Mistura conducted on 21 July 2020. The chapter first introduces the conflict context and early attempts at settlement and then maps the interaction between efforts to address the conflict violence and efforts to address the incompatibility.

CONTEXT: ISSUES, ACTORS, AND PAST PEACEMAKING ATTEMPTS

Issues and Actors

The Syrian armed conflict has its origin in popular mass demonstrations against the government of President Bashar al-Assad in March 2011 in the course of the Arab Spring. The toppling of the authoritarian regimes in Tunisia, Egypt, and Libya made Syrian protestors lose their fear of the notorious intelligence system (*mukhabarat*). They hoped that, under those new circumstances, their calls for democracy, dignity, freedom, and better governance would be heard. However, Syrian government forces brutally repressed the initially peaceful protesters from various religious backgrounds who took to the streets, responding first with rifles and later also with tanks, heavy weapons, and air power. Not all army members were ready to use violence against unarmed civilians, however, and many of them deserted. Months into the uprising, they formed what became known as the Free Syrian Army (FSA), on 29 July 2011.[5] On the political side of the crystallizing opposition, the Syrian National Council established itself in exile in Istanbul, on 23 August 2011, and merged with other opposition groups into the broader Syrian National Coalition of Revolutionary and Opposition Forces (SOC), on 11 November 2012. The main incompatibility between the opposition and the government was (and still is) the future of President Bashar al-Assad and his family dynasty. While the opposition groups insisted on his ousting at the outset of the political process, they have transformed their demands into calls for a political transition and reforms over the years. Meanwhile, Assad remains unwilling to step down or even only engage in meaningful political reforms.

Regional and international actors are strongly divided over the future of the Syrian president. At the regional level, the conflict particularly puts rivals Iran and Saudi Arabia at loggerheads. Iran is a close ally of Assad because it strives for an Iran-controlled land bridge from Teheran to Beirut (the Shia Crescent) as a link to the anti-Israeli Hezbollah party and militia in Lebanon. Therefore, Iran needs to keep an obedient government in place in Damascus. In 2013, Iran put pressure on Hezbollah to proactively engage in the Syrian war, to support the struggling President Assad. Gradually, Iran itself became more directly involved, deploying its Revolutionary Guard Corps to Syria and founding various militias on the ground, providing arms and ammunition, and sending money and thereby strengthening its currency, finances, and economy.[6] In contrast, Saudi Arabia, Qatar, the United Arab Emirates (UAE), and other Arab countries supported armed opposition groups of different shades with military assistance and training. Turkey did the same from the north, mostly in sync with Qatar. Later on in 2017, Saudi Arabia and the UAE led their own regional confrontation with Qatar. It was then Qatar and Turkey who supported the more Islamist sections of the armed opposition in the north, while Saudi Arabia and the UAE backed more secular rebels in the south. Saudi Arabia and the UAE, however, gradually opted out of this military struggle and put their weight behind an exclusively political solution to the conflict, in particular through the UN in Geneva. The SOC continued to be hosted in Istanbul, while the broader formation of the Syrian Negotiation Committee (SNC) (who, in 2017, represented the negotiating delegation of a broad spectrum of groups at the UN process in Geneva, including the SOC, but also the so-called Cairo and Moscow Platforms) took up its headquarters and meeting facilities in Riyadh.

International actors are equally divided on the question of the future of President Bashar al-Assad. European states and the United States strongly aligned behind the opposition in the early days of the uprising. Mainly the United States, France, and the United Kingdom have provided military assistance to opposition groups. While none of them intervened directly on behalf of the opposition, the United States conducted retaliatory air strikes on government targets. China and Russia, in turn, are firmly on Assad's side. They strictly oppose any form of external intervention (except when being invited by the Syrian government, as they point out when referring to their own presence) as well as regime change. Most decisively, Russian forces intervened militarily on 30 September 2015, which started a process of ever rising asymmetry in which the Syrian government gradually reclaimed large parts of lost territory. The step-by-step intervention of Hezbollah, Iran, and finally Russia paved the way for a largely military solution to this conflict.

The above shows that the main incompatibility (i.e., whether the Assad regime and his security apparatus should remain in power or be dismantled) divided national, regional, and international actors. At the same time, the conflict became more complex over the years with a fragmentation of armed groups on the ground and subconflicts emerging between various actors. Radicalization through violence, systematic torture, and the collapse of state and social structures became the fertile breeding ground for the formation of Islamist groups and the spread of the Islamic State (IS) in Syria. These groups emerged outside the main conflict that was raging between the Assad regime and large parts of the Syrian population but fought out their own agendas, partly in more or less silent cooperation with Damascus. Equally at the margins of the original conflict and with the exclusive target of fighting Islamist terrorism, the "Global Coalition to Defeat Daesh/ISIS" was formed in September 2014. It comprises eighty-two countries, including the United States, France, and the United Kingdom, and started air strikes against IS targets in 2014. The additional goal of fighting terrorists blurred the lines between pro-opposition and pro-government regional and international alliances, since the rise of IS rendered Assad's departure less of an immediate priority to the US and European states. This was particularly accentuated after terrorist attacks in Paris in 2015, Brussels and Nice in 2016, and

Manchester in 2017, which made the IS threat perception spill into European territory. Assad strategically used this development by portraying himself as a factor of stability and a champion of "secularism" while presenting all opposition groups as Islamist terrorists nurturing a narrative that in his absence Syria would descend into radicalism, chaos, and statelessness.

The rise of IS also gave a prominent role to Kurdish forces in northeast Syria (mostly represented by the Party of Democratic Unity, PYD). They are linked to the Kurdistan Workers' Party (PKK) in Turkey. The PYD's military wing (People's Protection Units, YPG) allied with Assad at the outbreak of the upheaval, after which they were handed over the northeastern territories by the militarily overstretched Assad regime. Years later, the PYD-Kurds changed sides and shouldered up with the United States while profiling themselves as effective fighters against IS on the ground. The PYD's rising profile and strife for autonomy reinvigorated the long-standing Kurdish–Turkish conflict that emerged in addition to the purely Syrian one. It further blurred the distinction between pro-opposition and pro-government alliances and opened up new subconflicts on an already complex map of actors. Turkey and the United States both support the opposition, but the United States also supported the Syrian Defence Forces (SDF) mainly run by the PYD as a key actor in the fight against IS, while Turkey considers the PKK, and therefore also the PYD, terrorists. Thus, the Syrian crisis has been playing out at national, regional, and international levels and has metastasized into various subconflicts. This rendered peacemaking efforts even more complicated.

Early Peacemaking Efforts

Peacemaking efforts in Syria started in 2011, but they remained in a preprenegotiation phase as they were blocked by a mostly deadlocked UN Security Council (UNSC). In September 2011, the United States, France, and the United Kingdom (P3) had proposed a UNSC resolution to condemn the government's heavy repression of the largely peaceful demonstrations and threatened sanctions. Russia and China, who supported the Assad regime, vetoed the resolution. Many Western countries consequently put bilateral sanctions on the Syrian regime.[7] The League of Arab States (LAS) also approved sanctions and suspended Syria's membership in November 2011. In light of the UN's inaction, the LAS proposed two peace plans that favored regime change.[8] It sent an observer mission to Syria in December 2011, upon agreement with Assad. Nevertheless, violence continued, and the mission had to withdraw at the end of January 2012.

The P3 proposed another UNSC resolution at the beginning of 2012, but Russia and China vetoed it again on 4 February 2012.[9] In response to the vetoes, the UN General Assembly adopted a resolution that called for the appointment of a UN special envoy for Syria.[10] On 23 February 2012, the UN secretary-general appointed one of his predecessors, Kofi Annan, who started his term in March of the same year.[11] Kofi Annan presented a Six-Point Plan on 16 March 2012, calling on the government to collaborate with the envoy, as well as agree to a UN-supervised cessation of hostilities, withdraw heavy weapons from urban areas, and allow for the provision of humanitarian assistance. Annan's priority was to stop the violence through a ceasefire. Indeed, the Syrian government and the opposition agreed to a ceasefire on 12 April 2012. The UNSC subsequently authorized the deployment of thirty unarmed military observers to Syria in its resolution 2042 on 14 April 2012 and approved the creation of a rather toothless UN Supervision Mission in Syria (UNSMIS) in its Resolution 2043 on 21 April 2012.[12] Yet, the violence did not stop after the UNSMIS observer mission deployed, and it had to suspend its activities on 16 June 2012.

On the international level, in light of the failure of a ceasefire on the domestic front, Annan hosted the Geneva I conference, attempting to move beyond the pre-prenegotiation phase and to mount political pressure on the parties. He invited the so-called Action Group for Syria, which consisted of the most important regional and international players in Syria. The Action Group adopted the Geneva Communiqué on 30 June 2012, which called on all parties to the Syrian conflict to recommit to the Six-Point Plan, mapping out steps for a Syrian-led political process. The communiqué read in elaborate diplomatic language that a Transitional Governing Body (TGB) was to be formed in Syria with the "mutual consent" of the two parties. It was clear, however, that a consensual solution was far out of reach in this polarized conflict where the stronger party would need to give up power voluntarily. Indeed, Annan maintained that the communiqué was a "de facto agreement on Assad's departure," since the "agreement on political transition required an end to the system of government that currently existed in Syria, leading to full, free and fair elections."[13] The P3 tabled the Geneva Communiqué as part of a Chapter VII resolution with the threat of nonmilitary sanctions under article 41 of the UN Charter in case of noncompliance by the Syrian authorities.[14] Russia and China vetoed the resolution on 19 July 2012, fearing that the P3 could use the resolution to justify a military intervention akin to what had happened in Libya, where they lamented "the West's manipulation of the UNSC humanitarian resolution . . . for purposes of military intervention and regime change."[15] Cognizant of this concern and having great power unity as a priority, Annan would have accepted a Chapter VI resolution, but the P3 were convinced that Assad's leaving was a mere question of time and were thus little worried about keeping the peace process alive.[16] The vetoed UNSC resolution containing the Geneva Communiqué, however, broke the Annan-led mediation process and Annan announced his resignation on 2 August 2012.

EFFORTS TO ADDRESS THE CONFLICT VIOLENCE AND THE INCOMPATIBILITY

In the established context, Lakhdar Brahimi and Staffan De Mistura found a highly polarized national, regional, and international environment in which they needed to address both the conflict's rising violence as well as the incompatibility between the parties. The following analysis shows the close interaction between the negotiations on military and political issues, as well as the benefits and risks of separating them.

Lakhdar Brahimi: Aiming at Nationwide Ceasefires and Political Negotiations

The UN and the LAS appointed Lakhdar Brahimi as joint special representative for Syria on 17 August 2012, and he started his mission on 1 September 2012. His mandate encompassed addressing both the conflict violence as well as the incompatibility, as depicted in figure 9.1. He carefully sequenced the two, acknowledging their circular interaction.

As a potential first CBM, Brahimi proposed to the parties a four-day cessation of hostilities[17] marking Eid al-Adha from 25 to 29 October 2012. The UNSC backed the proposal and urged the parties to respect it.[18] However, while the violence initially seemed to calm down, clashes soon reoccurred throughout the country. Indeed, both parties had retained the right to retaliate in case of attacks. The cessation of hostilities, therefore, did not transform into a preliminary ceasefire (that is to say, an agreement to stop the violence). Trying to move beyond the pre-prenegotiation phase toward prenegotiations or even direct negotiations, Brahimi then engaged in intensive diplomatic consultations, reiterating calls to the parties to engage in talks based on the Geneva Communiqué of 30 June 2012. He convened meetings

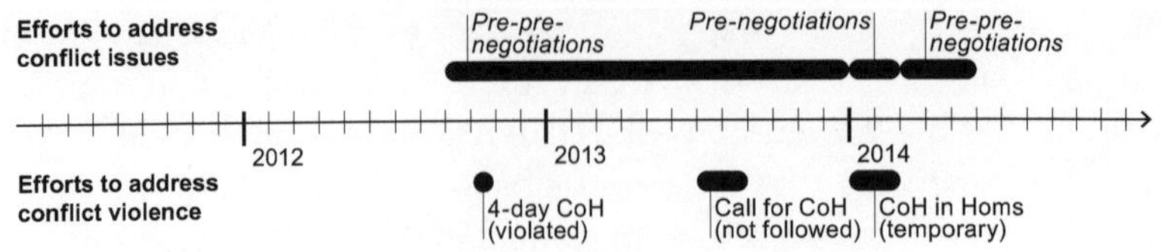

Figure 9.1 Summary of efforts during Lakhdar Brahimi's term

with the United States and Russia on 6 and 9 December 2012 as well as on 11 January 2013 to discuss options for a peace conference. Yet, a move toward prenegotiations was blocked over the government's unwillingness to engage. Assad refused to talk to Brahimi allegedly because Brahimi had suggested that Assad "hear the voices of the young people" and give power to a transitional government. He had asked in a closed-door briefing of the UNSC whether an appeal could be made to Assad "to voluntarily forego" the right to run in the upcoming elections.[19]

Developments at the international level unblocked the situation. With John Kerry's arrival as US secretary of state in February 2013, relations between the United States and Russia improved, with Kerry throwing "his full diplomatic energy into resuscitating talks."[20] When he met Putin on 7 May 2013, the two of them agreed on the importance of finding common ground, raising hopes for a new conference under UN auspices. Such a conference was intended to revive the peace process, which had stalled since the rejection of the Geneva Communiqué in the UNSC.[21] World leaders expressed their support for renewed talks at the G8 summit on 17–18 June 2013 in Northern Ireland.[22] The secretary-general welcomed this initiative, while Brahimi continued to organize discussions on how to implement the Geneva Communiqué.[23] Brahimi held two rounds of tripartite meetings with Russia and the United States on 5 and 25 June 2013, in order to prepare for a conference on Syria, to be held in Geneva.[24] In an attempt to strengthen this push to move toward prenegotiations with a reduction of violence, he also called for a cessation of hostilities during the month of Ramadan, from 8 July 2013 to 7 August 2013, but the parties did not follow the appeal.[25]

A decisive push toward a peace conference evolved after the government's use of sarin gas against civilians in the Damascus suburb of Ghouta, on 21 August 2013. After turbulent diplomatic efforts and Western military threats against Assad, this led to the adoption of UNSC Resolution 2118, on 27 September 2013, which required Syria to destroy its chemical weapons arsenal. In addition, it formally endorsed the Geneva Communiqué and officially called for an international conference.[26] To prepare for the conference that was to kick off UN-led negotiations between the Syrian parties, another set of trilateral meetings were held between the UN, the United States, and Russia. At the same time, the opposition met several times to form a credible delegation for the upcoming conference.[27] In the run-up to the conference, Brahimi, along with the secretary-general, also renewed appeals for unilateral CBMs by the parties, such as the release of prisoners, but the parties did not follow them.[28] In December, he announced the date of the international conference as 22 January 2014.[29] The conference started with a high-level opening in Montreux with all the important regional and international actors present, except for Iran. Brahimi had invited Iran but was forced to rescind the invitation as the United States opposed Iran's participation. The Syrian government and the opposition (the National Coalition of Syrian Revolutionary and Opposition Forces—SOC) were also present at the Montreux event.

Right after the Montreux Conference, direct talks with the two Syrian parties followed in the Palais des Nations in Geneva in two rounds, from 23 to 31 January 2014 and from 10 to 15 February 2014. The talks were a combination of face-to-face talks and bilateral meetings between the delegations and Brahimi and his team. It was the first time that the parties met since the beginning of the conflict in 2011.[30] They did not engage in negotiations, however, and remained at the level of prenegotiation, merely discussing ways to implement the Geneva Communiqué.

The reduction of violence was clearly also part of the agenda. The government agreed to a cessation of hostilities in Homs to let women and children leave the besieged city and allow access to humanitarian convoys. However, there was no agreement on a nationwide ceasefire.[31] At the end of the first round, Brahimi shared some points of commonality between the parties related to the acceptance of the Geneva Communiqué, as well as the acknowledgment of the need for a political process.[32] Yet, he also mentioned that "we haven't noticed any major change, to be honest, in the two sides' positions."[33]

This remained the case during the second round, which started with disagreements over the agenda of the talks and the sequence of issues, with the government wanting to talk about terrorism first (which in their eyes included their counterparts seated on the opposite side of the room) and the opposition wanting to discuss the TGB or, in their reading, Assad's departure.[34] In the last session, on 15 February, Brahimi suggested an agenda consisting of four points: violence and terrorism, TGB, national institutions, and national reconciliation and dialogue.[35] The government insisted on conditioning the sequence of the talks: terrorism first, and only when this issue would be resolved, a possible discussion of governance and transition. At the same time, it considered and publicly denounced the opposition figures in the SOC delegation as terrorists instead of negotiation partners.[36] This led to suspicion about the Syrian government's willingness to engage seriously in negotiations. Brahimi, therefore, did not announce another round but urged the parties to reflect on their commitment to the process.[37] In his press statements at the end of the talks, he said, "I am very, very sorry, and I apologize to the Syrian people that . . . on these two rounds we haven't helped them very much."[38] Another reason that brought the process to a quick collapse was of international nature. The revolution in Ukraine and the toppling of the pro-Russian government in Kyiv led to a diplomatic fall-out between the United States and Russia, the two main powers on which Brahimi had based his diplomatic efforts.

The political process had thus arrived at a standstill. Brahimi never convened a third round as the first two rounds had shown that the parties, particularly the Syrian government, were not willing to make any concessions and did not even agree on the agenda. US and Russian coordination had been instrumental in allowing the Geneva II conference to happen in the first place, but it was not enough to make the parties engage with serious intent. In a briefing to the UNSC on 13 March 2014, Brahimi mentioned that the Geneva process would end if the government organized "presidential elections" amid the ongoing war. On 28 March 2014, France proposed a draft press statement in the UNSC to support the resumption of talks, suggesting that real elections should be organized in the framework of the Geneva peace talks. In contrast, Russia objected to any language that referred to elections or to how the talks should be sequenced and refused to accept tackling terrorism in parallel with discussions on the transitional governing body.[39] The Homs cessation of hostilities agreement ended on 15 April 2014 when the government renewed attacks on the city. Brahimi announced his resignation on 13 May 2014 after Assad had publicized the date for state-run "elections," paving the way for his third seven-year term, ignoring any UN peace efforts.

During Brahimi's term, the process moved from pre-prenegotiations to prenegotiations as he managed to invite the parties to direct talks, but they collapsed. There were three attempts at cessations of hostilities, but these were limited in either time (during Eid al-Adha or Ramadan) or place (Homs), and none transformed into a preliminary ceasefire. The case shows the close interlinkage between the efforts to address the violence and the efforts to address the incompatibility. The strongest progress achieved on both aspects happened during the Geneva II talks with the political talks providing an arena for negotiations on the reduction of violence.

STAFFAN DE MISTURA: KEEPING THE POLITICAL PROCESS ALIVE

Staffan De Mistura became UN special envoy for Syria in September 2014. His term can be divided into two analytical phases (see figure 9.2). In the first phase from September 2014 to December 2016, he was formally in charge of mediating talks on both military and political issues. In a second phase from January 2017 to December 2018, he led the political process while Russia, Turkey, and Iran, on their own behalf, convened military talks on Syria in Astana.

Phase I: The Intra-Syrian Talks

Staffan De Mistura started with a different approach than his predecessor, seeing the failure of Geneva II as an indication that direct peace talks would make little sense given the parties' lack of willingness to negotiate on either a nationwide ceasefire or any political issues. He thus called for a reduction of violence from the bottom up, in the form of small clusters of so-called freezes of fighting that could eventually be linked to a nationwide ceasefire. His first initiative to negotiate such a freeze focused on Aleppo.[40] The Syrian government indicated a willingness to halt all aerial bombardment over Aleppo for a period of six weeks.[41] However, the freeze never happened. Fighting around Aleppo intensified when on 4 March 2015, the Syrian opposition allegedly attacked the government's Air Force Intelligence building. The government retaliated with barrel bombs, which was the prelude to a month of intensive fighting. The events showed that the government was not only unwilling to genuinely engage in a political process but also only feigning its willingness to stop the fighting, while the opposition forces withdrew from the agreement. The Aleppo freeze initiative was thus stillborn, and Ban Ki-moon asked De Mistura to relaunch the political process on 28 March 2015.[42]

De Mistura had to find an adequate approach to engage the parties on the political issues despite their lack of willingness. In this period of pre-prenegotiations, he opted for holding the so-called Geneva Consultations with a broad range of Syrian, as well as regional and international, stakeholders, on 5 May 2015, to explore options to reopen peace talks based on the Geneva Communiqué.[43] While this is the groundwork of any mediator and often happens without much public attention, De Mistura gave it an official label to suggest some advancement in the process. In the end, he announced

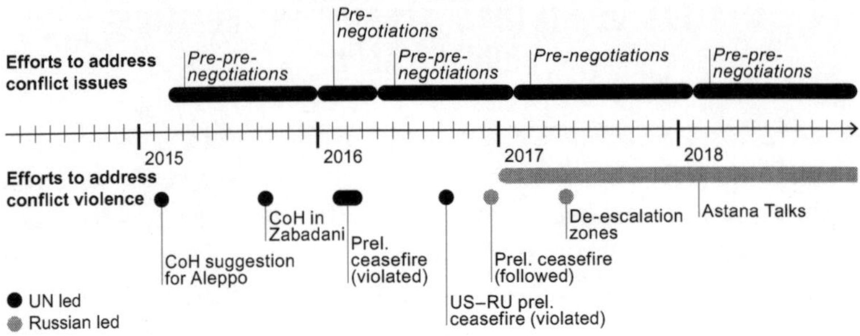

Figure 9.2 Summary of efforts during Staffan De Mistura's term

in a UNSC briefing on 29 July 2015 that he would facilitate Intra-Syrian Working Groups to generate a "Syrian-owned framework document" on how to implement the Geneva Communiqué. The idea was that four working groups would be set up on governance issues, constitutional processes, elections, and security and terrorism with specialized Syrian intellectuals and experts discussing these themes.[44] However, the working groups were never established, as the political process was soon to regain traction and allowed for a move toward prenegotiations in the form of political talks between the parties.

The political process regained traction after the signing of the Nuclear Deal (JCPoA) with Iran in the summer of 2015, which made it possible for the United States and Iran as an important stakeholder of the conflict to sit at one table. This led to a new dynamic, which merged into the Vienna Process at the end of 2015, a gathering of the main international and regional stakeholders of the Syrian conflict. It was the first time that Iran participated in such a forum on Syria. A first meeting in October 2015 led to an agreement on the need to revive the peace process. A second round of talks in November 2015 formed the International Syria Support Group (ISSG), which set January 2016 as a starting point for renewed formal negotiations between the Syrian government and the opposition under UN auspices. In light of this, the opposition met in Riyadh from 10 to 12 December 2015 to form a unified negotiation body and delegation. On 12 December 2015, they agreed to create the High Negotiation Committee (HNC), an umbrella delegation of thirty-four opposition groups. On 18 December 2015, the UNSC unanimously adopted Resolution 2254 calling for a "Syrian-led and Syrian-owned political transition based on the Geneva Communiqué." The resolution laid out a timetable for ending the war in Syria with UN-mediated political talks, a nationwide ceasefire, and a political transition. It thus clearly foresaw progress on both reducing the conflict violence by negotiating a preliminary ceasefire as well as addressing the contested political issues by moving beyond pre-prenegotiations. It looked, for a moment, as if there was finally a chance of achieving progress on both aspects in a coherent UN-led mediation process.

The talks officially started with the first round from 29 January 2016 to 3 February 2016. De Mistura opted for the term "talks" rather than negotiations, or Geneva III, to manage expectations. A heavy escalation of violence on the ground, however, overshadowed their onset, which in turn caused a controversy within the opposition about whether they should take part in the talks under those circumstances at all. After long bickering and some delay, they finally decided to take part. This became a recurrent pattern in subsequent rounds and, in more general terms, serves as a reminder of the circularity of events when seeking to end violence through political talks (as opposed to the idea that progress occurs in a linear sequence). As De Mistura said, "Most negotiations in conflict environments see a flare-up of the fighting prior to the negotiations. This is the hot negotiation approach to be in a better position when the discussions take place. It was sad and annoying, but not surprising."[45]

As a consequence of the escalated violence, chiefly in the form of barrel bombs on civilian and medical targets and air power against opposition areas from the regime side, the ISSG met in Munich on the margins of the Munich Security Conference and agreed to create a humanitarian and ceasefire task force, to be co-chaired by Russia and the United States under UN auspices in Geneva. On 22 February, the United States and Russia, as co-chairs of the ISSG, agreed on a preliminary ceasefire to take effect one week later. The UNSC endorsed the preliminary ceasefire in its Resolution 2268, which was officially adopted on 26 February 2016, entering into force on 27 February 2016. While there was no mechanism to sanction breaches, the ceasefire was monitored by US and Russian military staff at the UN. They had direct hotlines with both sides in order to control the ceasefire. As De Mistura mentioned, "This was actually quite remarkable. They were monitoring any type of breaking the ceasefire in order to be able to address it and to control it."[46] It was a moment of high hope among the Syrian population and external observers.

Against the background of the first (and last) successful nationwide ceasefire, Staffan De Mistura invited the conflict parties to a second round of talks from 14 to 24 March 2016. The arms had remained largely silent up to this point.[47] At the end of this round of talks, the special envoy published a document with what he called the envoy's "12 Living Essential Intra-Syrian

Principles" that he identified as a common basis for the Syrian parties to continue the negotiations.[48] The special envoy classified it as an important step to creating a common understanding of principles and expressed his hope that the next round of talks could see substantial discussions on political issues.[49] The third round of Intra-Syrian Talks followed swiftly, with the parties back in Geneva from 13 to 27 April 2016. The special envoy had set the political transition as an agenda item with the objective to help the parties find common ground. Given the lack of progress from the parties' side, he published a mediator's summary underlining three main points: the need for a political transition; a credible and inclusive transitional governance mechanism, including members of the government, opposition, independents, and others; and a new constitution.[50] However, this round was marred by escalating violence on the ground, with the nationwide ceasefire coming under severe strain and eventually breaking down. As the special envoy himself put it, "In the last 48 hours, we have had an average of one Syrian killed every 25 minutes. One Syrian wounded every 13 minutes."[51] The round ended with the opposition walking out of the talks due to the heavy violence and lack of progress on humanitarian access. This was followed by several months of blockage of any movement on political or military talks in the framework of the UN.

With the UN-led talks at a standstill, the outgoing US administration of President Obama was engaged with Russia in hammering out a comprehensive deal to include a lasting ceasefire and a common fight against Islamist Al-Nusra in Syria. This might have been a game-changer in the political process. Members of the ISSG met in Vienna from 9 to 10 September 2016. The United States and Russia reached an agreement to establish a ceasefire with effect on 12 September 2016. Moreover, the additional deal about the common fight against Al-Nusra was almost complete, with the situation looking highly promising. The Syrian government, however, ended the ceasefire on 17 September 2016 after US-led coalition air strikes on government targets. The United States admitted the air strikes but underlined that they had been accidental and were aimed at IS targets. The Russian and Syrian governments retaliated with a fatal attack on a UN aid convoy near Aleppo, which they also claimed to be accidental. The United States declared the suspension of diplomatic contacts with Russia, which ended the ceasefire deal. In a high-level international meeting on Syria, John Kerry called for a grounding of all aircraft to de-escalate the situation. However, tensions between the United States and Russia increased. At the same time, fighting intensified, particularly in Aleppo. In light of this, Staffan De Mistura proposed the "Aleppo initiative," which required a halt to the bombing and evacuation of Al-Nusra fighters from the city. However, Russia vetoed draft resolutions in the UNSC that would have demanded an end to military flights over Aleppo and a seven-day end to all attacks in the city. The bloody battle for Aleppo officially ended on 13 December. Syria's biggest city and commercial hub fell entirely into government hands. The UNSC unanimously adopted Resolution 2328 on 19 December 2016, allowing for evacuations from Aleppo. The fall or reconquest of the city definitively marked the asymmetric situation on the ground with the government winning the war militarily. It also showed the UN's powerlessness in the face of escalating violence. All this happened in a vacuum of the political process in Geneva, where no official meetings had been held for months since April.

In the time period from January to April 2016, the process had come closer to negotiations than ever before, strongly facilitated by the nation-wide ceasefire. De Mistura was formally in charge of both processes, but the ceasefire was negotiated by the United States and Russia in Munich (not by the parties in Geneva). This was the first indication that the two issues started to become increasingly separated before they were then addressed in entirely different forums in phase II.

Phase II: Parallel Tracks in Geneva and Astana

In light of the standstill of the UN-led political process, with the United States busy with a presidential change of extraordinary repercussions on the country's institutions, Russia increasingly took the lead on military issues. Together with Turkey, it brokered a nationwide ceasefire that was accepted by both parties, which came into effect on 30 December 2016. The UNSC backed the ceasefire in its Resolution 2336, adopted on 31 December 2016. Russia and Turkey invited the parties to talks in the Kazakh capital of Astana and thereby launched a new format outside the UN Geneva framework, the so-called Astana Process. From this time on, military and political negotiations were increasingly separate, with the former negotiated in Astana and the latter in Geneva, leading to the absence of a coherent overall strategy.

Addressing the Violence

The first round of talks in Astana was held from 23 to 24 January 2017 and was attended by the Syrian government, as well as Turkey-picked military figures from the armed opposition groups. They were not identical to the political opposition delegation in Geneva, while the Syrian government was present with basically the same delegates as in Geneva. The meeting was held under the auspices of Russia, Turkey, and Iran with the UN envoy invited as a guest. It took place despite breaches of the agreed-upon ceasefire, especially in Eastern Ghouta and Daraa countryside, and was focused on discussing ways to consolidate the ceasefire. The convening states agreed to set up a trilateral mechanism to monitor the ceasefire negotiated in December 2016 that would allow the Intra-Syrian Talks in Geneva to resume in February 2017. The Syrian parties, however, did not sign the agreement.[52]

After several rounds of talks in Astana, the three guarantor states changed their approach from a nationwide ceasefire to so-called de-escalation zones signing a memorandum to create four such zones in parts of the Idlib Governorate, the northern parts of the Homs Governorate, the Damascus suburb of Eastern Ghouta, and the Jordan–Syria border area, including Daraa. The agreement was to reduce fighting in these zones in order to allow for humanitarian access. It took effect on 6 May 2017. The UN qualified the agreement as a positive step in the right direction in the process of de-escalating the conflict.[53] The parties did not accept the agreement, however, and the talks were interrupted as the military opposition delegation walked out over intensified government bombardment on the ground. One month later, the Syrian Network for Human Rights, a UK-based war monitor, had already documented seventy-five violations of the agreement.[54] Shortly thereafter, Russia and the United States—along with Jordan—agreed on a ceasefire for the de-escalation zone in the southwest of Syria at the G20 summit in Hamburg on 7 July 2017. Moreover, on 16 July 2017, the guarantor states announced that they had found an agreement on the de-escalation zones and that Turkey would carry out monitoring in Idlib, and Russia and Iran would monitor the other zones.

This de-escalation approach heralded a fundamental shift in the course of the war. It had been carefully crafted by Russia and the Syrian regime to solidify the latter's military victory as it enabled it to gradually retake the territories monitored by Russia and Iran. The exception was Idlib, where Turkey's vital interests were at stake and which slowly became the last refuge of civilians, armed opposition groups, but also Al-Nusra fighters.

Addressing the Contested Political Issues

As it was haunted by a parallel format in Astana, the UN did everything to push the political process forward. Several rounds of Intra-Syrian Talks were convened between February 2017 and January 2018. During one of the rounds, De Mistura tried to make a step forward by presenting his updated version of the "12 Living Essential Intra-Syrian Principles" as a vision for a future for Syria without specifying the way toward it.[55] He shared them with the parties as a basis for further discussions, but no progress on any substance was made. At the same time, the team of the special envoy started a technical consultation process consisting of meetings with experts of the two sides (however mainly with the opposition groups) on constitutional and legal issues.[56] The stated goal was to deepen reflections on constitutional matters without replacing the other agenda items of the Intra-Syrian Talks. De Mistura rhetorically hinted at progress, but this stood in increasing contrast with reports by other sources[57] and the situation on the ground.

In light of the emerging military victory by the government, the opposition increasingly underlined the need for negotiations under UN auspices and thus tried to strengthen its representation in Geneva. The UN managed for the first time to invite different opposition groups—namely, the HNC, the Cairo Group, and the Moscow Group—to common technical talks in Geneva and Lausanne in the summer of 2017. Cooperation between those rivaling opposition groups gradually increased on constitutional matters and beyond. Building on this new dynamic from within the UN process, a few months later, in November, the three opposition groups, plus an increased number of independents, agreed to politically unite into one common Syrian Negotiation Committee (SNC) during the second Riyadh Conference. The Saudi government was instrumental in shaping this deal, which shifted the opposition toward more moderate and secular elements while more hardline factions, mostly supported by Qatar, were pushed out. HNC coordinator Riyad Hijab lost his position to Nasser Hariri from the SOC who subsequently led the SNC until June 2020. The SNC's headquarters became institutionalized with its own compound in Riyadh with an additional office in Geneva.

At this stage, with the key to reducing violence in Russia's hands, the UN gradually lost influence. Indeed, the interaction between the henceforth separate processes of addressing military and political issues led to a gradual loss of control by the UN over the trajectory of events.

The Interaction and Its Challenges

The UN had to position itself with regard to Astana. It had little other choice than deciding to treat the Astana format as a "compatible effort," while De Mistura underlined the strict difference in the purpose of the two processes:

Astana for military and Geneva for political issues. Thus, rhetorically, De Mistura always underlined complementarity. In a press briefing, for instance, he stated that "successful work in Astana on ceasefire, reinforces Geneva and vice versa," but in fact he had little room for maneuver.[58] For their part, Russia and Turkey in the driver's seat increasingly dealt with political issues in Astana. In the eighth round of Astana Talks from 21 to 22 December 2017, the guarantors created the Working Group on the release of detainees, the handover of corpses, and the identification of missing persons (hereafter the Working Group on Detainees) and confirmed their intention to hold a Congress of Syrian National Dialogue, the so-called Sochi National Congress.[59] The push for such a conference was a clear deviation from the division of labor between the formats in Astana (military) and Geneva (political). It put the UN in a tight spot, which held the ninth—and last—round of Intra-Syrian Talks (exceptionally in Vienna) from 25 to 26 January 2018, thus underlining that a political solution could only be reached under UN auspices.[60] The question of whether the UN would follow the Astana's trio invitation and participate in the Sochi National Congress was mainly a tug-of-war between the UN and Russia, as it meant that the UN legitimized the initiative. In the end, the UN decided to take part under the informally negotiated precondition that Sochi would result in a mandate to the UN to facilitate the establishment of a constitutional committee in the framework of the UN-led process in Geneva and not elsewhere.

The Sochi National Congress took place on 30 January 2018 and gathered up to 1,600 Syrian participants. The SNC and other opposition groups and individuals boycotted the Sochi Congress, leaving the event filled with almost only progovernment representatives. As previously agreed with the UN, the meeting ended with a declaration to "form a constitutional committee comprising the Government of the Syrian Arab Republic delegation along with wide-represented opposition delegation for drafting of a constitutional reform as a contribution to the political settlement under the UN auspices."[61] Yet, while Sochi officially gave the mandate to the UN to establish the constitutional committee, it gave Russia and Turkey decisive influence over its setup.

With a new political mandate, Staffan De Mistura held intensive consultations with both parties, as well as the three guarantor states in Sochi, to discuss the composition and terms of reference of the constitutional committee. However, these efforts happened against the backdrop of escalating violence, including in the so-called de-escalation zones.[62] Eastern Ghouta was especially subject to intensive fighting due to the Assad government's attempts to reconquest it. On 6 April 2018, fighting in Eastern Ghouta fully escalated, with sustained air strikes and shelling, the killing of civilians, destruction of civilian infrastructure, and attacks damaging several health facilities, alongside allegations of the use of chemical weapons in Douma on 7 April 2018.[63] The UN special envoy gave a briefing in an emergency meeting to the UNSC on 9 April 2018, urging the international community to act.[64] The events triggered air strikes by the United States, United Kingdom, and France on 13 April 2018 that targeted the Syrian government's chemical weapons capabilities.[65]

With the crumbling of the de-escalation zones, the opposition had lost almost all of its territory to the regime. It no longer had any moral or political responsibility to shield the population under its control from military violence from the regime. As such, escalating violence became a less influential factor in jeopardizing the political process in Geneva. The opposition had nothing to lose anymore but rather banked on the political process in Geneva to keep up its political relevance and message. Against this background, it even accepted that the Intra-Syrian Talks had silently come to a standstill and were replaced by a narrower process to establish the constitutional committee, stripped of broader discussions about a political transition.

Eight months after the Sochi conference, on 18 September 2018, De Mistura announced the agreement on a formula for the setup of the Constitutional Committee: fifty delegates from the government, fifty from the opposition, and fifty from the so-called middle third, meaning Syrian experts, civil society, independents, tribal leaders, and women. From each delegation, fifteen members would be part of a smaller commission.[66] The UN was supposed to be responsible for the list of the middle third, which would have presented an opportunity to include bridge builders between the Syrian government and the opposition. However, the process stalled and became heavily politicized, as the government, along with Russia, significantly questioned this list and the mediating role of the UN.[67] Thus, the UN was increasingly downgraded to a facilitator. Turkey also exerted its influence in compiling the "UN's Middle Third" by presenting objections. However, in the end, the opposition and Turkey accepted the list and the way to move forward.[68] The government presented an alternative middle third list, but the UN refused it as it was not balanced according to its standards, and it risked ending up with a list of questionable quality and legitimacy. The process remained blocked until the end of the year when Staffan De Mistura resigned.[69] De Mistura handed over to his successor, Geir Pedersen, who eventually convened the first meeting of the constitutional committee in Geneva in October 2019. By frontloading constitutional issues only, the rest of the substantial items mentioned in UNSC Resolution 2254 and labeled "baskets" in the UN's mediation process (governance, elections, security) have remained parked since then.

CONCLUSION

UN mediation in Syria has faced tremendous challenges. The conflict parties have arguably never reached the phase of negotiations, and a nationwide ceasefire has only been held temporarily. While, at the time of writing, violence has de-escalated and the government has emerged as the military winner of the war, a political and sustainable solution has not yet been found.

This chapter has shown that efforts to address the conflict violence and efforts to address the incompatibility have not followed a linear model and mediators have tried various approaches to come up with entry points for a reduction of violence or political negotiations. Brahimi proposed cessations of hostilities (even if temporary) as CBMs to get the parties engaged in discussing the incompatibility. In parallel, he tried to bring the parties to the negotiation table where ending the violence was a main concern and discussion topic, as illustrated by the cessation of hostilities in Homs negotiated during the Geneva II talks. While he aimed at forging a nationwide ceasefire and hosting an official peace conference, De Mistura initially started with a bottom-up attempt of local freezes, alongside more informal consultations with key stakeholders. Both failed, however, due to the lack of willingness among the conflict parties.

This chapter has also illustrated the benefits and risks of separating the negotiations on military and political issues. In the case of Syria, the first trimester of 2016 saw a relatively coherent process under UN auspices marked by substantive progress with the Intra-Syrian Talks starting in Geneva, with the United States and Russia agreeing on a nationwide ceasefire in Munich. However, hopes for a lasting ceasefire and a comprehensive political transition quickly evaporated over the US–Russia fallout and the subsequent standstill of the UN-led process. This left space for Russia to take over. The political capital Russia gained by having helped the government win the war militarily conferred it with important influence in the realm of addressing not only the conflict violence but also the conflict issues, as illustrated by it holding the Sochi National Congress and influencing the setup of the constitutional committee. The UN kept the responsibility for overseeing the constitutional committee, but it was a highly downgraded version of a political process stripped of its more ambitious goals for a political transition. In this sense, holding the key to a reduction of the fighting became a bargaining chip in deciding on an agenda for political talks. This chapter has shown that while separating political from military issues can allow for focused negotiations on ending the violence, it can also lead to a situation where violence de-escalates and thus offers much important relief to suffering populations, but without addressing the underlying issues. Any political process accompanying such a scenario thereby runs the risk of further legitimizing a victor's peace.

NOTES

We thank Marie Lobjoy for her research assistance.

1. See Janine di Giovanni, "The Man with the Toughest Job in the World," *The Guardian*, 30 July 2015, https://www.theguardian.com/world/2015/jul/30/staffan-de-mistura -man-with-toughest-job-in-world-syria.

2. Please see introduction of this book for definitions of pre-prenegotiations, prenegotiations, formal negotiation phase, and implementation phase.

3. Interview with Staffan De Mistura, 21 July 2020.

4. Please see introduction of this book for definitions of de-escalation mechanisms, cessation of hostilities, preliminary ceasefires, and definitive ceasefires.

5. Opposition groups on the ground splintered over the years into a heterogeneous group of secular nationalist fighters (Crocker et al., "Why Is Mediation So Hard? The Case of Syria," 151).

6. The secretary-general of Hezbollah, Hassan Nasrallah, acknowledged Hezbollah's involvement in the fighting on the side of the Syrian government on 25 May 2013.

7. Gowan, "Kofi Annan, Syria and the Uses of Uncertainty in Mediation."

8. Arab League, Council Resolution 7438; see also Crocker et al., "Why Is Mediation So Hard? The Case of Syria," 143; Akpınar, "The Limits of Mediation in the Arab Spring: The Case of Syria," 2293–2294.

9. Hill, "Kofi Annan's Multilateral Strategy of Mediation and the Syrian Crisis: The Future of Peacemaking in a Multipolar World?" 449.

10. See Resolution A/RES/66/25, https://www.un.org/en/ga/search/view_doc.asp ?symbol=A/RES/66/253.

11. At the same time, seventy countries, including the P3, created the so-called Group of Friends of the Syrian People in a meeting on 24 February 2012. They recognized the political opposition as a legitimate representative of Syrians seeking peaceful change, urged the government to cease violence and allow humanitarian access, and agreed on additional sanctions, including travel bans, asset freezes, stopping oil purchases, decreasing diplomatic ties, and preventing arms shipment (Crocker et al., "Why Is Mediation So Hard? The Case of Syria," 143).

12. See UNSC Resolution 2042, 14 April 2012, http://unscr.com/en/resolutions/2042; UNSC Resolution 2043, 21 April 2012, http://unscr.com/en/resolutions/2043.

13. Hill, "Kofi Annan's Multilateral Strategy of Mediation and the Syrian Crisis: The Future of Peacemaking in a Multipolar World?" 463.

14. The draft resolution said that in case of noncompliance of the Syrian authorities, the UNSC "shall impose immediately measures under Article 41 of the UN Charter,"

https://www.securitycouncilreport.org/atf/cf/%7B65BFCF9B-6D27-4E9C-8CD3
-CF6E4FF96FF9%7D/Syria%20S2012%20538.pdf.

15. Hinnebusch and Zartman, "UN Mediation in the Syrian Crisis: From Kofi Annan to Lakhdar Brahimi," 12.

16. Hill, "Kofi Annan's Multilateral Strategy of Mediation and the Syrian Crisis: The Future of Peacemaking in a Multipolar World?"; see also Hinnebusch and Zartman, "UN Mediation in the Syrian Crisis: From Kofi Annan to Lakhdar Brahimi," 12.

17. Brahimi officially called it a ceasefire, but it did not foresee monitoring mechanisms or longer-term disarmament measures.

18. See UNSC Press Statement on Ceasefire in Syria, 24 October 2012, https://www.un
.org/press/en/2012/sc10800.doc.htm.

19. See "Syria Envoy Says Assad Can't Be Part of New Government," 9 January 2013, https://
www.reuters.com/article/us-syria-crisis-brahimi/syria-envoy-says-assad-cant-be-part
-of-new-government-idUSBRE90819Q20130109; "Syria Accuses U.N. Envoy Brahimi
of Interfering," 24 April 2013, https://www.reuters.com/article/us-syria-crisis-brahimi
/syria-accuses-u-n-envoy-brahimi-of-interfering-idUSBRE93N10O20130424.

20. Crocker et al., "Why Is Mediation So Hard? The Case of Syria," 152.

21. Allison, "Russia and Syria: Explaining Alignment with a Regime in Crisis," 822.

22. See "Briefing to the UNSC on the Situation in the Middle East," 25 June 2013, https://
unsco.unmissions.org/sites/default/files/scb_25_june_2013.pdf.

23. See "Briefing to the UNSC on the Situation in the Middle East," 22 May 2013, https://
unsco.unmissions.org/sites/default/files/security_council_briefing_22_may_2013
.pdf; "Briefing to the UNSC on the Situation in the Middle East," 25 June 2013.

24. See "Transcript of Press Conference by Joint Special Representative for Syria (JSRS)
Lakhdar Brahimi," 25 June 2013, https://www.un.org/sg/en/content/sg/note
-correspondents/2013-06-25/transcript-press-conference-joint-special-representative.

25. See "Briefing to the UNSC on the Situation in the Middle East," 23 July 2015, https://
unsco.unmissions.org/sites/default/files/middle_east_situation_23_july_2013.pdf.

26. See UNSC Resolution 2118, 27 September 2013, http://unscr.com/en/resolutions
/2118.

27. See "Transcript of Press Conference by Joint Special Representative for Syria (JSRS)
Lakhdar Brahimi," 5 November 2013, https://www.un.org/sg/en/content/sg/note
-correspondents/2013-11-05/transcript-press-conference-joint-special-representative.

28. See "Transcript of Press Conference by Joint Special Representative for Syria (JSRS)
Lakhdar Brahimi," 20 December 2013, https://www.un.org/sg/en/content/sg/note
-correspondents/2013-12-20/transcript-press-conference-joint-special-representative.

29. See "Transcript of Press Conference by Joint Special Representative for Syria (JSRS)
Lakhdar Brahimi," 20 December 2013, https://www.un.org/sg/en/content/sg/note
-correspondents/2013-12-20/transcript-press-conference-joint-special-representative.

30. See "Full Transcript of Press Conference by Joint Special Representative for Syria (JSRS)
Lakhdar Brahimi," 31 January 2014, https://www.onug.ch/80256EDD006B8954
/(httpAssets)/EFB4470D9E3A9ACDC1257C71005B8C6F/$file/31+jan+press+co
nf+tanscript+Brahimi.pdf.

31. See "Transcript of Press Conference by Joint Special Representative for Syria (JSRS)
Lakhdar Brahimi Geneva," 27 January 2014, https://reliefweb.int/report/syrian-arab
-republic/transcript-press-conference-joint-special-representative-syria-jsrs-0.

32. See "Full Transcript of Press Conference by Joint Special Representative for Syria (JSRS) Lakhdar Brahimi," 31 January 2014.

33. See "Transcript of Press Conference by Joint Special Representative for Syria (JSRS) Lakhdar Brahimi," 30 January 2014, https://reliefweb.int/report/syrian-arab-republic/transcript-press-conference-joint-special-representative-syria-jsrs-2.

34. See "Transcript of Press Conference by Joint Special Representative for Syria (JSRS) Lakhdar Brahimi," 11 February 2014, https://reliefweb.int/report/syrian-arab-republic/transcript-press-conference-joint-special-representative-syria-jsrs-3.

35. See "Transcript of Press Conference by Joint Special Representative for Syria (JSRS), Lakhdar Brahimi," 15 February 2014, https://reliefweb.int/report/syrian-arab-republic/transcript-press-conference-joint-special-representative-syria-jsrs-5.

36. See "Transcript of Press Conference by Joint Special Representative for Syria (JSRS), Lakhdar Brahimi," 15 February 2014, https://reliefweb.int/report/syrian-arab-republic/transcript-press-conference-joint-special-representative-syria-jsrs-5.

37. See "Transcript of Press Conference by Joint Special Representative for Syria (JSRS), Lakhdar Brahimi," 15 February 2014, https://reliefweb.int/report/syrian-arab-republic/transcript-press-conference-joint-special-representative-syria-jsrs-5.

38. See "Transcript of Press Conference by Joint Special Representative for Syria (JSRS), Lakhdar Brahimi," 15 February 2014, https://reliefweb.int/report/syrian-arab-republic/transcript-press-conference-joint-special-representative-syria-jsrs-5.

39. See Security Council Report "Chronology of Events," https://www.securitycouncilreport.org/chronology/syria.php.

40. See "Briefing to the Press Following Security Council Closed Consultations, UN Special Envoy for Syria Staffan de Mistura," 29 October 2014, https://www.un.org/undpa/en/node/183363.

41. See Security Council Report, "March 2015 Monthly Forecast Syria," https://www.securitycouncilreport.org/monthly-forecast/2015-03/syria_17.php.

42. See Security Council 7497th meeting, 29 July 2015, https://undocs.org/en/S/PV.7497.

43. See UN News, "UN Syria Envoy to Hold Consultations on Re-start of Peace Talks," https://news.un.org/en/story/2015/04/495932-un-syria-envoy-hold-consultations-re-start-peace-talks.

44. See Security Council 7497th meeting, 29 July 2015.

45. Interview with Staffan De Mistura, 21 July 2020.

46. Interview with Staffan De Mistura, 21 July 2020.

47. See "Note to Correspondents: Near Verbatim Transcript of Press Conference by UN Special Envoy for Syria Staffan De Mistura," 24 March 2016, https://www.un.org/sg/en/content/sg/note-correspondents/2016-03-24/note-correspondents-near-verbatim-transcript-press.

48. See "UN Special Envoy's Paper on Points of Commonalities," 24 March 2016, https://reliefweb.int/report/syrian-arab-republic/un-special-envoy-s-paper-points-commonalities-24-march-2016-enar.

49. See "Note to Correspondents: Near Verbatim Transcript of Press Conference by UN Special Envoy for Syria Staffan De Mistura," 24 March 2016.

50. See "Mediator's Summary of the 13–27 April Round of UN Facilitated Intra-Syrian Talks," 28 April 2016, https://reliefweb.int/report/syrian-arab-republic/mediators-summary-13-27-april-round-un-facilitated-intra-syrian-talks-28; "Transcript of Press

Remarks by Staffan De Mistura, UN Special Envoy for Syria," 27 April 2016, https://reliefweb.int/report/syrian-arab-republic/transcript-press-remarks-staffan-de-mistura-un-special-envoy-syria.

51. See "Transcript of Press Remarks by Staffan De Mistura, UN Special Envoy for Syria," 27 April 2016.

52. Russia also proposed a project of the Syrian Constitution and tabled a ready-made draft of a new Syrian constitution to the Syrian parties in Astana. This was one of the rare moments where the Syrian government and Syrian (military) opposition rejected a move unanimously. Both of them found it appalling that a foreign power would impose a constitution on Syrians.

53. Participants also discussed the creation of a working group on the exchange of detainees.

54. See Syrian Network for Human Rights, http://sn4hr.org/blog/2017/06/17/42532/.

55. See "Note to Correspondents: Statement on Behalf of the UN Special Envoy for Syria, Staffan De Mistura (scroll down for Arabic)," 1 December 2017, https://www.un.org/sg/en/content/sg/note-correspondents/2017-12-01/note-correspondents-statement-behalf-un-special-envoy.

56. See "Transcript of Press Conference by UN Special Envoy for Syria, Staffan De Mistura Conclusion of the 6th round of Intra-Syrian talks," 19 May 2017.

57. See "Geneva Talks: Syria Constitution Proposal on Hold," 18 May 2017, https://www.aljazeera.com/news/2017/05/syrian-opposition-voice-concern-transitional-phase-170518090125408.html.

58. See "Transcript of Press Stakeout by the United Nations Special Envoy for Syria, Staffan de Mistura—End of the Fifth Round of the Intra-Syrian Talks," 31 March 2017.

59. See "Syria Peace Talks End in Astana with Joint Statement," https://www.tasnimnews.com/en/news/2017/12/22/1608207/syria-peace-talks-end-in-astana-with-joint-statement.

60. See "Note to Correspondents: Statement of Special Envoy for Syria Staffan De Mistura at the Conclusion of the Special Round 9 Meeting of the UN-Convened Intra-Syrian Talks in Vienna," 26 January 2018, https://www.un.org/sg/en/content/sg/note-correspondents/2018-01-26/note-correspondents-statement-special-envoy-syria-staffan.

61. See "Final Statement of the Congress of the Syrian National Dialogue, Sochi," 30 January 2018, https://www.google.com/url?sa=t&rct=j&q=&esrc=s&source=web&cd=&ved=2ahUKEwjr2f33loPqAhXD86YKHbInDoEQFjAAegQIBRAB&url=https%3A%2F%2Fwww.peaceagreements.org%2Fmasterdocument%2F2114&usg=AOvVaw3G_JRwfriuJhCGkHolRMPe.

62. UNSC 8206th meeting, 16 March 2018, http://www.securitycouncilreport.org/atf/cf/%7B65BFCF9B-6D27-4E9C-8CD3-CF6E4FF96FF9%7D/s_pv_8206.pdf.

63. See "Statement Attributable to the Spokesman for the Secretary-General on the Situation in Douma, Syria," 8 April 2018, https://www.un.org/sg/en/content/sg/statement/2018-04-08/statement-attributable-spokesman-secretary-general-situation-douma.

64. UNSC 8225th meeting, 9 April 2018, http://www.securitycouncilreport.org/atf/cf/%7B65BFCF9B-6D27-4E9C-8CD3-CF6E4FF96FF9%7D/s_pv_8225.pdf.

65. See "Secretary-General's Briefing to the Security Council on Syria," 14 April 2018, https://www.un.org/sg/en/content/sg/statement/2018-04-14/secretary-generals-briefing-security-council-syria-delivered.

66. See "Briefing to the UN Security Council by the Special Envoy of the UN Secretary-General for Syria, Mr. Staffan De Mistura," 18 September 2018, https://reliefweb.int /report/syrian-arab-republic/briefing-un-security-council-special-envoy-un-secretary -general-syria-2.

67. See "Briefing to the UN Security Council by the Special Envoy of the UN Secretary-General for Syria, Mr. Staffan De Mistura," 18 September 2018.

68. See "Briefing to the UN Security Council by the Special Envoy of the UN Secretary-General for Syria, Mr. Staffan De Mistura," 18 September 2018.

69. See "Briefing to the Security Council by Staffan De Mistura, United Nations Special Envoy for Syria," 20 December 2018, https://reliefweb.int/report/syrian-arab-republic /briefing-security-council-staffan-de-mistura-united-nations-special.

CHAPTER 10

Myanmar, 1989–2020
Conflict Management Ceasefires

Anonymous, Cate Buchanan, and Govinda Clayton

Since gaining independence from the British in 1948, Myanmar has experienced decades of armed conflict. Following a fleeting period of democracy (1948–1958) and a military coup, Myanmar was subject to rule by a military regime for the next three decades. From the perspective of many of the ethnic communities, agreements to respect ethnic nationality autonomy in the postindependence era were largely ignored, and successive regimes failed to provide adequate services for citizens (e.g., health, education, social protection), particularly in ethnic nationality locations, which fueled conflict drivers. Ethnic Armed Organizations (EAOs), which had formed over successive decades, grew to oppose the Armed Forces of Myanmar (the military) pursuing forms of self-determination and the control of territory and resources. Across Myanmar, there are multiple EAOs of different sizes, orientations, histories, and identities.

For years, the military made few attempts to broker peace with the EAOs. This changed in 1988 when the "new" military regime began to adopt selective ceasefires as part of a broader conflict management and economic "development" strategy in Myanmar's borderlands. Between 1988 and 2007, the junta sought bilateral informal cessation of hostility agreements with more than forty EAOs.[1] These were so-called gentlemen's agreements, and the details varied across groups. Generally, these secret agreements granted EAOs some local autonomy and economic rents in exchange for the suspension of armed violence and the tacit acceptance of central Burmese authority.[2]

In the 2000s, following the breakdown of several ceasefires, the regime renegotiated a series of new bilateral ceasefires, under similar terms, albeit with more formal agreements and a broad commitment to future discussion of contested political issues. For a range of reasons that go beyond the scope of this chapter, the regime reinvented itself, in 2010–2011, as a quasi-civilian-military government (hereafter, quasi-civilian).[3] This "transition" involved broad political and economic shifts, and eventually multilateral negotiations between the regime and multiple EAOs, as a bloc, in contrast to the prior experience of bilateral negotiations. The bloc of some twenty groups split, and in October 2015, eight EAOs signed the so-called Nationwide Ceasefire Agreement (NCA), with the quasi-civilian government one month ahead of the historic November 2015 elections, which then bought the National League for Democracy (NLD) to power—albeit in a parliament, economy, and governance systems heavily dominated and constitutionally controlled by the military.[4]

The NCA was not nationwide in scope despite the original ambition. Nonetheless, it was a notable achievement. For the first time, EAOs collectively negotiated a ceasefire agreement with the military, and the agreement included a commitment to political dialogue—a long-held aspiration of ethnic nationality communities. The achievement of the NCA also tallied with the growing confidence of civil society to stake claims to wide-ranging peace and human security issues in Myanmar.[5] However, several powerful EAOs opted not to sign, on account of disagreements surrounding who should be included or, more precisely, military conditionality on who should not be included. There was hope that the government led by Aung San Suu Kyi would offer a more genuine path to peace, and many ethnic nationality communities voted for the NLD with this in mind. Signatories to the NCA represented just 20 percent of the armed ethnic forces operating across Myanmar.[6] In April 2016, the NLD assumed formal power and implementation of the NCA, and formal political dialogue began to unfold.

The NCA signatories, the NLD, and the military were unable to secure agreement on substantial measures to bring an end to violence and the inequalities underpinning it. The peace process was inhibited by a deep lack of trust from ethnic nationalities in institutions, often related to their perception that they were dominated by the ethnic-majority Bamar, but also by the approach of the military, regarding who was formally included in the process and not. Unsteady Bamar relations between the military and NLD were also in constant tension, most prominently on the long-desired constitutional change by the NLD. The NLD saw the peace process as a pathway to secure such change. Against this backdrop, increasing instability and violence in Rakhine State was unfolding, which in turn resulted in the exodus of over 750,000 Rohingya people into Bangladesh.[7]

On 1 February 2021, a military coup abruptly halted a decade of incremental democratic and development gains, resulting in a multidimensional crisis. The junta initially declared it would rule for one year followed by elections, but this did not transpire. At the point of writing, successive declarations of state of emergency have been issued by the military. The takeover triggered unprecedented protests and a powerful civil disobedience movement, which ground the public sector to a near halt. Displacement is at an all-time high, and as of late December 2023, there have been over 4,200 deaths, over 25,500 arrests, and close to 19,900 detained.[8]

In this chapter, we detail how ceasefires have been framed, agreed upon, and instrumentalized in Myanmar. We explore the interaction between efforts to *address the conflict violence* and efforts to *address the contested issues*. We argue that, over at least thirty years, ceasefires have been primarily used to manage the cost of violence and to provide more opportunity to consolidate economic and military gains without the regime making significant concessions on the contested issues: ethnic nationality self-determination, federalism, and respect for human rights. The military managed and moderated relationships with some EAOs through ceasefires but has been resistant to enter any deeper political negotiation processes and never seriously negotiated the redistribution of power. Ceasefires have been used as an instrument of control, rather than a step toward conflict resolution. The willingness of EAOs to go along with this arrangement has varied across groups and over time. Some accepted ceasefire agreements as these generated beneficial pathways (e.g., economic concessions and types of recognition of territorial control). When groups demanded political issues be negotiated before or alongside ceasefires, the military resisted and sought to defeat them militarily and arguably through collective punishment of civilian communities. This led to successive waves of displacement, and hundreds of thousands of people fleeing Myanmar to seek asylum, alongside economic migrants. Despite successive ceasefires, political dialogue, conferences, and talks, there was no formal negotiation process with the genuine intention of producing a comprehensive peace agreement. Instead, ceasefires have been a means to an end; that civil society and EAOs argue has been used to sustain a status quo that primarily benefits the military.

Given the complexity of the conflict and the multitude of armed groups, we focus our discussion on four EAOs that have adopted different approaches to conflict management, ceasefires, and the negotiation of contested issues.

These exemplify the historical function of ceasefires across Myanmar and include the following:[9]

1. The United Wa State Army (UWSA)—the largest EAO with more than 20,000 troops and a well-equipped, modern fighting force.[10] Representing the Wa community in northeast Myanmar adjacent to China, the UWSA is also regarded as a powerful narcotic trafficking organization, one of the biggest in Southeast Asia.[11] They have had a bilateral ceasefire with the military for most of their existence but were not part of the NCA.

2. The Kachin Independence Organisation (KIO)[12]—the second largest EAO with some 10,000 troops and around 10,000 civilian reservists.[13] It represents Kachin people, mainly within Kachin State in northern Myanmar, bordering China and India. The KIO generates significant revenue from the rich natural resources in Kachin[14] and was one of the lead architects of the NCA, although ultimately not a signatory.

3. The Karen National Union (KNU)[15]—one of the oldest EAOs that represents the Karen people and holds territory that borders Thailand. Prior to 1 February 2021, their fighting forces declined on account of decades of counterinsurgency and military splits but generally maintained a force of around 5,000 troops.[16] The KNU is funded through local taxation, diaspora support, and mining and logging operations. They became one of the most significant signatories to the NCA (but have since withdrawn).

4. The Arakan Army (AA)—one of the newer EAOs. Formed in 2009 by disaffected Rakhine, it has trained and fought alongside the KIO and was excluded from the NCA by the military. It has arguably evolved to become one of the most militarily effective EAOs.[17]

Figure 10.1 presents an overview of the ceasefires between the military and these four EAOs over time. Figure 10.2 presents an estimation of violence in this period from the Uppsala Conflict Data Programme, providing an indicative overview of periods of conflict escalation and de-escalation. Readers should note that battle-related fatalities are only one indicator of violence. As with armed conflict elsewhere, indirect suffering and death is both significant and hard to "count," such as the pernicious effects of sexual violence by armed actors, lack of medical treatment, and food insecurity due to forced displacement.

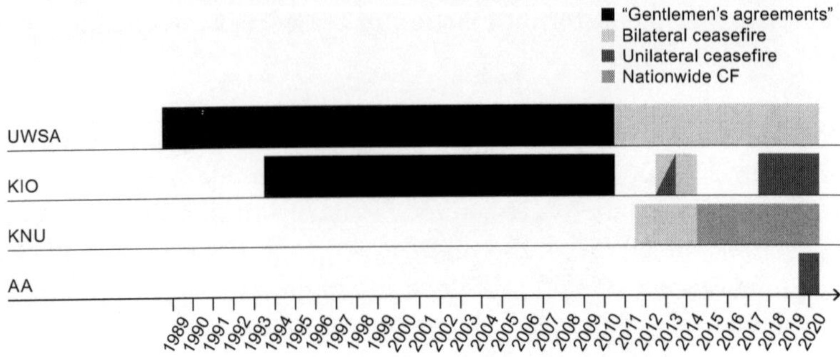

Figure 10.1 Overview of ceasefire agreements in Myanmar by EAO

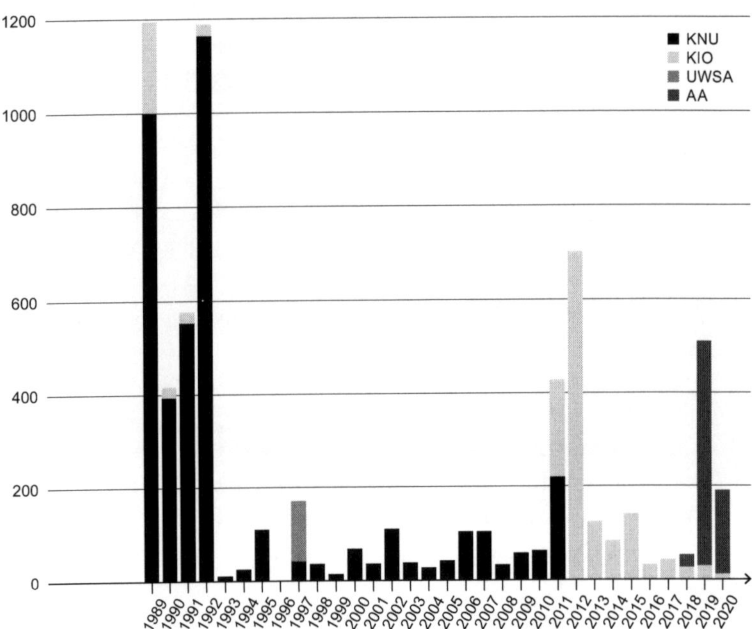

Figure 10.2 Overview of fatalities in Myanmar conflict by EAO

We provide a brief overview of violent conflict prior to 1989, then detail conflict management and peace efforts from 1989 to 1 February 2021, in which successive military regimes, the NLD government, and civil society pursued initiatives to generate ceasefires, focusing in particular on the four groups listed above. We then offer an overview of the interactions between the attempts to address violent conflict and contested issues in Myanmar.

CONFLICT BACKGROUND

Successive rulers of Myanmar—be that royal court, state, colonizing, and imperial powers—have largely concentrated their power in the Burmese "heartland," which is regarded as the more accessible valleys and plains in the center of what is understood to be modern Myanmar.[18] Meanwhile, they have maintained relatively limited (or nonexistent) control over the mountainous and jungle terrain of the borderlands, where distinct ethnic nationalities with unique languages and cultures live.[19] The 1947 Panglong Agreement between Bamar and Kachin, Karen, Karenni, Chin, and Shan leaders promising autonomy for ethnic nationalities postindependence was never implemented. This promised a federal Union of Burma (as it was then known) on the condition that ethnic nationalities received full autonomy and an equal share of the wealth. Indeed, following independence from Britain in 1948, the Burmese central state sought to expand its control over these communities and nations.

One of the first groups to resist was the Karen. They were well represented in colonial armed forces and given preference by the British for administrative, military, and policing posts and had been promised independence in return for siding against the Japanese in World War II. In 1949, fearing domination at the hands of the Bamar, when attempts to negotiate a solution with the Bamar-led government proved unsuccessful, the military wing of the KNU began what would become the world's longest-running civil conflict.

By the end of the 1950s, the new government of Burma had lost control of almost all its land borders to communist groups and EAOs.[20] The military, dominated by the Bamar, started to develop the now deeply entrenched narrative of saving the state from "insurgency." They came to dominate control of the state and seized power directly from 1958–1960 and then again in 1962, 1988, and 2021. They have never been able to militarily defeat the EAOs.

In the early 1960s, the Kachin Independence Organisation was formed and quickly grew in numbers as young recruits sought to push back against Burmese military, economic, and cultural dominance. The Kachin were disillusioned Panglong Agreement signatories.

The Wa community, who had never been directly colonized by the British, became the strongest resistance force in Myanmar. They did so under the auspices of the Communist Party of Burma and were supported by Chinese weapons and funding.

Over the coming decades, the military made few attempts to reach out to the EAOs to contain violence, most notably during the periods of

1963–1964 and 1980–1981. These limited attempts were largely ineffectual, due to irreconcilable positions, whereby the military demanded surrender and the EAOs demanded some form of self-rule and recognition of ethnic nationalities.[21] The status quo thus became the military controlling the Burmese "center" and EAOs controlling "states within a state," on the periphery.

A critical change began with the shifting geopolitics toward the end of the Cold War. This occurred at the same time as a broader wave of political resistance was sweeping across Myanmar. The ruling Burmese Socialist Programme Party collapsed in the face of growing urban pro-democracy protests. In response, another military regime assumed power in 1988 and launched an extensive campaign of violent repression, killing and imprisoning thousands, stifling dissent, and seriously restricting political activity.

Throughout the Cold War, the military and some EAOs benefited from significant external support. Black market trafficking of opium, precious stones, and timber profited the military and helped to fund some of the EAOs. By the late 1980s, this trade was worth around US$3 billion, or 40 percent of Burma's gross domestic product (GDP).[22] Concurrently, the Communist Party of Burma (CPB) received significant economic and military backing from China. Yet as the Cold War dynamics began to unravel, the situation in Myanmar shifted. The incentives for neighboring states to maintain Myanmar as a kind of buffer declined and were outweighed by the desire of regional actors to tap into Myanmar's lucrative resources.

As Chinese support for the CPB was weakened, it quickly collapsed under the weight of internal rivalries. In early 1989, a group of Wa troops occupied the CPB headquarters and seized their sizable armory. As the communist group fragmented into a multitude of ethnically aligned militia, the dominance of the ethnic Wa within the former CPB meant that the newly formed United Wa State Army became, overnight, one of the largest and best-equipped EAOs in Myanmar.[23]

Neighboring states, most significantly China, dropped their support of the CPB, as well as other EAOs, and began to build relations with the military regime.[24] The result was the growing embeddedness of a particular form of capitalism and what was seen by many in civil society and EAOs as predatory economics, through which the military established a powerful business empire.[25] The Burmese army remained fully committed to economic and military control of the borderlands, but given the unprecedented unrest and dire economic situation, it was forced to weigh up the different military threats around the country. Ultimately, it sought a new, pragmatic approach to reduce how many fronts it was fighting on and to consolidate its economic interests. This led the military to a conflict management approach and seeking ceasefire agreements with many of the EAOs.

OVERVIEW OF CEASEFIRE PROCESSES

"Gentlemen's Agreements"

In this era, responsibility for negotiating ceasefires fell to General Khin Nyunt, the head of the military intelligence (MI) division. The regime afforded the general significant autonomy and latitude to negotiate. General Khin Nyunt and his team were able to develop a channel of communication with many EAOs. Through a mix of pragmatism, incentives, and communication, most EAOs agreed to some violence management mechanisms. Ultimately, the aim was to create an environment that was more manageable for the military, but where the unfettered exploitation of natural resources was legitimized and licensed, a lucrative economic potential untapped.[26]

Significantly, General Khin Nyunt moved quickly to negotiate an arrangement with the UWSA. He offered the Wa a unique arrangement, due to his fear of a well-armed UWSA who might supply protestors and other EAOs with weaponry, and thus tip the balance of power against the military. They were allowed to keep their weapons, maintain control over their territory, and engage in *any* kind of business in return for not attacking the military or supplying those involved in the protest movement with weapons. This provided the Wa with the de facto autonomy they desired and shored up the position of the military regime.[27]

Other former communist groups also found themselves without their patrons, lacking sufficient military capacity and facing increasingly war-weary constituents. Without the promise of support from the Chinese or weapons from the UWSA, they had little option but to adopt similar arrangements.

Between 1989 and 2005, General Khin Nyunt agreed to a cessation of hostility arrangements with more than forty armed groups. These arrangements were labeled "gentlemen's agreements," which proved an accurate term since discussions were overwhelmingly dominated by men. They were informal, verbal deals, with no clearly prohibited conduct and no monitoring or lines of demarcation, albeit they were largely understood between the parties. The arrangements often involved civilian liaisons who acted as trusted go-betweens in the event of breaches. This, in turn, was a feature that became common in future agreements. These trusted individuals who could shuttle messages and quietly problem-solve were key to keeping violence at bay. These were, ultimately, elite pacts, *quid pro quos* that informally recognized the status quo and traded economic opportunities and a sense of stability for a willingness to drop, or at least pause, violence, alongside any significant political claims.[28]

In 1994, under growing military pressure and lacking the support of former patrons, the KIO entered into a ceasefire agreement with the military. Unlike other verbal agreements, uniquely, this was a written agreement, perhaps reflecting the KIO's status as a significant organization, that held resource-rich territory and perhaps the broader aspiration of some KIO leadership in using the arrangement as a potential path to peace. This agreement also benefited from "insider mediation" from trusted civil society actors such as the Baptist reverend Saboi Jum. Yet the written agreement was still very basic and lacked key details on demarcation, monitoring, or any political provisions. In return for the ceasefire, the KIO received promises of significant economic control of, and expanded business opportunities for, the elites.[29] Pragmatically, the KIO also gained an opportunity to expand its military strength, increasing its military numbers from 5,000 to 15,000 in the years following the ceasefire.[30]

In sum, these ceasefires were an example of political pragmatism on behalf of both the military and many of the EAOs involved.[31] They conferred a range of benefits: the EAOs maintained de facto control over territory, were allowed to retain their weapons, had protection from prosecution, received sizable economic concessions for the leaders, acquired access to the extraction of natural resources, and, of course, achieved a suspension of violence.[32] For populations fatigued by war, it promised some relief from poverty and arduous living conditions and lent some support for pursuing such agreements. In some cases, these benefits filtered down to the population, there were modest improvements in infrastructure and well-being, and for many, the agreements succeeded in creating the first sustained period with no violence in their lifetime.

While the EAOs and the wider population benefited from the ceasefire, the most significant rewards came to the Myanmar military leaders, who were able to build multigenerational businesses and become wealthy and influential with significant control over licit and illicit economies. The agreements also relieved the pressures of a multifront conflict, allowing the military to focus attention on groups posing the greatest threat or those resisting their ceasefire overtures. They were able to offer such lucrative financial incentives to various EAOs, in part because they, too, benefited economically from the break in fighting. The military was able to sign foreign trade deals and make profitable investment deals for mining and logging. Rents previously captured by the EAOs were either "allowed" as part of these agreements or slowly transferred to the military. Over time, it became clear that the military used its growing economic strength, alongside its leverage over the EAOs, to advance Burmese state building.[33] This process was helped by the incorporation of some ethnic elites into the economic system, a process labeled by Woods as "ceasefire capitalism."[34]

At the same time, the military resisted EAO attempts to negotiate on contested political issues. This was justified by arguing it was only intended to be a transitional "government," and negotiation on issues such as autonomy or federalism could only occur once "disciplined flourishing democracy" had been fully achieved. As Reverend Saboi Jum reported, the general narrative was to "discuss those matters with the politicians . . . we are military, we don't discuss political matters." This allowed the military to create the desired break in hostilities, consolidate their economic interests, and refocus their fighting energy elsewhere, without having to make any concessions that might have undermined the integrity of the Burmese state or affected their booming business empire.

While these "gentlemen's agreements" started with the former communist groups, once the process gathered momentum, other groups came into the fold. By the late 1990s, almost a decade after this military regime took power, only two major groups were still engaging in violence, one of which was the KNU.[35]

Unlike some other EAOs, the KNU was reluctant to enter a ceasefire or "gentlemen's agreement." This was driven by a strong commitment to their political aspirations: namely, separatism or a federal system with guaranteed protections.[36] In 1992, talks broke down due to the KNU's insistence that the military regime negotiate a ceasefire *and* a political settlement with the KNU and its allies.[37] Similarly, in 1995, the talks collapsed due to the military's refusal to discuss any political issues.[38]

The KNU was also facing significant internal problems. KNU leadership was predominately Christian, and internal tensions led to splintering with the organization's Buddhist forces. Several KNU brigades split from the main force and entered into bilateral ceasefire arrangements with the military. They then subsequently joined forces to attack the KNU. This helped the military to rapidly expand its control over KNU territory, embarking on an occupation that produced hundreds of thousands of refugees and displaced persons, leading the KNU leadership to relocate to neighboring Thailand.[39]

Despite this, the KNU remained opposed to a ceasefire and came to "view the term *ceasefire* as synonymous with *surrender*, and the term *development* as code for *personal profit*."[40] But this proved costly, for, having secured "gentlemen's agreements" with many of the other EAOs, the military was able to concentrate its forces against the KNU and so apply sufficient pressure to seriously weaken one of its strongest opponents.

The Breakdown of the Informal Ceasefires

Perhaps surprisingly, given their highly informal character, almost all of the ceasefires were honored for several years and, throughout General Khin Nyunt's tenure, were rarely violated.[41] Only one ceasefire agreement broke down completely.[42]

These agreements first began to unravel when a conflict within the military led to the purge of Khin Nyunt and the reconfiguration of the Directorate of Defence Service Intelligence in 2004–2005. This was then reestablished as the Office of the Chief of Military Security Affairs or simply MI, military intelligence. The purge largely destroyed the informal ties and system of EAO liaison offices that were an effective element in the conflict management approach to ceasefires. The new military security affairs section set about trying to restore and rebuild relations but failed to build the same level of trust as its predecessor. As a result, by early 2008, many of the EAOs, including the USWA and KIO, began to escalate their military preparedness, in concern for their safety and anticipation of a possible return to violent conflict.

Despite hopes that the agreements would lead to developments that would lift the population out of poverty, the ceasefires produced a narrow cadre of economic winners, as over time the military regime and its vast business empire took over greater control of lucrative industries. Seeing few benefits from this approach to conflict management, growing popular dissatisfaction with the ceasefires began to emerge.

Crucially, relations between the military regime and the EAOs were further damaged by the controversial constitution-making process that came to a head in 2008. The military sought to consolidate power by forging a new constitution to enshrine its power while creating a framework for "disciplined democracy." Many of the EAO leaders who had agreed a ceasefire were permitted to attend the national constitutional-making convention as delegates. While this was often not in their function as EAO leaders, they were nevertheless invited as cultural leaders or intellectuals.

One advantage of the ceasefire period was that it provided an opportunity for local civil society to further develop. Notably, Reverend Saboi Jum, who had helped to negotiate some of the earlier ceasefires in Kachin State, established the Nyein (Shalom) Foundation in 2000.[43] In 2002, the Ethnic Nationalities Mediators Fellowship was formed from a group of religious leaders who had been promoting and supporting ceasefires in their own states, and in 2004, the Nyein (Shalom) Foundation organized a ceasefire EAO leaders' meeting in Yangon and Myitkyina.

Building on these earlier initiatives, a new group of ethnic armed leaders was informally set up with thirteen of the seventeen key ceasefire groups who were attending the constitutional conference, including the KIO. Non-ceasefire groups, such as the KNU, remained outside of the process at this time. For more than three years, these leaders lived in close proximity and, under the guise of informal dinners and prayer meetings, received training on negotiation, debating, and discussing possible political solutions among themselves. The KIO and other EAOs submitted a nineteen-point proposal for a future federal state (although for political sensitivity reasons, the word "federal" was not used). They saw this as the "culmination of their ceasefire strategies,"[44] presenting it to the constitution drafters during the National Convention (although it was never discussed and eventually ignored). Ultimately, these groups were excluded from the political process, leading to a constitution almost entirely dictated by the military to consolidate power and resources at every turn.

The final nail in the coffin for the informal ceasefires arose when the military demanded that the EAOs transition into Border Guard Forces (BGF)—a form of military-aligned auxiliary fighting unit—in April 2009. The new, and heavily contested, 2008 constitution decreed that the military could be the only armed force, and thus any EAO would be illegal.[45] This has since been argued by many observers to be a strategic miscalculation that seriously underestimated the resistance of the stronger EAOs, placing their forces under the control of the Bamar- and military-dominated state. The military demanded that the stronger EAOs, most of which still accepted the ceasefire arrangements, should be transformed into BGFs. This would allow them to maintain some level of autonomy and control of their forces but would render them subject to some oversight as an auxiliary component of the military. The military proposed that weaker groups become militia, fully under military control. Many groups were extremely reluctant to be integrated into the military without any political settlement. This reluctance was made worse when the military insisted that the demobilization occur before the forthcoming election (i.e., as a precondition of involvement in the electoral process). Ultimately, many EAOs saw this as an attempt to weaken their position and an example of a divide-and-rule approach often used by the military.

At this point, many of the EAOs had experienced almost a decade of ceasefire, in which time they had come to develop sizable business opportunities. Coupled with the growing capacity of the military, this affected the will of most groups to return to violence. So, for many of the smaller, militarily weaker EAOs, transforming into a closer arrangement was deemed preferable to a return to conflict. As a result, out of the forty groups that agreed to a ceasefire with the military, thirty were disarmed or incorporated into a "people's militia," while five were transformed into a BGF. The BGFs and militias remain a significant source of instability, maintaining economic interests and control over local communities, and they are often accused of being perpetrators of violence. The five remaining groups were generally the larger and more powerful EAOs (including both the KIO and UWSA).[46] Yet, while the "gentlemen's agreements" broke down, most EAOs and the military generally tried to limit the return to violence. The only exception was the KIO, who some argue began to favor a return to violence on the back of growing political and economic grievances, with a new, younger generation of officers.[47] Violence restarted in June 2011 when the military broke the ceasefire by launching a serious attack on KIO positions. The subsequent air strikes on KIO populations and reciprocal attacks on military forces resulted in hundreds of deaths largely on the civilian side. Kachin civilians reported being subjected to displacement, sexual violence, extortion, and other forms of repression.

At the same time, across Myanmar, a growing appetite for conflict emerged. As a prominent civil society leader noted, ceasefire capitalism mainly benefited the military and some EAO leaders and their members, "but the people at the grassroots got no benefit at all."[48] Thus, the political economy tilted away from peace, the memory of violence faded, the benefits of the imperfect conflict management efforts failed to trickle down, and the lack of political settlement meant many ethnic nationality concerns— such as human rights, autonomy, self-determination, and equitable natural resource management—remained unaddressed. Opportunities arose for new armed groups to emerge, replacing and recruiting from those that had aligned with the military. By the time a quasi-civilian government took hold in 2011, there were at least sixteen significant armed conflicts, five EAOs that had refused to be transformed into a BGF (including the KIO and UWSA), two groups that had always resisted a ceasefire (including the KNU), and eleven groups who had not entered into a ceasefire with the regime, including the AA.

Bilateral Ceasefires

In August 2011, with the inauguration of a quasi-civilian regime, the new president, former general and leader of the State Peace and Development Council, U Thein Sein, spoke in an unprecedented way about the need to secure a lasting peace and to address ethnic nationality concerns and aspirations. It was the first time in the history of Myanmar that a military leader had publicly spoken so clearly of a desire for peace.

Following this, the new quasi-civilian government began reaching out to the EAOs. This included opening lines of communication with those groups who had previously had ceasefires, including the UWSA and KIO, and a number of groups that had not previously agreed a ceasefire, including the KNU.[49] In a clear break from prior negotiations, U Thein Sein enlisted the help of a nongovernmental organization (NGO) and a think tank, bringing together an unorthodox team, primarily composed of men who were exiled Burmese prodemocracy activists and advisors to assist in the negotiations.

As the process progressed, the U Thein Sein administration restructured its peacemaking infrastructure. U Aung Min, the former railways minister, became the chief negotiator, backed up by a new and well-funded Myanmar Peace Center (MPC). The MPC was effectively run as an NGO taking on secretariat functions for the Union Peacemaking Central Committee (UPCC) and the Union Peacemaking Working Committee (UPWC). It was funded by the European Union and composed of a mixture of Burmese ministers, senior officials, and technocrats, many of whom were returning to Myanmar after decades abroad. Shortly after, U Thein Sein announced a tiered approach to peacemaking. Herein, the EAOs would first negotiate an initial ceasefire at the state level, then hold union-level talks to discuss the more significant political issues, and finally a conference to agree a comprehensive peace agreement. The EAOs were unwilling to agree to disarmament before the negotiation of political solutions, and the quasi-civilian government had to quickly adapt this demand and promise to discuss some political issues earlier in the process.

Despite the growing peace bureaucracy and infrastructure, U Aung Min retained significant freedom to negotiate bilateral ceasefires. In effect, he could accept almost all EAO demands, including promoting economic incentives, withdrawing military forces, promising to address human rights abuses, and agreeing to move quicker to political dialogue around federalism.[50] This does not mean all these demands were met. The biggest red line remained that of consenting to anything that might imply independence or undermine the centralist integrity of the Burmese state.

In many ways, however, the approach was a return to the mutually beneficial arrangements of the past. The quasi-civilian government set about attempting to inspire a new wave of "ceasefire capitalism," offering significant economic incentives to bring them into bilateral arrangements. As before, the quasi-civilian government sought ceasefires to limit the use of arms and violence, which was necessary to enact their desired political and economic reforms and prevent an escalation on multiple fronts. Importantly, they remained unwilling to seriously discuss any of the contested political issues.

While the EAOs remained skeptical of the new regime, many were happy to go along with the process given the quasi-civilian government's seeming willingness to make notable concessions to sweeten the deals. The U Thein Sein negotiators had some important early successes and produced a new raft of written bilateral agreements. Once again, the UWSA, which retained the greatest military capacity of all EAOs, was one of the first groups to enter into a new bilateral agreement.[51] Notably, this was followed by a bilateral agreement with the KNU, who, having suffered greatly from resisting a ceasefire in the prior period—and were weakened, moreover, by the internal fractures and relocation of their central governing body to Thailand—came under increasing pressure to change tack.[52] Key Karen stakeholders argued that the organizational survival of the group and the well-being of its constituents required a break in the fighting and significant regional development. This was initially resisted by KNU leadership, who remained reluctant to agree any form of economic development or regulation of violence in the absence of a resolution of the key political issues (i.e., autonomy and democracy). In the end, the election of new KNU leadership produced a change in direction. Henceforth, while the KNU continued to resist major infrastructure projects (e.g., dam building), in the absence of political solutions, they agreed a ceasefire and embarked on forms of cooperation with the Burmese state. Meanwhile, they remained committed to working with other EAOs to promote the establishment of a democratic federal union. By mid-2012, thirteen groups had signed similar bilateral agreements with the quasi-civilian government.

The bilateral agreements in this period were more formal than the verbal "gentlemen's agreements." They were written documents, often covering several pages. Using the typology forwarded in this book, these were cessation of hostilities, as they lacked any formal monitoring, robust timelines, and accountability provisions.

The KIO, in contrast to some of the other long-standing groups, decided it had to continue violent struggle with the military. Attempts to negotiate a ceasefire failed, often due to their perception that the military was resistant to discussing any political issues prior to its emergence. As a result, throughout 2012 and early 2013, violence continued, leading to the displacement of more than 100,000 people who continue to remain in camps. In May 2013, China brokered a de-escalation agreement, which was developed in a follow-up agreement in October of the same year. Together, the agreements *inter alia* committed the parties to a cessation of hostilities, as well as to the endorsement of the EAOs' conference for a peace process, to be convened in Laiza (the headquarters of the KIO), and to the establishment of a monitoring mechanism (see below for more details).

As the process progressed, the EAOs learned from their earlier experiences and from each other. In initial bilateral arrangements involving the UWSA and KNU, agreement monitoring was included. Yet as the processes progressed, an NGO called the Nyein (Shalom) Foundation spearheaded discussions on the need for, and types of, available ceasefire monitoring. With the Centre for Humanitarian Dialogue, they organized workshops for civil society leaders focusing on training, promoting understanding of the value of ceasefire monitoring. These efforts bore fruit, leading to the inclusion of party-led monitoring in several agreements, including with the KIO, the likes of which may possibly be considered preliminary ceasefires. Thus, while the initial agreement involving the KNU was rather weak, including only a passing reference to monitoring, the later agreements had clearer and more elaborate details and a ceasefire monitoring mechanism that included a draft Code of Conduct document. Yet, despite the growing focus and understanding of monitoring, none of the agreements produced a functioning party-led monitoring system.

The individual knowledge of some of the EAO negotiating teams also shaped the bilateral agreements. Some EAOs had legal scholars in their teams such as the KNU and the Chin National Front (CNF), who brought references to international human rights and civilian protection into these discussions.

Negotiating a Nationwide Ceasefire Arrangement

The origins of the Nationwide Ceasefire Agreement (NCA) can be traced to the negotiations between the quasi-civilian government and the KIO. In the second union-level meeting (October 2013), the chief negotiator for the KIO, General Gun Maw, proposed to U Aung Min that they would convene an EAO conference in Laiza, which was a KIO stronghold. Up to this point, the EAOs had previously met together in Thailand and never officially before in Myanmar. For the EAOs, coming together in a formal meeting offered the chance to coordinate their bargaining approaches and to prevent the military and quasi-civilian government from adopting the "divide-and-rule" tactics that had proven so effective in the past. In prior negotiations, the regime did not allow any form of collective bargaining, and therefore all the cessation of hostilities (CoH) arrangements were agreed upon between the military and an individual group. This had previously undermined alliances between EAOs (e.g., the National Democratic Front and the Democratic Alliance of Burma). As General Gun Maw stated at the time, if the EAOs wanted a federal union, then they would ultimately have to start working together. President U Thein Sein was attending an Association of Southeast Asian Nations (ASEAN) meeting at this time and had given full permission to U Aung Min to make any concessions necessary to get a bilateral deal with KIO. In this context, without any backchannel negotiations or prior warning, General Gun Maw suggested an ethnic nationalities conference, and somewhat surprisingly for the EAOs, U Aung Min immediately accepted, keen to lock the KIO into a ceasefire.

The first-ever ethnic nationalities-led conference took place in Laiza in October 2013. At the request of the KIO, the United Nations secretary-general's special envoy to Myanmar and the Chinese ambassador for the Asia Pacific meeting were observers. At the Laiza meeting, a National Cease-fire Coordination Team (NCCT) was formed. Quickly, this group came to include all sixteen of the major EAOs, many of whom already had a bilateral agreement with the Burmese state (e.g., KIO, KNU), as well as others who did not (e.g., AA). Once the NCCT was formed, the EAOs could for the first time begin a process of collective bargaining with the UPWC. By working together, they could maximize collective power. For many of the EAO leaders—since they belonged to ethnic nationalities—Burmese was their second or third language. Thus, while they had no problem discussing and debating broader political concerns, when it came to the specifics to be included in an agreement, alongside any understanding of technical jargon, some lacked the necessary capabilities—a situation that is not uncommon for those involved in negotiating agreements. In the earlier negotiations, the military benefited from this weakness, often toning down or weakening what was agreed on verbally in the written agreement. By working together, the groups could better overcome these challenges.

The military and the U Thein Sein government failed to anticipate the formation of the NCCT and the EAOs' intention to move toward collective bargaining. There was a long pause in their response, although ultimately, they consented to the new arrangement as this was the only way forward to secure a ceasefire and cement the reputation of U Thein Sein as a peacemaker. The first meeting of the NCCT took place in November 2013 in Myitkyina, where the EAOs began to prepare their ideal version of a nationwide ceasefire arrangement. The agreement sought to incorporate the strongest elements from each of the different existing bilateral ceasefires and, where possible, international conventions to strengthen the legitimacy of their claims.

The mandate of NCCT was to negotiate. It did not have decision-making power. Therefore, once the negotiators agreed on the terms, they called an EAO summit in which the agreement was further debated and refined by the top leaders. At this point, it was considered more a collective than a nationwide ceasefire.

In January 2014, the two sides came together to discuss the two versions of the collective ceasefire. To come to an agreement, the parties decided on a single-text process. They first agreed on the chapters and then pulled apart the two agreements placing the different provisions into the relevant chapters. This resulted in a two-column version of the single text, in which the military, U Thein Sein government, and NCCT demands were placed either side, with the NCCT provisions in red and the former in blue. They then began what would become nine rounds of talks in which the red and blue points were negotiated, until a common text could be agreed upon, which was then added in black.[53]

The idea for a nationwide ceasefire emerged in the early meetings of the negotiation of NCCT and UPWC. The logic was chiefly based on locking the military into an arrangement, as under a nationwide agreement, any violation would be not only against one group but also against all, and this would risk undermining a unique moment where peace was possible across the entire country.[54]

A key distinction between this process and the prior ceasefire negotiations was the content. For many EAOs, this was their second or third ceasefire negotiation with the military, and thus they were no longer content to simply agree on an economically incentivized break in fighting. Some of the groups were stronger than in previous processes (in part because of the stronger economic position resulting from the earlier ceasefires), and they were now negotiating collectively. Therefore, for the EAOs, the purpose of the process was not just to stabilize the status quo but to move toward a political settlement and, moreover, the creation of a federal democratic union. This was mapped out in eleven common principles that the NCCT produced during the first EAO conference in Laiza.

The quasi-civilian government version of a collective agreement turned out to be wholly unacceptable to the EAOs, as it did not include any mention of political matters or what would happen after the ceasefire. The only reference to the post-ceasefire period in the original government draft was a statement committing them to arrange for the food and security for the EAOs. This deeply concerned the EAOs, as it seemed to imply that the ceasefire would place them totally at the mercy of the military and U Thein Sein's government, with the two entities inextricably linked.

The federalism question was a long and contentious topic during the negotiations. While generally all EAOs were in favor, groups such as the KNU and KIO were some of the strongest proponents of this position. The military itself remained steadfast in its opposition to even discussing such matters. At one point in the process, it seemed like a significant milestone had been reached, as U Aung Min and the military general in charge of the negotiation agreed to include a reference to a "democratic federal country" within the text. The following day, this concession was all over the media, as newspapers reported that the EAOs had secured agreement on federalism. The next day, the quasi-civilian government receded its commitment to the term, insistent that it be removed. Shortly after, the general was replaced on the negotiating team.

During this process, the Nyein (Shalom) Foundation provided technical assistance to the EAOs and played an important function connecting the EAOs with legal and other relevant practitioners. When the groups were concerned about the legality or implications of a provision, they would film a response from a lawyer and play this to the EAO leaders in Chiang Mai as it was not possible for lawyers to converse directly with the EAOs as they were proscribed. This method helped to reassure and advise the EAOs in a manner that did not pose a risk to the legal experts.

The negotiation of the precise ceasefire mechanisms was continually delayed in the earlier part of the process. Prior to agreeing to the composition and functions of a joint military commission, the EAOs sought to first reach an agreement on the definition of the key ceasefire-related terms. They felt that without a common understanding of the terms, it was irrelevant what was included in the deal. This includes terms like "ceasefire area" and "nonconflict zone" that were common within the text. Both sides developed working committees, and the Nyein (Shalom) Foundation worked with the EAOs to prepare definitions of more than thirty key terms. However, the quasi-civilian government continually resisted negotiations on these elements, and they remained missing in the final document, which in turn had significant implications for the implementation.

In terms of the ceasefire mechanism, only the bare bones were agreed, meaning that the agreement lacked many of the details that would have helped with implementation. It was agreed in principle that there would be a Joint Ceasefire Monitoring Committee (JMC), which would be tripartite and would include the EAOs, the military, and civilian representatives. But the specifics of this were not agreed, and the lack of agreed definitions on the key terms further weakened the agreement. Moreover, what little detail existed, including any commitments to any next steps, was moved to the annex of the agreement. This became problematic when the annex was relegated to a nonbinding document and not included in the published version of the NCA the MPC produced. This meant that many of the important details made in the process, defining terms, setting out next steps, and further commitments, were all effectively lost. Then as international representatives from donors, international nongovernmental organizations (INGOs), and even EAOs changed, many important agreements and points of progress were lost from memory. This weakened the NCA and further undermined the implementation process. But there were also those, such as the Nyein leadership, who retained deep historical knowledge of the nuances.

Violence continued during the negotiations, but at a relatively low level. There were, however, notable incidents, most prominently an air strike on a KIO officer training school, which was a direct violation of the bilateral ceasefire and threatened to derail the process. On several occasions, violence occurred on the day of the negotiations, in what appears to have been attempts by the military to undermine the talks. For example, when military matters were being negotiated, the negotiations would be chaired by General Gun Maw from the KIO, who was also the lead negotiator on the EAO side. When Gun Maw was due to chair meetings, air strikes often occurred in or around Laiza, General Gun Maw's headquarters. This led to the meetings being paused to allow the general to take phone calls to manage the situation and seemed intended to distract the general or lead to a breakdown in talks. These incidents suggested a possible fissure between the military and U Thein Sein's government negotiating the deal, as the armed attacks seemed an attempt to undermine the process. Ultimately, the parties remained at the table, hopeful that agreement was possible. On other occasions, divisions with the KNU led to low-level intragroup fighting, as those within the organization who were against negotiations attempted to undermine those at the table. There were also ceasefire infringements relating to contraband, under what the military referred to as clearance missions. This led to several clashes with the KNU, while all parties again remained within the negotiations.

The only parts of the NCA process that occurred bilaterally were the economic elements. As an agreement neared, the EAOs entered bilateral talks with U Thein Sein's government, agreeing to economic dividends within the process. As many of the groups were already in a ceasefire with the state, their bargaining powers were diminished. It was therefore extremely difficult for them to resist. At the same time, the economic terms agreed seemed to have been satisfactory and were not a reason for any parties to leave the process.

By March 2015, the agreement was in sight, and with a November election looming, U Thein Sein was keen to push ahead with signing, in the hope that his peacemaking endeavors would pay off electorally. Throughout January and February, a multitude of informal meetings had attempted to iron out the final details of the deal. In March, senior KIO leaders agreed on almost all of the final provisions in a meeting at Naypyidaw, with only the precise wording of a provision on security sector reform in dispute.[55]

Up to this point, it had been assumed by the EAOs that all NCCT members would be the signatories to the NCA. All EAOs supported the process and were generally happy with the almost complete agreement (this included the KIO, KNU, and AA). The military then surprised everyone by announcing that it would only consent to ten of the sixteen NCCT groups signing the NCA. The military's justification was twofold. First, the three smallest groups were excluded as they didn't hold any significant armed forces. Since they were not engaged in armed hostilities with the groups, the military argued there was no need for a ceasefire.[56] Second, and more significantly, they excluded other groups, including most notably the Arakan Army, due to what they claimed to be a recent attack on the sovereignty of Myanmar.[57] This related to an attack allegedly undertaken by the AA and its allied EAOs on an administrative office. As a result, the military was insistent these groups disarm before being allowed to sign the NCA—something that was clear the groups would never accept.[58]

The exclusion of the AA and two other EAOs (the Ta'ang National Liberation Army and the Myanmar National Democratic Alliance Army) was profound, as it triggered a domino effect that seriously weakened the NCA. First, the KIO, one of the largest EAOs in Myanmar, who had led in much of the NCA negotiations, was closely aligned with the AA (and the other EAOs), having trained their initial forces, and often conducted joint operations against the military. By excluding these groups, the military thus made it very difficult for the KIO to sign, due to the KIO commitment to inclusion of all EAOs and also because the agreement would have been near unimplementable.[59] The KIO was, at the time, also the chair of the United Nationalities Federal Council (UNFC), a coalition of EAO opposition groups; the KIO's exclusion from the process also made it exceedingly difficult for their other allies to sign and so resulted in the three other EAOs refusing to sign the NCA.[60] And so, with the agreement almost complete, of the sixteen EAOs who had been involved in the negotiations, the military's exclusion of six groups led to the subsequent loss of four further groups, meaning only six of the original EAOs became signatories of the NCA.

Then, in a further surprising twist, two EAOs who had not been involved in the major negotiations, the Restoration Council of Southern Shan (RCSS) and the All-Burma Students Democratic Front (ABSDF), were drafted in at the last minute to sign. These two groups had been part of the EAO conferences and so had been kept abreast of the developing NCA but had not played an active role in the process.

The exclusion and inclusion of EAOs had important implications for the peace process. All-inclusiveness was a principle shared by the EAOs, and this was deeply affected by the exclusionary conditions introduced by the military. First, the changes in the signatories radically shifted the composition and preferences of the parties signed onto the NCA. The KIO was out, having been a firm advocate for addressing the contested political issues and a strong supporter of a democratic federal union. This made the KNU and the RCSS the two centers of power on the EAO side in the NCA, as they held the most significant armed forces and controlled considerable territory. The RCSS had not previously taken a strong political position or shown any strong preference for federalism. They had also been absent from all the negotiations and so lacked any institutional memory of the process or commitment to the negotiated principles. In essence, the NCA is a highly developed form of prenegotiation or framework agreement, which set out some of the parameters for future negotiations. Thus, implementation was never going to be straightforward, as every provision required further negotiation. The late inclusion of the RCSS complicated the future negotiations, leading to disagreements with the KNU, which undermined the implementation and reduced the drive for a federal solution. Moreover, this meant that of the signatories to the NCA, only three groups had armed forces. Some regarded the five others as "more akin to non-governmental organizations (NGOs) or tiny militias."[61]

The exclusion of the AA also had a serious impact, as we discuss below. The group went on to become a savvy adversary, engaging the military in draining fighting in the years ahead.[62] Significantly, the UWSA, which was still the largest EAO, also resisted signing, albeit they were kept informed of the process and considered it as a prospect. Eventually, they determined that their existing bilateral ceasefire was sufficient and, with the growing Chinese influence in the region, were keen to avoid the Western-funded process. As a result, they saw no additional benefit in joining the NCA.

The NCA represented a landmark achievement, yet the weaknesses baked into the agreement in these final phases meant that implementing the agreement, as well as broadening participation to include the nonsignatures, was going to be challenging.[63] It was in this context that a landslide victory for Aung San Suu Kyi's NLD party further shifted the process.

Aung San Suu Kyi and the NCA Implementation

The NLD won a landslide election in November 2015, comprehensively defeating military representatives (in one form or another), ending the grip on power they had managed to exert for generations and thus also their decades of control over the conflict management process. However, the military still maintained a constitutional grip on powerful ministries, as well as 25 percent of seats in all parliaments, and a business empire. Parliamentary power was in principle shared with a civilian government, one that stated peace as a top priority.

The EAOs, both signatories and nonsignatories to the NCA, were hopeful that the new government would act more favorably and push the needle toward the long sought-after democratic federal state. These aspirations were not without justification. During the election period, the NLD promised that a better deal lay waiting for the EAOs once they were elected. The NLD was keen not to give the military a political win before going to the polls and discouraged the EAOs from pursuing the NCA. Yet, following the election, it quickly became apparent that the NLD, and Aung San Suu Kyi, were going to take a different approach. U Aung Min was replaced as chief negotiator, resulting in a loss of institutional memory and relationships. The MPC was folded and converted into a less active institution, the National Peace and Reconciliation Centre. Aung San Suu Kyi gave preference to building trust and relations with the military, and the views of the NLD and Tatmadaw on the peace process appeared to grow more closely aligned. Aung San Suu Kyi's nationalistic tendencies and Bamar Buddhist outlook, with her reticence toward ethnic nationality aspirations and experiences of oppression, were hiding in plain sight. The entrenched military power was going to make concessions or further progress difficult, and so the peace process began to stall. As time passed, Aung San Suu Kyi's focus on the peace process—perhaps primarily as a vehicle for the constitutional change the NLD so desperately sought—began to wane. She attended meetings less frequently until ceasefire implementation was largely passed over to the military.

For the EAO NCA signatories, this complicated the process of implementation and made it hard to significantly advance the political dialogue framework set out in the NCA. In accordance with the hybrid (though, importantly, not joint) nature of the NCA, Aung San Suu Kyi presided over major events. First, she oversaw the Union Peace Conference (UPC) in September 2016, then she rebranded them with a Panglong link, calling them the 21st Century Panglong Conferences (May 2017, July 2018, August 2020).[64] These meetings had the stated aim of agreeing on a framework for political dialogue and forging a path to a democratic federal union. The four UPCs resulted in minor agreements on economic and social issues, and the fourth conference in August 2020 produced an agreement on the general principles designed to establish a federal union, but ultimately, the key political and security issues have remained unaddressed.

Beyond the spectacle of the union conferences, the peace process infrastructure was intensely complicated, with structural problems hindering progress. Most of the civilian representatives chosen by the military to join the JMC, for example, were former members of the military, which meant that incidents were viewed through a partisan lens, thereby contributing to the body's general ineffectiveness. The JMC operated at three levels: union, state, and local. Civilian representatives were most prominent at the local level. At least one member was drawn from the civilian ceasefire monitoring community, which was quietly operating in parallel to these formal efforts, attempting to build accountability and civilian confidence in the process.[65]

Similarly, the promised interim committee to address social issues was not formed, resulting in no platform to address community-based concerns, such as humanitarian problems, the prohibition of sexual violence, and development efforts for local conflict-affected populations. In gray areas (i.e., those governed by an EAO and the military), disputes were common around the implementation of political aspects of the agreement. With no commission, however, these political violations of the agreement went unchecked and undiscussed, as the JMC only examined violent incidents.

The NCA document was vague in places and was arguably an example of "constructive ambiguity" in contentious agreements. As the NCA included multiple groups, it was deemed impractical to negotiate all of the key details, such as lines of demarcation and clearly defined details on violations, as part of the agreement. Instead, it was agreed that a commission would be formed after the signing, one that would oversee bilateral negotiations between the military and the EAO signatories to agree on specific details with each group. This commission was not formed, leaving no clear lines of demarcation, in many cases, or clear details on prohibited behaviors, in turn making it challenging to maintain and monitor the ceasefire. As a result, low-level violence continued between the EAO signatories and military, including both the KNU and the RCSS. Notably, the KNU stepped back from the formal NCA peace process in 2018, citing a lack of progress, in particular with regard to bringing EAO nonsignatories into the process.

With regards to the nonsignatories, the NLD government continued to insist that joining the NCA is a necessary precondition for engaging in peace negotiations that hindered attempts to secure all-inclusiveness in the political dialogue process.[66] Only two groups subsequently joined the NCA, the New Mon State Party (a small group) and Lahu Democratic Union (also small and predominantly Thailand based). While this might have been conceived with the intention of giving the appearance of momentum, it was generally not understood as a significant advance.

The experience of the other nonsignatories was mixed. The UWSA continued to honor its longstanding ceasefire with the military and, in 2019, celebrated the thirtieth anniversary of this agreement.[67] Concurrent negotiations attempted to bring the UWSA into the NCA process, but the military's and government's unwillingness to discuss significant political matters—most notably the UWSA's desire to create an autonomous Wa state and make amendments to the NCA and the 2008 constitution—saw them remain outside the NCA and formal peace talks.

In contrast, following its decision not to sign the NCA, the KIO was on the receiving end of increasing military attacks, sparking a new phase of violent hostilities. The KIO leadership indicated that they were unwilling to join the NCA until the military and the NLD government showed a willingness to focus on contested political issues absent in the NCA process.

At this point, the former government's decision to exclude the AA, in line with demands made by the military, was indicative of the Bamar power struggles and tensions. Between 2016 and 2020, the AA went from a few hundred fighters to over 7,000. This was achieved by tapping into salient grievances within the Arakan population, as well as long historical objections to Burmanization and militarization. The AA was deft at making strategic use of social media and modern communications to increase support and recruit people, quickly growing into a "formidable fighting force . . . employing modern guerrilla tactics to inflict serious damage."[68] The AA demanded "confederate status" and greater autonomy, which again the military had resolved not to discuss. The military responded with an approach common across the years. Major offensives against the AA, while seemingly calling unilateral ceasefires with EAOs in other parts of the country, enabled attention on the AA and its allies.[69] Concurrently, the militarization of Myanmar continued unabated and underpinned the military takeover in 2021. The military strengthened its fighting capabilities, investing in new aircraft, as well as helicopter gunships and drones, purchased from weapons manufacturers from Russia and China in particular.[70] The result was a major war producing thousands of casualties and hundreds of thousands of displaced people.[71]

In 2017, the AA joined the UWSA, the KIO, and other northern EAOs to form the Federal Political Negotiation and Consultative Committee (FPNCC). This body, de facto led by the UWSA, demanded the then government negotiate collectively through the FPNCC. The group also has strong connections to China, which, through its significant leverage over these groups, exerted notable influence over the process. Collectively, the FPNCC represents 80 percent of Myanmar's armed groups, far exceeding the 20 percent who chose to sign the NCA. Obstacles to peace were multifaceted. The NLD government's unwillingness to consent to negotiations before the EAOs signed the NCA was heavily influenced by the military, and the EAOs were unwilling to sign yet another ceasefire in the absence of political progress.

The 2021 Coup d'État

This chapter focuses on ceasefire dynamics up to 2020. Space precludes detailed exploration of the effects of the 2021 military takeover. We would be remiss to not note that following a second landslide election victory for the NLD, the military contested the results and staged a coup. This sparked mass protests, as well as a powerful civil disobedience movement (CDM). The CDM, catalyzed by feminized sectors such as health and education, was successful in removing labor and various forms of support to the militarized state.[72] The National Unity Government, the Committee Representing the Pyidaungsu Hluttaw, and the National Unity Consultative Council were swiftly established. The military did not appear to anticipate the multiple forms of resistance and rejection, particularly by the Bamar population in the Burmese "heartland" in the center of the country. In response, the military declared a unilateral ceasefire, repeating its common approach of reducing hostilities in some areas to concentrate forces in another. Concurrently, it unleashed widespread violence, mass arrests, and detention, coupled with reports of sexual violence and torture in detention sites. In addition, the military's collective punishment against the protests was unprecedented in terms of scale, locations, and the diversity of identity groups directly involved.[73] While several EAOs, notably the KNU, came out in support of the protestors,[74] the protesters themselves have attempted to garner wider support from the EAOs with the promise of a new constitution.[75] At the time of writing, it remains unclear how the situation will develop. With more armed actors than ever before, Public Defence Forces (some aligned to the National Unity Government and some to the broader revolution), and more militia (aligned to the military), there are complex challenges ahead to agree on a political settlement linked to effective and genuine ceasefires that are underpinned by a transformed and federal security sector.

THE INTERACTION BETWEEN EFFORTS TO ADDRESS THE CONFLICT VIOLENCE AND EFFORTS TO ADDRESS THE CONTESTED ISSUES

The preceding discussion has summarized efforts to manage the conflict violence and the move toward peace in Myanmar over the past sixty years, thus following independence from colonialism up to 2020. In line with the central focus of this book, we reflect more broadly on how, throughout the process, ceasefires have influenced, and were in turn influenced by, attempts to address the issues underlying the violent conflict.

Ceasefires have been an ever-present feature of conflict in Myanmar over the past thirty years, from informal "gentlemen's agreements" to bilateral ceasefires and the nationwide ceasefire agreement. For the most part, these agreements have proven to be relatively durable, limiting violence between the parties and often lasting many years. In many other contexts, several of which are discussed in this volume, durable ceasefires have aided attempts to build confidence and trust between the parties and proved vital steps toward a political settlement (i.e., produced a positive feedback loop). In Myanmar, this has not been the case. For, rather than serve as stepping stones to more substantive political negotiations and agreements, ceasefires have been used as a respite for the military on multiple fighting fronts, as well as to sustain and strengthen the status quo in favor of the military, alongside some of the EAO elite. It has meanwhile not served to move the parties—and the millions of people caught up in the conflict—any closer to a political agreement, since it appears this was never the point of the ceasefires.

A core issue is how power is distributed across Myanmar. Most significant EAOs, including the UWSA, KIO, KNU, and AA, seek forms of self-determination (e.g., autonomy, federalism, or a confederate status) while the military has largely sought to preserve its solid grip on the economy and power through a Bamar Buddhist nationalist authoritarian centralized order. The military has proven extremely resistant to discussing alternatives with *any* of the EAOs. The move toward a civilian-led government and forms of democracy with the 2015 NLD landslide election was a critical period. It was largely quarantined within a system that was rigged to the military's benefit through the constitution and the economy, with militarism pervading many aspects of life in Myanmar. Ultimately, in more than sixty years of post-colonialism conflict, the military and its various political affiliates have *never* initiated discussions, let alone a formal negotiation process with the stated goal of producing a genuine political settlement with EAOs and ethnic nationality populations.

Instead, an almost perpetual cycle of siloed ceasefires and economic incentives has prevailed. Political dialogue has largely stalled at the nascent phases, that is, at the question of which actors ought to be discussing which issues and when. The most significant example of this has been the NCA process, which, despite significant achievements, never reached its full potential. This hybrid agreement—outlining a ceasefire and also the pathways for political dialogue—lacks many important ceasefire-specific provisions, most notably the lines of demarcation, clarity of violations, and a clear timetable of activities. The NCA hybridity was hugely ambitious. While it did provide a path for future discussions with some EAOs, the subsequent Union Peace Conferences and the resulting peace architecture were not able to make meaningful gains.

Ceasefires have provided one form of de facto recognition of EAO territorial control and meanwhile economic incentives to enrich some leaders and business elites. That so many have been reasonably durable reflects the preference of many EAOs to also protect communities from military attacks and predation, albeit some EAOs have also secured access to lucrative natural resources and opportunities for narcotics production. In the bilateral ceasefire era, in return for a mitigation of direct violence by the military, EAOs were expected to consent to the suspension of any broader political aspirations. In stopping violence, they would allow the military to focus attention on its economic objectives and redirect its attention toward other "noncooperative" groups.

For the UWSA, this arrangement has largely prevented violent conflict with the military. As it is located in relatively inaccessible terrain on the Myanmar–China border, maintaining the most significant ethnic nationality army, the military has been keen to avoid direct confrontation with the powerful group (and so has China). The UWSA has benefited from its de facto autonomy and freedom to develop a wide range of economic activities. Up to 2020, the parties have maintained a long-standing ceasefire, without moving to a more permanent settlement as the status quo was acceptable to both parties.

The KIO and the KNU have had a more varied relationship with the military, particularly through to 2021, when dynamics dramatically shifted. Both groups have been strong proponents of political reform in Myanmar, advocating for a democratic federal state, with full recognition of ethnic nationalities, and equitable access and control of natural resources. Yet, given the military's unwillingness to make significant political concessions, both groups have been faced with the choice of accepting a ceasefire that provides lucrative economic opportunities or stand firm to their political aspirations. The latter would mean rejecting a ceasefire and facing the full range of the military's aggression. For a long time, the KNU stood firm to its political aspirations and hence opted for the military approach. But in the hope of a political settlement with changes in Burmese politics and fatigued by a long period of struggle (hoping there would be more progress with the NLD), the KNU opted to accept a ceasefire and subsequently become part of the NCA. In contrast, the KIO, who benefited from a long period of ceasefire up until 2011, decided not to enter the NCA. Now, as their vice chair General Gun Maw stated (prior to the 2021 coup), they prefer to remain in a state of conflict rather than to go for a quicker settlement that would not address their political grievances in a sustainable manner.

The AA, in contrast, has not yet held a long period of ceasefire with the military. In 2018–2019, the military exchanged unilateral ceasefires with the alliance of EAOs (of which the AA is a part), and in 2020, an informal ceasefire was agreed upon to facilitate elections in AA areas of operations. Yet, for the most part, both have pursued military conflict over a ceasefire. Dynamics in Rakhine State are subject to considerable flux. The postcoup effects have been markedly different in Rakhine compared to the rest of Myanmar, and it remains to be seen how relations with the AA and military will unfold.

Arguably, the duration of these limited ceasefires has contributed to the difficulties in resolving the underlying conflict drivers (e.g., negative feedback loop). By stopping the conflict violence, ceasefires can reduce the pressure on the conflict parties to make the concessions necessary to reach an agreement.[76] It is worth asking, for example, Why should the military make concessions when multiple ceasefires protect them from costly violence or the challenges of fighting a war on multiple fronts? Why would an EAO concede to more Burmese authority over an area that, during a ceasefire, they have maintained de facto control? Yet, ceasefires have also provided invaluable periods without direct violence for long-suffering communities and enabled forms of much-needed development across Myanmar.

CONCLUSION

Myanmar is home to the world's longest-running civil conflict(s). Following British colonialism and its problematic legacies, there have been numerous drivers of grievance and the growth of multiple nonstate armed groups. Successive military regimes have used ceasefires as a tool to manage and contain armed groups, as well as ethnic nationality communities, through costly direct and indirect violence. Ultimately, the military has resisted making substantive political concessions. Some EAOs have benefited from ceasefires that have limited the military's constant violence and thereby brought various forms of economic gain and development. But these gains are considered by many to be outweighed by the economic, military, and political benefits gained by the military. By design, these ceasefires have not translated into fulsome political negotiations and related agreements to establish an equitable federal union. Neither have they meant an end to militarization and violent conflict. The limited ceasefires in Myanmar have wrought a range of political, social, economic, and cultural consequences. In sum, they highlight that long-running ceasefires are no guarantee of a path to durable and inclusive peace.

NOTES

Given the state repression in Myanmar since the military takeover, it is necessary to redact the name of the lead author of this article for their safety.

1. Zaw Oo, "Understanding Myanmar's Peace Process: Ceasefire Agreements."
2. Woods, "Ceasefire Capitalism: Military–Private Partnerships, Resource Concessions, and Military–State Building in the Burma–China Borderlands."
3. For perspectives on the rationale for this shift, see Yamahata and Anderson, *Demystifying Myanmar's Transition and Political Crisis*; Cheesman, Skidmore, and Wilson, *Myanmar's Transition: Openings, Obstacles, and Opportunities*.
4. Under the military-designed 2008 constitution, the military guaranteed themselves 25 percent of seats in all parliaments, full control of key ministries (Home Affairs, Defence, Border Affairs), and a veto on any constitutional changes.
5. For reflections on civil society, see Paung Sie Facility, *Unlocking Civil Society Contributions to Peace in Myanmar*; Brenner and Schulman, "Myanmar's Top-Down Transition: Challenges for Civil Society"; Kramer, *Civil Society Gaining Ground: Opportunities for Change and Development in Burma*. The pre-2011 analysis is important to consider; Hlaing, "Associational Life in Myanmar: Past and Present"; Hlaing, "Burma: Civil Society Skirting Regime Rules."

6. Lintner, "The United Wa State Army and Burma's Peace Process," 2. For broader reflections, also see Transnational Institute, *The Nationwide Ceasefire Agreement in Myanmar: Promoting Ethnic Peace or Strengthening State Control.*

7. UN Human Rights Commissioner, *Statement,* 11 September 2017.

8. These figures are accurate as of 19 December 2023. Source: Daily briefing from the Assistance Association for Political Prisoners (Burma), https://aappb.org/?p=26983. It is important to note that these data do not capture all deaths and do not, as with most conflict incident data, reflect indirect death and suffering.

9. Other literature details other armed groups; for example, for an excellent analysis of militias in Myanmar, see Buchanan, *Militias in Myanmar.*

10. Lintner, "The United Wa State Army and Burma's Peace Process."

11. Lintner, "The United Wa State Army and Burma's Peace Process."

12. The Kachin Independence Organisation (KIO) is the political organization, and its military wing is the Kachin Independence Army (KIA). We use KIO throughout this text to refer to both groups.

13. Myanmar Peace Monitor, *Kachin Independence Organization.*

14. Dukalskis, "Why Do Some Insurgent Groups Agree to Cease-Fires While Others Do Not? A Within-Case Analysis of Burma/Myanmar, 1948–2011."

15. The Karen National Union (KNU) is the political organization, and its military wing is the Karen National Liberation Army (KNLA). We use KNU throughout this text to refer to both groups.

16. Jolliffe, "Ceasefires, Governance and Development: The Karen National Union in Times of Change."

17. Mathieson, "The Arakan Army in Myanmar: Deadly Conflict Rises in Rakhine State."

18. Scott, *The Art of Not Being Governed: An Anarchist History of Upland Southeast Asia;* Aung-Thwin and Aung-Thwin, *A History of Myanmar since Ancient Times: Traditions and Transformations.*

19. Dukalskis, "Why Do Some Insurgent Groups Agree to Cease-Fires While Others Do Not? A Within-Case Analysis of Burma/Myanmar, 1948–2011," 851.

20. Jones, "Understanding Myanmar's Ceasefires Geopolitics, Political Economy and State-Building."

21. Zaw Oo, "Understanding Myanmar's Peace Process: Ceasefire Agreements"; Dukalskis, "Why Do Some Insurgent Groups Agree to Cease-Fires While Others Do Not? A Within-Case Analysis of Burma/Myanmar, 1948–2011," 852.

22. Smith, *State of Strife: The Dynamics of Ethnic Conflict in Burma.*

23. Lintner, "The United Wa State Army and Burma's Peace Process."

24. Battersby, "Border Politics and the Broader Politics of Thailand's International Relations in the 1990s: From Communism to Capitalism"; Jones, "Understanding Myanmar's Ceasefires Geopolitics, Political Economy and State-Building."

25. Callahan, *Making Enemies: War and State Building in Burma.*

26. Woods et al., *Developing Disparity: Regional Investment in Burma's Borderlands.*

27. Lintner, "The United Wa State Army and Burma's Peace Process."

28. Woods, "Ceasefire Capitalism: Military–Private Partnerships, Resource Concessions, and Military–State Building in the Burma–China Borderlands"; Jones, "Understanding Myanmar's Ceasefires Geopolitics, Political Economy and State-Building."

29. Zaw Oo and Min, *Assessing Burma's Ceasefire Accords*; Dukalskis, "Why Do Some Insurgent Groups Agree to Cease-Fires While Others Do Not? A Within-Case Analysis of Burma/Myanmar, 1948–2011."

30. Zaw Oo and Min, *Assessing Burma's Ceasefire Accords*, 25; Dukalskis, "Why Do Some Insurgent Groups Agree to Cease-Fires While Others Do Not? A Within-Case Analysis of Burma/Myanmar, 1948–2011."

31. Smith, *Burma: Insurgency and the Politics of Ethnicity*, 332–333.

32. In some cases, especially in Karen, Kachin, and Mon states, villages often had dual governance structures from both the Burmese state and the EAO. These were called "brown areas" in contrast to the "black areas" that are under total EAO control.

33. Woods, "Ceasefire Capitalism: Military–Private Partnerships, Resource Concessions, and Military–State Building in the Burma–China Borderlands."

34. Woods, "Ceasefire Capitalism: Military–Private Partnerships, Resource Concessions, and Military–State Building in the Burma–China Borderlands."

35. The other EAO not to agree a ceasefire was the Restoration Council for Shan State (RCSS).

36. South, "Karen Nationalist Communities: The 'Problem' of Diversity."

37. Thawnghmung, *The Karen Revolution in Burma: Diverse Voices, Uncertain Ends.*

38. Jolliffe, "Ceasefires, Governance and Development: The Karen National Union in Times of Change."

39. Callahan, *Political Authority in Burma's Ethnic Minority States: Devolution, Occupation, and Coexistence*, 31; Jolliffe, "Ceasefires, Governance, and Development: The Karen National Union in Times of Change," 10.

40. Jolliffe, "Ceasefires, Governance and Development: The Karen National Union in Times of Change," 12 (emphasis in original).

41. Zaw Oo, "Understanding Myanmar's Peace Process: Ceasefire Agreements."

42. This was the Karenni National Progressive Party in response to military threats to retract some of their business opportunities.

43. Sadan, *War and Peace in the Borderlands of Myanmar: The Kachin Ceasefire 1994–2011.*

44. Smith, *State of Strife: The Dynamics of Ethnic Conflict in Burma*, 34.

45. Williams, "What's So Bad about Burma's 2008 Constitution?"

46. Zaw Oo, "Understanding Myanmar's Peace Process: Ceasefire Agreements." The other groups were the New Mon State Party (NMSP), the Karen Peace Council (KPC), and the National Democratic Alliance Army (NDAA).

47. Brenner, "Ashes of Co-optation: From Armed Group Fragmentation to the Rebuilding of Popular Insurgency in Myanmar."

48. Jones, "Understanding Myanmar's Ceasefires: Geopolitics, Political Economy and State-Building."

49. The AA came into the negotiation later as a member of NCCT; see below. Until the formation of NCCT in November 2013, they were not party to the ceasefire discussions.

50. For a perspective on federalism and ethnic nationality historical understandings, see Ohn, "Building a Lasting Federal Union in Myanmar."

51. The other EAO to quickly enter into an agreement as an early adopter was the Nationalities Democratic Alliance Army (NDAA).

52. The Restoration Council for Shan State (RCSS), the other group that had resisted a ceasefire in the prior period, then approved a bilateral agreement.

53. There was also green text used for text that was accepted by the negotiators but still requiring authorization from the group's leadership.

54. Myint-U, *The Hidden History of Burma: Race, Capitalism, and the Crisis of Democracy in the 21st Century*.

55. Saferworld, *Security Integration in Myanmar: Past Experiences and Future Visions*. The quasi-civilian government wished to label the reforms "security integration," a relatively ambiguous term with no international precedent. The EAOs preferred the term "security sector reform" (SSR), which was more widely understood.

56. The excluded groups were the Lahu Democratic Union, Wa National Organization, and the Arakan National Council.

57. The other groups were the Myanmar National Democratic Alliance Army (MNDAA) and the Ta'ang National Liberation Army (TNLA).

58. Burmese government negotiators also argued that because the AA was not based in the territory of its ethnic identity, Rakhine State, it could not meet provisions relating to territorial rights and monitoring arrangements contained in the Nationwide Ceasefire Agreement (NCA). Mathieson, "The Arakan Army in Myanmar: Deadly Conflict Rises in Rakhine State."

59. At the same time, the KIO remained unhappy with the lack of clarity in key parts of the agreement, in particular the arrangements concerning monitoring and security sector reform.

60. These groups were the New Mon State Party, the Karenni National Progressive Party, and the Shan State Progress Party.

61. Lintner, "The United Wa State Army and Burma's Peace Process."

62. See International Crisis Group, "Avoiding a Return to War in Rakhine State."

63. For a gendered analysis of the NCA, see AGIPP, *If Half the Population Mattered: A Critique of the Myanmar Nationwide Ceasefire Agreement and Joint Monitoring Committee Framework from a Gender Perspective*.

64. When the NLD took power, these became known as the 21st Century Panglong Conferences, harkening back to the original Panglong Agreement between the Burmese government led by Aung San—father of Aung San Suu Kyi—and the Shan, Kachin, and Chin nationalities in 1947.

65. For more detailed analyses of the civilian monitoring ecosystem, see Mercy Corps, *Building a Robust Civilian Ceasefire Monitoring Mechanism in Myanmar: Challenges, Successes and Lessons Learned*.

66. Lintner, "The United Wa State Army and Burma's Peace Process."

67. Sithu, "The UWSA: 30 Years of Going Its Own Way."

68. Mathieson, "The Arakan Army in Myanmar: Deadly Conflict Rises in Rakhine State."

69. Bynum, "Ceasefires and Conflict Dynamics in Myanmar."

70. International Crisis Group, "Coming to Terms with Myanmar's Russia Embrace"; UN Special Rapporteur on the situation of human rights in Myanmar, A/HRC/49/CRP.1, *Enabling Atrocities: UN Member States' Arms Transfers to the Myanmar Military*.

71. Mathieson, "The Arakan Army in Myanmar: Deadly Conflict Rises in Rakhine State."

72. For a span of perspectives and analysis of concerns, see Naw, "Raising Our Flag High. A Kachin Activist on Reimagining an Inclusive Society after the coup in Myanmar"; Burma News International, *Briefing Paper on Violations of Media Freedom by Myanmar Military Council*; Potkin and Mcpherson, "How Myanmar's Military Moved In on the Telecoms Sector to Spy on Its Citizens"; International Crisis Group, "Myanmar's

Military Struggles to Control the Virtual Battlefield"; Jap, "Protesters and Bystanders: Ethnic Minorities in the Pro-Democracy Revolution"; Thawnghmung, "Back to the Future? Possible Scenarios for Myanmar."

73. UN Human Rights Council, A/HRC/49/72, "Situation of Human Rights in Myanmar since 1 February 2021"; UN Human Rights Council, A/HRC/50/CRP.1, "Losing a Generation: How the Military Junta Is Attacking Myanmar's Children and Stealing Their Future"; UN Human Rights Council, A/HRC/51/4, "Report of the Independent Investigative Mechanism for Myanmar."

74. Roth, Hu, and Barnes, "Myanmar Junta Offers Ceasefire to Some, as UN Envoy Warns of 'Bloodbath.'"

75. Associated Press, "Junta's Foes Woo Ethnic Allies with New Myanmar Constitution."

76. Clayton et al., "Ceasefires in Intra-state Peace Processes."

CHAPTER 11

Conclusion
The Role of Ceasefires in Peace Processes

Govinda Clayton, Simon J. A. Mason, Valerie Sticher,
and Andreas Wenger

Peacefully ending intrastate conflict requires conflict parties to agree to a settlement of the contested issues *and* the terms under which conflict violence will stop. The nine case studies show the benefit of distinguishing these two tasks. They illustrate several ways in which the ceasefire and political process interact and how this interaction is conditioned by context factors. Every peace process is unique, and the interaction between the ceasefire and political negotiation process had distinctive elements in each of the cases covered. While acknowledging and recognizing these differences, this chapter strives for a broader perspective, trading a focus on the individual complexities of the single cases for more general insights. In essence, we strive to *connect the dots* between each of the individual chapters to draw out common patterns, trends, and learnings for research and practice.[1]

Figure 11.1 presents an overview of our analysis. We particularly focus on what we call the ceasefire opportunity space, a heuristic device that indicates the full range of potentially acceptable ceasefire arrangements and sequencing approaches in relation to the political negotiations in any given period. The ceasefire opportunity space is determined by the convergence in the parties' political and security interests and various contextual factors. The parties' interests (i.e., their preferences on whether to progress the political negotiation and/or ceasefire process) are shaped by the international, domestic, and military contexts. Ultimately, whether the opportunity for a (certain type of) ceasefire and sequence (in relation to the political

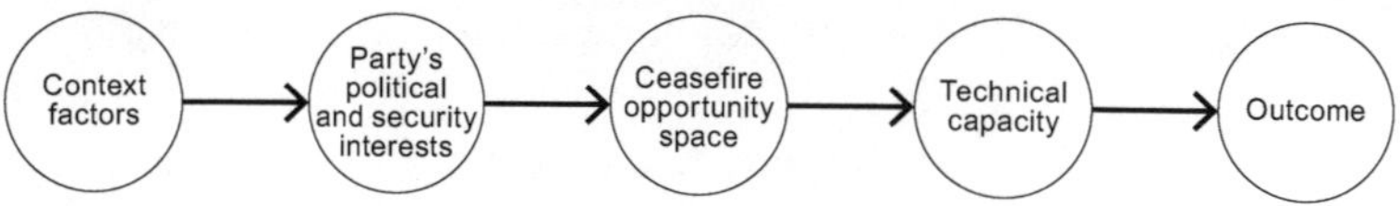

Figure 11.1 Factors shaping use and outcome of ceasefires

negotiations) is seized depends on various factors. Particularly, we focus on the technical capacity and competence of the negotiating actors and the mediation team.

In what follows, we discuss each of these steps. In the first section, we discuss how the overlap in the parties' interests regarding the ceasefire and political negotiation process shapes the ceasefire opportunity space. Second, we identify the contextual factors that impact this space. We conclude with a closing section on key insights and reflections for researchers and practitioners, in particular noting the importance of technical capacity, as a way to maximize the opportunity space provided by the interest profile of the involved parties and a given context.

CEASEFIRE OPPORTUNITY SPACE

The *ceasefire opportunity space* is a heuristic device that helps identify the range of potentially acceptable ceasefire arrangements and sequencing approaches in any given period. Ceasefire sequencing refers to when in the political negotiation process conflict parties adopt various kinds of ceasefires. Ceasefire arrangements are rarely stand-alone agreements. As discussed more comprehensively in the introductory chapter, there is often a feedback loop between ceasefire and political negotiation processes: progress in one track facilitates progress in the other, whereas an impasse or breakdown in one process often spills over to the other track. The empirical analyses in the case chapters indicate that, beyond a simple feedback loop, the interests of conflict parties to move each of these two tracks forward also influences ceasefire sequencing options, that is, shapes at which point in the political negotiation process conflict parties may choose to adopt a (specific class of) ceasefire. The "ceasefire opportunity space" therefore refers to the potential to reach and implement ceasefires. It is determined by the parties' convergence of interests in ending conflict violence and dealing with the contested issues in the broader transition from war to peace.

Drawing on the case chapters, we derive a 2 × 2 table that identifies four distinct ideal type combinations of the parties' interests. These four combinations are defined by the conflict parties' shared interest (or lack thereof) in progressing the political negotiation process and/or stopping violence (see figure 11.2). Importantly, a shared interest in progressing negotiations does not necessarily imply that both actors have an inherent stake in finding a political solution. One or all parties may genuinely seek to address the contested issues to end the armed conflict, or they may enter talks merely to probe and explore potential gains. Alternatively, they may be willing to go along with their opponent's preference to address the conflict issues as the price of achieving their desired end to violence. A shared interest in stopping the violence therefore indicates that both actors see the need to address the conflict violence, either as an end in and of itself, as a tactical move, or to facilitate the political negotiation process.

The combinations of parties' political and security interests shape the ceasefire opportunity space. Specifically, they determine the likelihood of reaching (specific types of) ceasefires and shape the ceasefire sequencing logic parties will likely adopt. Each of the four different spaces offers unique incentives for the parties to adopt different types of ceasefires at different stages of the political negotiation process, with broader implications on the likelihood of ending conflict violence and resolving the contested issues.

We next discuss the four combinations of parties' political and security interests and how they define the ceasefire opportunity space. It is important to note, however, that these combinations are ideal types: they may only relate to a specific phase of a conflict and shift over time. As we discuss below, contextual factors—such as the distribution of military power or international pressure—shape parties' interests, and these context factors change

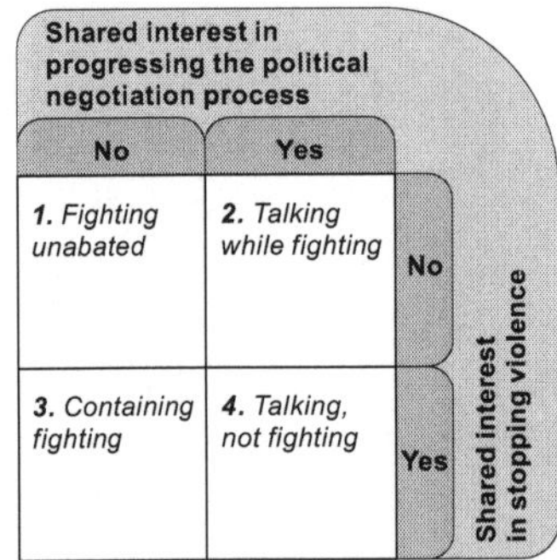

Figure 11.2 A 2 × 2 table of interaction between the political negotiation and ceasefire processes

over time. Consequently, parties' alignments of interests often shift over the course of a conflict, shaping the ceasefire opportunity space and conditioning what sequencing strategies are most feasible. Identifying such shifts and adapting the ceasefire and political negotiation process to them constitutes an important part of conflict and context-sensitive policy engagement.

Fighting Unabated

A first typical situation exists when conflict parties lack a shared interest in both progressing the political process *and* stopping violence. This can occur when all conflict parties prefer to pursue their goals through solely military means, or where the preferences of the actors are unaligned (e.g., one party may wish to limit violence, while the other seeks progress on the political level, and neither are willing to make concessions on the other track).

In any case, when parties lack a common interest in pushing forward the political negotiation process or stopping the violence, the opportunity space for any ceasefire is limited if not nonexistent. However, there is still a minimal "opportunity space" for limited types of confidence-building or de-escalation measures. In many conflicts, as soon as violence starts, there are often attempts to curtail, restrain, or at least not escalate certain kinds of violence. However, only extremely limited and brief arrangements that serve some mutually beneficial short-term goal are likely in these types of situations. Examples include prisoner and corpse exchanges, unwritten agreements to refrain from using certain weapons to attack certain targets; brief truces to collect bodies from the battlefield; and limited breaks to celebrate religious holidays. Identifying such efforts and trying to build on them is one way to move from this extremely limited opportunity space into one of the following quadrants with more space for cooperation.

These situations are commonly found when conflict breaks out, as it is the parties' inability to satisfactorily progress the political process and/or agree to mechanisms to stop violence that bring about the start of an armed conflict. They are thus particularly common in the pre-prenegotiation and prenegotiation phases, but parties can return to this space throughout a conflict—often repeatedly—if talks or a ceasefire breaks down.

In Myanmar, for example, as argued in chapter 10, the Arakan Army and the Tatmadaw suffered prolonged periods of unabated fighting as the non-state group was reluctant to temper hostilities in the absence of progress on the political level, while the military regime sought the limitation of violence without offering any concessions in the political process.

Talking While Fighting

A second typical situation exists when parties have a shared interest in progressing the political negotiation process, but at least one of the parties is resistant to stopping the violence. This can occur when parties both see the benefit of progressing the political process, but at least one side has concerns about stopping violence potentially prematurely or believes that it benefits militarily or politically from continued fighting.

This situation is common in pre-prenegotiation and prenegotiation phases when the parties agree to discuss the terms of political talks but are not yet trusting enough to agree a stop to the violence. However, in some cases, it extends to the negotiation phase. A party that favors an immediate stop to violence might agree to prioritize progress in political negotiations in the hope that this will eventually lead to their desired cessation of violence. This was the case in Colombia, where the FARC—despite favoring an immediate suspension of violence—agreed to the government's demand to focus on the political negotiations in the understanding that progress here was necessary to ultimately achieve the desired end to the violence.

There are limited opportunities for bilateral ceasefires in this context, as by definition, the parties do not agree on the need to stop the violence. This does not, however, preclude unilateral ceasefires or other de-escalation measures. Alongside other confidence-building measures, these more limited arrangements can perform important functions like signaling commitment and limiting violence during political negotiations.

As the cases of El Salvador and Colombia demonstrate, a political process can make considerable progress, even in the absence of a preliminary ceasefire. Somewhat counterintuitively, parties operating in such a context can more easily signal their genuine commitment to finding a settlement and are less likely to be accused of progressing talks to achieve some devious military goal (e.g., rearming under the cover of a ceasefire). For in the absence of a ceasefire, there is less likely to be a *military* incentive to engage in or prolong negotiations (unless perhaps pressed to do so by third parties). Ongoing violence is also accepted as part of this approach, so *in principle*, the threat of the process breaking down due to violence is also less pertinent than when a ceasefire is in place.

One of the challenges of this approach is that it seeks to delink the ceasefire from the political negotiation process, while conflict violence and issue contestation are intrinsically linked. It is difficult to negotiate while violence continues, and violent incidents are hard for both elites and their constituents to ignore. In Colombia, the parties explicitly agreed to "fight as if they weren't talking and talk as if they weren't fighting." Nevertheless, conflict violence continued to affect the political negotiation process, and public support for the process soured in the aftermath of significant battlefield events. This made it difficult for the leadership to justify their continued engagement. As a result, the parties agreed to adopt several unilateral de-escalation measures to address the violence (e.g., unilateral ceasefires and suspension of air strikes). By the time the peace agreement was signed, despite no preliminary ceasefire being in effect, a shared interest in stopping the violence had arisen, and the violence had effectively stopped.

Ultimately, the aim of any peace process is to stop the violence—at the latest when the parties have satisfied their most essential political aims. However, as the experiences from Colombia and El Salvador demonstrate, even when the parties agree to postpone the end of violence to the signing of a peace agreement, it may become apparent over time that measures to stop or limit the violence are needed to facilitate the signing of such an agreement in practice. Such measures may be in the form of a bilateral ceasefire toward the end of a process (El Salvador) or, if a bilateral ceasefire is not possible for political or historical or domestic reasons, in the form of reciprocal unilateral measures in the lead-up to an agreement (Colombia). While finding context-appropriate measures should be up to the conflict actors, third parties can support them in making such decisions, by highlighting different available arrangements and helping parties think through the advantages and challenges of each of them.

Containing Fighting

A third context exists when parties lack a common desire to progress the political talks but hold a shared interest in stopping or at least limiting conflict violence. In this case, progress toward a peaceful resolution of a dispute is undesirable for one or more conflict parties, but collectively they see a common benefit in cooperating to reduce violence, either to move toward a political settlement or as an end in itself.

Parties might favor ceasefires over political progress for several reasons, from saving lives and reducing civilian suffering to reducing their conflict costs to a sustainable level, or because they have no interest in resolving the contested issues and see a ceasefire as a de facto alternative to both fighting and settlement. Conversely, one side may strongly favor progress in political negotiations, but the power holder dominates militarily and so imposes their preferences in the process. Finally, parties may be interested in a ceasefire for military reasons (e.g., to rearm and reorganize) and have no genuine desire to end conflict violence in the long term. Here ceasefires serve so-called devious intentions, where parties engage in peacemaking to further their interests—but not necessarily with the aim of moving toward a peaceful solution.[2]

This space creates a significant opportunity for several types of ceasefires, although as noted, there is a risk that one or both actors may use a ceasefire for military purposes, which may lead to short-term de-escalation but risk escalating or prolonging the conflict violence in the long term. Depending on the conflict and the underlying objectives of the conflict parties, everything from limited cessation of hostilities to fully monitored agreements is possible. This can involve long-term arrangements spanning many years (e.g., KNU in Myanmar) to more limited periods of de-escalation (e.g., Syria).

When parties prioritize reducing conflict violence over political negotiations, it can often have the effect of impeding progress on the political level. Containment ceasefires can create a mutually, or unilaterally, beneficial negative peace that reduces any incentives to progress political negotiations (e.g., the Wa in Myanmar). Impeding progress in the political process can sometimes be an unintended outcome of containment ceasefires, while on other occasions, ceasefires are called precisely to undermine the political process. In Syria, for example, as argued in chapter 9, the Russia-led peace process deliberately delinked the ceasefire process from efforts to negotiate the conflict issues as part of the broader war-fighting strategy.

Despite these risks, third-party actors may often find it preferable to promote a freeze or containment of a conflict to save lives and reduce suffering, even if it comes at the expense of potentially perpetuating the underlying conflict.[3] Third-party actors choosing to push for such so-called containment ceasefires need to be clear on purpose (e.g., humanitarian) and specify the conditions under which a ceasefire should be renewed or not. They also need to recognize that actors may engage in a ceasefire for military purposes, with possible negative long-term consequences for the trajectory of violence. Mitigating the risks of such negative consequences requires third-party engagement beyond the parties' signing of a ceasefire arrangement. Third-party actors should carefully assess their own ability and willingness for such a sustained engagement before pushing for a containment ceasefire.

Talking, Not Fighting

The fourth context exists when both parties have a shared interest in advancing political talks *and* stopping conflict violence. This does not mean both parties are necessarily equally favorable to both processes. In many cases, different parties might have different preferences regarding political progress versus stopping violence. Yet, in this fourth context, both parties understand that achieving their desired outcome requires progress on both tracks, with progress on one track reinforcing progress on the other. Thus, parties seek to progress the ceasefire process broadly in unison with political negotiations, ensuring that as talks progress, violence on the battlefield is progressively reduced.

This ultimately creates the greatest opportunity space for the full range of ceasefires, ranging from limited short-term arrangements in the earlier phases of a negotiation process to preliminary and definitive ceasefires as the talks progress. In this context, different ceasefires are used to promote progress in the political negotiations, which then provides further impetus to progress further in efforts to stop violence—a mutually reinforcing feedback loop. Parties may decide to enter a ceasefire prior to formal negotiations and build and expand on it during talks, or they may agree on a ceasefire after the onset of formal negotiations. In either case, ceasefires help build trust and incrementally test more significant forms of cooperation. For example, in the Philippines, the parties agreed on a preliminary ceasefire that came into effect at the start of political negotiations. The ceasefire architecture expanded as the political talks progressed, making the ceasefire increasingly more resilient to nonstrategic violations. Similarly, in Sudan (North–South), the parties incrementally built the ceasefire process alongside developments in the political process.

The advantage of this approach is that it allows parties to develop and test out forms of cooperation before a final agreement. Doing so can help to save lives, allow conflict parties to build confidence and working relations incrementally, and help them prepare for permanent arrangements. As it is preliminary, the actors do not give up their fighting force and thus retain the ability to return to conflict if the political negotiations fail. The logic is to disentangle the military violence from the negotiation process, but without giving up the option of returning to military fighting, as giving this up would minimize the parties' incentive to agree to it. This disentanglement is key, as it is hard to build trust and find a compromise at the negotiation table if at the same time parties are killing each other.

The disadvantage of this approach is that it removes some pressure from the political negotiation process and sometimes leads to a longer, more drawn-out process. There seems to be a far greater risk of this if the preliminary ceasefire is poorly crafted from a technical point of view, with unclear time frames, and lacking in detail on a monitoring and verification mandate. Furthermore, there may be unhelpful incentives for third parties to push for a preliminary ceasefire, irrespective of the conflict parties' readiness for such an agreement (e.g., to access funds and gain media attention). A technically flawed preliminary ceasefire may be worse than no ceasefire at all, as it raises expectations, and if the ceasefire is not kept, it can lead to an escalation of violence—and a negative feedback loop. This is particularly regrettable if the conflict parties do have a shared interest in moving ceasefire and political negotiation processes forward.

Ultimately, all peaceful terminations require the conflict parties reach the "talking, not fighting" quadrant. But how "early" or "late" in a process this occurs can vary greatly. When parties enter this context earlier in a process, it makes it easier to save lives, build confidence, and prepare for permanent arrangements,[4] as it is often very hard to talk and build trust while fighting is ongoing. Yet an "early" ceasefire can also sometimes lead to a longer, more drawn-out political negotiation process as the impetus to move to settlement is reduced once violence is stopped (as was discussed as a possible interpretation of the Philippines case in chapter 5). As political negotiations are so clearly linked to the ceasefire (and vice versa), there is also a risk that impasses on the political stage trigger the collapse of a ceasefire, or that ceasefire violations lead to crises at the negotiation table (i.e., a negative feedback loop). Parties' readiness and "ripeness" are therefore important considerations, even if an early end of violence often seems most attractive from a third-party or humanitarian perspective.

Implications

The four distinct combinations of parties' political and security interests have different prospects for several types and timing of ceasefires, and the probable impact any ceasefire is likely to have on political negotiations. Several useful implications can be derived from this analytical approach.

First, parties' interests are likely to shift over time, potentially widening or tightening the opportunity space for different ceasefires and enabling or impeding different ceasefire sequencing strategies. Most conflicts begin with an initial period of unabated fighting where any ceasefire is unlikely. Whereas ultimately, a peaceful termination almost always requires that the parties converge on *talking, not fighting* and agree on some form of ceasefire or other de-escalation mechanisms prior to the final agreement. Yet there is likely to be significant variation in how "early" or "late" in the process the parties agree to talk and not fight, and the extent to which the path to peace involves periods in which the parties' interests converge on containing fighting, talking while fighting, or even returning to *unabated fighting*. Parties' interests are perhaps less likely to switch during formal negotiation when they settled on a common sequencing strategy during the prenegotiation phase. However, processes often break down and restart later, requiring parties to renegotiate the sequencing strategy. In some cases, formal negotiations begin without a clear sequencing strategy and are contested throughout the talks (e.g., Syria, El Salvador). However, separate periods of negotiation in the same conflict can operate in different contexts, no doubt in part due to learning across processes. This was the case in Colombia, where a failed talking, not fighting approach led the government in the subsequent peace process to insist on a talking while fighting model. Part of a peacemaker's job is helping the parties to navigate this journey, balancing the benefits and limitations of different sequencing options as the process develops.

Second, the type of ceasefire arrangement should reflect the ceasefire opportunity space it is operating in. For example, a preliminary ceasefire is only likely to be possible when parties' shared interests converge on talking, not fighting. In other contexts, this is unlikely to be an effective approach, and attempts to impose this approach externally are likely to do more harm than good.

Third, the convergence of interests creates an opportunity for a ceasefire sequencing approach but does not automatically mean that ceasefire and political negotiation processes will be successful. Several process factors shape the extent to which an opportunity for a ceasefire can be seized, including the capacity of the negotiating actors. As we saw across several cases, military forces are trained for fighting but seldom for ceasefires and peace processes. Parties, therefore, benefit from support and training on how to develop a ceasefire and sequence a peace process and are less likely to resist entering a ceasefire if they understand the process. Training can also be necessary to ensure that there is sufficient knowledge down the chain of command, as we saw in the Sudan North–South process. Training can also help to develop the necessary technical expertise to negotiate an agreement. The extent to which all the practical details are agreed upon and included is crucial, as the risk of a ceasefire collapse increases with misunderstandings, even when there is an opportunity space and sufficient political will from parties to stop fighting. More specifically, training and support can help parties think through different sequencing approaches to use a given ceasefire opportunity space. Another factor shaping the party's ability to seize an opportunity space is the extent to which the chief mediator, topical mediators, advisory, and experts are able to work together (e.g., Sudan North–South process) or not (e.g., Darfur).

Fourth, with the benefit of hindsight, the context is often easy to identify, and the most effective ceasefire sequencing approach appears quite clear. Yet during ongoing conflict, it is obviously far harder to determine if there are any shared interests across conflict parties, and which ceasefire sequencing approach would most likely favor conflict settlement, not least because actors often have an incentive to misrepresent their true objectives for engaging in a ceasefire.[5] Ceasefire sequencing is also likely to be keenly contested by conflict parties, as it can have significant implications for the broader conflict dynamics. On the one hand, failure to agree on a ceasefire sequencing strategy can provide essential information about the parties' political and security interests, and about conflict ripeness in a broader sense, indicating that parties may still perceive continued fighting as a preferable option. On the other hand, failure to agree on ceasefire sequencing can also be due to a lack of knowledge of implications and different options. If this is the case, intermediaries might help by talking the parties through different scenarios and sequencing strategies. Thus, this heuristic device (i.e., the ceasefire opportunity space) is primarily analytical rather than operational in character and could feature as part of a broader conflict analysis, rather than prescribe any clear actions in any particular context. The operational implication for third parties, beyond analysis, is that discussing the pros and cons of different sequencing strategies with conflict parties can also potentially shift parties' perceptions of what is favorable.

So far, we have discussed how convergence in the parties' interests creates or shapes the opportunity space for ceasefires. However, these interests are shaped by broader contextual factors that we will now discuss.

HOW THE CONTEXT SHAPES THE CEASEFIRE OPPORTUNITY SPACE

In this section, we identify the most influential international, domestic, and military context factors that shaped the political and security interests of the conflict parties in our case chapters and reflect on how these factors impacted

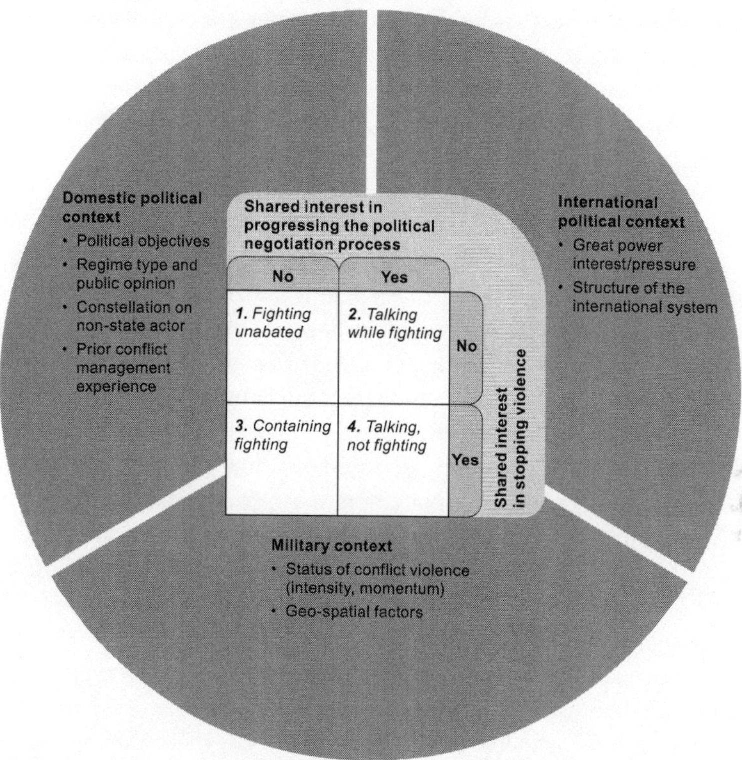

Figure 11.3 Key elements of the three context factors conditioning the parties' political and security interests.

the ceasefire opportunity space (see figure 11.3). We use examples from the case chapters to illustrate these effects, mindful that our examples always provide only one analytical perspective and that convergence of interests is generally explained through a combination of factors.

Domestic Political Context

The domestic political context covers any elements that shape the peace process that originate within the contesting groups. We focus on those elements that, across the cases in this book, were most influential in terms of shaping the parties' political and security interests and consequently the ceasefire opportunity space.

The political objectives of the conflict parties are crucial here. Political objectives are the starting point upon which conflict parties develop their approach. When the conflict parties lack a common goal for the political process, ceasefire sequencing options are limited to *fighting unabated* or *containing fighting,* as no serious political process can occur.

In Myanmar, for example, the Tatmadaw has for decades sought to primarily maintain the system of military dominance and has been willing to use violence, ceasefires, economic incentives, and strategic alliances to achieve this. This often did not overlap with the goals of the ethnic armed groups, meaning *containment* has often been the only viable option. Similarly in Syria, President Bashar Hafez al-Assad's main objective has arguably been to keep the regime in place and retain full control of political power. At the same time, the nonstate groups were (initially) committed to replacing Assad. Given these diametrically opposed positions, and the fact that both sides were supported by external actors that prevented exhaustion and a mutually hurting stalemate, it is not surprising that the political negotiation process never really gained traction. Ceasefires still occurred, but these were either disconnected from the political negotiations altogether or used strategically to gain some military advantage (i.e., containment).

In contrast, the emergence of a minimal overlap of political goals opens the path to talking while fighting and talking, not fighting. In Burundi, the primary objective for the Tutsi minority was to safeguard their group from the threat of Hutu extermination. The primary objective of the Hutu majority was to gain a fair share of the political and economic power and have "one person, one vote." A minimal common objective of the peace process was thus to share power, return to the rule of law, and safeguard certain interests of the minorities. Once this was clear, the parties adopted a series of ceasefires in support of the political process. Similarly, in Colombia, the FARC gave up on the objective of overthrowing the government after its forces greatly diminished in the early 2000s and sought to trade guns for votes instead. This allowed for a minimal common goal between the FARC and the government for the peace process, namely, to end the armed conflict, though they mainly agreed to a "talking while fighting" approach due to other historical factors.

Indeed, the outcome of prior conflict management efforts is another domestic factor that shapes the ceasefire opportunity space. We observed a form of path dependency, where prior efforts colored shared incentives that define the actor's preferences when it comes to stopping violence during talks. Where ceasefires had previously been tried and failed or, worse, been manipulated by a conflict party for some political or military gain, we observe stiffer resistance to similar efforts in the future. The clearest example of this was in Colombia, where in a prior peace process, the FARC was widely considered to have used a ceasefire in a demilitarized zone to develop their military position. This led to the Colombian military, government, and broader population being extremely resistant to offering the FARC another ceasefire and giving them an opportunity to exploit the process in an analogous way. In Myanmar, decades of ceasefires without any considerable progress on the political level subsequently led several groups to resist signing the nationwide ceasefire agreement without the government committing more firmly to political progress. In both cases, prior failures in talking, not fighting led actors (both state and nonstate) to prefer a talking while fighting approach (at least initially).

In contrast, prior successes often created positive feedback loops, where the parties were subsequently willing to undertake similar initiatives in the future. In the Philippines, for example, the success of earlier ceasefires built trust in the ceasefire architecture and between the parties, meaning that when the political process stalled, or violence flared up, the parties were able to restore the prior arrangements, often adding new provisions to fix former failures. In essence, the *talking, not fighting* approach was never seriously questioned as the most effective and desirable for the peace process. Similarly, in Burundi, the success of the Arusha accords created a context in which the rebel group saw the benefits of a deal as a route to power and so were willing to give political negotiations, and ultimately *talking, not fighting*, a chance.

Identifying shared goals and learning from the past both depend to a certain extent on the coherence of the nonstate groups. Our cases covered contexts with various configurations of nonstate groups, ranging from processes involving a single, centralized, and relatively strong nonstate armed group (e.g., Colombia, El Salvador, Sudan North–South, Burundi, and the Philippines), to cases with a plethora of armed groups with strikingly different capacity (e.g., Myanmar, Syria, Darfur). Generally, it seems that agreeing on a ceasefire sequencing strategy was more feasible in contexts with a smaller number of stronger and more coherent armed groups.[6] It was "easier" to develop a negotiation process with a single group that has a relatively centralized structure, as elite bargaining tended to be more straightforward, and challenging questions of inclusion and sequencing were easier to resolve. At the same time, centralized leadership also made it easier for the conflict parties to design and implement a ceasefire strategy and integrate this into a broader political negotiation process. In particular, the inevitable setbacks throughout the process (e.g., ceasefire violations) were easier to resolve.

Strong centralized movements were also more likely to have a clear political goal, which helped negotiations. In contrast, containment was more likely when parties were fragmented.

Collectively, the case studies highlight the importance of considering the parties' overarching, and often shifting, objectives and how these shape the ceasefire opportunity space.[7] These objectives are often shaped by the military balance or external pressure, as conflict parties may consider a shift toward less maximalist objectives if they are losing on the battlefield or face massive costs from external actors (see discussions on international and military context). Often only by considering the degree of overlap between the objectives of conflict parties can we make sense of the approach taken toward the political negotiation process, ceasefires, and the interaction between the two. Identifying group objectives can be incredibly challenging, namely in fragmented contexts where actors might lack a clear overarching objective. However, from an analytical and a practical standpoint, they should be a central consideration. Similarly, prior experiences seem to have an influence on the ceasefire opportunity space, as certain sequencing approaches are more likely to be adapted and work when the parties have already had positive experiences with previous similar initiatives. This provides an important argument against adopting ceasefires immaturely, as failing initiatives often have long-term consequences on the trajectory of violence.

Military Context

The military context is crucial in shaping the interests of the conflict parties. Parties are more likely to converge on a shared interest in progressing political talks when a "mutually hurting stalemate"[8] exists, that is, when significant conflict costs make ongoing violence unmanageable for all parties, and both sides believe that a favorable military outcome on the battlefield is unlikely in the future. The presence of a mutually hurting stalemate means parties are more inclined to moderate their goals and make the concessions necessary to advance political talks and eventually stop the violence. This can be through fighting while talking, for example, in El Salvador, where the hurting stalemate emerged because FMLN's military success put enormous pressure on the government, but their inability to overthrow the government made victory unlikely. Another example is Colombia, where the military had significantly weakened the FARC but remained unable to overcome the non-state group in the inhospitable Colombia periphery. Or it may be achieved through talking, not fighting—for example, in Sudan, where decades of war between the North and South had proven the inability of either side to produce a decisive victory, and in the Philippines, where the conflict parties began to experience the ongoing war as painful and costly and recognized that they could not easily escalate to victory.[9]

Prior research has established that a hurting stalemate often leads to political progress but says little about the factors that shape the ceasefire sequencing strategy in this context. Here, our cases offer useful additional insights. In each case, the ceasefire opportunity space was shaped by the military balance. While a hurting stalemate implies a shared perception as to the unlikelihood of victory, that does not mean that the parties evenly share the costs of continued conflict or are balanced militarily, politically, and economically. In our cases, it was the interests of the relatively more powerful actor that tended to determine the sequencing approach of whether the parties would talk with or without fighting. For example, in El Salvador, the nonstate armed group held the upper hand and the military initiative and sought to talk while fighting as a means of maintaining pressure on the state. In Colombia, it was instead the state that held the advantage and so favored talking while fighting as a means of protecting itself against possible manipulation of any ceasefire by the FARC. In Sudan, the government also dominated militarily but ultimately favored the talking, not fighting approach on account of external pressure from the escalating war on terror. In each of these cases, it was the mutual acceptance as to the unlikelihood of victory that shifted the parties' interests in terms of engaging in political talks, but the stronger actor that ultimately leveraged their favorable position to determine whether violence should be stopped early or late in the talking process.

The preferences of the stronger party in turn tended to reflect the geospatial realities on the ground. Powerful actors seem to have been more reluctant to stop violence when this risked locking in losses that would make it more challenging to regain ground in the future. In contrast, in those cases in which the nonstate group had demonstrated control of a region, ceasefires often appeared easier to design and implement. This did not necessarily make political negotiations any easier but, akin to interstate conflict, allowed parties to identify lines of control and demarcation more easily. This helped the process of negotiating ceasefires in the Philippines and North–South Sudan and complicated the process in El Salvador and Colombia.

When the military context instead led one side to believe that they could achieve victory by sustaining their military endeavors, they were unlikely to progress political talks (unless for devious intentions) and more likely to fight unabated or seek to contain the conflict. In this case, the crucial factor shaping the parties' interests seems to have been the extent to which conflict costs could be sustained. When parties could both sustain the conflict (and maintained an aspiration of victory), fighting unabated appears to have been more likely. Whereas when the costs of conflict became unmanageable for all parties, the likelihood of conflict containment increased. In some cases, this involved a mutually beneficial ceasefire in one part of the country that allowed one of the actors to escalate or sustain violence elsewhere (e.g., Myanmar and Syria).

International Political Context

The United Nations guidance argues that for mediation to be effective, "there must be general consensus at the regional and international levels to support the process."[10] The case chapters offer evidence to support this. Peace agreements more often emerged in periods when the regional or international powers converged in support of a deal (e.g., El Salvador, Burundi, Bosnia, North–South Sudan, Philippines, and Colombia), whereas periods or cases in which this consensus was absent were less likely to produce an agreement (e.g., Syria, Darfur, Myanmar).

The alignment of international actors is connected to the broader geopolitical environment. The international consensus that emerged in the period following the end of the Cold War led to several peace agreements, and limited cooperative engagement remained possible even in the period that followed 9/11 when international unity began to unravel. But in recent years, the increasingly polarized international environment has made consensus more difficult (e.g., Syria), and only cases where powerful international actors have little or no competing interests appeared ripe for resolution (e.g., Colombia).

However, the broader shifts in the geopolitical environment do not appear to be a strong factor in shaping the ceasefire opportunity space as far as talking while fighting versus talking, not fighting. Talking while fighting was the dominant approach adopted in both El Salvador in the early 1990s and Colombia in the mid-2010s. Talking, not fighting was a significant part of the process in both the Philippines and Sudan, which both spanned the 1990s and 2000s, whereas containing fighting has been the dominant approach in Myanmar since Cold War times and in Syria throughout a significant part of the conflict. In short, there is no clear temporal trend in ceasefire sequencing approaches, although a polarized geopolitical context would intuitively imply more situations of "fighting unabated" and "containment ceasefires."

Where the international context does appear to exert a significant impact relates to the use of military, economic, or diplomatic pressure. As we set out in the prior discussion, the shared interests of the parties shape the ceasefire opportunity space. Processes tended to be more effective when third parties worked within the existing opportunity space to help the parties develop a mutually acceptable sequencing approach or prepare the parties to expand or develop future opportunities for a ceasefire.

In the Philippines, for example, the government and the MILF engaged in on-off talks for nearly two decades, with limited engagement of external actors, although as the process progressed, internationals did play supportive roles in helping to monitor the ceasefire, facilitating talks, and generally helping the process move forward, without putting undue pressure on the conflict parties to adopt a different sequencing approach.

In Colombia, prior to the 2012–2016 Havana talks, the United States helped "ripen" the conflict by supporting the military engagement against the FARC, strongly shifting the balance of power in favor of the government. When President Santos reversed the hardline approach of his predecessor and provided an opening for political negotiations, the United States let the process move forward, leaving it in the hands of the conflict parties. Smaller countries played a limited but key role, with Cuba hosting the process, and Cuba and Norway (among other actors) helping the conflict parties overcome moments of crises and impasses. The talking while fighting approach fits well with the specific context of Colombia and the opportunity space that existed.

In other cases, more third-party involvement was needed. When effective, rather than directly impose or pressure the parties into accepting a specific ceasefire sequencing approach, third parties allowed the process to develop organically or used leverage to push the parties to engage in talks. They provided positive and negative inducements that incentivized actors to seize the opportunities before them and offered appropriate training and technical support to help the parties achieve their goals effectively.

In El Salvador, for example, the United States used its significant leverage to support the process at critical junctures. At times, the United States also sought to pressure the parties on the issues and into a premature ceasefire that would have been at odds with the existing opportunity space and the sequencing approach agreed between the conflict parties. The process was ultimately a success because the UN-led mediation team was able to redirect this pressure, ensuring that US pressure incentivized cooperation without disrupting the parties' sequencing logic.

Similarly, in Sudan, US pressure was instrumental in pushing Khartoum to engage in the North–South process. This helped to incentivize the parties to engage in a geographically limited ceasefire in the Nuba Mountains, an agreement that was in line with the parties' shared interests, bringing the IGAD-led peace process back to life. As the process continued, US and international pressure also threatened to undermine the process by pushing for agreement on the conflict issues that the conflict parties were not yet ready for. Here again, the mediator played a pivotal function, protecting the process and sequencing approach from international pressure on the issues.

In contrast, when external parties pressured or imposed an outcome or particular sequencing approach that was not in alignment with the parties' shared interests, the results were often disastrous. The clearest example of this is the Darfur case where the British and Americans applied significant pressure through deadline diplomacy first to push the parties into *talking, not fighting*, and subsequently a peace agreement, both of which were arguably not aligned with the parties' interests. By pushing the parties into a preliminary ceasefire, irrespective of their readiness for such an agreement, third-party actors created a situation where conflict parties accepted an agreement without any genuine interest in implementing it. In Syria, international calls for a ceasefire were continually undermined by the diametrically opposed preferences of the United States and Russia (as well as regional actors). Their actions undermined any hope of developing a shared interest between the parties in progressing the political negotiation process, meaning that only containment ceasefires proved even marginally effective at reducing violence (in the short term).

The case of Bosnia is an interesting exception in that it shows that external pressure can fundamentally reshape the opportunity space beyond a short-term ceasefire, but only if pressure can be maintained over time in such a way as to force interests to align across the parties. In the latter phases of the process, a combination of willingness to use force—combined with a long-term commitment and Western powers acting in unison—helped build a shared interest in stopping violence and agreeing a settlement that resolved at least some of the contested issues.

In summary, an absence of external pressure increases the chance of homegrown negotiated outcomes and a sequencing approach that naturally reflects the shared interests of the parties. However, pressure can also be effective, but only when it works within a sequencing approach that matches the existing opportunity space. Pressure from external actors that messes with the natural ordering is unlikely to be effective (unless backed up by extreme support over a longer period, which seems unlikely in the current geopolitical context).

Implications

It has long been understood that the international, domestic, and military context shapes peace processes. This analysis provides additional specificity by showing how several context factors shape the ceasefire opportunity space and thus the likely sequencing approaches. Several useful implications can be derived from this discussion.

First, the context shapes conflict parties' preferences on both progressing political talks and stopping conflict violence. The context is therefore central in determining where the parties' interests converge and the degree to which an opportunity space for ceasefires and joint ceasefire sequencing strategies exists.

Second, it is the combination of contextual factors that jointly shapes the process interests and preferences of the actors. No one factor alone determines the preferences of the parties. Instead, it is the combination of factors, including international pressure, party objectives, prior conflict management experience, and the military situation, that together shapes a party's preferred approach in terms of moving the ceasefire and/or political negotiation process forward.

Third, while acknowledging the above, the distribution of (military) power within a conflict was shown to be particularly influential in shaping the sequencing approach adopted. The military situation on the ground—particularly the existence or lack of a mutually hurting stalemate—was crucial in determining the party's willingness to progress political talks. However, whether negotiations took place with or without a ceasefire was often a reflection of the preferences of the party with stronger bargaining leverage, which is an important consideration for peacemakers.

Finally, combining the contextual analysis with the prior analysis of ceasefire opportunity space reveals an important insight. Figure 11.4 presents each of the cases discussed in this text in relation to the dominant approach adopted during the pivotal phases of negotiation discussed in the chapter.[11] As figure 11.4 sets out, in Bosnia, Darfur, and Syria (at least at the national level), this was fighting unabated; in Colombia, El Salvador, and Burundi, talking while fighting; in Syria (at the local level[12]) and Myanmar, containing fighting; and for the Philippines and Sudan, talking, not fighting.

In the left column (i.e., fighting unabated and containing fighting) are those cases that involve multiple often fragmented actors and a lack of geopolitical alignment. Thus, in those cases with more challenging domestic and international contexts, it appears harder to develop a coherent approach linking efforts to stop violence and advance the political process. In contrast, the right-hand column involves those cases with more centralized and stronger nonstate groups, as well as contexts with more coherent geopolitical support for the process or at least less geopolitical interference. Thus, in cases with more "favorable" contexts, we appear more likely to observe a coordinated and coherent process design. Whether this involves talking while fighting or talking, not fighting depends (as we discuss above) on the historical factors and military situation on the ground. Identifying the different context factors that most often shape the overall coherency of the process (i.e., left or right column) or specific strategy (i.e., upper or low row) is a fruitful topic for future research. For practitioners, our cases confirm that analysis of the geopolitical context can indicate if a mediation sequencing strategy is more or less likely to be effective: less likely on the left (with a divided geopolitical context) and more likely on the right (with a supportive geopolitical context).[13] Geopolitical context analysis, however, *cannot* indicate which specific sequencing strategy is better (talking while fighting or talking, not fighting) as this depends on case-specific historical factors and relations between the parties. In any given case, an in-depth analysis and communication with the actors is thus required.

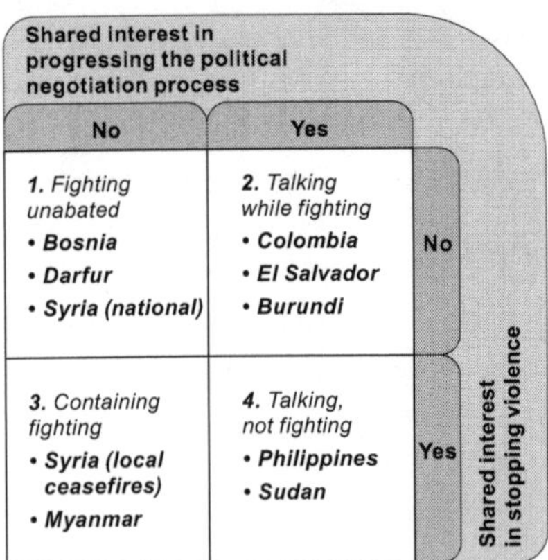

Figure 11.4 A 2×2 table of interaction between the political negotiation and ceasefire processes across the cases in this book

CONCLUSION

This book represents one of the first attempts to study the interaction between ceasefire and political negotiation processes across multiple cases.[14] Connecting the dots across cases reveals several new insights into how ceasefires operate within peace processes. We have shown that the international, domestic, and military context shapes conflict parties' interests (i.e., their preferences on whether to advance the political negotiation and/or ceasefire process). Convergence of the parties' interests then determines the ceasefire opportunity space, that is, what types of arrangements are possible to limit, manage, or resolve violence and the impact ceasefires are likely to have on the political negotiation process. Ultimately, whether the opportunity for a (specific type of) ceasefire is seized will always depend on numerous factors, but we particularly noted the importance of the technical capacity and competence of the negotiating actors and the mediation team.

Therefore, an important conclusion from this book is that there is no one most effective approach to ceasefire sequencing. Instead, we argue that any sequencing approach is possible if it respects the existent ceasefire opportunity space and therefore reflects the convergence of the parties' interests in that period. Even though a peace agreement ultimately requires that the parties' interests converge on talking, not fighting, any attempt to prematurely impose this approach (e.g., through an imposed preliminary ceasefire) is likely to be ineffective—and quite possibly counterproductive.

Over the course of a conflict, the ceasefire opportunity space is likely to vary, meaning the optimal sequencing approach might also change. In the early phases of a conflict, it is more likely to be unclear what opportunities exist for a ceasefire. But as the process develops and (pre)negotiations begin, identifying and agreeing on a joint sequencing strategy should be a key objective, even if this is likely to require updating as the process develops.

Another crucial point to stress is that the existence of a ceasefire opportunity space does not mean that this will be seized by the parties. Third parties can play an important function in helping actors make better-informed decisions by talking through the advantages and disadvantages of different sequencing approaches. Effective ceasefire and political negotiations call for a broader negotiation or mediation strategy, with clear roles and teamwork to develop and implement an integrated strategy. Third parties can play a vital role in supporting this process and helping to bring into reality the latent opportunity for a particular type of ceasefire.

None of this should be taken to mean that peacemakers should not be working toward limiting, managing, and resolving violence, whatever the context. A lack of effort to end violence quickly and effectively is problematic, as battlefield dynamics can hinder trust building and progress in the negotiation process, as well as increase civilian suffering. At the same time, a premature ceasefire can also destroy trust and extend conflict, or potentially reduce the impetus to move toward peace altogether. Finding the right balance is therefore key. And while we argue that third parties are best to avoid imposing their sequencing preferences, this in no way means that they should not work with the parties to help to widen the opportunity space, through training, joint problem solving, or positive and negative inducements.

Even when talking, not fighting remains elusive, there is still much to be gained from working within the existing opportunity space. As the cases in this book illustrate, talking while fighting can prove an effective means of moving toward peace and presents different opportunities to manage or mitigate violence. Similarly, while containment might often seem a less desirable goal for peacemakers when the opportunity space is limited to this approach, much can still be done to limit the suffering of civilians, reduce the costs of conflict, and prepare the ground for a future political process.

The cases in this book demonstrate that we need to view the ceasefire process and the political negotiation process as separate but closely related integral features of a peace process. We also provide case evidence for some principles that are commonly considered in the mediation practitioner community but less known in the academic mediation community, thereby helping to move insights from practice closer to theory.[15] While this is to date the most significant qualitative comparison of ceasefire processes, our focus is still limited to only a handful of cases. As such, we are mindful to avoid overextrapolation. Demonstrating the external validity of key findings should be the focus of further work. Future research could also expand on our sequencing models, exploring in greater detail the conditions under which different sequences tend to perform differently. Equally, for practitioners, our conceptual work provides a new lens through which to understand many principles that are often intuitively grasped. There are multiple approaches to ending violence, with advantages and challenges of both an "early" and a "late" end of violence in a peace process. Being more aware of each approach, the factors that shape conflict parties' strategic calculations, and what can be done on a technical level, irrespective of where the parties' interests converge, is useful to match the strategy to the case and context and avoid that violence or conflict unnecessarily persists.

NOTES

1. While several trends were observed, it is important to note that our focus is limited to the cases included in this book. As we note below, further work will be required to demonstrate the external validity of our key findings.

2. Sosnowski, "Redefining Ceasefires: Wartime Order and Statebuilding in Syria"; for similar examples relating to negotiation and mediation more generally, see Min, "Talking While Fighting: Understanding the Role of Wartime Negotiation"; Min, "Painful Words: The Effect of Battlefield Activity on Conflict Negotiation Behavior"; Richmond, "Devious Objectives and the Disputants' View of International Mediation: A Theoretical Framework."

3. See discussions in Sticher, "Healing Stalemates: The Role of Ceasefires in Ripening Conflict."

4. Brickhill, "Mediating Security Arrangements in Peace Processes: Critical Perspectives from the Field."

5. See Clayton, Nathan, and Wiehler, "Ceasefire Success: A Conceptual Framework."

6. In line with Zartman's ripeness theory criteria, see Zartman, "The Timing of Peace Initiatives: Hurting Stalemates and Ripe Moments."

7. See also Sticher and Vuković, "Bargaining in Intrastate Conflicts: The Shifting Role of Ceasefires."

8. See Zartman, "The Timing of Peace Initiatives."

9. See Zartman, "The Timing of Peace Initiatives."

10. United Nations, *United Nations Guidance for Effective Mediation*, 5.

11. In each of the cases discussed in this book, the parties moved across different opportunity spaces and approaches over the course of the conflict.

12. For more information on local ceasefires in Syria, see Lundgren, Svensson, and Karakus, "Local Ceasefires and De-escalation: Evidence from the Syrian Civil War"; Karakus and Svensson, "Between the Bombs: Exploring Partial Ceasefires in the Syrian Civil War, 2011–2017."

13. "There are some indicators that suggest the potential for effective mediation . . . there must be general consensus at the regional and international levels to support the process" (UN Guidance for Effective Mediation, 5).

14. Although see Åkebo, *Ceasefire Agreements and Peace Processes. A Comparative Study* for a cross-case comparison of Sri Lanka and Aceh (Indonesia).

15. Examples are the principle of the UN Guidance for Effective Mediation about the necessity for regional and international consensus for a process to be effective or the distinction between pressure on process and pressure on issues/content, presented by Julian Th. Hottinger in the MAS ETH MPP.

BIBLIOGRAPHY

Abdul-Jalil, M. A., M. A. Azzain, and A. A. Yousuf. "Native Administration and Local Governance in Darfur: Past and Future." In *War in Darfur and the Search for Peace*, edited by A. De Waal, 39–67. Cambridge: Global Equity Initiative, 2007.

Abinales, Patricio N. "War and Peace in Muslim Mindanao: Critiquing the Orthodoxy." In *Mindanao: The Long Journey to Peace and Prosperity*, edited by Paul D. Hutchcroft, 39–61. Mandaluyong City: Anvil Publishing Inc., 2016.

Abubakar, Ayesah, and Kamarulzaman Askandar. "Defining the Bangsamoro Right to Self Determination in the MILF Peace Process." In *Breaking the Silence*, edited by Azmi Sharom, Sriprapha Petcharamesree, and Yanuar Sumarlan, 144–161. Bangkok: Human Rights in Southeast Asian Series 1, 2018. http://shapesea.com/wp-content/uploads/2018/03/06b-Defining-the-Bangsamoro-Right-to-Self-Determination-in-the-MILF-Peace-Process.pdf.

"Acuerdo Sobre Cese al Fuego y de Hostilidades, Bilateral y Definitivo y Dejación de Las Armas Entre El Gobierno Nacional y Las Farc-EP." Havana: Government of Colombia and FARC-EP, 23 June 2016.

Advisor to the USAID, interviewed by Haven North. "Interview #26." United States Institute of Peace, The Association for Diplomatic Studies and Training, 4 October 2006. https://www.usip.org/sites/default/files/file/resources/collections/histories/sudan/26.pdf.

African Security Analysis. *The Sudan–IGAD Peace Process Signposts for the Way Forward.* Institute for Security Studies (ISS) Paper 86, March 2004. https://www.files.ethz.ch/isn/112148/PAPER86.PDF

Åkebo, Malin. *Ceasefire Agreements and Peace Processes. A Comparative Study.* Routledge Studies in Peace and Conflict Resolution. London: Routledge, 2016.

Åkebo, Malin. "Ceasefire Rationales: A Comparative Study of Ceasefires in the Moro and Communist Conflicts in the Philippines." *International Peacekeeping* 28, no. 3 (2021): 366–392.

Åkebo, Malin. "'Coexistence Ceasefire' in Mindanao." *Peace & Change* 44, no. 4 (2019): 468–496.

Åkebo, Malin. "The Politics of Ceasefires: On Ceasefire Agreements and Peace Processes in Aceh and Sri Lanka." Umea: Department of Political Science, Umea University, 2013.

Akpınar, P. "The Limits of Mediation in the Arab Spring: The Case of Syria." *Third World Quarterly* 37, no. 12 (2016): 2288–2303.

Alliance for Gender Inclusion in the Peace Process (AGIPP). *If Half the Population Mattered: A Critique of the Myanmar Nationwide Ceasefire Agreement and Joint Monitoring Committee Framework from a Gender Perspective.* Policy Brief No. 4, 2018. https://asiapacific.unwomen.org/sites/default/files/2024-03/mn-c748-myanmar-wps-brief_march2024_eng.pdf.

Allison, R. "Russia and Syria: Explaining Alignment with a Regime in Crisis." *International Affairs* 89, no. 4 (2013): 795–782.

Antonov, Nikola. "Bosnian President Asks Army to Protect People." *Reuters News [Factiva]*, 20 April 1992.

Antonov, Nikola. "Bosnia's Rival Ethnic Groups Agree Ceasefire." *Reuters News [Factiva]*, 4 December 1992.

Antonov, Nikola. "New Fighting in Bosnia Dims Peace Hopes." *Reuters News [Factiva]*, 19 April 1992.

Arabie, B. *Darfur: Road to Genocide.* Bloomington, IN: AuthorHouse, 2012.

Arab League. Council Resolution 7438 [Plan of Action], 2011.

Armed Forces of the Philippines. "Restoring a Fragile Peace: The 2000 Battle for Central Mindanao." Fort Bonifacio, Taguig: Operations Research Center, 2020.

Arnson, Cynthia. *Crossroads: Congress, the President, and Central America, 1976–1993.* University Park: Pennsylvania State University, 1993.

Aronson, B. "Interviewed by Jean Krasno for Yale–UN Oral History Project," 10 September 1997. http://ugspace.ug.edu.gh/handle/123456789/2765.

Aspinall, Edward, and Harold Crouch. *The Aceh Peace Process: Why It Failed.* Policy Studies. Washington, DC: East-West Center, 2003.

Associated Press. "Junta's Foes Woo Ethnic Allies with New Myanmar Constitution." *ABC News,* 2021. https://abcnews.go.com/International/wireStory/attack-myanmars-kachin-minority-signals-deepening-crisis-76784547.

Aung-Thwin, Michael, and Maitrii Aung-Thwin. *A History of Myanmar since Ancient Times: Traditions and Transformations.* 2nd ed. London: Reaktion Books, 2012.

Bara, Clayton, and Aas Rustad, "Understanding Ceasefires." *International Peacekeeping* 28 no. 3 (2021): 329–340.

Bara, Corinne, and Govinda Clayton. "Your Reputation Precedes You: Ceasefires, Credibility, and Bargaining during Civil Conflict." Working paper, 2022.

Barometer Initiative, Peace Accords Matrix. "State of Implementation of the Colombia Peace Agreement." Report 2. Bogotá: Kroc Institute for International Peace Studies, 2018.

Battersby, Paul. "Border Politics and the Broader Politics of Thailand's International Relations in the 1990s: From Communism to Capitalism." *Pacific Affairs* 71, no. 4 (1998): 473–488.

BBC Mundo. "Colombia: FARC Aseguran Que Ataque a Batallón Fue Una Acción Defensiva," 16 April 2015. https://www.bbc.com/mundo/noticias/2015/04/150416_colombia_farc_comunicado_ataque_cauca_ng.

Beardsley, Kyle. "Agreement without Peace? International Mediation and Time Inconsistency Problems." *American Journal of Political Science* 52, no. 4 (2008): 723–740.

Beardsley, Kyle, and Nigel Lo. "Third-Party Conflict Management and the Willingness to Make Concessions." *Journal of Conflict Resolution* 58, no. 2 (2014): 363–392.

Bell, Christine. "Peace Agreements: Their Nature and Legal Status." *The American Journal of International Law* 100, no. 2 (2006): 373–412.

Bell, Christine, and Sanja Badanjak. "Introducing PA-X. A New Peace Agreement Database and Dataset." *Journal of Peace Research* 56, no. 3 (2019): 452–466.

Bermúdez, Andrés. *Los Debates de La Habana: Una Mirada Desde Adentro.* Bogotá: IFIT, 2018.

Boban, Mate, Alija Izetbegović, and Radovan Karadžić. "Bosnia-Herzegovina Ceasefire Agreement." PA-X Peace Agreement Database, 4 December 1992. https://www.peaceagreements.org/view/1470/Bosnia-Herzegovina%20Ceasefire%20Agreement.

Boshoff, Henri, and Waldemar Vrey. *A Technical Analysis of Disarmament, Demobilisation, and Reintegration: A Case Study from Burundi.* Pretoria: Institute for Security Studies, 2006.

Boshoff, Henri, Waldemar Vrey, George Rautenbach, and Institute for Security Studies (South Africa). *The Burundi Peace Process: From Civil War to Conditional Peace.* Pretoria: Institute for Security Studies, 2010.

"Bosnia-Herzegovina: Croat." In *Uppsala Conflict Data Program*, 21 April 2021. https://ucdp .uu.se/conflict/398.

Brenner, David. "Ashes of Co-optation: From Armed Group Fragmentation to the Rebuilding of Popular Insurgency in Myanmar." *Conflict, Security & Development* 15, no. 4 (2015): 337–358.

Brenner, David, and Sarah Schulman. "Myanmar's Top-Down Transition: Challenges for Civil Society." *International Development Studies (IDS) Bulletin* 50, no. 3 (2019): 17–36.

Brickhill, Jeremy. "Mediating Security Arrangements in Peace Processes: Critical Perspectives from the Field." CSS Mediation Resources. Zurich: Center for Security Studies, ETH Zurich, 2018.

Brickhill, Jeremy. "Protecting Civilians through Peace Agreements: Challenges and Lessons of the Darfur Peace Agreement." ISS Paper 138. London: Institute for Security Studies, 2007.

Brooks, S. P. "Enforcing a Turning Point and Imposing a Deal: An Analysis of the Darfur Abuja Negotiations of 2006." *International Negotiation* 13, no. 3 (2008): 413–440.

Brosché, J., and A. Duursma. "Hurdles to Peace: A Level-of-Analysis Approach to Resolving Sudan's Civil Wars." *Third World Quarterly* 39, no. 3 (2018): 560–576.

Buchanan, Cate, Govinda Clayton, and Alexander Ramsbotham. "Ceasefire Monitoring: Developments and Complexities." London: Accord Spotlight: Conciliation Resources, 2021.

Buchanan, Cate, and Joaquín Chávez. "Negotiating Disarmament: Guns and Violence in the El Salvador Peace Negotiations." Country Study. Negotiating Disarmament. Geneva: Center for Humanitarian Dialog, March 2008. https://www.hdcentre.org/wp-content /uploads/2016/08/84GunsandViolenceintheElSalvadorPeaceNegotiations-March -2008.pdf.

Buchanan, John. *Militias in Myanmar.* Yangon: The Asia Foundation, 2016.

Burma News International. *Briefing Paper on Violations of Media Freedom by Myanmar Military Council.* April 2021. https://progressivevoicemyanmar.org/2021/04/23/briefing-paper -on-violations-of-media-freedom-by-myanmar-military-council/.

Burr, J. M., and R. O. Collins. *Sudan in Turmoil: Hasan Al-Turabi and the Islamist State 1889– 2003.* Princeton, NJ: Markus Wienner Publishing, 2010.

Burr, M., and R. O. Collins. *Africa's Thirty Years War: Libya, Chad, and the Sudan, 1963–1993.* Boulder, CO: Westview Press, 1999.

Bynum, Elliott. "Ceasefires and Conflict Dynamics in Myanmar." *Acled Data*, 2019. https:// www.acleddata.com/2019/05/13/ceasefires-and-conflict-dynamics-in-myanmar/.

Byrne, Hugh. *El Salvador's Civil War: A Study of Revolution.* Boulder, CO: Lynne Rienner, 1996.

Callahan, Mary. *Making Enemies: War and State Building in Burma.* Ithaca, NY: Cornell University Press, 2003.

Callahan, Mary. *Political Authority in Burma's Ethnic Minority States: Devolution, Occupation, and Coexistence.* Washington, DC: East-West Center Washington; Institute of Southeast Asian Studies, 2007.

Canal, Margarita, and David Aponte. "A Collaborative Peace." Bogotá: Universidad de los Andes, 2019.

"Ceasefire Agreement between the Transitional Government of Burundi and the Conseil National Pour La Défense de La Démocratie—Forces Pour La Défense de La Démocratie." 2002. https://peacemaker.un.org/node/161.

Center for Preventive Action. "Civil War in South Sudan." Council on Foreign Relations Global Conflict Tracker, 12 May 2022. https://www.cfr.org/global-conflict-tracker/conflict/civil-war-south-sudan#:~:text=Since%20civil%20war%20broke%20out,or%20fled%20to%20neighboring%20countries.

"Cessation of Hostilities Agreement between the Transition Government of Burundi and the Armed Political Parties of Burundi," signed in Dar es Salaam, Tanzania, on October 7, 2002, between the Government of Burundi, CNDD-FDD (Ndayikengurukiye) and PALIPEHUTU-FNL (Mugabarabona).

Cheesman, Nick, Monique Skidmore, and Trevor Wilson, eds. *Myanmar's Transition: Openings, Obstacles, and Opportunities.* Singapore: Institute of Southeast Asian Studies, 2012.

Chernick, Marc W. "Negotiated Settlement to Armed Conflict: Lessons from the Colombian Peace Process." *Journal of Interamerican Studies and World Affairs* 30, no. 4 (1988): 53–88.

Chounet-Cambas, Luc. "Negotiating Ceasefires: Dilemmas & Options for Mediators." Mediation Practice Series. Geneva: The Centre for Humanitarian Dialogue, 2011.

Clayton, Govinda, Simon Mason, Valerie Sticher, and Claudia Wiehler. "Ceasefires in Intrastate Peace Processes." *CSS Analysis in Security Policy* no. 252 (2019). https://css.ethz.ch/content/dam/ethz/special-interest/gess/cis/center-for-securities-studies/pdfs/CSSAnalyse252-EN.pdf.

Clayton, Govinda, Laurie Nathan, and Claudia Wiehler. "Ceasefire Success: A Conceptual Framework." *International Peacekeeping* 28, no. 3 (2021): 341–365.

Clayton, Govinda, Håvard Mokleiv Nygård, Håvard Strand, Siri A. Rustad, Claudia Wiehler, Tora Sagård, Peder Landsverk, Reidun Ryland, Valerie Sticher, Emma Wink, and Corinne Bara. "Introducing the ETH/PRIO Civil Conflict Ceasefire Dataset." *Journal of Conflict Resolution* 67, nos. 7–8 (2022): 1279–1643. https://doi.org/10.1177/00220027221129183.

Clayton, Govinda, and Valerie Sticher. "The Logic of Ceasefires in Civil War." *International Studies Quarterly* 65, no. 3 (2021): 633–646. https://doi.org/10.1093/isq/sqab026.

CNMH. *¡Basta Ya! Colombia: Memoria de Guerra y Dignidad.* Bogotá: Centro Nacional de Memoria Histórica, 2013.

Cockett, R. *Sudan: Darfur and the Failure of an African State.* New Haven, CT: Yale University Press, 2010.

Collins, R. O. *A History of Modern Sudan.* Cambridge: Cambridge University Press, 2008.

Colombia Reports. "Timeline." Fact sheet, 25 September 2016. https://colombiareports.com/colombia-peace-talks-fact-sheet/#2016.

The Comprehensive Peace Agreement between the Government of the Republic of the Sudan and the Sudan People's Liberation Movement/Sudan People's Liberation Army, 2005. https://peacemaker.un.org/sites/peacemaker.un.org/files/SD_060000_The%20Comprehensive%20Peace%20Agreement.pdf.

Cooper, Adam. "Dag Nylander on Salmon Diplomacy." Mediator's Studio, 14 July 2020.

Córdova Macías, Ricardo. *El Salvador: las negociaciones de paz y los retos de la postguerra.* [San Salvador, El Salvador]: Instituto de Estudios LatinoAmericanos, 1993.

Coronel Ferrer, Miriam. *Region, Nation and Homeland: Valorization and Adaptation in the Moro and Cordillera Resistance Discourse.* Singapore: ISEAS Yusof Ishak Institute, 2020.

Cortés, Omar, and Juanita Millán Hernández. "The Role of the Armed Forces in the Colombian Peace Process." Report. NOREF Norwegian Centre for Conflict Resolution, September 2019.

Council on Foreign Relations. "1903–2022. U.S. Colombia Relations," 2022. https://www.cfr.org/timeline/us-colombia-relations.

Crocker, Chester A., Pamela R. Aall, and Kofi A. Annan. *The Fabric of Peace in Africa. Looking beyond the State.* Waterloo, Canada: Centre for International Governance Innovation, 2017.

Crocker, Chester A., Fen Osler Hampson, and Pamela R. Aall. *Herding Cats: Multiparty Mediation in a Complex World.* Washington, DC: United States Institute of Peace Press, 1999.

Crocker, Chester A., Fen Osler Hampson, and Pamela Aall. *Taming Intractable Conflicts. Mediation in the Hardest Cases.* Washington, DC: United States Institute of Peace, 2004.

Crocker, Chester A., Fen Osler Hampson, Pamela R. Aall, and Simon Palamar. "Why Is Mediation So Hard? The Case of Syria." In *Handbook of International Negotiation: Interpersonal, Intercultural, and Diplomatic Perspectives,* edited by M. Galluccio, 139–156. Cham: Springer, 2015.

Curran, Daniel, James K. Sebenius, and Michael Watkins. "Two Paths to Peace. Contrasting George Mitchell in Northern Ireland with Richard Holbrooke in Bosnia–Herzegovina." *Negotiation Journal* 20, no. 4 (2004): 513–537. https://doi.org/10.1111/j.1571-9979.2004.00041.x.

Daalder, Ivo. *Getting to Dayton. The Making of America's Bosnia Policy.* Washington, DC: The Brookings Institution, 2000.

Darby, John, and Roger MacGinty. *Contemporary Peace Making: Conflict, Violence and Peace Processes.* New York: Palgrave Macmillan, 2003.

Daugherty, Arron. "'FARC Has Suffered 2 Historic Blows': Santos." Colombia Reports, 29 March 2012. https://colombiareports.com/farc-has-suffered-2-historic-blows-santos/.

De Waal, A. "Counter-Insurgency on the Cheap." *Review of African Political Economy* 31, no. 102 (2004): 716–725.

De Waal, A. "Darfur and the Failure of the Responsibility to Protect." *International Affairs* 83, no. 6 (2007): 1039–1054.

De Waal, A. "Darfur's Deadline: The Final Days of the Abuja Peace Process." In *War in Darfur and the Search for Peace,* edited by A. De Waal, 267–283. London: Global Equity Initiative, 2007.

De Waal, A. "I Will Not Sign." *London Review of Books* 28, no. 23 (2006): 17–20.

De Waal, A. "Sudan: Darfur." In *Responding to Conflict in Africa: The United Nations and Regional Organizations,* edited by J. Boulden. New York: Palgrave Macmillan, 2013.

De Waal, A. "Sudan: The Turbulent State." In *War in Darfur and the Search for Peace,* edited by A. De Waal, 1–38. Cambridge: Global Equity Initiative, 2007.

De Waal, A. "The DPA and Its National Context." In *Peace by Piece: Addressing Sudan's Conflicts,* edited by M. Simmons and P. Dixon. London: Conciliation Resources, 2006.

Debié, Franck. "Paper Tiger. Europe and the Crisis in the Former Yugoslavia (1991–1996)." *Cambridge Review of International Affairs* 10, no. 2 (1997): 122–140. https://doi.org/10.1080/09557579708400139.

De Jesus, Edilberto C., and Melinda Quintos de Jesus. "The Mamasapano Detour." In *Mindanao: The Long Journey to Peace and Prosperity,* edited by Paul D. Hutchcroft, 159–198. Mandaluyong City: Anvil Publishing Inc., 2016.

De Soto, Alvaro, and Graciana del Castillo. "Obstacles to Peacebuilding." *Foreign Policy*, no. 94 (Spring 1994): 69–83.

De Soto, Alvaro. "Ending Violent Conflict in El Salvador." In *Herding Cats: Multiparty Mediation in a Complex World*, edited by Chester A. Crocker, Fen Osler Hampson, and Pamela Aall, 349–385. Washington, DC: United States Institute of Peace Press, 1999.

De Soto, Alvaro. "UN Negotiations Not among Casualties of War in El Salvador." *Wall Street Journal*, 11 January 1991.

Di Giovanni, Janine. "The Man with the Toughest Job in the World." *The Guardian*, 30 July 2015. https://www.theguardian.com/world/2015/jul/30/staffan-de-mistura-man-with-toughest-job-in-world-syria.

Dukalskis, Alexander. "Why Do Some Insurgent Groups Agree to Cease-Fires While Others Do Not? A Within-Case Analysis of Burma/Myanmar, 1948–2011." *Studies in Conflict & Terrorism* 38, no. 10 (2015): 841–863. https://doi.org/10.1080/1057610X.2015.1056631.

Dulic, Tomislav. "Perpetuating Fear. Insecurity, Costly Signalling and the War in Central Bosnia, 1993." *Journal of Genocide Research* 18, no. 4 (2016): 463–484. https://doi.org/10.1080/14623528.2016.1226433.

Duursma, Allard. "He Who Pays the Piper, Calls the Tune? Non-African Involvement in Sudan's African-Led Mediation Processes." *Journal of Eastern African Studies* 13, no. 3 (2019): 1–17.

Duursma, Allard. "When to Get out of the Trench: Using Smart Pressure to Resolve Civil Wars." *Civil Wars* 17, no. 1 (2017): 43–61.

El-Tom, A. O. *Darfur, JEM and the Khalil Ibrahim Story*. Trenton, NJ: Red Sea Press, 2011.

Fadul, A., and V. Tanner. "After Abuja: A View from the Ground." In *War in Darfur and the Search for Peace*, edited by A. De Waal, 284–313. Cambridge: Global Equity Initiative, 2007.

FARC-EP. "Unilateral Cease-Fire for an Indefinite Period: FARC-EP." Communiqués FARC-EP. Havana, December 17, 2014. https://www.farc-epeace.org/peace-process/news/item/617-unilateral-cease-fire-for-an-indefinite-period-farc-ep.html.

FARC-EP and Government of Colombia. "Expedite in Havana and De-Escalate in Colombia." Joint Communique #55. Havana, 12 July 2015.

Fearon, James D. "Rationalist Explanations for War." *International Organization* 49, no. 3 (1995): 379–414.

Fearon, James D. "Domestic Political Audiences and the Escalation of International Disputes." *American Political Science Review* 88, no. 3 (1994): 577–592.

Flint, Julie, and Alex de Waal. *Darfur: A New History of a Long War*. London: Zed Books, 2008.

Flint, J. "Darfur's Armed Movements." In *War in Darfur and the Search for Peace*, edited by A. De Waal, 140–172. London: Global Equity Initiative, 2007.

Flint, Julie. *Rhetoric and Reality: The Failure to Resolve the Darfur Conflict*. Sudan Human Security Baseline Assessment Working Paper 19. Geneva: Small Arms Survey, 2010.

Flint, Julie. "Without Foreign Chancelleries and Hollywood's Finest, Can Darfur Peace Deal Succeed?" *Pambazuka News*, no. 254, 11 May 2006.

Forero, Juan. "Colombia's FARC Rebels Say They'll Stop Kidnapping." *The Washington Post*, 26 February 2012, sec. The Americas. https://www.washingtonpost.com/world/the_americas/colombias-farc-rebels-say-theyll-stop-kidnapping/2012/02/26/gIQAi4UWcR_story.html.

Fortna, Virginia Page. "Scraps of Paper? Agreements and the Durability of Peace." *International Organization* 57, no. 2 (2003): 337–372.

"Framework Agreement for the Federation." United Nations Peacemaker, 3 April 1994. https://peacemaker.un.org/bosniawashingtonagreement94.

Galbraith, Peter W. "Washington, Erdut and Dayton. Negotiating and Implementing Peace in Croatia and Bosnia-Herzegovina." *Cornell International Law Journal* 30, no. 3 (1997): 643–652.

GALLUP. "Gallup Poll #115 Colombia." Summary of Survey Data, October 2016. http://www.eltiempo.com/contenido/politica/proceso-de-paz/ARCHIVO/ARCHIVO-16741542-0.pdf.

George, Alexander L., and Andrew Bennett. *Case Studies and Theory Development in the Social Sciences.* Cambridge, MA: MIT Press, 2005.

Global Security.org, Sudan People's Liberation Army (SPLA). Sudan People's Liberation Movement (SPLM), n.d. https://www.globalsecurity.org/military/world/para/spla.htm.

Global Security.org. Sudan Army, n.d. https://www.globalsecurity.org/military/world/sudan/army.htm.

Global Security.org. Sudan Air Force, n.d. https://www.globalsecurity.org/military/world/sudan/air-force.htm.

Goulding, Marrack. Interviewed by James S. Sutterlin for Yale–UN Oral History Project, 30 June 1998. http://ugspace.ug.edu.gh/handle/123456789/2893.

Goulding, Marrack. *Peacemonger.* London: John Murray, 2002.

Gowan, R. "Kofi Annan, Syria and the Uses of Uncertainty in Mediation." *Stability: International Journal of Security and Development* 2, no. 1 (2013): 1–6.

Granada, Soledad, Jorge Restrepo, and Andrés R. Vargas. "El Agotamiento de La Política de Seguridad." In *Guerra y Violencias En Colombia*, edited by Jorge Restrepo and David Aponte, 27–124. Bogotá: Pontificia Universidad Javeriana, 2009.

Grauvogel, Julia. *Regional Sanctions against Burundi: A Powerful Campaign and Its Unintended Consequences.* Berlin: German Institute of Global and Area Studies, 2014. https://www.files.ethz.ch/isn/183814/wp255_grauvogel_0.pdf.

Gutiérrez Sanín, Francesco. *Clientelistic Warfare: Paramilitaries and the State in Colombia.* Oxford: Peter Lang, 2019.

Hanson, Kolby. "Live and Let Live: Explaining Long-Term Truces in Separatist Conflicts." *International Peacekeeping* 28, no. 3 (2020): 393–415.

Hara, Fabienne. "Burundi: A Case of Parallel Diplomacy." In *Herding Cats: Multiparty Mediation in a Complex World*, edited by Chester A. Crocker, Pamela R. Aall, and Fen Osler Hampson, 135–158. Washington, DC: United States Institute of Peace, 1999.

Hartwell, Leon. "Conflict Resolution. Lessons from the Dayton Peace Process." *Negotiation Journal* 35, no. 4 (2019): 443–469.

Haspeslagh, Sophie. "The Effect of Proscription on Pre-Negotiation: A Comparative Analysis of Making Peace with Colombia's FARC before and after 9/11." London: The London School of Economics and Political Science, 2018.

Haspeslagh, Sophie. "The 'Linguistic Ceasefire': Negotiating in an Age of Proscription." *Security Dialogue* 52, no. 4 (2021): 361–379. https://doi.org/10.1177/0967010620952610.

Haysom, Nicholas, and Julian Hottinger. "Do's and Don'ts of Sustainable Ceasefire Arrangements." Briefing paper, 2004. https://peacemaker.un.org/sites/peacemaker.un.org/files/DosAndDontofCeasefireAgreements_HaysomHottinger2010.pdf.

Henderson, Christian, and Noam Lubell. "The Contemporary Legal Nature of UN Security Council Ceasefire Resolutions." *Leiden Journal of International Law* 26, no. 2 (2013): 369–397. https://doi.org/10.1017/S0922156513000083.

Hill, Christopher. *Outpost. A Diplomat at Work.* New York: Simon & Schuster, 2014.

Hill, T. "Kofi Annan's Multilateral Strategy of Mediation and the Syrian Crisis: The Future of Peacemaking in a Multipolar World?" *International Negotiation* 20, no. 3 (2015): 444–478.

Hinnebusch, R., and I. W. Zartman. "UN Mediation in the Syrian Crisis: From Kofi Annan to Lakhdar Brahimi." New York: International Peace Institute, 2016.

Hlaing, Kyaw Yin. "Associational Life in Myanmar: Past and Present." In *Myanmar: State, Society, and Ethnicity,* edited by N. Ganesan and Kyaw Yin Hlaing, 143–171. Singapore: Institute of Southeast Asian Studies, 2007.

Hlaing, Kyaw Yin. "Burma: Civil Society Skirting Regime Rules." In *Civil Society and Political Change in Asia: Expanding and Contracting Democratic Space,* edited by M. Alagappa, 389–418. Stanford, CA: Stanford University Press, 2004.

Högbladh, Stina. "UCDP GED Codebook Version 19.1." Uppsala: Department of Peace and Conflict Research, Uppsala University, 2019.

Höglund, Kristine. "Tactics in Negotiations between States and Extremists: The Role of Cease-Fires and Counterterrorist Measures." In *Engaging Extremists: Trade-Offs, Timing, and Diplomacy,* edited by I. William Zartman and Guy Olivier Faure, 221–244. Washington, DC: United States Institute of Peace Press, 2011.

Holbrooke, Richard C. *To End a War.* New York: Modern Library, 1999.

Holslag, Jonathan, "China's Diplomatic Manoeuvring on the Question of Darfur." *Journal of Contemporary China* 17, no. 54 (2008): 71–84.

Hottinger, Julian Th. "Throw Your Prejudice over Board and Listen." In *For Peace, Human Rights, and Security: Switzerland's Commitment to the World,* edited by Federal Department of Foreign Affairs, 12–13. Bern: FDFA, 2012.

International Crisis Group. "Avoiding a Return to War in Rakhine State." *Asia Report,* no. 325. Brussels: ICG, 2022.

International Crisis Group. "Coming to Terms with Myanmar's Russia Embrace." *Crisis Group Asia Briefing,* no. 173. Bangkok/Brussels: ICG, 2022.

International Crisis Group. "CrisisWatch. Colombia, January 2013." Colombia: International Crisis Group, January 2013.

International Crisis Group. "CrisisWatch. Colombia, January 2014." Colombia: International Crisis Group, January 2014.

International Crisis Group. "God, Oil and Country Changing the Logic of War in Sudan," 2002. https://www.crisisgroup.org/africa/horn-africa/sudan/god-oil-and-country-changing -logic-war-sudan.

International Crisis Group. "In the Shadow of 'No': Peace after Colombia's Plebiscite." Latin America Report. Bogotá/Brussels: International Crisis Group, 31 January 2017.

International Crisis Group. "Myanmar's Military Struggles to Control the Virtual Battlefield." *Asia Report,* no. 314. Brussels: ICG, 2021.

International Crisis Group. "On Thinner Ice: The Final Phase of Colombia's Peace Talks | Crisis Group." Latin America Briefing. Bogotá/Brussels: International Crisis Group, 2 July 2015.

International Crisis Group. "The Burundi Rebellion and the Ceasefire Negotiations." Nairobi/Brussels: International Crisis Group, 2002. https://d2071andvip0wj.cloudfront.net/the-burundi-rebellion-and-the-ceasefire-negotiations.pdf.

International Crisis Group. "The Cost of the Coup: Myanmar Edges Toward State Collapse." *Crisis Group Asia Briefing*, no. 167. Yangon/Brussels: ICG, 2021.

International Crisis Group. "The Day after Tomorrow: Colombia's FARC and the End of the Conflict." Latin America Report. Bogotá/Brussels: International Crisis Group, 11 December 2014.

International Crisis Group. "The Mandela Effect: Prospects for Peace in Burundi." ICG Central Africa Report. Bujumbura/Nairobi: International Crisis Group, 18 April 2000.

International Crisis Group. "Unifying Darfur's Rebels: A Prerequisite for Peace." *Africa Briefing* 32 (2005).

IFIT. "The Colombian Peace Talks: Practical Lessons for Negotiators Worldwide." Institute for Integrated Transitions, September 2018. https://www.ifit-transitions.org/files/documents/colombia-peace-talks-final-web.pdf/view.

Iyob, R., and G. M. Khadiagala. *Sudan: The Elusive Quest for Peace.* Boulder, CO: Lynne Rienner, 2006.

Izetbegović, Alija, Radovan Karadžić, and Miljenko Brkic. "Sarajevo Declaration on the Humanitarian Treatment of Displaced Persons." PA-X Peace Agreements Database, November 4, 1992. https://www.peaceagreements.org/view/1469/Sarajevo%20Declaration%20on%20the%20Humanitarian%20Treatment%20of%20Displaced%20Persons.

Izetbegović, Alija, Franjo Tuđman, and Slobodan Milošević. "General Framework Agreement for Peace in Bosnia and Herzegovina." PA-X Peace Agreements Database, 21 November 1995. https://peacemaker.un.org/bosniadaytonagreement95.

Jap, Jangai. "Protesters and Bystanders: Ethnic Minorities in the Pro-Democracy Revolution." *Tea Circle Blog Post,* 22 March 2021. https://teacircleoxford.com/politics/protesters-and-bystanders-ethnic-minorities-in-the-pro-democracy-revolution/.

Jaramillo, Sergio. Interview about the use of battlefield violence in the context of the Colombian peace negotiations. Conducted by Valerie Sticher in Zurich (Switzerland) on 24 June 2019.

Jaramillo, Sergio. "The Possibility of Peace." Transcript of Inaugural Lecture. Chicago: The Pearson Institute, University of Chicago, 24 March 2017.

"Joint Communique # 42." Joint Communique by the negotiating delegations of the Government of Colombia and the FARC. Havana, 22 August 2014.

"Joint Declaration of Agreement Reached between President Buyoya, Representing the Transitional Government of Burundi, and Pierre Nkurunziza, the Legal Representative of the CNDD-FDD in Pretoria on 27 January 2003." 2003.

Jolliffe, Kim. "Ceasefires, Governance, and Development: The Karen National Union in Times of Change." *The Asia Foundation, Policy Dialogue Brief Series,* no. 16 (2016).

Jones, Lee. "Understanding Myanmar's Ceasefires Geopolitics, Political Economy and State-Building." In *War and Peace in the Borderlands of Myanmar.* Copenhagen: NIAS Press, 2016.

Karakus, Dogukan Cansin, and Isak Svensson. 2017. "Between the Bombs: Exploring Partial Ceasefires in the Syrian Civil War, 2011–2017." *Terrorism and Political Violence* 32 (4): 681–700.

Keels, Eric, and Krista Wiegand. "Mutually Assured Distrust: Ideology and Commitment Problems in Civil Wars." *Journal of Conflict Resolution* 64, no. 10 (2020): 2022–2048. https://doi.org/10.1177/0022002720928414.

Khadiagala, Gilbert. In *Dealing with Conflict in Africa The United Nations and Regional Organizations*, edited by Jane Boulden, 215–251. New York: Palgrave Macmillan, 2003.

Ki-moon, Ban. "A Climate Culprit in Darfur." *UN Secretary General via The Washington Post*, 16 June 2007. https://www.un.org/sg/en/content/sg/articles/2007-06-16/climate-culprit-darfur.

Kitchener-Waterloo Record [Factiva]. "Acceptance of Peace Pact Fails to Quell Balkan Strife," 22 January 1993.

Kolås, Åshild. "Naga Militancy and Violent Politics in the Shadow of Ceasefire." *Journal of Peace Research* 48, no. 6 (2011): 781–792. https://doi.org/10.1177/0022343311417972.

Kramer, Tom. *Civil Society Gaining Ground: Opportunities for Change and Development in Burma*. Amsterdam: Transnational Institute Burma Center Netherlands, 2011.

Kristof, Nicholas D. "Genocide in Slow Motion." *New York Review of Books* 53, no. 2 (2006).

Verdad Abierta. "La Hoja de Ruta Para Lograr La Paz," 4 September 2012. https://verdadabierta.com/la-hoja-de-ruta-de-santos-para-logar-la-paz/.

Lintner, Bertil. "The United Wa State Army and Burma's Peace Process." *Peaceworks*, no. 147. Washington, DC: United States Institute of Peace USIP Press, 2019.

Lounsbery, M. O., F. Pearson, and F. S. Pearson. *Civil Wars: Internal Struggles, Global Consequences*. Toronto: University of Toronto Press, 2009.

Lundgren, Magnus, Isak Svensson, and Dogukan Cansin Karakus. "Local ceasefires and de-escalation: Evidence from the Syrian Civil War." *Journal of Conflict Resolution* 67.7-8 (2023): 1350-1375.

Luttwak, Edward N. "Give War a Chance." *Foreign Affairs* 78 (1999): 36–44.

Machakos Protocol between the Government of Sudan and the Sudan People's Liberation Movement/Army, 20 July 2002. https://peacemaker.un.org/sites/peacemaker.un.org/files/SD_020710_MachakosProtocol.pdf.

Mack, Michelle. *Increasing Respect for International Humanitarian Law in Non-International Armed Conflicts*. Geneva: International Committee of the Red Cross, 2008. https://www.icrc.org/sites/default/files/topic/file_plus_list/0923-increasing_respect_for_international_humanitarian_law_in_non-international_armed_conflicts.pdf.

Mahieu, Sylvie. "When Should Mediators Interrupt a Civil War? The Best Timing for a Ceasefire." *International Negotiation* 12, no. 2 (2007): 207–228.

Maloney, Sean M. "Operation Bolster. Canada and the European Community Monitor Mission in Former Yugoslavia, 1991–92." *International Peacekeeping* 4, no. 1 (1997): 26–50. https://doi.org/10.1080/13533319708413650.

Marchal, R. "The Unseen Regional Implications of the Crisis in Darfur." In *War in Darfur and the Search for Peace*, edited by A. De Waal, 173–198. Cambridge, UK: Global Equity Initiative, 2007.

Martínez, A. G. Interviewed by Jean Krasno for Yale–UN Oral History Project, 21 June 1997. http://ugspace.ug.edu.gh/handle/123456789/3104.

Martínez Peñate, Óscar. *El Salvador: Las Negociaciones de Los Acuerdos de Paz (1990–1992)*. San Salvador: Editorial Nuevo Enfoque, 2011.

Mason, Simon J. A., and Matthias Siegfried. "Confidence Building Measures (CBMs) in Peace Processes." In *Managing Peace Processes: Process Related Questions. A Handbook for*

AU Practitioners, vol. 1, 57–77. Geneva: African Union and the Centre for Humanitarian Dialogue, 2013.

Mashal, Mujib. "Countdown Begins to Possible End of U.S. War in Afghanistan." *The New York Times*, 4 March 2020. https://www.nytimes.com/2020/02/21/world/asia/afghanistan-cease-fire-peace-talks.html.

Mathieson, David Scott. "The Arakan Army in Myanmar: Deadly Conflict Rises in Rakhine State." *United States Institute of Peace: Special Report*, no. 486 (2020).

Maxwell, Daniel, Martina Santschi, and Rachel Gordon. *Looking Back to Look Ahead? Reviewing Key Lessons from Operation* Lifeline *Sudan and Past Humanitarian Operations in South Sudan*. Secure Livelihoods Research Consortium, 2014. https://securelivelihoods.org/wp-content/uploads/Reviewing-key-lessons-from-Operation-Lifeline-Sudan-and-past-humanitarian-operations-in-South-Sudan.pdf.

Mecanismo de Monitoreo y Verificación. "Informe de Cierre de Actividades Del Mecanismo de Monitoreo y Verificación." Bogotá, 22 September 2017. https://unmc.unmissions.org/sites/default/files/informe_final_publico_221530r_sept_17_v_final_-_prensa_i.pdf.

Medina, Carlos. *FARC-EP. Temas y Problemas Nacionales 1958–2008*. Bogotá: Universidad Nacional, 2008.

Memorandum of Understanding on Cessation of Hostilities between the Government of the Sudan and the Sudan People's Liberation Movement/Army. 2002. https://peacemaker.un.org/sites/peacemaker.un.org/files/SD_021015_MoU%20on%20Cessation%20of%20Hostilities%20between%20the%20GoS%20and%20the%20SPLMA.pdf.

Mercy Corps. *Building a Robust Civilian Ceasefire Monitoring Mechanism in Myanmar: Challenges, Successes and Lessons Learned*. Working Paper and Recommendations Report, 2016.

Millán Hernández, Juanita. "Connecting Practice and Research: What Can We Learn from the Colombian Ceasefire between the Government and the FARC (2016 to 2017)?" MAS thesis, ETH Zurich, 2019.

Min, Eric. "Painful Words: The Effect of Battlefield Activity on Conflict Negotiation Behavior." *Journal of Conflict Resolution* 66, nos. 4–5 (2022): 595–622.

Min, Eric. "Talking While Fighting: Understanding the Role of Wartime Negotiation." *International Organization* 74, no. 3 (2020): 610–632.

Moreno, Rafael E. "El Proceso de Negociación Salvadoreño Desde La Perspectiva Del FMLN." Ponencia presented at the Seminario Internacional Sobre Negociación de Conflictos Armados, 27 October 1994. http://www.cedema.org/ver.php?id=2853.

Myanmar Peace Monitor. *Kachin Independence Organization*. 2021. https://web.archive.org/web/20180312204620/http://mmpeacemonitor.org/stakeholders/stakeholders-overview/155-kio.

Myint-U, Thant. *The Hidden History of Burma: Race, Capitalism, and the Crisis of Democracy in the 21st Century*. London: Atlantic Books, 2020.

NATO. "Peace Support Operations in Bosnia and Herzegovina." NATO, 26 April 2019. http://www.nato.int/cps/en/natohq/topics_52122.htm.

Nathan, Laurie, and Ajay Sethi. "Holding the Peace in Intra-State Conflict? The Relevance of Ceasefire Agreement Design." Unpublished manuscript, 2020.

Nathan, L. "The Failure of the Darfur Mediation." *Ethnopolitics* 6, no. 4 (2007): 495–511.

Nathan, L. "The Making and Unmaking of the Darfur Peace Agreement." In *War in Darfur and the Search for Peace*, edited by A. De Waal, 245–266. London: Global Equity Initiative, 2007.

Nathan, L. "No Ownership, No Peace: The Darfur Peace Agreement." *Working Paper* 5, Crisis States Research Centre, London School of Economics (2006): 3–5.

Nathan, L. "The Mandate Effect: A Typology and Conceptualization of Mediation Mandates." *Peace & Change* 43, no. 3 (2018): 318–343.

Naw, Stella. "Raising Our Flag High. A Kachin Activist on Reimagining an Inclusive Society after the Coup in Myanmar." *Adi Magazine*, Spring 2021. https://adimagazine.com /articles/raising-our-flags-high/.

Neuman, William, and Jenny Carolina Gonzales. "Colombian Rebels Free 10, Raising Hopes of Peace Talks with Government." *The New York Times*, 2 April 2012, sec. World. https://www.nytimes.com/2012/04/03/world/americas/farc-frees-10-hostages-in-colombia .html.

Nindorera, Willy. *The CNDD-FDD in Burundi: The Path from Armed to Political Struggle*. Berlin: Berghof-Stiftung für Konfliktforschung, 2012.

Nuba Mountains Cease-Fire Agreement, 2002. https://www.peaceagreements.org /viewmasterdocument/470.

Nussio, Enzo. "The Colombian Trap: Another Partial Peace." *CSS Analyses in Security Policy*, no. 258 (March 2020).

Nussio, Enzo. "Violencia, terrorismo y guerra de discursos. Dos décadas de amenazas a la seguridad vistas por los presidentes colombianos." *Bulletin de la Société Suisse des Américanistes*, no. 75 (2013): 43–54.

Nussio, Enzo, and Juan E. Ugarriza. "Why Rebels Stop Fighting. Organizational Decline and Exit from Colombia's Insurgency." *International Security* 45, no. 4 (2021): 167–203.

OACP. *Biblioteca Del Proceso de Paz Con Las FARC*. Vol. 1. Bogata: Oficina del Alto Comisionado para la Paz, 2018.

O'Ballance, Edgar. *Civil War in Bosnia, 1992–94*. Hampshire: Macmillan Press Ltd, 1995.

Oberschall, Anthony. *Conflict and Peace Building in Divided Societies. Responses to Ethnic Violence*. New York: Routledge, 2007.

Ohn, U Shwe. "Building a Lasting Federal Union in Myanmar." In *Prisms on the Golden Pagod: Perspectives on National reconciliation in Myanmar*, edited by Kyaw Yin Hlaing, 84–109. Singapore: NUS Press, 2014.

Paczulla, Jutta. "The Long, Difficult Road to Dayton. Peace Efforts in Bosnia-Herzegovina." *International Journal* 60, no. 1 (2004): 255–272.

Paung Sie Facility. *Unlocking Civil Society Contributions to Peace in Myanmar*. Yangon: PSF, 2018.

Pérez de Cuéllar, Javier. *Pilgrimage for Peace: A Secretary-General's Memoir*. Basingstoke: Macmillan, 1997.

Phayal, A. "UN Troop Deployment and Preventing Violence against Civilians in Darfur," *International Interactions* 45, no. 5 (2019): 757–780.

Pinaud, Margaux. "Home-Grown Peace: Civil Society Roles in Ceasefire Monitoring." *International Peacekeeping* 28, no. 3 (2021): 470–495.

Pizarro, Eduardo. *Una Democracia Asediada: Balance y Perspectivas Del Conflicto Armado En Colombia*. Bogotá: Editorial Norma, 2004.

Posso, Camilo González. "Negotiations with the FARC: 1982–2002." In *Alternatives to War. Colombia's Peace Processes*, edited by Mauricio García-Durán, vol. 14, 46–51. Accord. London: Conciliation Resources, 2004.

Potkin, Fanny, and Poppy Mcpherson. "How Myanmar's Military Moved In on the Telecoms Sector to Spy on Its Citizens." *Reuters*, 19 May 2021. https://www.reuters.com /world/asia-pacific/how-myanmars-military-moved-telecoms-sector-spy-citizens -2021-05-18/.

"Pretoria Protocol on Outstanding Political, Defence, and Security Power-Sharing Issues in Burundi." 2003. https://www.un.org/sg/en/content/sg/statement/2003-11-03/statement-attributable-the-spokesman-for-the-secretary-general-the-signing-of-the-pretoria-protocol-outstanding-political-defence-and-security-power-sharing-issues.

Prunier, G. *Darfur: The Ambiguous Genocide*. London: Hurst, 2005.

Purrer Guardado, Ulrike. *Diplomacia pastoral: la Iglesia y Arturo Rivera y Damas en el proceso de paz salvadoreño*. San Salvador, El Salvador: UCA Editores, 2015.

Rabasa, Angel, and Peter Chalk. *Colombian Labyrinth. The Synergy of Drugs and Insurgency and Its Implications for Regional Stability*. Monograph Reports. Washington, D.C.: RAND Cooperation, 2001.

Reiter, Dan. *How Wars End*. Princeton, NJ: Princeton University Press, 2009.

Reuters News [Factiva]. "Moslems Accept Ceasefire in Fighting against Croats," 20 January 1993.

Reuters Staff. "TIMELINE: Events in Sudan since the Start of Civil War," 22 July 2009. https://www.reuters.com/article/us-sudan-south-events-timeline-sb-idUSTRE56L2KA20090722.

Richmond, Oliver. "Devious Objectives and the Disputants' View of International Mediation: A Theoretical Framework." *Journal of Peace Research* 35, no. 6 (1998): 707–722.

Rood, Steven. "Forging Sustainable Peace in Mindanao: The Role of Civil Society." *East-West Center Policy Studies*, no. 17. Washington, DC: East-West Center, 2005.

Roth, Richard, Caitlin Hu, and Taylor Barnes. "Myanmar Junta Offers Ceasefire to Some, as UN Envoy Warns of 'Bloodbath.'" CNN, 2021. https://www.cnn.com/2021/03/31/asia/myanmar-military-crackdown-halt-intl/index.html.

Rothchild, Donald. "Third Party Incentives." In *Ending Civil Wars: The Implementation of Peace Agreements*, edited by Stephen John Stedman, Donald Rothchild, and Elizabeth M. Cousens, 117–145. Boulder, CO: Lynne Rienner, 2002.

Sadan, Mandy, ed. *War and Peace in the Borderlands of Myanmar: The Kachin Ceasefire 1994–2011*. Copenhagen: NIAS Press, 2016.

Saferworld. *Security Integration in Myanmar: Past Experiences and Future Visions*. London: Saferworld, 2017.

Samayoa, Salvador. *El Salvador: La Reforma Pactada*. Colección Estructuras y Procesos, v. 19. San Salvador: UCA Editores, 2002.

Santos, Juan Manuel. "Tweet by @JuanManSantos: Dejemos de Felicitarnos Por Las Muertes de La Guerra. Todos Somos Colombianos. Recordemos a Ghandi: 'Ojo Por Ojo y El Mundo Quedará Ciego,'" 25 May 2015. https://x.com/JuanManSantos/status/602971177305378816.

Santos, Juan Manuel. "Tweet by @JuanManSantos: Lamento Muerte de Soldados En Cauca. Esta Es Precisamente La Guerra Que Queremos Terminar," 15 April 2015. https://twitter.com/juanmansantos/status/588308298962755584?lang=en.

Santos, Juan Manuel. "Tweet by @JuanManSantos: Mindefensa y Cdte Gral: Quiero Que Me Expliquen Por Qué BG Alzate Rompió Todos Los Protocolos de Seguridad y Estaba de Civil En Zona Roja," 17 November 2014. https://twitter.com/JuanManSantos/status/534167188459249664.

Santos, Soliman M., Jr. "War and Peace on the Moro Front: Three Standard Bearers, Three Forms of Struggle, Three Tracks (Overview)." In *Primed and Purposeful: Armed Groups and Human Security Efforts in the Philippines*, edited by Soliman M. Santos and Paz Verdades M. Santos, 58–90. Geneva: Small Arms Survey, 2010.

Schirmer, Jennifer. "To End the War in Colombia: Conversatorios among Security Forces, Ex-Guerrillas, and Political Elites, and Cease Re Seminars—Workshops for the Technical Sub-Commission." In *The Politics of Violence in Latin America*, edited by Pablo Policzer. Calgary: University of Calgary Press, 2019.

"School of the Dictators." *The New York Times*, 28 September 1996, sec. Opinion. https://www.nytimes.com/1996/09/28/opinion/school-of-the-dictators.html.

Scott, James C. *The Art of Not Being Governed: An Anarchist History of Upland Southeast Asia*. New Haven, CT: Yale University Press, 2010.

Segura, Renata, and Delphine Mechoulan. "Made in Havana: How Colombia and the FARC Decided to End the War." New York: International Peace Institute, February 2017.

Sisk, Timothy D. "Peacemaking Processes: Preventing Recurring Violence in Ethnic Conflicts." In *Preventive Negotiation: Avoiding Conflict Escalation*, edited by I. William Zartman, 67–90. Lanham, MD: Rowman & Littlefield, 2001.

Sithu, Aung Myint. "The UWSA: 30 Years of Going Its Own Way." *Frontier Myanmar*, 2019. https://www.frontiermyanmar.net/en/the-uwsa-30-years-of-going-its-own-way/.

Smith, James. *Stopping Wars: Defining the Obstacles to Cease-Fire*. Boulder, CO: Westview Press, 1995.

Smith, Martin. *Burma: Insurgency and the Politics of Ethnicity*. London: Zed Books, 1999.

Smith, Martin. *State of Strife: The Dynamics of Ethnic Conflict in Burma*. Washington, DC: East-West Center Washington; Institute of Southeast Asian Studies, 2007. https://www.amazon.com/State-Strife-Dynamics-Conflict-Studies/dp/9812304797.

Sosnowski, Marika. "Ceasefires as Violent State-Building: Local Truce and Reconciliation Agreements in the Syrian Civil War." *Conflict, Security & Development* 20, no. 2 (2020): 273–292.

South, Ashley. "Karen Nationalist Communities: The 'Problem' of Diversity." *Contemporary Southeast Asia* 29, no. 1 (2007): 55–76.

Stedman, Stephen John. "Spoiler Problems in Peace Processes." *International Security* 22, no. 2 (1997): 5–53.

Sticher, Valerie, and Siniša Vuković. "Bargaining in Intrastate Conflicts: The Shifting Role of Ceasefires." *Journal of Peace Research* 58, no. 6 (2021): 1284–1299. https://doi.org/10.1177/0022343320982658.

Sticher, Valerie. "Ceasefires as Bargaining Instruments in Intrastate Conflicts: Ceasefire Objectives and Their Effects on Peace Negotiations." PhD thesis, Leiden University, 2021. https://scholarlypublications.universiteitleiden.nl/handle/1887/3176458.

Sticher, Valerie. "Ceasefire Violations: Why They Occur and How They Relate to Strategic Decision-Making Processes." *International Studies Review* 24, 4 (2022). https://doi.org/10.1093/isr/viac046.

Sticher, Valerie. "Healing Stalemates: The Role of Ceasefires in Ripening Conflict." *Ethnopolitics* 21, no. 2 (2022): 149–162.

Sticher, Valerie. "Negotiating Peace with Your Enemy: The Problem of Costly Concessions." *Journal of Global Security Studies* 6, no. 4 (2021): 1–18. https://doi.org/10.1093/jogss/ogaa054.

Sticher, Valerie. "War of Narratives: Elite Framing and Peace Negotiations." In *The Causes and Consequences of Civil War Ceasefires*. Oslo, Norway: PRIO, ETH Zurich, 2019.

Sullivan, Joseph G. "How Peace Came to El Salvador." *Orbis* 38, no. 1 (1994): 83–98. https://doi.org/10.1016/0030-4387(94)90107-4.

Sundberg, Ralph, and Erik Melander. "Introducing the UCDP Georeferenced Event Dataset." *Journal of Peace Research* 50, no. 4 (2013): 523–532.

Tate, Winifred. *Drugs, Thugs, and Diplomats: U.S. Policymaking in Colombia.* Anthropology of Policy. Stanford, CA: Stanford University Press, 2015.

Thawnghmung, Ardeth Maung. "Back to the Future? Possible Scenarios for Myanmar." *ISEAS Yusof Ishak Institute Blog post,* 12 March 2021. https://www.iseas.edu.sg/articles-commentaries/iseas-perspective/2021-30-back-to-the-future-possible-scenarios-for-myanmar-by-ardeth-maung-thawnghmung/.

Thawnghmung, Ardeth Maung. *The Karen Revolution in Burma: Diverse Voices, Uncertain Ends.* Washington, DC: East-West Center Washington, Institute of Southeast Asian Studies, 2008. https://bookshop.iseas.edu.sg/publication/1350.

The International Crisis Group. *The Mandela Effect: Prospects for Peace in Burundi.* Bujumbura/Nairobi: The International Crisis Group, 2000.

"The Pretoria Protocol on Political, Defence, and Security Power Sharing in Burundi," 2003. https://peacemaker.un.org/node/165.

Toft, Monica Duffy. "Ending Civil Wars: A Case for Rebel Victory?" *International Security* 34, no. 4 (2010): 7–36.

Toga, D. "The African Union Mediation and the Abuja Peace Talks." In *War in Darfur and the Search for Peace,* edited by A. De Waal, 214–244. London: Global Equity Initiative, 2007.

Touval, Saadia. "Ethical Dilemmas in International Mediation." *Negotiation Journal* 11, no. 4 (1995): 333–337.

Transnational Institute. *The Nationwide Ceasefire Agreement in Myanmar: Promoting Ethnic Peace or Strengthening State Control.* Amsterdam: Transnational Institute, 2023.

Trnka, K., D. Kalinic, J. Djogo, A. Kurjak, and S. Sito Coric. "Geneva Agreement on Humanitarian Principles." PA-X Peace Agreements Database, May 22, 1992. https://www.peaceagreements.org/view/1475/Geneva%20Agreement%20on%20humanitarian%20principles.

Trnka, K., D. Kalinic, S. Sito Coric, and I. Sarac. "Agreement (ICRC Humanitarian Principles)." PA-X Peace Agreements Database, 6 June 1992. https://www.peaceagreements.org/view/1589/Agreement%20(ICRC%20Humanitarian%20Principles).

Tubiana, J. *The Chad-Sudan Proxy War and the 'Darfurization' of Chad: Myths and Reality.* HSBA Working Paper No. 12. Geneva: The Small Arms Survey, 2008.

Tubiana, J. "Darfur: A Conflict for Land?" In *War in Darfur and the Search for Peace,* edited by A. De Waal, 68–91. Cambridge: Global Equity Initiative, 2007.

UN. *United Nations Guidance for Effective Mediation.* New York: United Nations, 2012.

UN Department of Political and Peacebuilding Affairs, *Guidance on the Mediation of Ceasefires.* New York: United Nations, 2022.

UN Department of Public Information. *The United Nations and El Salvador, 1990–1995.* Vol. 4. The United Nations Blue Books Series. New York: United Nations, Dept. of Public Information, 1995.

UN Human Rights Commissioner. *Statement,* 11 September 2017. https://www.ohchr.org/en/statements/2017/09/darker-and-more-dangerous-high-commissioner-updates-human-rights-council-human?LangID=E&NewsID=22041.

UN Human Rights Council. A/HRC/49/72. "Situation of Human Rights in Myanmar since 1 February 2021," 15 March 2022. https://www.google.com/url?sa=t&rct=j&q=&esrc=s&source=web&cd=&cad=rja&uact=8&ved=2ahUKEwjw8r2RhKH8AhVs_7sIHTUIAQ0QFnoECA8QAQ&url=https%3A%2F%2Fwww.ohchr.org%2Fsites%2

Fdefault%2Ffiles%2F2022-03%2FA_HRC_49_72_AdvanceEditedVersion.docx&usg =AOvVaw37UCdnuXcLA8Usv_ic89_Q.

UN Human Rights Council. A/HRC/50/CRP.1. "Losing a Generation: How the Military Junta Is Attacking Myanmar's Children and Stealing Their Future," 13 June 2022. https:// www.ohchr.org/en/documents/thematic-reports/ahrc50crp1-conference-room-paper -special-rapporteur-losing-generation.

UN Human Rights Council. A/HRC/51/4. "Report of the Independent Investigative Mechanism for Myanmar," 12 July 2022. https://iimm.un.org/wp-content/uploads/2022/08 /A-HRC-51-4-E.pdf.

UN Security Council. *Resolution 781*, 1992. http://www.ohr.int/other-doc/un-res-bih/pdf /s92r781e.pdf.

UN Security Council. *Resolution 816*, 1993. http://www.ohr.int/other-doc/un-res-bih/pdf /816e.pdf.

UN Security Council. *Resolution 819*, 1993. https://undocs.org/S/RES/819(1993).

UN Security Council. *Resolution 824*, 1993. https://undocs.org/S/RES/824(1993).

UN Special Rapporteur on the situation of human rights in Myanmar. A/HRC/49/ CRP.1. *Enabling Atrocities: UN Member States' Arms Transfers to the Myanmar Military*. Geneva: OHCHR, 22 February 2022. https://reliefweb.int/report/myanmar/enabling -atrocities-un-member-states-arms-transfers-myanmar-military-ahrc49crp1.

UN Sudan. *United Nations Mission in Sudan (UNMIS) Background*. UN, 2005a. https:// peacekeeping.un.org/en/mission/past/unmis/background.shtml.

UN Sudan. *United Nations Mission in the Sudan Mandate*. UN, 2005b. https://peacekeeping .un.org/en/mission/past/unmis/mandate.shtml.

Van der Zwan, Jost. "Evaluating the EU's Role and Challenges in Sudan and South Sudan. Sudan and South Sudan Case Study." *International Alert*, September 2011. https://www .international-alert.org/sites/default/files/publications/092011IfPEWSudan_0.pdf.

Vickers, George. "El Salvador a Negotiated Revolution." *Report on the Americas* 25, no. 5 (1992): 4–8. https://doi.org/10.1080/10714839.1992.11723101.

Von Mittelstaedt, Juliane, and Helene Zuber. "'Waging War Is More Popular Than Negotiating.' SPIEGEL Interview with Colombian President Juan Manuel Santos." *Spiegel*, 21 May 2014.

Wade, Christine J. *Captured Peace: Elites and Peacebuilding in El Salvador*. Ohio University Research in International Studies. Latin America Series 52. Athens: Ohio University Press, 2016.

Wagner, R. Harrison. "Bargaining and War." *American Journal of Political Science* 44, no. 3 (2000): 469–484.

Wallensteen, P., and I. Svensson. "Talking Peace: International Mediation in Armed Conflicts." *Journal of Peace Research* 51, no. 2 (2014): 315–327.

Walter, Barbara F. "Re-Conceptualizing Conflict Resolution as a Three-Stage Process." *International Negotiation* 7, no. 3 (2002): 299–311.

Waterman, Alex. "Ceasefires and State Order-Making in Naga Northeast India." *International Peacekeeping* 28, no. 3 (2020): 496–525.

Werner, Suzanne, and Amy Yuen. "Making bind Keeping Peace." *International Organization* 59, no. 2 (2005): 261–92.

White, Richard A. *The Morass: United States Intervention in Central America*. New York: Harper & Row, 1985.

Whitfield, Teresa. *Paying the Price: Ignacio Ellacuría and the Murdered Jesuits of El Salvador.* Philadelphia: Temple University Press, 1995.

Williams, D. "What's So Bad about the Burma's 2008 Constitution?" In *Law, Society and Transition in Myanmar,* edited by M. Crouch and T. Lindsey, 117–139. London: Bloomsbury Publishing, 2014.

Winokur, Justin. "Before the Peace. Ceasefire Durability in Ethnic Civil Wars." *Government and International Relations Honors Papers* 52 (2018). https://digitalcommons.conncoll.edu/govhp/52/.

Wood, Elisabeth Jean. *Forging Democracy from Below: Insurgent Transactions in South Africa and El Salvador.* Cambridge Studies in Comparative Politics. Cambridge: University Press, 2000.

Woods, Kevin, Tom Kramer, Jennifer Franco, and Joseph Purugganan. *Developing Disparity: Regional Investment in Burma's Borderlands.* Amsterdam: Transnational Institute and Burma Center Netherlands, 2013.

Woods, Kevin. "Ceasefire Capitalism: Military–Private Partnerships, Resource Concessions, and Military–State Building in the Burma–China Borderlands." *The Journal of Peasant Studies* 38, no. 4 (2011): 747–770. https://doi.org/10.1080/03066150.2011.607699.

Yamahata, Chosein, and Bobby Anderson, eds. *Demystifying Myanmar's Transition and Political Crisis.* Singapore: Palgrave Macmillan, 2022.

Zartman, I. William. "The Timing of Peace Initiatives: Hurting Stalemates and Ripe Moments." *The Global Review of Ethnopolitics* 1, no. 1 (2001): 8–18.

Zaw Oo, Min. "Understanding Myanmar's Peace Process: Ceasefire Agreements." *SwissPeace Catalyzing Reflection,* no. 2 (2014). https://www.themimu.info/sites/themimu.info/files/documents/Report_Catalyzing_Reflections_SwissPeace_Feb2014.pdf.

Zaw Oo, Min, and Win Min. *Assessing Burma's Ceasefire Accords.* Washington, DC: East-West Center Washington, Institute of Southeast Asian Studies, 2007.

INDEX

Page numbers followed by *f* or *t* indicate material in figures or tables, respectively

Abéché ceasefire Agreement, 166

Abuja mediation process, 183

Ad Hoc Joint Action Group (AHJAG), 119–20, 127, 129, 130

African Union Mission in Sudan (AMIS), 167, 169, 175, 178, 180, 181

analytical framework, 2*f*, 4, 18, 19

analytical strategy, 10, 17–19

Arakan Army (AA), 247

Arusha Peace and Reconciliation Agreement, 82, 87, 94, 96, 99

Bangsamoro Development Agency (BDA), 128

Bangsamoro Islamic Freedom Fighters (BIFF), 124, 126, 127

Bantay ceasefire, 126

bilateral ceasefire, 6, 131, 191, 194, 199, 203, 207–9

Black Book, 164

Border Guard Forces (BGF), 255, 256

Bosnia (1992–1995): Carrington–Cutileiro plan, 63, 64; ceasefire process, 72–78; conflict (1991–1994), 64*f*; Contact Group plan, 67–69, 68*f*; democratization process, 60; final peace agreement, 69–72; international and military contexts, 72–78; Juppe–Kinkel plan, 65; lift-and-strike policy, 66; NATO, 59, 61, 70; negative feedback loop, 74; overview, 60–62; peace agreement, 76; peace-making, 73; peace process, 62–63; political negotiation process, 72–78; separate initiatives by EU, 63–67; shuttle diplomacy, 69; Vance–Owen plan, 65

Bosniak–Croat coalition, 67, 70, 74, 75

Burundi (1996–2003): Arusha Peace and Reconciliation Agreement, 82; ceasefire process, 98–101; CNDD-FDD, 82, 83, 86*f*, 89*t*, 90–91; conflict actors, 84–86; implementation phase, 97–98; negotiation phase, 93–97, 94*f*; overview, 83–84; PALIPEHUTU-FNL, 82, 85; peace process, 88*t*–89*t*; political negotiation process, 98–101; prenegotiation phase, 91–93; pre-prenegotiation phase, 90–91; pro-Tutsi government, 84; regional and international efforts, 86–87; UPRONA, 85

Burundi National Defense Force (BNDF), 95, 96

Burundi peace process, 88*t*–89*t*

Caraballeda meeting, 42

Caracas agreement, 37

Carrington–Cutileiro plan, 63, 64

case selection, 23–24

Ceasefire Agreement, 99, 113–14, 167

ceasefire/ceasefire process, 2, 2*f*, 5–8, 7*t*; arrangements, classes of, 6–8, 7*t*; containing fighting, 283–84; context factors, 288, 289*f*; contextual conditions impacting, 22–23; defined,

5–6; domestic political context, 289–92; factors shaping use and outcomes, 278, 279*f*; fighting unabated, 281; geopolitical context analysis, 298; impact on political negotiation process, 10–16; implications, 286–88, 297–98, 298*f*; importance of, 6; international political context, 294–97; military context, 292–94; political and security interests, 280; talking, not fighting, 285–86; talking while fighting, 282–83

ceasefire opportunity space, 279–81, 280*f*

ceasefire sequencing strategies, 1, 17, 21–22, 47–49, 286, 291

cessation of hostilities (CoH), 6, 44–46, 112, 114, 116, 145

civil disobedience movement (CDM), 269

Civilian Protection Component (CPC), IMT, 111

Cold War, 24, 33, 63, 68, 136, 250, 294

Colombia (2012–2016): aftermath of the plebiscite, 199; battlefield dynamics and de-escalation, 210–12; bilateral ceasefire, 207–9; ceasefire arrangement in, 1; ceasefire considerations, 201–3; change in military balance, 190–91; conflict and negotiations, 189; definitive ceasefire, 198; disarmament as initial stumbling block, 209–10; FARC perspective, 206–7; government perspective, 200–201; Havana peace process, 188; negotiation and battlefield dynamics, 190–91; negotiation phase, 194–96; overview, 188–89; political negotiations, 191, 192*f*; prenegotiation phase, 193–94; pre-prenegotiation phase, 193; previous negotiation attempts, 189–90; shift in dynamics, 204–6; shift in negotiations and

in battlefield dynamics, 196–97; unilateral ceasefires, 195*t*; unilateral cessation of hostilities, 207–9

command control, ceasefire to demonstrate, 12

Communist Party of Burma (CPB), 249, 250

2014 Comprehensive Agreement, 105

Comprehensive Peace Agreement (CPA), 134, 172, 173; implementation process, 153, 154; Machakos Protocol, 134; mediation team, 144; negotiation process, 156; security-related clauses, 138; Sudan's peace process, 172

conducive environment for negotiations, 11

confidence-building measure, ceasefires as, 12

conflict party, 5–7, 14, 15, 199–200, 290; signaling peaceful intentions, 11

Conseil National Pour la Défense de la Démocratie—Forces pour la Défense de la Démocratie (CNDD-FDD), 1, 82, 83, 86*f*, 89*t*, 90–91

Contact Group plan, 67–69, 68*f*

contentious issues: belligerency status, 114; cessation of hostilities, 114, 116; GRP-MILF talks, 115; legal jurisdiction, 116; MILF camps, 117; participatory process, 116

Darfur (2000–2007): AU-mediated peace, 170; ceasefire negotiations, 165–70; comprehensive negotiation phase, 170–72; context, 164–65; declaration of principles (DoP), 169; final flurry, 176–77; implementation phase, 177–78; movement negotiators, 176; N'djamena Humanitarian Ceasefire Agreement, 168*f*, 169; North–South peace process, 165; overview, 163; ripeness theory,

183; serious negotiations, 172–74; subsequent mediation process, 163; timeline, 182*t*; undue pressure on mediators, 174–75
Darfur Peace Agreement (DPA), 163, 174–78, 183
Dayton agreement, 71
de-escalation mechanisms, 7–8, 7*t*, 191, 219
definitive ceasefires, 5–7, 13, 15, 31, 42, 44–47
devious intention, 14, 284, 293
Disarmament, Demobilization, and Reintegration (DDR) process, 71, 96; challenges, 149, 150; coordination framework, 151; joint commission, 152; preparing parties, 148–53; security-related process, 149

El Salvador peace negotiations (1989–1992): conflict and precursors, 31–32; dialogue without negotiation, 34–35; FMLN military pressure, 30; government of El Salvador (GOES), 30; parties to the conflict, 32; political and ceasefire negotiations, 31, 47–51; pre-prenegotiations, 32–34; timeline, 52*t*–54*t*; UN-assisted negotiations, 35–47; UN mediation team, 30
Ethnic Armed Organizations (EAOs): Arakan Army (AA), 247; Border Guard Forces (BGF), 255, 256; ceasefire agreements, 246, 248*f*; constitution-making process, 254; fatalities in, 248*f*; gentlemen's agreements, 244, 251–54, 256; Kachin Independence Organisation (KIO), 247, 258; Karen National Union (KNU), 247, 255, 258; National League for Democracy (NLD), 245; Nationwide Ceasefire Agreement (NCA), 245; United Wa State Army (UWSA), 247; Uppsala Conflict Data Programme, 247
EU Action plan, 65, 67
European Community Monitor Mission (ECMM), 64, 73

Federacion Nacional Sindical de Trabajadores Salvadorenos (FENASTRAS), 34
Federal Political Negotiation and Consultative Committee (FPNCC), 269
feedback loops, 19–21, 49–51, 60, 83, 99, 100
Forces Technical Agreement (FTA), 96
formal negotiation phase, political negotiation process, 9
Framework Agreement on the Bangsamoro (FAB), 111, 128
Frente Democratico Revolucionario (FDR), 32
Frente Farabundo Marti para la Liberacion Nacional (FMLN): ceasefire proposal, 49; democratic reforms, 32; GOES, 36, 40; government's conception, 43; grassroots and peasant organizations, 32; guerrilla tactics, 31; left-wing insurgency, 31; left-wing revolutionary movement, 32; military pressure, 30; ONUSAL, 45, 46; preliminary ceasefire, 50; surface-to-air missiles, 48; UN General Assembly, 33, 39; unilateral declaration, 50; UN secretary-general (UNSG), 35
Front pour la Democratie au Burundi (FRODEBU), 85–87, 94

gentlemen's agreements, 244, 251–54, 256
Global Ceasefire Agreement, 82, 96–98, 101
government of El Salvador (GOES), 30, 42
GRP-MILF Agreement, 114

Havana peace process, 188, 191
Humanitarian, Rehabilitation, and
    Development Component (HRDC),
    121
2004 Humanitarian Ceasefire Agree-
    ment, 178
Hutu majority, 84, 85, 290

IGAD mediation team, 142, 145, 147
implementation phase, political
    negotiation process, 8, 9
inclusion, in peace process, 12
Independent Fact-Finding Committee
    (IFFC), 119
International Monetary Fund (IMF), 32
Intra-Syrian Talks, 229–38

Janjaweed, 165, 178
Japan International Cooperation and
    Assistance (JICA), 128
Joint Ceasefire Commission (JCC),
    95, 98
Juppe–Kinkel plan, 66
Justice and Equality Movement (JEM),
    164, 166–68, 173–75, 177–79

Kachin Independence Organisation
    (KIO), 247, 254–60, 262–65,
    268–70, 272
Karen National Union (KNU), 247,
    249, 253–60, 265, 268, 270

lift-and-strike policy, 66
long-term conflict management, 13

Memorandum of Agreement on
    Ancestral Domain (MOA-AD),
    109, 121, 124
Mexico agreement, 41
Mindanao Trust Fund (MTF), 128
Moro Islamic Liberation Front
    (MILF), 1; BIFF, 124; CCCH mech-
    anism, 129; ceasefire agreement

negotiations, 113–14; commanders
    and central committee members,
    130; conflict landscape, 107;
    contentious issues, 114–18; disavow
    criminality, 130; domestic stage
    process, 108; peace agreement, 113
Moro National Liberation Front
    (MNLF), 107
multilateral ceasefire, 6
Muslim–Croat federation, 66, 71
Myanmar (1989–2020): bilateral
    ceasefires, 257–59; black market
    trafficking, 250; breakdown of
    informal ceasefires, 254–56; civil dis-
    obedience movement (CDM), 269;
    Communist Party of Burma (CPB),
    249, 250; conflict background,
    249–51; conflict violence and
    efforts, 270–73; contested issues,
    270–73; 2021 Coup d'État,
    269–70; EAOs. See Ethnic Armed
    Organizations (EAOs); gentlemen's
    agreements, 244; NCA Implemen-
    tation, 266–69; NCA negotiations,
    259–66; quasi-civilian regime, 257;
    successive rulers of, 249; 21st Century
    Panglong Conferences, 267
Myanmar Peace Center (MPC), 257

Naivasha negotiations, 153
National Democratic Front of the Phil-
    ippines (NDFP), 112
National League for Democracy
    (NLD), 245, 248, 266, 268, 269
National Unification Commission
    (NUC), 112
Nationwide Ceasefire Agreement
    (NCA), 245, 259–66
N'djamena Agreement, 168, 178
N'djamena Humanitarian Ceasefire
    Agreement, 167, 168f, 169
negotiations, conducive environment
    for, 11

Nepali peacekeeping battalion, 45
North Atlantic Treaty Organization
    (NATO), 59, 61, 65–70, 75, 77
Nuba Mountains ceasefire, 136–39

ongoing violence, 11, 82, 190, 282, 292
onset/timing, of political negotiation
    process, 15
ONUSAL, 38, 45–47, 51
Operation Deliberate Force, 62, 69, 75
Organization of Islamic Cooperation
    (OIC), 107, 119
Owen–Stoltenberg plan, 65

122-page Chapultepec Agreement, 46
Panglong Agreement, 249
Parti pour la liberation du peuple
    Hutu—Forces nationales de libera-
    tion (PALIPEHUTU-FNL), 82, 85,
    87, 97, 98, 101
peace processes, components of, 2, 2*f.*
    See also ceasefire process; political
    negotiation process
Philippines and the MILF, Mindanao:
    AHJAG protocols, 129, 130; armed
    conflict, 106–8; ceasefire and imple-
    mentation mechanisms, 118–21;
    ceasefire and political negotiations,
    121–24, 124*f*; cessation of hostilities
    agreement, 112; GPH-MILF peace
    process, 120*f*; issues and conflict
    violence, 106; overview, 105–6;
    peace negotiations, 109–12; peace
    talks, 127–28; quick response team
    (QRT), 119; security cooperation,
    129–30; timeline, 110*t*–11*t*; violent
    ceasefire breakdowns, 124–27
political and ceasefire negotiations:
    ceasefire sequencing strategy, 48–49;
    positive feedback loops, 49–51;
    talking while fighting, 47–48
political negotiation process, 2, 2*f*,
    8–10, 9*f*; Bosnia (1992–1995),

72–78; Burundi (1996–2003),
    98–101; contextual conditions
    impacting, 22–23; formal negoti-
    ation phase, 9; impact of ceasefire
    process on, 10–14; impact on cease-
    fire process, 14–16; implementation
    phase, 8, 9; onset/timing of, 15;
    prenegotiation phase, 8, 9;
    pre-prenegotiation phase, 8–9;
    progress in, 15; United Nations-
    assisted negotiations, 39–41
preliminary ceasefires, 5–7, 13, 38–39,
    41–43, 48
prenegotiation phase, political negotia-
    tion process, 8, 9
pre-prenegotiation phase, political
    negotiation process, 8–9
Pretoria I agreement, 95

quantitative research, 17
quasi-civilian regime, 257

Reform the Armed Forces (RAM), 112
research, 16–17
Revolutionary Armed Forces of Colom-
    bia (FARC), 1, 188, 189; aftermath
    of the plebiscite, 199; battlefield
    dynamics and de-escalation, 210–12;
    bilateral ceasefire, 207–9; ceasefire
    considerations, 201–3; change in mil-
    itary balance, 190–91; conflict and
    negotiations, 189; definitive ceasefire,
    198; disarmament as initial stum-
    bling block, 209–10; government
    perspective, 200–201; Havana peace
    process, 188; negotiation and battle-
    field dynamics, 190–91; negotiation
    phase, 194–96; overview, 188–89;
    perspectives, 206–7; political nego-
    tiations, 191, 192*f*; prenegotiation
    phase, 193–94; pre-prenegotiation
    phase, 193; previous negotiation
    attempts, 189–90; shift in dynamics,

204–6; shift in negotiations and in battlefield dynamics, 196–97; unilateral ceasefires, 195*t*; unilateral cessation of hostilities, 207–9

San Jose Agreement, 38
sequencing strategies, 21–22
Serbian military dominance, 72
Socio-Economic Assistance Components (SEAC), 121
Sudan North–South negotiations (2002–2005): advising parties and preparation, 145–48; background, 134–36; build mediation strategy, 141–44; coherent mediation strategy, 158–59; confidence-building measures (CBMs), 158; IGAD mediation team, 142; implementation process, 153–55; Machakos protocol, 139–41; from Machakos to Torit, 144–45; Nuba Mountains ceasefire, 136–39; overview, 133–34; parties for DDR negotiations, 148–53; political negotiation and ceasefire process, 158; process timeline, 137; special envoy, 143; SPLM/A troops, 138; teamwork, 141–44; technical knowledge, 159–60
Sudan People's Liberation Movement/Army (SPLM/A), 134–38, 140, 142, 144–47, 154, 155
Syria (2012–2018): aim at nationwide ceasefires, 225–28; ceasefire arrangement, 1; confidence-building measures (CBMs), 220; contested political issues, 234–35; interaction and challenges, 235–38; Intra-Syrian Talks, 229–33, 235; issues and actors, 220–23; overview, 219–20; parallel tracks in Geneva and Astana, 233; peacemaking efforts, 223–25; political negotiations, 225–28, 226*f*; political process alive, 229–33, 230*f*;

United Nations (UN) mediator, 219; violence, 233–34

Taliban, ceasefire called by, 12
talking, not fighting, 285–86
talking while fighting, 282–83
timing, of political negotiation process, 15
Tripoli Agreement, 118, 119, 128

UN-AU Hybrid Operation in Darfur (UNAMID), 178, 181
UNICEF's Child Soldiers Rehabilitation Programme, 155
unilateral ceasefire, 6, 195, 196
Union Peacemaking Central Committee (UPCC), 257
Union Peacemaking Working Committee (UPWC), 257, 260, 261
Union pour le Progres national (UPRONA), 85, 87, 97
United Nations-assisted negotiations: Caraballeda meeting, 42; Caracas agreement, 37; ceasefire implementation, 46–47; demobilization, 46; political negotiation process, 39–41; preliminary ceasefire, 38–39; prenegotiations, 35–37; rethinking preliminary ceasefire, 41–43; sequencing the ceasefire, 37–38; from unilateral cessation of hostilities, 44–46
United Nations (UN) mediator, 219
United Nations Protection Force (UNPROFOR), 61, 63–65, 73, 75, 77
United Wa State Army (UWSA), 247, 251, 256–59, 265, 268–71
UN mediation team, 30, 43–45, 47, 51
Uppsala Conflict Data Programme, 247

Vance–Owen Geneva negotiations, 73
Vance–Owen plan, 65

Washington Framework Agreement, 66, 67, 74, 75

CONTRIBUTORS

MALIN ÅKEBO is an associate professor at the Department of Political Science, Umeå University. Her research interests concern ceasefire agreements, the dynamics of postwar transitions, and varieties of peace. Åkebo completed her PhD in 2013 on the politics of ceasefires in relation to peace processes within a comparative framework (*The Politics of Ceasefires: On Ceasefire Agreements and Peace Processes in Aceh and Sri Lanka*), and she has studied ceasefires in different empirical contexts, including in Indonesia, Sri Lanka, and the Philippines. She is the author of *Ceasefire Agreements and Peace Processes: A Comparative Study* (Routledge 2016).

JEREMY BRICKHILL is an international expert on the mediation, management, and implementation of security sector transformation, including ceasefire and peace-building processes and security sector reform. He has provided expert advice to governments and other armed actors in many countries and has worked as a program manager and advisor for the United Nations and the African Union and designed and delivered training programs for several academic and military training institutions.

CATE BUCHANAN specializes in mediation and process design, conflict sensitivity, and inclusion. She was senior adviser to the Nyein (Shalom) Foundation Myanmar supporting national dialogues and negotiation approaches. In 2018–2019, she was a member of the UN Mediation Support Unit's Standby Team of Experts. In 2020–2021, she was a senior adviser to the Office of the Special Envoy of the UN Secretary-General for Yemen. From 2001–2013, she was a programme manager and senior adviser with the Centre for Humanitarian Dialogue. She is conflict adviser to the Myanmar Livelihoods and Food Security Fund and manages an initiative on conflict-related sexual violence in Myanmar.

GOVINDA CLAYTON is a mediation support manager and thematic lead on ceasefires and security arrangements at the Centre for Humanitarian Dialogue (HD). He has published widely on topics including mediation, ceasefires and security arrangements, negotiation, and conflict dynamics. He is the leader of the Ceasefire Project, a collaboration with researchers and practitioners seeking to improve mediation practice relating to the integration of security arrangements within mediation processes. He holds a doctorate in international conflict analysis and was formerly a senior researcher in peace processes at ETH Zurich.

ALLARD DUURSMA is an assistant professor in Conflict Management and International Relations at ETH Zurich. His research focuses on how mediation and peacekeeping can help to prevent and end armed conflict. One of the case studies in his PhD dissertation focused on mediation in Darfur. To this purpose, he has conducted many interviews with mediators and representatives of the Darfurian conflict parties in Sudan, South Sudan, and Ethiopia, among others. Allard's work has been published in the *Journal of Conflict Resolution, International Studies Quarterly*, and *International Organization*. He is editor-in-chief at *International Peacekeeping*.

ALMA EVANGELISTA is an independent consultant on peace and development in the Philippines. She served as Team Leader for Crisis Prevention and Recovery with the United Nations Development Programme–Philippines, undersecretary and executive director of the Office of the Presidential Advisor on the Peace Process, and chair of the Technical Committee of Philippine government's peace panel for initial negotiations with the Moro Islamic Liberation Front (MILF), which negotiated and signed the GRP-MILF General Agreement on Cessation of Hostilities.

MBAYE FAYE is an international expert in security arrangements. With a decade-plus tenure as a UN advisor in Burundi, he notably served as Security Sector Reform Adviser for the Secretary-General's Conflict Prevention Office. His UN roles spanned diverse crises in Libya, Cote d'Ivoire, Georgia, South Sudan, and the Central African Republic. Beyond the UN, Faye contributed as senior adviser for CMI–Martti Ahtisaari Foundation, focusing on African Union collaboration. Prior to his UN career, Faye held pivotal military positions in the Senegalese armed forces, commanding operations in Saudi Arabia, Guinea-Bissau, and the Gambia.

MIRIAM CORONEL-FERRER is a professor in political science at the University of the Philippines, founding member of the Southeast Asian Network of Women Peace Mediators and Negotiators, chair of the Philippine government panel that signed the Comprehensive Agreement on the Bangsamoro with the Moro Islamic Liberation Front in 2014, and a member of the UN Standby Team of Mediators for three years.

OWEN FRAZER is currently senior advisor Conflict Transformation with Helvetas, a Swiss development NGO. He previously worked as a negotiation and mediation advisor with the Berghof Foundation; as a senior programme officer in the Mediation Support Team of the Center for Security Studies at the Swiss Federal Institute of Technology, Zurich; and as a delegate of the International Committee of the Red Cross. A certified mediator, he is the author of several publications on conflict transformation topics. His forthcoming book on peace mediation with Routledge is based on a study of the El Salvador peace negotiations.

SARA HELLMÜLLER is a senior researcher at the Center for Security Studies (CSS) at ETH Zurich. Prior to that, Sara held positions as SNSF assistant professor at the Geneva Graduate Institute, senior researcher at swisspeace, and lecturer at the University of Basel and was a visiting scholar at Oxford University, University of Montreal, Columbia University, and the University of Bunia. Sara's research focuses on peace processes, particularly UN peace missions in various world orders, the role of norms in peace promotion, local and international peacebuilding, and knowledge production on peace and conflict.

CHRISTOPHER R. HILL is an American diplomat who has served across multiple regions, including as ambassador to Iraq, the Republic of Korea, Poland, North Macedonia, and currently in the Republic of Serbia. As assistant secretary of state for East Asian and Pacific Affairs under presidents George W. Bush and Barack Obama, he led US efforts to end North Korea's nuclear weapons program. He was a lead Department of State negotiator in negotiations that ended the Bosnian war in 1995 and was the US special envoy in negotiations that ended the Kosovo war in 1999.

EEMELI ISOAHO manages the Master of Advanced Studies ETH Mediation in Peace Processes (MAS ETH MPP) program at ETH Zurich in partnership with the United Nations, Switzerland, Germany, and Finland. From 2011–2017, Eemeli worked at CMI—Martti Ahtisaari Foundation, where he specialized in the provision of mediation support to African regional organizations and was involved in high-level mediation efforts, including for instance in South Sudan (2014–2015) and Burundi (2015–2017). Eemeli continues to provide training and advisory support in peace mediation, catering to diverse audiences from regional organizations and governments to private mediation actors.

SIMON J. A. MASON heads the Mediation Support Team at the Center for Security Studies (CSS) at ETH Zurich. He holds a doctorate in environmental science. His research interests include the use of mediation in peace processes, mediation of conflicts involving religious dimensions, and the mediation of ceasefires. He works in the Mediation Support Project, a joint initiative of CSS and swisspeace, in collaboration with the Swiss Federal Department of Foreign Affairs. With Dekha Ibrahim Abdi, he coauthored "Mediation and Governance in Fragile Contexts: Small Steps to Peace." He is advisor to the MAS ETH Mediation in Peace Processes.

JUANITA MILLÁN HERNÁNDEZ is a retired lieutenant commander from the Colombian Navy (2006–2020). She was part of the government negotiating team in the Havana Peace Talks between the Colombian Government and the FARC and the only woman from the security forces in that process. She holds a Master of Advanced Studies in Mediation in Peace Processes from ETH Zurich, Switzerland. She also carried out postgraduate studies in conflict resolution from Javeriana University in Bogota. She has extensive experience with mediation, conflict analysis, DDR, SSR, security arrangements, ceasefires, and the Women Peace and Security agenda.

LAURIE NATHAN is professor of the Practice of Mediation and director of the Mediation Program at the Kroc Institute for International Peace Studies, University of Notre Dame. He has served on the UN Academic Advisory Council on Mediation and as a senior mediation advisor to the UN, the African Union, and several subregional bodies in Africa. He was a member of the AU mediation for Darfur in 2005–2006 and facilitated negotiations on security arrangements and a ceasefire. He is the author of four books, including *Community of Insecurity: SADC's Struggle for Peace and Security in Southern Africa* (Ashgate, 2012; University of Cape Town, 2013).

ENZO NUSSIO is a senior researcher at the Center for Security Studies (CSS) at ETH Zurich working on the causes and consequences of violence. He holds a doctorate in International Affairs and Governance from the University of St. Gallen. Prior to his work at the CSS, he worked in Colombia for the Universidad de los Andes and the Universidad Nacional, specializing in the reintegration of ex-combatants and peacebuilding. His research appeared in academic journals like the *American Journal of Political Science* and *International Security* and was featured in the *New York Times* and *Neue Zürcher Zeitung*.

ALVARO DE SOTO is a Peruvian diplomat and renowned international mediator. He led the negotiations that brought an end to the war in El Salvador; he has also served as political advisor to Boutros Boutros-Ghali, special envoy for Myanmar, the special advisor on Cyprus, and the special coordinator for the Middle East Peace Process.

GEORG STEIN works as senior mediation adviser and ceasefire expert, at the Swiss Federal Department of Foreign Affairs (FDFA). He was posted in Africa, as well as in Southeast Asia. Working in a number of conflict contexts worldwide, he specializes in dialogue facilitation, in negotiation and mediation support, in particular in regard to process design and in building ceasefires and security arrangements.

VALERIE STICHER combines academic research with over ten years of practitioner experience to assist opposing parties in transitioning from war to negotiated peace. Her PhD research at Leiden University focused on the role of ceasefires as strategic bargaining instruments. In her ongoing postdoctoral research project, funded by the Swiss National Science Foundation, she explores the effects of artificial intelligence on strategic decision-making in armed conflicts. Valerie was previously a senior program officer in mediation support at the Center for Security Studies, ETH Zurich, and worked for the United Nations Integrated Mission in Timor-Leste.

ANDREAS WENGER is professor of International and Swiss Security Policy at ETH Zurich. He studied History and Political Science at the University of Zurich. His main research interests include security and strategic studies and the history of international relations. He has been the director of the Center for Security Studies (CSS) at ETH Zurich since 2002. The CSS is a center of excellence for national and international security policy. He teaches seminars on political violence and security politics and serves as director of studies for the Master of Advanced Studies ETH Mediation in Peace Processes (MAS ETH MPP).

CLAUDIA WIEHLER is a practice-oriented researcher focusing on armed groups and peace mediation, in particular ceasefires. Her work combines quantitative and qualitative methods, including data generation in conflict-affected contexts. Her research has been published in the *Journal of Conflict*

Resolution and the *Journal of Peacekeeping,* among others. She has work experience in West Africa, Latin America, and South Asia, and currently completes her PhD at ETH Zurich.

CARSTEN WIELAND is a senior German diplomat, former UN consultant, Middle East, and conflict expert with high-ranking mediation experience. He served with three UN Special Envoys for Syria and is a senior policy adviser for the Middle East in the Green Party Group in the Bundestag, an associate fellow at the Geneva Centre for Security Policy (GCSP), and senior fellow at the Peace Research Institute in Oslo (PRIO). He worked in the Syria team of the Foreign Office in Berlin and director of the German Information Center for the Arab World in Cairo. Wieland has published widely on Middle East, nationalism, ethnic conflicts in the Balkans, and South Asia.